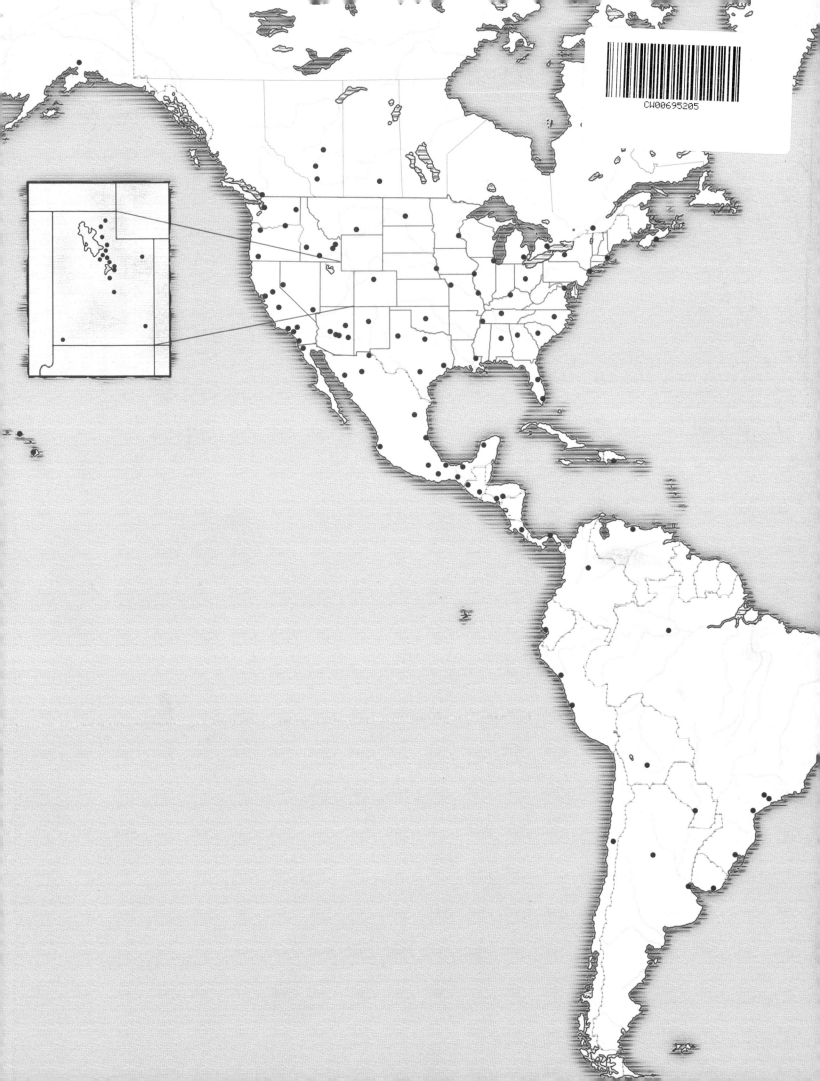

TEMPLES
OF THE NEW MILLENNIUM

Facts, Stories, and Miracles from the First 150 Temples

CHAD S. HAWKINS

DESERET
BOOK

Salt Lake City, Utah

*To my dear wife, Stephanie, and my
amazing children (Jacob, Anne, Rachel, Mary, and Jared).
You all make every day better than the day before.*

———

*This book is a tribute to all the individuals
who quietly strive for perfection while
building temples in the latter days.*

The artwork of temples included in this volume is available in many sizes of fine-art prints and on temple recommend holders. For more information about the artwork or to learn more about the artist/author, please visit www.chadhawkins.com.

Library of Congress Cataloging-in-Publication Data

Names: Hawkins, Chad S., 1971– author.
Title: Temples of the new millennium : facts, stories, and miracles from the first 150 temples / Chad Hawkins.
Description: Salt Lake City, Utah : Deseret Book, [2016] | Includes bibliographical references. | Description based on print version record and CIP data provided by publisher; resource not viewed.
Identifiers: LCCN 2015045789 (print) | LCCN 2015044902 (ebook) | ISBN 9781629734200 (ebook) | ISBN 9781629721491 (hardbound : alk. paper)
Subjects: LCSH: Mormon temples. | The Church of Jesus Christ of Latter-day Saints—History.
Classification: LCC BX8643.T4 (print) | LCC BX8643.T4 H39 2016 (ebook) | DDC 246/.9589332—dc23
LC record available at http://lccn.loc.gov/2015045789

Printed in Hong Kong
RR Donnelley, Kwun Tong, Kowloon, Hong Kong

10   9   8   7   6   5   4   3   2   1

Contents

CHRONOLOGICAL LIST OF TEMPLES

ALPHABETICAL LIST OF TEMPLES

Introduction

It was a sunny morning and I was standing at the construction site of the Paris France Temple. The temple's concrete shell was formed and the ornate stone cladding was being adhered to the walls. The tall stationary crane was efficiently unloading the contents of a recently arrived semi-truck. It was an exciting day for the temple builders because the temple's imported windows had cleared customs and were scheduled to arrive within the hour. As I stood envisioning how the temple would appear with the soon-to-be installed windows, a man approached and casually introduced himself. He seemed eager to share his thoughts on how wonderful it was that a Christian religion was building a new "church." Although his country had many church buildings, he explained regrettably how most were in disrepair. "No one goes anymore," he said. "Churches aren't growing, and it seems there is no need for new religious buildings." He walked away saying, "This new church will bring light into the city!"

Although our conversation was brief, his observations have stayed with me. Indeed, it is wonderful that The Church of Jesus Christ of Latter-day Saints has a growing membership resulting in the need for more church buildings and temples. With this expansion comes the light of the restored gospel. This perceptive man rightfully observed how the temple would be a beacon of light and a witness of good. President George Q. Cannon once said, "Every foundation stone that is laid for a Temple, and every Temple completed . . . lessens the power of Satan on the earth, and increases the power of God and Godliness" (George Q. Cannon, in "The Logan Temple," *Millennial Star*, Nov. 12, 1877, 743). And so it is in our own lives; the more the temple is a part of our personal being, the power of the adversary lessens and the influence of God becomes more abundant.

The Church has become one large family scattered across the earth. As of the date of this book's publication, about 15.4 million members are found in nearly two hundred nations and territories. A marvelous and wonderful work is coming to pass. With a sense of urgency, temples are continually being built closer to members. Humble people in rural corners of developing nations are entering into binding eternal covenants and becoming forever families. The Lord is fulfilling His promise that His gospel shall be as the stone cut out of the mountain without hands which would roll forth and fill the whole earth (see Daniel 2:31–45). Today's Church members are blessed to witness and participate in this historic season of vast temple expansion.

An important part of the gospel filling the whole earth pertains to the increase of latter-day temples. In the words of Elder Bruce R. McConkie, "We expect to see the day when temples will dot the earth, each one a house of the Lord; each one built in the mountains of the Lord; each one a sacred sanctuary to which Israel and the Gentiles shall gather to receive the blessings of Abraham, Isaac, and Jacob. Perhaps they will number in the hundreds, or even in the thousands, before the Lord returns" (*The Millennial Messiah: The Second Coming of the Son of Man* [Salt Lake City: Deseret Book Co., 1982], 277).

While collecting reference photography for my artwork and gathering historical research for this book, I had the privilege of visiting over one hundred temples. Most of these temples were visited during their construction, open house, or dedication. The timing of these visits allowed me to meet and interview hundreds of people involved with temple construction. Interviewing these dedicated people has been a highlight of my life, and I consider many of them to be friends. My journey has involved translators, schedules in different time

Chad and Stephanie Hawkins visiting the Hamilton New Zealand Temple

zones, hard hats, meetings in construction trailers, persistence, and ignoring the effects of jet lag. This book would not be possible without the help of others and the heavens coordinating events beyond my control. I wish to express my gratitude to all those who helped bring this book to fruition.

Since the time of antiquity until the latter days, temples of the Lord have been monuments to sacrifice, faith, and dedication. They are the result of man's best effort given to the Creator. The scope of work required to build modern-day temples is huge and unlike any other in the world. From the large and noticeable features to the most hidden and menial task, care is given to achieve the best possible result. President Brigham Young established this high standard while supervising the construction of the Salt Lake Temple, when he proclaimed, "We are building this temple to stand through the millennium" (LeGrand Richards, "Laying a Foundation for the Millennium," *Ensign*, Dec. 1971, 81).

Visiting the Perth Australia Temple

On numerous occasions, I met with construction missionaries, project supervisors, tradespeople, and artisans who used their talents to ensure that temples were built with the highest possible construction standards. Their sincere quest for perfection is a magnificent reflection of their devotion to the Lord. A temple project superintendent shared with me the following: "No one will ever know the quality that is behind the walls. The quality is not just the paint and trim. No one will know the late hours, early hours, and times in below-freezing weather builders go to make temples as perfect as man can make them." The many stories of outstanding service contained in this book are only a few among the countless examples that could be referenced on every temple. Although those who provide their best effort and talent to build temples do not seek the accolades of man, I will nonetheless express my gratitude by offering this book as a tribute to them.

Chad and his family (from left to right: Rachel, Stephanie, Anne, Jacob) with a Nauvoo Illinois Temple sunstone

I have personally witnessed this pursuit of perfection. On three separate occasions while visiting three different temples, I was given in-depth tours by those involved in the temple's construction. On each tour, I was shown examples of high-quality workmanship and building materials that often exceeded local building code requirements. All tours concluded with the escorts sharing how they believed their temple was the best-built temple in the Church. With time transpiring between these three temple visits, I did not recognize the repeated statement until I heard it a third time. After hearing the familiar phrase the third time, I concluded for myself that all temples are the best-built temple in the Church.

Temple architects and designers are masterful at their craft and dedicated to their profession. This publication highlights many of the artistic treatments, motifs, and designs that make every temple unique. Although temple art, architectural features, window designs, and landscaping have great value, it should be remembered that their primary purpose is to enhance and not overshadow the essential purpose of the temple. In the words of Elder Kent F. Richards, a member of the Seventy

Chad and his son Jake at the Bern Switzerland Temple

and Executive Director of the Temple Department, "It is the ordinances that define the temple. It is about receiving ordinances for eternity, learning about the nature of Heavenly Father and receiving all the blessings that are important" (Genelle Pugmire, Payson LDS Temple Magazine, *Daily Herald*, April 2015, 17).

Observing how Church members around the world universally embrace and cherish the temple has strengthened my own reverence for the Lord's house and its divine purpose. I have met with and interviewed many members living in the world's remote locations. The Lord's kingdom encompasses members who are experiencing their mortal existence in entirely different ways. Individuals across the spectrum of human experience join together to speak the gospel of Jesus Christ. Unification among the Latter-day Saints is solidified further as members gather as equals to partake of temple blessings. For me, this

Chad at the Copenhagen Denmark Temple

powerful unification among the family of God is a profound witness of the divinity of the restored gospel of Jesus Christ.

Temples are more than stone and mortar. They are built of faith and fasting, of trials and testimonies, and are sanctified by sacrifice and service. In the temple, the things of earth are joined with the things of heaven and our perspective of eternity is increased. It is my hope that those who read this book will develop a deeper appreciation for the temple and a greater desire to partake of temple blessings. In the words of President Thomas S. Monson, "Those who understand the eternal blessings which come from the temple know that no sacrifice is too great, no price too heavy, no struggle too difficult in order to receive those blessings. There are never too many miles to travel, too many obstacles to overcome, or too much discomfort to endure. They understand that the saving ordinances received in the temple that permit us to someday return to our Heavenly Father in an eternal family relationship and to be endowed with blessings and power from on high are worth every sacrifice and every effort" ("The Holy Temple—a Beacon to the World," *Ensign*, May 2011, 92).

Chad drawing in his art studio

St. George Utah Temple

The pioneers of Southern Utah suffered years of physical hardships as they struggled to establish St. George and other communities. They endured scorching summer heat and heavy spring rains, which frequently flooded the nearby Virgin and Santa Clara Rivers. But despite the difficulties of establishing themselves on the desert frontier, the Saints began building a magnificent temple within ten years of their arrival.

After a selection committee had considered several possible temple sites, President Brigham Young chose a location at the lowest part of the valley. Local Saints argued that the place he had chosen was too boggy—for months after the stormy season the ground could not support even horses and wagons. President Young, however, remained resolute.

The dedication of the temple site on November 9, 1871, marked the beginning of a great and difficult undertaking for the Saints of Southern Utah. Heber Jarvis recorded that President Young said "there would not be any persons who would lose their lives on any of the works on this Temple." Brother Jarvis later declared, "I lived to see this prediction fulfilled as I saw many persons hurt but none of them died." While still serving as chief architect of the Church, Truman Angell drew up the original plans for the temple. Many of the exterior features on the St. George Temple were patterned after the Salt Lake Temple. The side elevations, buttresses, battlements, and window designs are almost the same as those found on the Salt Lake Temple. Other architectural

1

influences originate from earlier temples of the Restoration, including Kirtland and Nauvoo.

Workers moved tons of black volcanic rock from the ridges above the town to the temple site to prepare the boggy ground to hold the footings and foundation of the temple. With great ingenuity, they used a cannon to pound the footings deep into the ground. Using a system of pulleys fastened to a team of horses, the workers lifted the cannon, which was filled with lead, about thirty feet in the air and then dropped it onto the stone footings, where it bounced three times before coming to rest. This tedious task continued until solid footings were firmly set in the soft ground.

The amount of materials needed to construct a building of this magnitude was staggering. Building the foundation alone cost more than one hundred thousand dollars. Some seventeen thousand tons of black volcanic rock and sandstone were hauled by mule teams to the temple site. Most of the million feet of lumber used in the temple had to be transported from a forest eighty miles away. On January 1, 1877, the lower story of the temple was dedicated by Elder Wilford Woodruff, president of the temple from 1877 to 1884. Baptisms for the dead were first administered in the temple on January 9, 1877, and endowments for the dead were begun two days later. President Woodruff described the occasion as being "the first time endowments for the dead had been given in any Temple in this dispensation." After an amazingly short period of five and a half years and much backbreaking effort, the temple was dedicated in its entirety on April 6, 1877, by Daniel H. Wells, Second Counselor in the First Presidency.

Brigham Young watched the progress of the building with great satisfaction. There was one thing he did not like about the temple, however. He felt the tower on the temple was "short and squatty," and he boldly encouraged the members to rebuild it higher. The people, worn out after their nonstop efforts to build the temple, resisted. Five months after the temple was dedicated, President Young died in Salt Lake City at age seventy-six. Several weeks later, on the night of October 16, 1878, a severe storm hit St. George, and the tower was destroyed by lightning. The unanimous feeling of the St. George Saints was that President Young had had his way. The tower was rebuilt taller, thus meeting his original specifications.

Significant spiritual experiences in the St. George Temple have been recorded. Perhaps the best known of these happened to President Wilford Woodruff. He was in the temple late one evening when the spirits of many of America's Founding Fathers gathered around him. He said, "Every one of those men that signed the Declaration of Independence, with General Washington, called upon me . . . two consecutive nights, and demanded at my hands that I should go forth and attend to the ordinances of the House of God for them."

During his service as temple president, Wilford Woodruff received revelations that would shape the way Latter-day Saints performed their temple worship. He also received revelation that allowed proxy ordinances to be done by people other than direct descendants.

The temple was renovated in 1935 and again in the 1970s. It has remained relatively untouched in the years since, but an earthquake in 1992 caused the walls to lean out. At the time, some Church officials considered building a new temple or demolishing the St. George site due to the damage sustained, but President Gordon B. Hinckley told his workers to "check again." Upon further inspection, it was determined that the building was fit and would stand.

The pristine whiteness of the St. George Utah Temple contrasts dramatically with the brilliant red hills of Utah's Dixie. The temple's grandeur amid the rugged terrain reflects the sacrifice of a people whose faith and diligence conquered the wilderness and created a mighty edifice to their God.

SITE
6 acres

GROUNDBREAKING
November 9, 1871, by Brigham Young

DEDICATION
April 6–8, 1877, by Daniel H. Wells
(with Brigham Young presiding)

REDEDICATION
November 11–12, 1975,
by Spencer W. Kimball

EXTERIOR
Native red sandstone quarried north
of the city and plastered white

TOTAL FLOOR AREA
110,000 square feet

DIMENSIONS
142 feet by 96 feet; to top
of buttresses, 80 feet;
after remodeling, 249 feet
by 282 feet

HIDDEN IMAGE
In memory of the signers of the
Declaration of Independence
appearing in the St. George
Temple, the words "We the
people" are written in the bluffs.

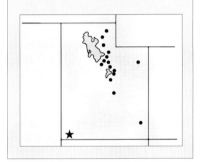

Logan Utah Temple

Excavation for the Logan Temple began on May 28, 1877, just one month after the dedication of the St. George Temple. The prominent east-bench temple site, designated by Brigham Young on May 15, 1877, overlooks Cache Valley. The temple is "the spiritual symbol of the valley. It stands in the midst of this very fertile and productive area as a reminder that life is more than the struggle for physical survival or the acquisition of material wealth. It symbolizes a long-range view of things—an eternal view." It stands as a reminder to the Saints of Cache Valley that life's greatest successes come through eternal families and the keeping of sacred covenants.

From the beginning of the settlement of Cache Valley, the Saints had a vision of a future temple on the bench in Logan. Bishop William H. Maughan recorded an event that took place at a religious gathering in Maughan's Fort (later called Wellsville) two years before the settlement of Logan: "Brother John Thirkell was appointed orator of the day. . . . He soon got to prophesying and he said there would be a temple built on the ground at Logan. . . . He said he could see these things and could not help telling it."

On August 22, 1863, while in Logan, Elder Wilford Woodruff prophesied: "Yea, the day will come . . . when you will have the privilege of going into the towers of a glorious Temple built unto the Name of the Most High (pointing in the direction of the bench), east of us upon the Logan bench." Knowing that a temple was to be built on "the bench," the

2

❖

Saints set aside this property and used it as a city park.

Before building the Logan Temple, the local Saints had generously donated their means and labor toward building the St. George and Salt Lake Temples and the newly completed Logan Tabernacle. Speaking to the Saints at the groundbreaking ceremony on May 18, 1877, President Young explained that building the temple would require continued great sacrifice: "From the architect to the boy who carries the drinking water and the men that work on the building, we wish them to understand that wages are entirely out of the question."

Many of those who labored on the temple used this means of working out the accounts they owed to the Perpetual Emigrating Fund, which had assisted them in coming from Europe. Many others donated diverse forms of provisions and goods. The ledger book of the Logan Temple shows contributions of quilts, eggs, honey, books, shoes, garden sheds, vegetables, grains, meat, livestock, clothing, a threshing machine, a covered carriage, and even a Mason and Hamblin organ. Everything was accepted.

As the Saints willingly sacrificed time and money to build the temple, God's power was witnessed in the preservation of many lives, including that of nineteen-year-old Brother James, who, in the words of Nolan P. Olsen, "had loaded up about two tons of lumber and headed down stream toward the temple. . . . All went well for a short distance, until the wagon wheel hit a soft spot. The riverbank caved in, dropping the two wheels and throwing Brother James on the bottom of the stream, with his big load upside down on top of him. It took the workmen nearly a half hour to break the binding and to roll the wagon and lumber from the river. Brother James had been under water for this full length of time. They laid his body on the bank, covered it with a blanket and

SITE
9 acres

GROUNDBREAKING
May 18, 1877, by John W. Young

DEDICATION
May 17–19, 1884, by John Taylor

REDEDICATION
March 13–15, 1979,
by Spencer W. Kimball

HIDDEN IMAGE
The young Prophet Joseph Smith can be seen shielding his eyes as he looks into the light of the First Vision.

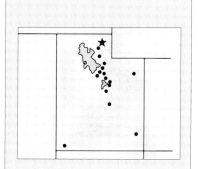

told one of the boys to get on a horse and come to Logan to tell the parents what had happened to their son.

"Before the horse could be bridled, the blanket began to move and Brother James was up on his feet. Evidently his wind had been knocked out as his load went over, and he had not breathed for thirty minutes, and had no water in his lungs. The ice cold water had slowed his body processes, and he had no brain or bodily damage of any kind. He was none the worse for the experience, and reloaded his wagon and brought it on down to the temple."

Another manifestation of divine protection was witnessed when high scaffolding that had been supporting three men gave way. One of the men, who fell fifty-three feet, said: "I landed so hard that it bounced my spirit right out of my body. . . . [And when] a worker administered to me saying, 'In the name of Israel's God, we command you to be made whole,' my spirit entered my body and I opened my eyes. After it was all over, they put me in the buggy and took me home. I have testified to hundreds of people as to how I was brought back to life through the Priesthood of God." Another accident transpired when someone unknowingly pushed a hand axe off the scaffolding, causing the axe to fall about fifty feet. An unfortunate young man was struck by the axe, resulting in the loss of his nose. Although a local doctor (Dr. Lamoreaux) was able to restore his nose to proper function, it remained crooked the rest of his life.

The Logan Temple has been an important site of latter-day temple work for the living and the dead. From its dedication until 1976, more than eighteen percent of all temple ordinances were performed in the Logan Temple. The temple continues to exert much influence for righteousness and contributes greatly to the spirituality of the Saints throughout the region.

Manti Utah Temple

The majestic Manti Utah Temple sits on a hill at the base of a rock mountain and commands a superb view of the Sanpete Valley. The twenty-seven-acre temple hill is richly landscaped with hundreds of evergreens and grass. The temple is one of the best-known landmarks in central Utah.

Manti, founded in 1849 by 224 pioneers, was one of the first settlements established by the Latter-day Saint pioneers. Most of the immigrants who settled the area originated from Scandinavia. In 1854, President Heber C. Kimball prophesied that the settlement would succeed and that a temple of God would be built on the hill above Manti. "The rock will be quarried from that hill to build it with," he proclaimed, "and some of the stone from that quarry will be taken to help complete the Salt Lake Temple." This prophecy was fulfilled in every detail, as stone from the Manti quarry was used for both the Manti Temple and for decorative tablets at the east and west ends of the Salt Lake Temple.

On the morning of April 25, 1877, President Brigham Young determined where the temple should be built when he took Elder Warren S. Snow to temple hill with him. Brother Snow related: "We two were alone: President Young took me to the spot where the Temple was to stand; we went to the southeast corner, and President Young said: 'Here is the spot where the prophet Moroni stood and dedicated this piece of land for a Temple site, and that is the reason why the location is made here, and we can't move it from this spot; and if

3

you and I are the only persons that come here at high noon today, we will dedicate this ground.'"

Lewis Anderson, who served as Manti Temple President for twenty-seven years (1906–1933), had a vision of the temple at age fifteen. As a young man, he was knocked to the ground while hauling a load of wood. His daughter shares the following account: "He had broken his collar bone, arm, a leg in two places, ribs, and a finger. . . . Father had to lie in bed at home for weeks for all those bones to knit. . . . Father was afraid he would always be crippled and a burden to [his parents]. One day when he was feeling very depressed, a picture came before him. It was a picture of a building. He said it looked as though someone was holding it, but he could not see any hands. It stayed long enough for him to study it. He remembered all the details of the outside of the building. And he didn't have any idea what the building was, because he had never seen a building or picture like it before. Well, it just disappeared, faded away. Father got well, grew up, married, and went on two missions to the Northern States. When he came home from his last mission, the Temple was ready for dedication. He hadn't seen it during construction. . . . When he got to the south side of Ephraim, . . . he saw the Temple. The vision he had long ago all came back to him. He exclaimed, "There is the building I saw when I was a boy!"

The Saints laboring on the temple worked swiftly and felt protected in their labors. One night Edward L. Parry, the master mason of the temple, was awakened from a very realistic dream in which a man fell from the temple's scaffolding. Brother Parry immediately arose from his bed and went to the site to examine the scaffolding. There he found that an important support rope had worked its way loose. After repairing the scaffolding, he returned home to his bed. Because he heeded the warning, no one was injured.

The quality of the workmanship and materials had the highest of standards. The temple's master mason, Edward Parry, exemplified this high standard when he observed a stoneworker

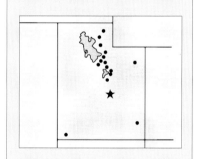

about to use a cracked stone on the building. "I will put the crack on the inside. No one will know it is there," said the stone layer.

"That is not quite right!" replied Brother Parry. "You will know it, I will know it, and the Lord will know it. Now remove the stone and replace it with one without flaws!"

President Anthon H. Lund, the second president of the Manti Temple and a member of the First Presidency, related a story of divine assistance concerning vicarious temple ordinances: "I remember one day in the temple at Manti, a brother from Mount Pleasant rode down to the temple to take part in the work, and as he passed the cemetery in Ephraim, he looked ahead (it was early in the morning), and there was a large multitude all dressed in white, and he wondered how that could be. Why should there be so many up here; it was too early for a funeral, he thought; but he drove up and several of them stepped out in front of him and they talked to him. They said, 'Are you going to the temple?' 'Yes.' 'Well, these that you see here are your relatives and they want you to do work for them.' 'Yes,' he said, 'but I am going down today to finish my work. I have no more names and I do not know the names of those who you say are related to me.' 'But when you go down to the temple today you will find there are records that give our names.' He was surprised. He looked until they all disappeared, and drove on. As he came into the temple, Recorder Farnsworth came up to him and said, 'I have just received records from England and they all belong to you.' And there were hundreds of names that had just arrived, and what was told him by these persons that he saw was fulfilled. You can imagine what joy came to his heart, and what testimony it was to him the Lord wants this work done."

In 1988, during the temple's centennial year, the First Presidency commemorated the occasion by stating: "Our thoughts go back to those Latter-day Saints who first made the trek to Manti. As the first 50 families came into the valley, the hill upon which the temple now stands seems to have marked their destination. . . . One hundred years of temple ordinance work is a great contribution to the Lord's work."

Salt Lake Temple

The Salt Lake Temple expresses in stone the religious faith and pioneer endurance of the thousands who built it. It stands as a monument to the beleaguered Saints who had been persecuted and driven from their homes and across the desolate plains to a valley where they could worship in peace. The Salt Lake Temple, recognized worldwide as the centerpiece of nineteenth-century Mormon industry, symbolizes the Saints' efforts to build Zion and establish the Lord's house "in the top of the mountains" (Isaiah 2:2).

On July 28, 1847, four days after President Brigham Young entered the Salt Lake Valley, he chose the site for the future temple. As he and a few others walked across the area that would one day become Temple Square, he struck the ground with his cane

and declared, "Here will be the Temple of our God." Wilford Woodruff then placed a stake in the ground to mark the spot that would become the center of the Salt Lake Temple and the symbolic center of God's kingdom in the latter-days.

During the April 1853 general conference, President Young said: "I have never inquired what kind of a temple we should build. Why? Because it was represented before me. I have never looked upon that ground, but the vision of it was there. I see it as plainly as if it was reality before me." President Young also firmly directed that the temple should be built using the best stone. The stone to be used was granite from Little Cottonwood Canyon. The permanence of the stone was a fitting symbol of eternal temple covenants.

4

Ground was broken for the temple on February 14, 1853, and the cornerstones laid with great ceremony on April 6, 1853. The first pioneer company had arrived in the valley only five and a half years earlier, and the Saints were still trying to get a foothold. One who attended the groundbreaking described their situation: "I walked [to the meeting] the morning the ground was broken for the foundation of the Temple . . . on the Temple Block. I went through frozen mud and slush with my feet tied up in rags. I had on a pair of pants made out of my wife's skirt, a thin Scottish plaid. . . . These were all the clothes I had. It was either go that way or stay home. . . . I was not alone in poverty. . . . There were many who were fixed as badly as I was."

Remaining true to Brigham Young's desire for the temple to stand through time, the builders skillfully shaped each individual granite stone. The robust structure featured walls nine feet thick at their base and six feet thick at their top. Nearly a century later, Elder Mark E. Petersen attested to the temple's solid construction. He was in the temple when an earthquake hit, which severely damaged several buildings throughout the Salt Lake Valley. "As I sat there in that temple I could feel the sway of the quake and that the whole building groaned." Afterward, he recalled, the engineers "could not find one semblance of damage" anywhere in the temple.

The tireless commitment that raised the temple walls slowly over the next twenty-five years is exemplified by the story of John Rowe Moyle. A stonemason and farmer from Alpine, Utah, he had been called as a work missionary to use his talents in building the temple walls. Early each Monday morning Brother Moyle walked some twenty miles north to the Salt Lake Temple site. There he spent the week laboring on the temple until he returned home on Friday. On Friday and Saturday he tended to his farm, and following a restful Sabbath, he began the cycle all over again. But one weekend while he was working on his farm, a cow kicked him, badly breaking his leg. The best medical advice available was to amputate the leg. While his stump healed, Brother Moyle carved himself a wooden leg. He put on the prosthetic leg as soon as he was able and "walked into Salt Lake as was his custom to take up his

SITE
10 acres

GROUNDBREAKING
February 14, 1853, by Brigham Young

DEDICATION
April 6–24, 1893,
by Wilford Woodruff

EXTERIOR
Quartz monzonite (similar
to granite) quarried from
Little Cottonwood Canyon, twenty
miles southeast of Salt Lake City

TOTAL FLOOR AREA
253,000 square feet

DIMENSIONS
117 feet by 184 feet; height of
the east center pinnacle is 210
feet; center of the three towers
on the west end is 204 feet

HIDDEN IMAGE
Representing how we should build
our lives upon the foundation of
the gospel, the Lord's right hand
is outlined supporting the entire
foundation of the temple.

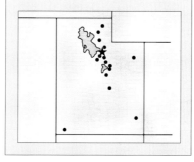

work, for he had been called as a work missionary on the Temple. And there, the story goes, he climbed up the scaffolding on the east side of the Temple and carved 'Holiness to the Lord.'"

In the summer of 1890 as the temple neared completion, Church leaders called John Hafen, Lorus Pratt, and John B. Fairbanks, all promising artists, to travel to Paris and enroll in the Julian Academy. They were set apart as "missionaries with a special purpose" to create murals on the interior temple walls. After arriving in the exciting city of Paris, these three artists avoided the city's abundance of worldly offerings by losing themselves in rigorous study. They were first to arrive to class in the morning and the last to leave at night. They avoided cafes and bars and would just "go home and write letters to their wives."

The ceremony on April 6, 1892, to place the capstone of the temple marked the completion of the stone work. Some fifty thousand members attended the ceremony, making it the largest gathering to that date in Utah history, a record unchallenged for several decades. After the sacred Hosanna Shout, the choir and some fifty thousand members joined in singing "The Spirit of God," a hymn that had been written for the dedication of the Kirtland Temple fifty-six years earlier.

The temple interior was completed and ready for dedication by noon on April 5, 1893, just a few hours ahead of President Woodruff's requested deadline of April 6. Forty years of effort and sacrifice to build the Salt Lake Temple concluded on the last day of the Church's annual conference. The Associated Press carried news of the dedication over its wire service, and newspapers from the *New York Times* to the *Los Angeles Times* ran stories about the completion of Mormonism's most important symbol.

Through the years, the Salt Lake Temple has continued to be a spiritual center for the Saints. Along with the ordinances that are performed in the temple, it is used for Church governance during the weekly meetings of the First Presidency and the Quorum of the Twelve Apostles and for solemn assemblies. Thus, the Salt Lake Temple continues to play a key part as God's kingdom rolls forth to fill the whole earth.

Laie Hawaii Temple

A temple in the Hawaiian Islands was the dream of many devoted and faithful Saints in the Pacific from the time the gospel was first proclaimed to them in 1850 by George Q. Cannon. In 1900, while attending the fiftieth anniversary of the founding of the Hawaiian Mission, President Cannon, then a member of the First Presidency, said that if the Hawaiian Saints would be faithful, they would one day be able to be sealed as families for eternity. The Saints saw this as a prophecy that a temple would be built in Hawaii.

This prophecy was partially realized in June 1915, when President Joseph F. Smith dedicated part of the "Plantation of Laie" for a temple. Purchased by the Church in 1865 for fourteen thousand dollars, the sugarcane and pineapple plantation had become the gathering place for the Hawaiian Saints. The property was approximately six thousand acres and included more than three miles of beach frontage, five hundred head of cattle, five hundred sheep, two hundred goats, and twenty-six horses. The "Hawaiian Temple" was formally proposed by President Joseph F. Smith during the Eighty-Sixth Semiannual General Conference of the Church. The proposition was embraced unanimously and signaled by what one publication described as a "great forest of uplifted hands which gave affirmation to the proposal."

Several features of the site presented problems for the workers on the temple. For one, the ground was unstable coral and sand, necessitating a large excavation to provide solid footings for the building.

5

Because large machinery was not available, the entire excavation had to be done using picks, shovels, and blasting powder. The remote location of the temple made it difficult to obtain building materials. Crushed lava and coral were added to the concrete that was used to form the entire edifice.

Even with this innovation, construction often had to wait while the contractors tried to locate necessary materials. At one point, when construction was at a standstill due to lack of lumber, temple contractor Ralph Woolley prayed for help in obtaining the needed supplies. Two days later, a freight ship became stranded on a nearby coral reef during a severe storm. The captain offered the Saints his cargo of lumber if they would help him unload his ship. The Saints agreed, and work on the temple was resumed.

Raising funds for the temple among the scattered Hawaiian Saints was a challenge that was overcome with faith and ingenuity. The Saints in Hawaii participated in a variety of fund-raising projects, including holding concerts and creating and selling mats, fans, and other craft items at local bazaars. Even though the Saints were already sacrificing a great deal for the temple, mission president Samuel E. Woolley noted that tithing paid by Hawaiian Saints had increased by nearly one-third during this time.

On the temple's exterior are four sculptured panels, one on each side of the building, with 123 figures. The friezes, sculpted by Leo and Avard Fairbanks, illustrate four gospel dispensations. The north frieze is of particular significance. It depicts the Book of Mormon dispensation and includes figures representing Hagoth and his companions, who are believed to be among the ancestors of the Polynesian peoples. In front of the temple is an ascending, palm-lined water court consisting of four reflecting pools. The climax to this wondrous scene is a bas-relief panel of a Hawaiian mother and her three children.

The temple was dedicated on November 27, 1919, four and a half years after the dedication of the site. Since the dedication, Saints from around the Pacific have attended the temple for their own ordinances and to perform ordinances for their kindred dead. The rate of temple work slowed significantly when Pearl Harbor was attacked on December 7, 1941, bringing the United States into World War II. The next day, Hawaii was placed under martial law, and the army governed the territory until October 1944. During the war, temple attendance

SITE
11.4 acres

SITE
DEDICATION
June 1, 1915, by Joseph F. Smith

DEDICATION
November 27–30, 1919,
by Heber J. Grant

EXTERIOR
Concrete made of the crushed
lava rock of the area and tooled
to a white cream finish

TOTAL FLOOR AREA
47,224 square feet

DIMENSIONS
157 feet by 283 feet

HIDDEN IMAGE
In the first reflection pool is
the Savior, in the second pool
are plumeria flowers, and
in the third pool are each of
Hawaii's eight main islands.

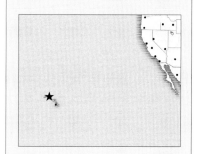

dropped by more than eighty percent. The temple was kept open only by the great faith of its patrons and was used only for a weekly endowment session and occasional weddings.

Through the years, additions and modifications have been made to the temple, including two wings at either side of the entrance to provide additional office space. Expansion over the years has increased the temple from 10,500 square feet to nearly 41,000 square feet. At one time the white temple was painted pale green to blend in with the landscaping. But most people preferred the original color, and eventually the white exterior was restored to the temple walls. As tourism continued to increase, a visitors' center was built to accommodate visitors from around the world.

In most recent decades, the temple and its surrounding grounds have been further beautified and modernized. In 1988, thick plant growth was cleared from a pioneer cemetery behind the temple, where some two hundred early Hawaiian Saints are buried. The area has now become the Laie Pioneer Memorial Cemetery. In 2003, the approaching Hale La'a Boulevard was dramatically transformed into a scenic and stately promenade to the temple. The boulevard extends from the temple to "temple beach" at the edge of the Pacific Ocean, where an enclosed garden is prepared for ocean baptisms. On January 1, 2009, a nearly two-year extensive temple renovation began, which included original art restoration, remodeling, refurbishing, and structural upgrades. Interior designer Greg Hill included "designs, motifs, colors, woods and styles that reflect the Hawaiian culture."

The beauty of the temple grounds, the serenity of the view, and the "Aloha" attitude of the guides and staff provide a warm welcome to the quarter of a million people who visit Laie each year. Thousands of missionary referrals are received annually from nonmembers who visit the visitors' center and the neighboring Polynesian Cultural Center.

The Hawaii state motto is "Ua mau ke ea o ka aina i ka pono," which translates to "The life of land is perpetuated in righteousness." The righteousness of many faithful Hawaiian Saints made the Laie Hawaii Temple a reality. Since its dedication in 1919, this temple has represented for them a timeless vision of paradise, white and gleaming, between the emerald mountains and the sapphire sea.

Cardston Alberta Temple

By 1900, Latter-day Saint settlements had become well established in areas far from Utah. In the April 1901 general conference, President Joseph F. Smith stated, "I foresee the necessity arising for other temples or places consecrated to the Lord for the performance of the ordinances of God's house, so that the people may have the benefits of the house of the Lord without having to travel hundreds of miles for that purpose."

Under President Smith's leadership, ground was broken in 1913 for a temple in Cardston, Alberta, Canada, on an eight-acre site set aside for Church use in 1887 by Charles Ora Card, an early settler. The temple grounds were enlarged by two more acres in the 1950s. Although the Laie Hawaii Temple was the first temple completed outside the United States, the

Cardston Alberta Temple was the first outside the United States to be announced.

For the first time, Church leaders invited leading architectural firms to submit architectural proposals for a temple. The design chosen was created by Salt Lake City architects Hyrum C. Pope and Harold W. Burton. Their design presented a radical shift in temple design. Their innovative concept did not include spires or a large assembly room. The temple would be stately, solid, and dignified. The work of American architect Frank Lloyd Wright heavily influenced the building's bold form and geometric, decorative details. Another prominent feature was the sculptured art on the temple's exterior. Positioned near the temple doors is a large bas-relief depicting the Savior and

6

the Samaritan woman at the well. Created by Norwegian artist Torleif Knaphus, the beautiful scene is mirrored in a reflecting pool at its base and seems to welcome visitors to the temple.

Construction on the Cardston Alberta Temple began in 1913 and was completed ten years later. Many factors combined to make constructing such a large building a difficult undertaking for the Saints in this small community. Progress on the temple was greatly hindered by World War I. Other factors that contributed to slow progress on the temple were insufficient funding, severe winters, and the need to transport materials long distances.

Yet the workers building the temple felt the hand of the Lord guiding their labors. Matthew Leavitt, a worker on the temple excavation, was driving a large plow team when a harness trace broke and a tree struck him in the leg. "There was a doctor on the job," Leavitt recorded of the experience, "and he came and examined my leg and found there were no broken bones. He said that a miracle had been performed here, that there was no reason in the world why [my] leg was not cut right off with that severe blow."

The four ordinance rooms of the temple are arranged both practically and symbolically. The rooms are placed around the center of the building, each room facing one of the cardinal directions, and each successive room is a few steps higher than the one before. As patrons move through the ordinance rooms, they follow a circular path until they finally enter the celestial room at the center of the temple. Each room is also richer in its materials and decoration than the one before. Thus, the architectural arrangement and interior decor of the temple ordinance rooms reinforce the concept of spiritual progression so central to the temple ceremony.

The construction of the temple sparked great interest throughout the Church. The Relief Society general board received letters from many women expressing "a wish to donate their mite toward this glorious project." The board decided to establish a penny subscription modeled after one started by Mercy Fielding Thompson and Mary Fielding Smith for the Nauvoo Temple. By saving a penny each week, the women of the Relief Society were able to contribute more than $13,000 to the construction of temples in Alberta and Hawaii. Local area Relief Society sisters organized a project to raise money for furnishings and temple clothing. Each sister was to save the

SITE
8 acres

GROUNDBREAKING
November 9, 1913

DEDICATION
August 26–29, 1923,
by Heber J. Grant

REDEDICATION
June 22–24, 1991, by
Gordon B. Hinckley

EXTERIOR
White granite quarried near Kootenai Lakes in Nelson, British Columbia; additions of artificial precast granite

TOTAL FLOOR AREA
Originally 29,471 square feet;
81,700 square feet after remodeling

DIMENSIONS
118 feet square, 85 feet high;
footprint 165 feet by 311 feet

HIDDEN IMAGE
The Savior and Samaritan woman are hidden within the trees and flowers to the right of the temple. Old Chief Mountain is included in the lower left-hand corner.

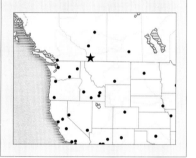

chicken eggs laid on Sunday and donate either the eggs or their value to the project. By their own labor, the Relief Society sisters thus raised fifteen hundred dollars for the temple.

So many General Authorities attended the dedication of the temple (August 26–29, 1923) that Cardston temporarily "became the capital of Mormondom." Elder John A. Widtsoe commented that "it was the first time in the history of the Church that so many of the General Authorities of the Church had been assembled at one time outside the boundaries of the United States."

During the sixth session of the dedicatory services, President Heber J. Grant offered the following counsel to the Saints: "Now, we as Latter-day Saints have everything in the world to be grateful for. We have not only the benefits of the Gospel for ourselves, but we can do a marvelous work for those who have died without a knowledge of the Gospel. . . . And I want to bear my witness here today in connection with others, that the unseen powers, that those who are working for us beyond the veil, never lose their interest in the work of those who are living here upon the earth."

Many temple workers and patrons have experienced strong spiritual manifestations as they have sought to perform saving ordinances. During a sealing of a woman to her children and deceased husband, President Edward J. Wood, the temple's first president, stopped in the middle of the ordinance and asked the woman if all her children were present. The woman said they were, and President Wood attempted the ordinance again. But again he stopped at the same place and asked if all her children's names were listed on the ordinance sheet. She said they were. After stopping again at the same place, the president asked, "Sister, didn't you ever have any other children?" To this the woman replied that she'd had a daughter who had died in infancy and whose name had not been included on the sheet. To this, President Wood said that he had heard a voice saying, "I am her child." The ordinance was performed again, this time including all the children. Despite the temple's remote location in a small community, the growth of the Church and subsequent temple attendance required the temple to be significantly renovated and expanded multiple times. Although upgraded with the latest technology, great effort has been made for it to visually maintain its 1923 splendor. In 1992, the temple was named a National Historic Site by Parks Canada.

Mesa Arizona Temple

Latter-day Saints settling parts of Arizona in the 1870s eagerly anticipated the time when a temple would be built there. By the end of World War I, plans for a temple in Arizona were under way. The recent construction of the Cardston Alberta and Laie Hawaii Temples strongly influenced the planning of the Mesa Arizona Temple. Proposed designs included Spanish baroque elements and a stepped dome in the center topped with a spire and a statue of the angel Moroni. The design that was finally chosen had elegant classical details with suggestions of both pre-Columbian temples and the temple of Herod.

On February 1, 1920, President Heber J. Grant selected the site for the temple at what was then the eastern edge of Mesa. The twenty-acre plot was immediately south of the "Apache Trail" section of the transcontinental highway, an artery that would carry thousands of tourists past the temple each year. Mesa was an ideal location for a temple because it was central to LDS settlements in Arizona, Southern California, and Mexico.

The exterior of the temple is faced with eggshell-colored terra cotta. At each corner of the building are sculptured friezes by Torlief Knaphus, based on sketches by A. B. Wright. On the north end of the temple, the sculptures depict the gathering of the elect in the Old World; on the south end, the figures represent the gathering in the Americas and the Pacific.

The temple's internal floorplan symbolically represents mankind's upward progression back to

7

the presence of Heavenly Father. The design centers on the grand staircase that patrons see as they enter the temple. Patrons ascend the staircase after they have received instruction and completed an endowment session. They then proceed up the staircase and into the celestial room, symbolizing the achievement of exaltation.

For most of its history, the Mesa Arizona Temple has been considered the temple of the Lamanites. This is partly due to the original temple district encompassing areas where the Navajo tribe is located. Visual reminders are included in paintings and other aspects of the temple's design. In the dedicatory prayer, President Heber J. Grant petitioned the Lord to bless the Lamanites "that they may not perish as a people but that from this time forth they may increase in numbers and in strength and in influence . . . and that many of them may have the privilege of entering this holy house and receiving ordinances for themselves and their departed ancestors."

Due to the immense public interest in the temple, the Church offered public tours during its final two years of construction. The *Mesa Journal Tribune* estimated that at least 200,000 people toured the structure. To put that staggering number in context, Mesa's total population was less than 4,000, and 200,000 was about half the population of Arizona. The public tour was such a massive success that the *Journal Tribune* noted, "Thousands and thousands of words will be telegraphed all over the world by writers for large press associations sent here to cover the dedication. It is declared that few affairs of a religious nature have ever excited so much comment or attracted more public attention." At the time of the temple's completion, the building was the costliest building ever erected in Arizona, costing several times more than the elegant Arizona Capitol Building.

Dedicated October 23, 1927, the temple was important for all members of the Church but especially for Native Americans, who joined the Church in large numbers during the middle decades of the twentieth century. A landmark event for temple

SITE
20 acres

GROUNDBREAKING
April 25, 1922, by Heber J. Grant

DEDICATION
October 23–26, 1927,
by Heber J. Grant

EXTERIOR
Concrete reinforced with 130 tons of steel; exterior is faced with glazed, eggshell-colored terra cotta tiles

TOTAL FLOOR AREA
113,916 square feet

DIMENSIONS
220 feet by 243 feet, and 50 feet in height above the foundation

HIDDEN IMAGE
A full-length image of the Savior, Jesus Christ, is found in the palm trees on the left.

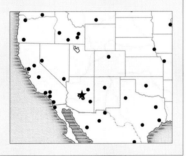

work took place at this temple in 1945. Because the endowment had been presented only in English up to that point, it was difficult for Latin American Saints to fully understand and participate in the ordinances. In November of that year, two hundred Spanish-speaking Saints from all over the Southwest and from as far away as Mexico City, Mexico, gathered in Mesa to participate in the first non-English presentation of the endowment. This was a spiritual boon to the members who participated in it; numerous similar conferences were held over the succeeding years.

An important tradition began early on Easter morning in 1938, when the youth of the Mutual Improvement Association from the Maricopa Stake presented a sunrise service on the temple grounds. A narrative and choir numbers recounted the story of Christ's life and sacrifice. The service was so successful that organizers made it an annual event, and it has grown to include some four hundred cast members, who present Christ's humble birth, inspiring ministry, and glorious resurrection in dance, drama, and music. The pageant now has a modern, two-hundred-foot-long stage, state-of-the-art sound and light systems, and a soundtrack featuring the London Symphony Orchestra. Even with these changes, however, the meaning remains the same—to bring people unto Christ by reenacting scenes from the beautiful story of His life. In April 1998, its sixtieth year, the Mesa Easter Pageant attracted more than 120,000 people from all over the world.

The Mesa Arizona Temple Garden Christmas Festival also inspires thousands of visitors each year. It includes a nativity scene with the scriptural account of the Savior's birth read over loudspeakers. Preparations for the display of 600,000 Christmas lights begin in October. Twenty-five hundred volunteers arrange the lights along pathways and fountains and in the trees. In 1998, more than a million visitors from every state and three hundred countries saw the lights illuminating the grounds of the Lord's holy house in Mesa, Arizona.

Idaho Falls Idaho Temple

The Idaho Falls Idaho Temple is located on seven acres of spacious grounds on the banks of the Snake River. Nearby, the wandering river cascades over the edge of a broad waterfall. The 1937 decision to build a temple in the Snake River Basin in southeastern Idaho was the fulfillment of a prophecy made to the pioneers of that area. These Saints had struggled to establish themselves on the harsh, desolate prairie. In 1884, President Wilford Woodruff and Elder Heber J. Grant encouraged them in their endeavors. Standing in a wagon, President Woodruff, then President of the Quorum of the Twelve Apostles, said to a small group, "Be not discouraged; be not disheartened, because God's blessing is upon this land." He then foretold the time when the Basin and its inhabitants

would prosper and develop into a strong community. "Yes," he continued, "as I look into the future of this great valley I can see temples—I can see beautiful temples erected to the name of the Living God where holy labors may be carried on in his name through generations to come."

Once the temple location was selected, each member of the Church board of temple architects was assigned to submit a proposal. The board agreed upon the concept prepared by John Fetzer Sr., who later said that after praying for inspiration, he "saw in vision an ancient Nephite temple which he used as the basis for his design."

Brother Fetzer expressed his belief that his one-spire temple design fulfilled the following prophecy

8

proclaimed by Brigham Young: "The time will come when there will be one [spire] in the center of temples we shall build." The warm white temple is symmetrical, with bladed pilasters rising up to a final shaft 148 feet high. The temple's exterior design results in vertical lines casting shadows toward the heavens.

Recent visitors to the temple will find it hard to believe that the temple's picturesque setting was once covered with wind-swept sand dunes, cactus, and sagebrush. The soft sand served as a playground for children and an ideal campsite for Native Americans and migrant travelers. Transforming the barren setting into a serene temple landscape started with the planting of more than 1,600 pine trees. Adding to the peaceful setting are colorful gardens, reflecting pools, and paths with multiple benches.

The temple's floor plan, which places the celestial room at the center of the structure, incorporates elements from the Cardston Alberta and Mesa Arizona Temples. To progress through the ordinance rooms of the temple, patrons move through successively brighter rooms on the way upward to the celestial room in the temple's tower, symbolizing mankind's progression back into the presence of God.

The beautiful walls of the temple sparkle in the sunlight from a two-inch-thick facing of white quartz aggregate and white cement that covers the sixteen-inch-thick exterior walls. The United States' entrance into World War II caused delays in the temple's building schedule. The exterior of the temple was nearly completed, but the interior still needed significant work. As an increasing number of Church members, both men and women, entered the armed forces or went to work in defense industries, a labor shortage delayed or halted most construction projects, including the temple. Wartime restrictions greatly limited the availability of building materials, but steel and other structural materials had been stockpiled for the temple, and most of its marble, from France, Italy, and Sweden, had been imported before the war. A major setback during this period came when it was discovered that mural fabrics in the temple had been damaged by condensation from insufficient insulation of the exterior concrete walls.

Despite the delays and difficulties, however, the temple was completed and then dedicated by President George Albert

SITE
7 acres

GROUNDBREAKING
December 19, 1939, by David Smith

DEDICATION
September 23–25, 1945, by
George Albert Smith

EXTERIOR
Reinforced concrete; a mixture made
from aggregate and white cement
covers the sixteen-inch thick exterior
walls in two-inch thick slabs

TOTAL FLOOR AREA
92,177 square feet

DIMENSIONS
192 feet by 234 feet; tower 148
feet high; two annexes added
7,700 square feet; a twelve-foot
statue of angel Moroni was added
to the tower September 5, 1983

HIDDEN IMAGE
Five oxen are placed beneath the
temple among the river scene.

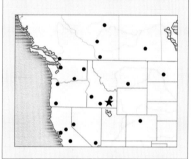

Smith just one month after the war ended. Not only was the Church able to complete the Idaho Falls Temple, but with the end of gasoline and tire rationing, the Saints could attend the temple more easily, making this an important period of revitalization in temple attendance.

In the early 1980s, representatives of the Idaho Falls Idaho Temple district asked the Church to consider adding a statue of the angel Moroni to the temple. The First Presidency approved the request, and on September 5, 1983, thirty-eight years after the temple was dedicated, a twelve-foot statue of the angel Moroni, identical to the statue on the Atlanta Georgia Temple, was positioned by helicopter on the temple spire.

The blessings of the temple cannot be gained anywhere else on earth. In the priesthood session of general conference in April 1993, President Russell M. Nelson counseled: "Brethren, please remember: the highest degree of glory is available to you only through that order of the priesthood linked to the new and everlasting covenant of marriage (see D&C 131:1–4). Therefore, your first priority in honoring the priesthood is to honor your eternal companion."

A tender demonstration of this understanding of priorities took place on a cold winter's morning at the Idaho Falls Temple. An elderly brother and his wife were walking arm in arm to the temple. Rain had made the walkways slick and hazardous. As the couple carefully made their way toward the temple's front doors, the wife gently took her husband's hand from her arm and placed it on the door handle. He opened the door for her and waited for her to enter. The touching scene was repeated at the next set of doors as the blind man opened the door for his beloved companion.

The solid structure of the Idaho Falls Idaho Temple standing beside the flowing Snake River aptly symbolizes the spiritual foundation of a community rich in pioneer heritage and devoted to the eternal goal of linking families in eternal bonds. The far-reaching spire seems to tell of eternal values ascending above material things. And as the river nourishes innumerable farms across southern Idaho, so do light and knowledge flow from the "temple by the river," feeding all who will accept them.

Bern Switzerland Temple

The Bern Switzerland Temple was the ninth Latter-day Saint temple to be built but the first to be built overseas. The temple is located in Zollikofen, a northern suburb of Bern, the capital of Switzerland. The construction of the "Swiss Temple" brought significant attention to the worldwide Latter-day Saint growth after World War II. No longer would faithful Saints have to cross the Atlantic to go to a temple. Constructing temples abroad allowed Saints to remain in their homelands and build up the Church there. Since its dedication in 1955, the Bern Switzerland Temple has been a mighty symbol for the Church in Europe.

While in Glasgow, Scotland, on July 22, 1952, President David O. McKay announced that the First Presidency and the Quorum of the Twelve Apostles

had decided to build a temple in Switzerland. Switzerland was the logical choice for the first temple in Europe for many reasons. The nation's constitution, adopted in 1848, guaranteed religious freedom, and the nation's neutrality during World Wars I and II kept it free from the divisive influences in Europe. Switzerland was also a natural choice for a temple because of its central geographic location and diversity of languages. Because so many languages and ethnic backgrounds are represented at the temple, former Bern Temple president Percy K. Fetzer referred to the sacred edifice as "the United Nations of Europe."

In 1952, President McKay assigned Samuel E. Bringhurst, the president of the Swiss-Austrian Mission, to obtain the land that had been selected

9

for a temple site. After several months of negotiations, the Church's bid to purchase the property was denied. Writing President McKay to inform him of the developments, and noting that he was disappointed to have all his efforts come to naught, President Bringhurst wrote that he felt a strange sense of relief and thought things would work out well in the end. President McKay mentioned a similar impression in his response: "My disappointment soon disappeared and was replaced by an assurance that the Lord will overrule all transactions for the best good of His Church, not only in Switzerland but throughout Europe." One week after his first letter to President McKay, President Bringhurst wrote again, this time with better news. He had found an available parcel of land in Bern that was twice the size of the original site and half as expensive. In his letter he noted that all his missionaries had "fasted and prayed, and immediately after the property became available."

To properly serve all the European Saints, new technology and methods needed to be developed to clearly and efficiently communicate endowment instructions in nearly a dozen languages in a much smaller space. To solve this problem, President McKay asked a young staff member in the Missionary Department named Gordon B. Hinckley to create a method of presenting the temple ordinances to many. "It was a charge of enormous significance," Brother Hinckley declared. "The ramifications of this project were enormous, as they would extend far beyond the temple in Switzerland."

After weeks of studying temple ordinances and counseling with President McKay in the Salt Lake Temple, Brother Hinckley proposed portraying the ordinances in movie form. Once the idea was approved by the First Presidency and the Quorum of the Twelve, the fifth-floor assembly room of the Salt Lake Temple was organized into a makeshift movie set. Huge floor-to-ceiling backdrops were hung, and large pulleys lifted props through the room's large windows. After a year of grueling work, the English version was completed. In the following months, versions in other languages were completed using immigrants and returned missionaries who spoke the various languages. To provide the best audio technology, the temple's architect sought the advice of motion picture studios, including MGM, Fox, and Paramount. Because President McKay had a personal friendship with MGM film producer Cecil B. DeMille, that studio was

SITE
7 acres

GROUNDBREAKING
August 5, 1953

DEDICATION
September 11–15, 1955,
by David O. McKay

EXTERIOR
Reinforced concrete with a cream gray terra cotta facing trimmed in white; tower is white; base and spire are gold-colored

TOTAL FLOOR AREA
35,546 square feet

DIMENSIONS
152 feet by 84 feet; top of tower rises 140 feet

HIDDEN IMAGE
An image of the Savior can be seen to the left of the temple.

especially helpful in suggesting solutions to logistical problems with the new method.

Once completed, care needed to be taken to safeguard the sanctity of these temple films while being imported through customs to Switzerland. Technology was used to develop the films in such a way that only authorized persons would ever see them.

Many acts of personal devotion helped make the construction of this temple possible. One eighty-two-year-old member, Therese Leuscher, sent one hundred francs in half-franc pieces to the home of Swiss-Austrian Mission president Samuel E. Bringhurst with a note stating: "It is my wish that the Almighty God may accept the temple just as sure as He did the Kirtland Temple, although I will not be living when this holy building will be dedicated." As she had predicted, this sister passed away before the dedication of the temple.

Workers labored around the clock for several nights to complete the final details as the dedication approached. On September 11, 1955, President McKay dedicated the Swiss temple. After welcoming those present, he said, "I welcome also an unseen, but, I believe, a real audience among whom are former presidents and apostles of the Church, headed by the Prophet Joseph." President McKay later remarked, "The veil between those who participated in those exercises and loved ones who had gone before seemed very thin."

The temple was closed from 1990 to 1992 for extensive remodeling and refurbishing. The temple's cream colored terra cotta exterior was replaced with gleaming white stone. The interior was expanded by adding more endowment and sealing rooms. So thorough were the modifications that the refurbished temple was almost entirely new. Before the rededication of the temple, a public open house was held. Although only about 6,500 members live in Switzerland, some 33,000 people toured the remodeled building.

President Gordon B. Hinckley rededicated the temple on October 23, 1992, with nearly nine thousand members from throughout Europe attending the ten dedicatory sessions. Among his comments during the service, President Hinckley expressed gratitude for "this nation of Switzerland, which through centuries of time has been a land of peace while nations round about have been nations at war." He prayed that Switzerland "may continue to be a land of peace, a land of freedom, a land of opportunity and an example to other nations of the world."

Los Angeles California Temple

The Los Angeles California Temple was built to meet the needs of expanding Church membership in Southern California. Situated on a prominent hill, the highest point between Los Angeles and the Pacific Ocean, the temple can be seen from Catalina Island and from ships twenty-five miles out to sea. In March 1937, the Church purchased 24.23 acres from silent comedy film legend Harold Lloyd. It has since become the site of the temple, a mission home, a meeting-house, a family history building, a temple clothing building, and lodgings for patrons.

One early reference to a temple in California came in a letter of encouragement to the California Saints from President Brigham Young and Elder Willard Richards in August 1847. The message stated:

"In the process of time the shores of the Pacific may yet be overlooked from the temple of the Lord." In 1937 President Heber J. Grant announced that the Church had purchased property for a temple on the top of a hill near Westwood Village. The location's legal description dates back to 1542, when it was claimed by "Charles I, King of Spain, and his successors in interest, by right of discovery and settlement."

Although construction of the temple was delayed by the outbreak of World War II, the First Presidency developed a plan for the building to seat two hundred patrons in each session. After the war, they directed that the temple design be enlarged to accommodate up to three hundred per company. This change, along with the addition of a priesthood

10

assembly room on the upper floor, made this the largest temple built in the twentieth century. The temple's 257-foot spire is 47 feet taller than the Salt Lake Temple's highest spire, and its six levels include about four and a half acres of floor space. The temple's reinforced concrete and structural steel make the exterior fireproof and resistant to earthquakes.

In February 1952, President David O. McKay encouraged local Saints to bear part of the cost of building the temple. Meeting with twelve hundred ward and stake leaders, President McKay challenged the Saints of Southern California to raise $1 million for the temple. He encouraged them to have the "young people, even the children in the 'cradle roll,' contribute to the temple fund, for this is their temple, where they will be led by pure love to take their marriage vows." The enthusiastic Saints responded with generous pledges, and within three months they raised over $1.6 million.

Much attention was given to the landscape surrounding the temple. The temple was surrounded by more than four acres of lawn and twelve species of transplanted trees as well as ornamental plants, shrubs, and flowers. Twenty-two large olive trees had to be moved to the temple site at night under special permits. Two of the largest pine trees on the grounds were seventy feet tall. When transplanted, one tree with its soil weighed seventeen tons. The grounds were further beautified by a reflecting pool and a rose garden.

The building's interior is decorated with eight types of marble. Original murals are featured throughout the temple. Los Angeles artist Joseph Gibby was commissioned to paint a mural of the Savior's baptism by John the Baptist in the River Jordan. As the project neared completion, Gibby spoke with President McKay about a problem he had encountered. "I cannot paint the Savior's face to my satisfaction," he told the prophet. "I need to know His complexion and coloring." Without hesitation, President McKay described the Savior's features.

Millard F. Malin was selected to create the angel Moroni statue for the temple's spire. The nearly fifteen-and-a-half-foot statue was made of aluminum instead of bronze to meet the Los Angeles building code. With gold leaf added, the statue weighed some twenty-one hundred pounds. Malin's angel Moroni has Native American features, wears a Mayan-style cloak, carries the gold plates with his left arm, and with his

SITE
13 acres

GROUNDBREAKING
September 22, 1951, by
David O. McKay

DEDICATION
March 11–14, 1956, by
David O. McKay

EXTERIOR
Covered with 146,000 square feet
of Mo-Sai stone facing, a mixture of
crushed quartz and white Portland
cement quarried in Utah and Nevada;
the wainscot around the exterior is
Rockville granite from Minnesota

TOTAL FLOOR AREA
190,614 square feet

DIMENSIONS
269 feet by 369 feet; overall
height is 257 feet

HIDDEN IMAGE
Based upon the spirit of the temple
and the hymn "The Spirit of God,"
subtle flames are placed throughout
the temple's landscaping.

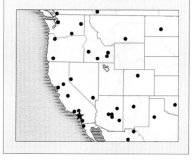

right hand holds an eight-foot trumpet to his lips.

The architectural plans depicted the statue of the angel Moroni facing southeast. During one of his frequent visits to the temple site, President McKay told the architect and newly appointed temple president that the statue "was not correct in that position" and asked the architect to adjust the statue so that it would face due east.

Public interest in the temple was clearly evident during the temple's fifty-one-day open house, when nearly 700,000 people visited the temple. President David O. McKay dedicated the temple March 11 to 14, 1956. The proceedings were carried throughout the temple by closed-circuit television. In reference to this technology, President McKay commented, "How easy it must be in the spirit world to tune in on an occasion of this kind."

In recent years, a much-anticipated annual event has brought thousands of people, members and nonmembers alike, to Temple Hill. Each Christmas season, nearly half a million lights set the entire grounds ablaze with festivity and celebration, symbolizing the great light that came into the world through Christ's birth. During the annual lighting ceremony, those in attendance hear the Christmas story as told in the Bible and Book of Mormon. A Church official explained: "This is the one opportunity during the year that we have to represent to the public the unique Christmas story as found in the Book of Mormon. We share the story of Christmas both from the Book of Mormon and the Bible, which really seems to move the hearts of those in attendance."

Although the temple is often admired for its beauty, its true value lies in the ordinances performed within. Jan Dickson agonized over being unable to attend the temple because she was unable to sit for long periods of time. She prayed for months that the Lord would make it possible for her to attend the temple. Then one day, Rosa Rice, a member in Sister Dickson's ward, called and said she had felt prompted to talk to her about the temple. Sister Dickson explained her medical condition. In turn, Sister Rice explained Sister Dickson's situation to the temple presidency, and they gave permission for her to lie on a gurney during the session. Soon Sister Dickson was attending the temple every month. To her friends who made this blessing possible, she said, "Thank you . . . for following the Spirit's prompting, for opening a door I didn't know could be opened."

Hamilton New Zealand Temple
==

Before the missionaries began proselyting among the Maori people in New Zealand, several *Tohungas* (Maori spiritual leaders) told of the coming of the "true religion." In 1879, King Tawhiao said that ministers of the true church would come in the future and would travel two by two. He said, "They will not come to you and return to European accommodations but they will stay with you, talk with you, eat with you, and abide with you." This is among the many predictions fulfilled with the beginning of Latter-day Saint missionary work among the Maoris in 1881. Several Maoris were baptized in 1882, and the first branch among their people was established in 1883.

In 1955, President David O. McKay arrived to look for property for a temple site. Of their meeting on the hill west of the Church College of New Zealand, Elder Wendell B. Mendenhall, director of the Church's building program in the Pacific, recalled, "President McKay called me to one side. By the way he was looking at the hill, I could tell immediately what was on his mind. . . . He asked, 'What do you think?' I knew what his question implied, and I simply asked in return, 'What do you think, [President] McKay?' And then in an almost prophetic tone he pronounced, 'This is the place to build the temple.'"

Purchasing the land was difficult because the family that owned the property did not want to sell. President McKay met with members of the family on the site to discuss possibilities, but the family members departed without agreeing to sell. As they

11

drove away, President McKay said with a tone of reassuring confidence, "They will sell it; they will sell it." Within a few days, the family changed their mind, but their selling price was much higher than the Church was willing to spend. The family's attorney agreed to analyze the property value himself and propose a price based upon his methods. The attorney's valuation turned out to precisely match the Church's property appraisal. The sale was quickly made.

Before the property acquisition could be finalized, the purchase had to be approved by the local government. The country's National Minister of Lands, Ernest Corbett, visited the property with Elder Mendenhall. As he visited the site, he was amazed with the college and the Church's efforts to develop the Maori people to the highest standard. Genuinely impressed, he turned to Elder Mendenhall and asked him to take this dictation: "Received personal assurance this day from the Minister of Lands and Maori Affairs that the New Zealand Government will not oppose the acquisition of this property."

Ground was broken for the temple on December 21, 1955. Work on the temple began immediately, with all of the construction being done by volunteer laborers, many of whom were just out of high school. Some were experienced builders from throughout the Pacific and the United States who responded to mission calls. Local Saints supported the labor missionaries with food and housing while they worked on the temple. Other workers received on-the-job training and were later able to start their own businesses using their newly developed trade.

Workers hurried to finish construction, but it appeared that the building would not be completed in time for the scheduled open house and dedication. Many who had already given their time and energy from dawn to dusk began working even longer shifts. At the peak of the construction, more than 400 labor missionaries were engaged simultaneously at the neighboring college and the temple. The day before the open house, workers laid carpet and hung wallpaper. Furniture was moved into the temple until one o'clock that morning.

Many noteworthy events occurred during the building's construction. While the concrete foundation was being poured, many workers witnessed an aberration in the weather. One worker, not a member of the Church, observed: "I have never

SITE
86 acres (including college grounds)

GROUNDBREAKING
December 21, 1955, by Ariel Ballif, Wendell B. Mendenhall, and George R. Biesinger

DEDICATION
April 20–22, 1958, by David O. McKay

EXTERIOR
Reinforced concrete block manufactured at site; white painted structural steel

TOTAL FLOOR AREA
44,212 square feet

DIMENSIONS
159 feet by 84 feet; height of tower is 157 feet

HIDDEN IMAGE
Placed on the temple grounds is Jesus Christ, the Good Shepherd, with His flock of sheep.

seen the rain act this way. The rain stops when it comes to this hill. Sometimes the clouds divide and go around the hill." This reprieve from the rains made it possible to not lose time while the concrete was poured.

Soon after topsoil had been spread over the hill in preparation for landscaping, a large storm hit the area, washing most of the topsoil from the temple hill. Leaders called on members to help fix the damage. Some 450 men, women, and children responded. Within three days, the workers had transported all of the topsoil back onto the hill.

During the three-week open house, nearly 113,000 people toured the temple. On April 20, 1958, President McKay gave thanks in his dedicatory prayer, saying, "We express gratitude that to these fertile Islands Thou didst guide descendants of Father Lehi, and hast enabled them to prosper and to become associated in history with leading and influential nations among mankind."

In early 1986 the temple received three Maria Theresa Czechoslovakian chandeliers for the celestial room. Each chandelier weighed approximately 500 pounds and displayed 2,755 pieces of cut crystal. One night, after one chandelier had been hung, temple president Glen L. Rudd woke up with an uneasy feeling. He said, "I thought to myself, 'something is wrong.' . . . Early the next morning I contacted our temple engineer. He expressed that he too had an uneasy feeling. We went into the temple and looked at the chandelier, and immediately we were able to see that the ceiling was sagging a little from the additional weight it was bearing." Before the other two chandeliers were installed, a structural engineer designed some large plates to correct the problem. President Rudd summarized: "There is no doubt in my mind but what we were impressed by the Spirit of the Lord to the fact that there was a problem and to not hang the other chandeliers until corrections were made."

The Hamilton New Zealand Temple has become an important landmark of Mormonism and a beacon visually and spiritually. Indeed, a marvelous work and a wonder has taken place on the hill at Tuhikaramea in Aotearoa—"the land of the long, white cloud"—as it was named by the Maori who settled these islands over 1,000 years ago.

London England Temple

An important milestone for British Latter-day Saints came with the construction and dedication of the beautiful London England Temple, located at Newchapel in Surrey. The thirty-two-acre temple site features formal gardens that occupy about one-third of the property. Towering oaks listed in a British registry, spacious lawns, an ornamental pond, and colorful rhododendrons and azaleas beautify the grounds throughout the year. The peace and beauty of the temple's picturesque English setting have a calming effect on all who visit.

The London Temple stands on historic ground that can be traced back to early Christianity. The area around Newchapel was successively occupied by the Celts, Romans, Saxons, and Danes. Anciently,

the property was split in half by the Roman highway that ran between London and the sea. The property was also included in William the Conqueror's *Doomsday Book,* recorded in about 1086, which was instrumental in establishing the feudal system. Old Pilgrim's Way, made famous by Chaucer's *Canterbury Tales,* ran nearby.

Two oak trees on the property—one in the garden and one near the temple—are thought to have existed at the time of Columbus's discovery of the Americas. Before the construction of the temple began, President David O. McKay gave instructions that the five-hundred-year-old tree in front of the temple should not be removed. Local members thought of their prophet with affection when viewing the oak and

12

subsequently attached a plaque to it identifying the tree as "The David O. McKay Oak."

After decades of enhancing the temple's pastoral setting, the tree eventually died. Several years prior to the tree's demise, Church landscaping supervisor Irvin T. Nelson brought nearly two hundred of the ancient tree's acorns to Salt Lake City. He planted and nurtured the acorns in pots located on Temple Square. Of the many acorns planted, two of them matured into small trees. When the trees were four years old, Brother Nelson showed them to President McKay, who received them with a big smile. Brother Nelson affectionately named each of the trees "President David O. McKay Oak Jr."

In 1972, Peter Lassig succeeded Irvin Nelson as Temple Square landscaping supervisor. Brother Lassig planted one of the "McKay Oak Jr." trees behind the Aaronic Priesthood monument. There in the shadows of the Salt Lake Temple, it grew well and matured into an attractive and large tree. In 2002, construction work on Temple Square required that the oak tree be removed. Thankfully, six months prior to construction, Brother Lassig had the foresight to harvest hundreds of acorns from the tree and send them to the London Temple to be planted on the grounds as the "grandchildren" of the original "David O. McKay Oak."

The impressive baronial mansion on the grounds, with its flagged floors, hand-hewn oak beams, and wrought-iron fixtures, is referred to as the Manor House and dates back to Elizabethan times. A previous owner developed the country estate into a horse farm. The Church rented the horse pastures on the property to Sir Winston Churchill, who had purchased an adjoining estate. More recently, the mansion has served as a home to the temple president and as a bureau of information. In 1985 it became a Missionary Training Center for much of Europe.

After the property was purchased, President David O. McKay and Church architect Edward O. Anderson spent time on the grounds deciding on the best placement for the temple. The site finally selected by President McKay had previously been partially covered by a lily pond, which had left the ground marshy, and the construction engineers feared it would prove unsuitable for the temple's foundation. President McKay, however, insisted that this was where the temple was

SITE
32 acres

GROUNDBREAKING
August 27, 1955, by David O. McKay

DEDICATION
September 7–9, 1958, by
David O. McKay

REDEDICATION
October 18–20, 1992, by
Gordon B. Hinckley

EXTERIOR
Reinforced concrete on structural steel skeleton; walls of brick masonry faced with white cut Portland limestone; spire sheathed in copper

TOTAL FLOOR AREA
42,652 square feet

DIMENSIONS
84 feet wide, 159 feet long, 56 feet to the square; tower rises 156 feet from ground level, spire 33 feet above that

HIDDEN IMAGE
Among the trees and foliage to the right of the temple is a full-length image of the Savior.

to be built. Upon further investigation, workers discovered that beneath the boggy ground was solid shale at the proper depth to support the temple. After the discovery, a project engineer commented, "You could build the city of London on that site."

On August 27, 1955, again visiting Europe, eighty-one-year-old President McKay broke ground for the temple. The services were held under a cove of trees in the garden. The Mormon Tabernacle Choir, then on tour in Europe, sang at the groundbreaking. Fine craftsmen from around England built the temple according to the highest architectural standards of the day. One of these craftsmen observed, "Why, you've put such steel and stone in this building that it might well stand 2,000 years."

British Mission president A. Hamer Reiser recognized the hand of the Lord in preparing the way for the London England Temple: "It may seem nothing spectacular or unusual has occurred during the building, but I nevertheless acknowledge the hand of the Lord in every detail. He has worked out His will in very natural ways and brought to pass many, many favourable conditions and factors that made this project possible."

On October 18, 1992, the London England Temple was rededicated by President Gordon B. Hinckley after being closed for two years for extensive remodeling and refurbishing. A three-week open house was held when the work was completed. There were advertisements and stories in local and national newspapers, a feature story on BBC (British Broadcasting Corporation), and some 200,000 flyers distributed to every home in the vicinity of the temple. Above a color photograph of the temple were the words, "The last time you could tour this building was in 1958." Beneath the photograph, the flyer said, "The next time is for six days during October 1992." Many of the more than 55,000 people who visited this open house had attended the one held thirty-four years earlier. Bryan J. Grant, public affairs director for the Europe North Area, said it was "the best single event in terms of its effect on the general public that we've ever had in Britain." Some will say that the temple was finally completed on December 15, 2008, when a helicopter placed an eight-foot angel Moroni statue on the temple's spire. The London England Temple has been a crowning achievement for Church members in the British Isles.

Oakland California Temple

The Oakland California Temple rests upon a site that is separate from the noise and bustle of the surrounding metropolis and yet accessible to the millions it serves. The unobstructed view from the East Bay Hills overlooks Oakland, Berkeley, San Francisco, and the waters of the famous bay leading out to the Pacific Ocean through the Golden Gate.

The history of the Oakland California Temple began in the summer of 1924, when Elder George Albert Smith, then a member of the Quorum of the Twelve Apostles, visited the San Francisco Bay area. Elder Smith sat on the roof terrace of a hotel with W. Aird MacDonald, a local Church leader. While admiring the view of the bay from atop the hotel, Elder Smith ceased talking and for several minutes gazed intently toward the hills above Oakland. He then said: "Brother MacDonald, I can almost see in vision a white temple of the Lord high upon those hills, an ensign to all the world travelers as they sail through the Golden Gate into this wonderful harbor. . . . A great white temple of the Lord will grace those hills, a glorious ensign to the nations, to welcome our Father's children as they visit this great city."

When this prophecy was made in 1924, the Church in that part of California consisted of only a few small branches, which were struggling to gain a foothold in the community. But the anticipation of a temple in central California brought these Saints hope.

In the April 1943 general conference, President Heber J. Grant announced: "I am happy to tell you

13

that we have purchased in the Oakland area another temple site. . . . The site is located on the lower foothills of East Oakland on a rounded hill overlooking San Francisco Bay. We shall in due course build there a splendid temple." Long before the temple was built, the future temple site was known as "Cow Hill," where children would slide down the grassy slope on cardboard.

Following the announcement, a committee was formed and given responsibility to raise funds for the temple. It was suggested that the local stakes contribute $500,000. The Saints gave an immediate and generous response, donating more than $750,000 for the temple.

The Oakland Temple's innovative interior made it the first temple capable of holding more than one endowment session at a time. The design of the temple's exterior is modern contemporary and has some Far-Eastern influence as well. The towers are perforated and covered in a blue glass mosaic and gold leaf.

Two sculptured granite panels, heroic in size, are displayed on the temple's north and south facades. The panel on the north depicts Christ and His Apostles in the Old World; the south panel shows Christ appearing to the Nephites in Bountiful. Lifting and securing the massive panels to the walls of the temple posed an especially difficult problem. The men working on the granite exterior found there was no way to put the twelve-ton panels into place without damaging them. Glen R. Nielsen, a Church member and contractor, prayed for a solution. "I went to my Father in Heaven with our problem and I asked Him to please show us the way to pick up these panels . . . without accident. One Sunday just before we were going to set the panels I was shown the way we were to pick up the panels. It was as clear to me as if I looked at someone face to face. . . . I knew the exact number of bolts to use, their size, the metal to use and how it was to be constructed."

During the public open house of the temple, a man arrived in a chauffeured government car and introduced himself as a commander of a ship in the U.S. Navy. He said, "I brought my ship through the Golden Gate early this morning and observed . . . on the foothills of East Oakland, a new landmark which I had not seen before. I immediately berthed my ship and made the necessary arrangements so that I could come here to determine what . . . this new landmark [is]." Some members saw this statement as being a partial fulfillment of

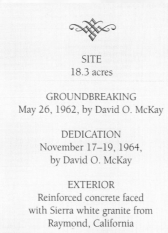

SITE
18.3 acres

GROUNDBREAKING
May 26, 1962, by David O. McKay

DEDICATION
November 17–19, 1964,
by David O. McKay

EXTERIOR
Reinforced concrete faced
with Sierra white granite from
Raymond, California

TOTAL FLOOR AREA
95,000 square feet

DIMENSIONS
210 feet by 302 feet with a
central tower rising 170 feet

HIDDEN IMAGE
A lighthouse among the trees
focuses a beam of light toward
the San Francisco Bay

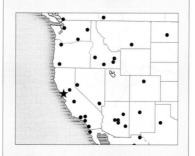

Elder George Albert Smith's prophecy that the temple would serve as an ensign to travelers as they entered through the Golden Gate into San Francisco Bay.

When the temple was dedicated on November 17, 1964, most people at the ceremony did not expect President David O. McKay, who had recently suffered a stroke, to offer the dedicatory prayer. His mind was whole, but his physical condition made it very difficult for him to speak or even to stand. Of these struggles, his son said: "His fluency of speech was gone. . . . He hated to talk because nearly always we could not understand him the first time and had to ask him to repeat what he had said." But when it came time to dedicate the temple, President McKay was helped to the pulpit, which he grasped tightly, and began to speak clearly and easily to the audience. His son recorded: "[My wife], with tears running down her cheeks, whispered, 'Lawrence, we are witnessing a miracle.' I nodded in agreement. Father finished his talk and, still standing, dedicated the building." The temple has served as a literal beacon in a very important way. Lorenzo N. Hoopes, who served as temple president from 1985–1990, explained, "During an energy crisis, when people cut back on their use of electricity, the Church dutifully turned off the temple's exterior lights. He said a frantic call came in from air traffic control asking the Church to turn the lights back on because the temple was a marker to guide pilots to the airport."

The Oakland California Temple has been protected from natural disasters. The powerful earthquake that shook central California on October 17, 1989, caused damage to the region estimated at $7 billion. But the temple escaped with only a few minor cracks. Two years later, wildfires in the area caused up to $5 billion in damage. Although the fire devastated the mountain ridge behind the temple, it was controlled before it reached the sacred edifice.

In 2014, activities throughout the year celebrated the temple's fiftieth year of service. An Oakland California Temple ordinance worker of more than fifteen years stated, "There is an ongoing process of learning in the temple. Many of the deeper and more significant principles of life are revealed. Faith is increased. Conviction is attained. A 'nobler estimate of man' is attained. In short, one gets a glimpse of the Celestial Kingdom."

Ogden Utah Temple

The first mention of a temple in Ogden came on December 12, 1920, when Elder Hyrum G. Smith, Patriarch to the Church, told the Saints in Ogden that they would one day have a temple. In 1921, President Heber J. Grant inspected potential sites for a temple in Ogden but concluded that the time had not yet come for a temple to be built there. The Saints in the area continued to travel to the Logan Utah Temple to perform their temple work.

In the early 1960s, President David O. McKay initiated research on the use of the temples then in operation. The study revealed that fifty-two percent of all ordinance work was being done in just three of the thirteen existing temples: the Salt Lake, Logan, and Manti temples. Instead of expanding these

temples to meet the ever-increasing needs of Church members in northern Utah, the First Presidency decided to build two new temples along the Wasatch Front—one in Ogden and one in Provo. Even though Saints in other areas of the Church had to travel much greater distances to attend the temple, the Brethren decided that adding two temples in Utah would serve the largest number of people.

Church members along the Wasatch corridor in northern Utah were elated to learn of the two new temples, the first to be constructed in Utah since the Salt Lake Temple had been completed in 1893. The site finally chosen for the Ogden temple was in downtown Ogden on the ten-acre, Church-owned Ogden Tabernacle block. To make room for the

14

30

temple, the historic pioneer tabernacle on the site had to be demolished. Knowing that removing this landmark might offend some in the community, Church leaders explained the decision at a press conference, emphasizing that although they loved the tabernacle and appreciated its significance in the community, the Church was a growing organization that could not jeopardize the future in preserving the past. The Church planned to replace the old tabernacle with a new one elsewhere on the same block.

Since its dedication on January 18, 1972, by President Joseph Fielding Smith, the Ogden Utah Temple has blessed the lives of all those who have served and worshipped within its walls. After nearly forty years of serving as one of the most productive temples in the Church, the most extensive renovation project in Church history was to be made. On February 17, 2010, Church and city officials announced plans to "remodel and architecturally change the appearance of the Ogden Utah Temple and its grounds." Bishop Keith B. McMullin of the Presiding Bishopric said, "These improvements will not only help us meet the increasing needs of a busy temple but will also be a part of the enhancement and beautification of downtown Ogden."

More than a single building renovation, the "Temple Square in Ogden" project included a tabernacle renovation, adding a parking facility, moving the Daughters of Utah Pioneers Museum, and moving the Miles Goodyear Cabin. Although these significant modifications were designed to accommodate the needs of the future, honor was given to those who made decisions in the past. As Elder William R. Walker stated, "When the decision was made by the First Presidency to do the renovation, there was obvious respect for [President David O.] McKay and others considered, and it is being built on the footprint of the first temple."

Without a formal decommission ceremony, renovation work began on April 25, 2011. Among the first tasks were to remove the original cornerstone plaque and time capsule box. The unopened copper time capsule was taken and stored at Church Headquarters, where it remained until it was repositioned in the new edifice on May 24, 2014.

GROUNDBREAKING
September 8, 1969, by Hugh B. Brown

DEDICATION
January 18–20, 1972, by
Joseph Fielding Smith

REDEDICATION
September 21, 2014, by
Thomas S. Monson

EXTERIOR
Granite, quarried and
fabricated in China

TOTAL FLOOR AREA
112,232 square feet

HIDDEN IMAGE
The original 1972 temple is softly silhouetted in the distant trees to the left of drawing. Additionally, the Savior is seen kneeling in prayer among the trees and landscaping.

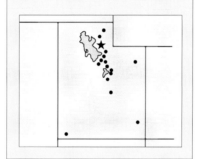

The exterior of the temple is clad in magnificent granite stone from China. Each piece arrived to the temple site precut, numbered, and ready for installation. With as many as 200 to 300 workers on the job at a time, the entire project was a constant beehive of activity. A construction milestone was reached on May 6, 2013, when the temple's 63,000-pound spire was successfully hoisted into position. The very next morning, amid the cheers and applause from the onlookers below, the spire was adorned with an angel Moroni statue. The newly refurbished angel is the same one that had been removed from the original Ogden Temple spire in 2011.

An estimated 550,000 visitors toured the temple during its five-week public open house. Among the visitors was a special group of about ninety blind individuals. Mike and Bonnie King, chairpersons of the usher committee, escorted the unique tour. They described their moving experience: "We were charged in helping the blind to visualize the majesty of the temple. As we entered the baptistry, they commented on how they could feel the cool air that fills the room." In the sealing room, some visitors chose to get on their hands and knees so they could feel the sculpting of the carpet and the craftsmanship of the granite altars. "A special moment was when we had them look towards the mirrors," said Sister King, "knowing they couldn't see, but describing to them what they would see if they could. As they envisioned looking eternally into their past and then into their future we taught the sacred truths of what blessings are found in the eternal gospel of Jesus Christ."

Due to the fact that the temple was a renovated and remodeled building, there was not a cornerstone ceremony at the time of its rededication. The transformation of the exquisite house of the Lord was completed on September 21, 2014, when President Thomas S. Monson rededicated the Ogden Utah Temple. During the ceremony, President Monson said, "As its doors open once again for the accomplishment of the purposes for which it was originally constructed and dedicated, lives will be blessed. It stands as a beacon of righteousness to all who will follow its light—the light of the gospel of Jesus Christ."

Provo Utah Temple

As the early Saints settled Utah Valley and began developing Provo City, they grew anxious for a temple in their midst. For years, the area on the hill where Brigham Young University now stands was known as Temple Hill. President Brigham Young is credited with saying: "We have ascended to the summit of this beautiful Hill and now you are standing on Holy Ground. The day will come when a Magnificent Temple will be erected here to our God and I want you to look and behold the scenic beauty of this wonderful Valley."

The idea of a temple in Provo revived during the 1950s as the enrollment of Brigham Young University soared from 4,510 to 10,305. The first student stake was organized in 1956. During this time, Church leaders began considering the possibility of doing missionary language training at BYU and having a temple nearby.

In the early 1960s, stake presidents in Utah Valley and nearby areas were called to a meeting with the First Presidency, who spoke with them about building a temple in Provo. Ben E. Lewis, one of those stake presidents, was assigned to chair the site-selection committee and raise funds from local Church members. President Lewis spoke privately after the meeting with President N. Eldon Tanner about a site he knew was available.

Some years before, a German immigrant named Leathy, who owned several acres of land near Rock Canyon on Provo's east bench, had approached President Lewis after having a vivid dream of a

15

beautiful temple being erected on his property. He had been so moved by the dream that he offered the land to President Lewis for a temple site. President Lewis, involved in BYU and Church land acquisition in Provo, communicated the information to President Harold B. Lee, who declined the offer. Instead, the property was purchased for BYU.

When President Tanner heard of the dream and the subsequent transaction, he was interested in the information but suggested considering other sites as well. After examining various sites around Provo, the committee recommended unanimously that the temple be placed on the Leathy property.

When President McKay announced the new temple to the members of the Church, the fund-raising response was immediate. An *Ensign* article reported on the Saints' enthusiasm for the temples in both Provo and Ogden: "One bishop discussed the quota for his ward in priesthood meeting, and by the time Sunday School was over, the total quota had been contributed in cash. One family had saved for a special vacation, but they voted in their family home evening to donate the total amount to the temple fund and save again for their postponed vacation. For Christmas of 1967 many families gave to the temple fund rather than to each other. Piggy banks were emptied, children's savings accounts were donated, and the widow's mite was contributed to make these beautiful buildings a reality."

The design for both the Ogden Utah Temple and the Provo Utah Temple was created by Church architect Emil B. Fetzer to maximize efficiency and accommodate the largest possible number of patrons. In this new design, small ordinance rooms on the second floor surround and open into the celestial room at the center of the temple. With six ordinance rooms, it would be possible for a session to begin every twenty minutes, accommodating many more patrons each day than any other temple then in operation. And having the two temples nearly identical in design kept construction costs relatively low. Thus, while the Ogden and Provo temples can accommodate as many individuals in a day as the largest temples in the Church, they were built at a fraction of the cost.

Almost a quarter of a million visitors toured the temple during the twenty days it was open to the public. The dedicatory prayer, written by President Joseph Fielding Smith, was read by President Harold B. Lee on February 9, 1972. Because

SITE
17 acres

GROUNDBREAKING
September 15, 1969, by
Hugh B. Brown

DEDICATION
February 9, 1972, by Joseph Fielding
Smith (read by Harold B. Lee)

EXTERIOR
White cast stone; gold anodized
aluminum grills; bronze glass
panels; single painted spire

TOTAL FLOOR AREA
128,325 square feet

DIMENSIONS
200 feet by 184 feet; 175
feet high with a 118-foot
spire on top of building

HIDDEN IMAGE
Christ is placed in the mountains
overlooking the temple with
His arms outstretched.

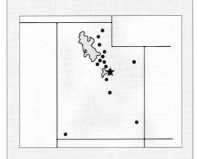

members could view the dedication on closed-circuit television in many locations, including Brigham Young University's Marriott Center, which seated 23,000, only two dedicatory sessions were required to accommodate all who wished to attend the services.

Since its dedication, the Provo Utah Temple has consistently been one of the Church's busiest temples. During its first full year of operation, 17.7 percent of all temple ordinances performed in the Church's fifteen operating temples were performed in the Provo Temple. For the next twenty-five years, this temple led the Church in the total number of endowments performed for the dead, even when subtracting the contributing numbers from nearby Brigham Young University and the Missionary Training Center.

According to Arthur S. Anderson, a past president of the Provo Utah Temple, the amount of temple work performed and the reverent atmosphere maintained in the temple are largely due to the more than two thousand workers who regularly serve in the temple. President Anderson gave an example of one dedicated temple worker from Heber City. One wintry day the worker couldn't make the twenty-eight-mile drive through Provo Canyon because of a storm that had closed the canyon. Instead of missing his shift that day, he took the circuitous route north to Park City, west to Salt Lake City, and then south to Provo. He traveled one hundred miles, not twenty-eight, to perform his temple duties. As decades have passed, numerous upgrades and renovations have taken place on the temple's exterior and interior. The most noticeable occurred on May 12, 2003, when an angel Moroni statue was placed on the spire. The spire's highest section was removed to make room for the statue and its base. Despite being an unpublished event, crowds quickly increased as news of the historic occasion spread. Later in the week, the spire was painted an off-white. After three-and-a-half years, a significant landscaping renovation was completed in 2006. The vast improvements included modifying the entry driveway, relocating the flagpole, expanded flowerbeds, and adding fountains and waterfalls.

Although the Ogden Utah Temple's extensive renovation project was completed in 2014, the Church has indicated that there are currently no similar plans for the temple in Provo. Thus, its design stands alone as it remains a unique spiritual beacon to faithful Saints throughout Utah Valley.

Washington D.C. Temple

In a city famous for its monuments to freedom, the Washington D.C. Temple was designed as a monument to the Lord, the Source of that freedom. Sitting amid lush greenery atop one of the highest points in the area, the temple is seen by millions every year who travel on the Capital Beltway (Interstate 495). The seven-story structure rises 288 feet, making it the tallest temple in the Church. A woman visiting from Florida observed, "Your temple preaches a profound sermon without saying a word."

The site for the temple was secured in 1962 for $850,000. It is situated on a wooded hill overlooking beautiful Rock Creek Park. Only eleven of the fifty-two acres were cleared for construction, thus creating a remote feeling and separating the temple from the distractions of the metropolitan area nearby.

In January 1969, a committee was formed to raise $4.5 million from the Saints living in the temple district. The remainder of the projected $15 million needed to build the temple would come from the general tithing funds of the Church. The Saints responded enthusiastically, contributing more than $6 million to the temple fund.

A team of four Utah architects was organized to create a structure that would impress upon viewers the grandeur of the gospel plan. For the temple to stand prominently above the surrounding wooded area, it would need to be quite tall. Accordingly, they designed the body of the temple to a height of 120

16

feet. They later learned that local building ordinances set 120 feet as the maximum height for that area.

Keith W. Wilcox described the architects' desires for the temple: "Our constant prayer was that the Washington Temple would 'glow with the spirit of enlightenment,' and that it would 'truly represent the majesty, dignity and vital message of the Church to all the world.'" Elsewhere Brother Wilcox said, "I have a feeling of deep humility, realizing that we have been instruments in the Lord's hands in helping to give direction to the design of one of his temples."

The Washington D.C. Temple is reminiscent of the Salt Lake Temple, with its six towers and similar shape. The towers on both temples symbolize the priesthood. The temple's vertical lines are a visual representation of our relationship to Deity. Another interesting feature is that the temple does not have any clear windows; however, the marble exterior is thin enough in some places to be translucent.

On the east and west ends of the temple are seven-foot-wide windows that run from the ground to the top of the temple. Near the ground, the glass is colored in rich and vibrant reds and oranges that give way to progressively lighter tones of blue, violet, and finally white. This succession of colors suggests the way the temple can shift visitors' minds from earthly concerns to thoughts of eternity. The windows rise unbroken to the top of the building, symbolizing the possibility of man's eternal growth.

Avard Fairbanks's representation of the angel Moroni was chosen from nine different designs. Positioned atop the temple, the statue holds a trumpet to its lips with one arm; in the other are the gold plates. "I wanted the angel Moroni statue to conform to the spirit and architecture of the temple, that of aspiring upward," Fairbanks said. "I wanted the feeling of that upward reach, accomplished by the stress of vertical lines." Fairbanks's three-foot model was enlarged in Italy and cast in bronze before a gold-leaf finish was added. When complete, the eighteen-foot statue weighed approximately two tons. A smaller bronze casting of this statue was used on the Seattle Washington, Jordan River Utah, and México City México Temples.

As the structure of the temple began to rise above the trees, travelers on the beltway became interested in this new and imposing building. A stream of visitors to the construction site

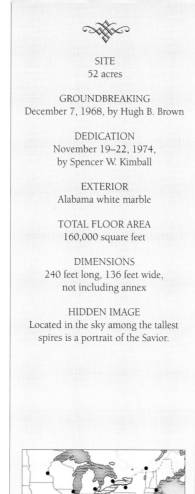

SITE
52 acres

GROUNDBREAKING
December 7, 1968, by Hugh B. Brown

DEDICATION
November 19–22, 1974,
by Spencer W. Kimball

EXTERIOR
Alabama white marble

TOTAL FLOOR AREA
160,000 square feet

DIMENSIONS
240 feet long, 136 feet wide,
not including annex

HIDDEN IMAGE
Located in the sky among the tallest
spires is a portrait of the Savior.

encouraged Church leaders to finish a visitors' center on the grounds even before the temple itself was completed. During its first year of operation, the center welcomed more than 115,000 visitors. In 2004, the annual visitor count was an estimated 250,000.

On January 10, 2015, a large model exhibit of the Washington D.C. Temple was opened at the visitors' center. The model was built using three-dimensional scans of the temple's interior and exterior to create the 1:48-scale replica. The model is about nine feet high and has an open cross section that shows all levels of the temple, including minute details such as furniture, light fixtures, and doors.

Because of the temple's proximity to the nation's capital, the first week of the open house was set aside for government officials from the United States and other countries. Betty Ford, wife of United States president Gerald R. Ford, participated in one of these tours and asked to have her photograph taken with President Spencer W. Kimball. Nearly three-quarters of a million people visited the temple during its seven-week open house. The Washington D.C. Temple was dedicated in ten sessions from November 19 to 22, 1974, becoming the first modern temple in use east of the Mississippi River.

The temple experienced a rattling event on August 23, 2011 when a 5.9-magnitude earthquake's epicenter occurred about 100 miles away near Richmond, Virginia. The violent shaking resulted in pieces of marble facing breaking loose and the tips of four spires falling off. Thankfully, no one was injured and the temple never closed.

With a press of a button, a highly anticipated Christmas holiday tradition comes to life on the temple grounds. The annual "Festival of Lights" features more than 600,000 lights and draws more than 200,000 visitors each year. In 2001, ambassadors from thirty-five nations joined the event to honor the victims of the September 11th attacks. In honor of the victims, only red, white, and blue lights were featured.

For years, the Washington D.C. Temple was the only temple that served Church members living in the eastern United States and Canada and in all of South America. During its first twenty-five years of operation, some 38,520 marriages were performed in this temple. The Washington D.C. Temple has become "a light unto the world."

São Paulo Brazil Temple

"I have an important announcement," President Spencer W. Kimball said even before the opening hymn and prayer of the Brazil area conference in 1975. "A temple will be built in Brazil, it will be built [here] in Sao Paulo." The audience gasped, and many began to weep as he unveiled a painting of the planned temple. Elder L. Tom Perry called this "the greatest audience reaction I have ever seen."

As the structure of the temple grew, so too did the maturity and stability of the Church in South America. Many historic and divinely-led events transpired during the temple's construction. During this time, the calling of native missionaries began to build momentum. In 1977, over seventy percent of missionaries in Brazil were native members, with over 400 called

during the first eight months of that year. Additionally, the first Brazilian mission presidents were called between 1974 and 1978. The calling of missionaries had a direct impact on the increased number of Melchizedek Priesthood holders who could serve in the temple and in stake callings.

A major difficulty that missionaries encountered was the question of race and the Church's ban on ordaining men of black African descent to the priesthood. Despite this policy, many members of African descent rejoiced equally in the announcement of a temple, despite not knowing whether they would ever be able to enter. The pinnacle moment regarding race, priesthood, and the temple took place just weeks prior to the temple's dedication. On September 30, 1978, the

17

Church reversed its ban on priesthood ordination for men of African descent and allowed men and women of all races to participate in temple ordinances. All of these historic events during the temple's construction had dramatic ramifications on the temple and the future of Church growth throughout South America and the world.

To take part in building the first temple on their continent since the end of Book of Mormon times, Saints from all over South America made significant sacrifices to donate to the temple fund. "They didn't have any money to contribute to the temple fund, or, the money that they managed to save wasn't worth much because of inflation," Elder James E. Faust said. "So they started offering their wedding rings, bracelets, gold medals, diamond rings, graduation rings and many other personal objects of gold, silver and precious stones. One member of the Church in Argentina even offered his gold dental cap." When the Saints in South America had reached sixty percent of their quota for donation, a member in Sao Paulo said: "A lot of [the members] already contributed everything they had. From now on they will have to start giving what they don't have. That is where the real sacrifice will begin." Many members from the far-reaching corners of Brazil and the rest of South America faced the trial of their own faith as they contributed to the construction of a temple that they might never be able to enter due to their financial situation. After donating whatever possible to the temple fund, members began again to sacrifice and save for their anticipated journeys to the temple.

Evidence of that sacrifice shines forth from the temple's shimmering white exterior, the work of eight hundred members who, financially unable to import white stone, donated their time to produce fifty thousand blocks of cast stone composed of quartz, marble, and white concrete. The high quality of construction required by the Church for the temple set new building standards for the city. "I have never seen anything like it before," commented Josef Weinberger, the nonmember engineer of the project. "It is the most perfect building I have ever seen."

Architects went to great lengths to make the temple sturdy (its foundation is said to be strong enough to sustain thirteen additional stories) and capable of withstanding a major earthquake with minimal damage. At the time, Brazil was considered an earthquake-free country, but during construction a small

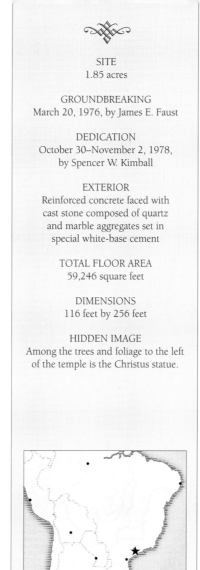

SITE
1.85 acres

GROUNDBREAKING
March 20, 1976, by James E. Faust

DEDICATION
October 30–November 2, 1978,
by Spencer W. Kimball

EXTERIOR
Reinforced concrete faced with
cast stone composed of quartz
and marble aggregates set in
special white-base cement

TOTAL FLOOR AREA
59,246 square feet

DIMENSIONS
116 feet by 256 feet

HIDDEN IMAGE
Among the trees and foliage to the left
of the temple is the Christus statue.

earthquake shook downtown Sao Paulo. The following day, newspapers were filled with articles citing local scientists as saying that more earthquakes of a greater magnitude were likely in the future.

When the temple was dedicated, President Spencer W. Kimball said, "I believe the Lord's Spirit is very close to us: He may be here in person. It would not be the first of the temples built to Him that He has occupied." In a dedicatory service, Elder Gordon B. Hinckley made particular reference to black members by saying, "Their contributions to a building they would not be allowed to enter was the greatest test those members would ever have to endure."

Former temple president Athos Marques de Amorim related a story of a family from Paraguay who had exceptional faith and determination to obtain temple blessings. The poor family had spent all their resources to make the long bus trip. When the bus reached Sao Paulo, however, the family missed the appropriate stop and were taken to the central bus station some seventeen miles from the temple. Because they didn't have enough money to take a bus back, the family, most of whom were barefoot, walked the distance back to the temple. They were overjoyed when they finally reached their destination. Instead of asking for any relief from their exhausting journey, they said simply that they wanted to be sealed together as a family. While the family was in Sao Paulo, Church members there collected clothing and shoes to give them. When the family returned to Paraguay, they felt spiritually recompensed for their journey to the temple, which had cost them all that they had.

In 2002, twenty-four years after its dedication, the temple was closed for significant renovation and expansion. The expansion included the addition of an angel Moroni statue, a modernized interior, a remodeled basement, and upgrading of mechanical systems. Once completed, the temple was opened to the public and received 99,000 visitors. The temple was rededicated on February 22, 2004, by President Gordon B. Hinckley.

When the temple was dedicated in 1978, Brazil had a Church membership of some 51,000 and twelve stakes. At the time of its rededication, it had some 867,000 members in 184 stakes. As the Church in Brazil continues to grow, the São Paulo Brazil Temple will remain a great symbol of the Lord's love for His people and of their commitment to Him.

Tokyo Japan Temple

Soon after World War II ended, the Church reopened its mission in Japan, with headquarters in the devastated city of Tokyo. In 1948, mission president Edward L. Clissold purchased an old building that had been hit by two bombs during the war. Though the building had to be completely reconstructed, the property was ideal for a mission home. In 1949, Elder Matthew Cowley of the Quorum of the Twelve Apostles stood in the library of the newly completed mission headquarters and offered the dedicatory prayer. In his prayer he was inspired to prophesy, "There will some day be many Church buildings, and even temples in [Japan]."

Considering the Church's condition in Japan at that time, this prediction was truly a wonder to those who heard it. Twenty-five years later, at the Japan area conference in 1974, President Spencer W. Kimball announced: "We bring you a matter of grave importance to all the people of the Asian countries and the world. Brother Matthew Cowley, one of the Twelve Apostles, made a prediction that there would be temples in Asia and in Japan. . . . And many of us have been almost holding our breath until the time could come when we could build a temple in this land. We, therefore, propose to you assembled here that we establish a temple in Tokyo, Japan, for all of Asia." Although generally reserved in their outward reactions, the Japanese Saints spontaneously broke into applause and wept for joy.

Members all over Asia and the Pacific expressed

18

their joy at the announcement. Baltazar G. Frederico, who was then serving as a branch president in the Philippines, declared: "Now I can work for the building of a temple. I have been saving every penny I could since December to save for a trip to the temple in Hawaii or New Zealand. But now I will work for the temple in Japan and take my family there." He noted that the announcement of a temple brought "warm brightness" to his life. One Japanese Saint exclaimed, "I can't express in words what this means to us as a family. We will be able to be sealed together in two or three years when the temple is finished. I can't believe it yet."

Work soon began at the temple site across from picturesque Arisugawa Park, just a few miles from downtown Tokyo, on the very spot where Elder Cowley had made his prophecy. An advantage of this location is its easy access to Tokyo's mass transit system. Temple patrons coming to Tokyo by air, train, or boat may go directly from their arrival points by way of the Tokyo central subway system to the Hiroo Station, which is a five-minute walk from the temple.

Materials for building the Tokyo Japan Temple were gathered from all over the world. The tower and ornate entranceway were built from granite native to Japan and onyx from Mexico. Black quartz from the Andes Mountains in South America was imported to use in the outer walls, and the stained-glass windows were created in Seattle, Washington. The international flavor of the temple extends to the interior, which is furnished with carpets woven in the United States, decorative glass imported from Ohio and France, and chandeliers for the celestial room created in Czechoslovakia.

In April 1978, construction on the temple began. Two years and two months plus 30,000 man-hours later, the completed temple stood as one of the safest, best-constructed buildings in Tokyo. Crowded living conditions and a shortage of land in Tokyo prompted the Church to develop unique features for the building, including a parking garage and an apartment for the temple president.

One of the more challenging tasks was the structural engineering of the central spire. It had to be designed to withstand an earthquake and typhoon conditions. Temple architect Emil B. Fetzer explained, "Some challenges can result in blessings. The workmanship was of exceptional quality and we are

SITE
0.46 acres

GROUNDBREAKING
Not formally held

DEDICATION
October 27–29, 1980, by
Spencer W. Kimball

EXTERIOR
Structural steel and reinforced
concrete faced with 289 panels
of precast stone, having the
appearance of light gray granite

TOTAL FLOOR AREA
52,590 square feet

DIMENSIONS
Ground floor is 103 feet by 134
feet; upper levels are 103 by 105
feet; height to square is 70.5 feet,
to top of tower is 178 feet

HIDDEN IMAGE
Christ is placed among the trees
overlooking the temple.

most gratified with the result. The craftsmen in the metal manufacturing shops who fashioned the spire are some of the finest workmen I have ever seen. But we also have an added bonus with the stainless steel of the tower we didn't anticipate." He continued, "We found after the spire was assembled in a place, that it takes on the color of the early morning sunlight, which is a beautiful pinkish color. Then during the daylight hours, it reflects the color of the sky and the clouds, and in the evening when the sun goes down, the tower lights up in the beautiful, warm colors of the sunset. We are absolutely delighted with how the tower is changing colors all day long from hues of soft pink to blues and whites. An unexpected, delightful thing has occurred!"

Five years after announcing the Tokyo Japan Temple, President Kimball dedicated it on October 27, 1980. The ceremony was considered by the Saints to be the most important event in the history of the Church in Asia. In the midst of a lengthy tour of the Far East, the eighty-five-year-old prophet was nonetheless able to stand at the pulpit to deliver the dedicatory address and prayer.

Much of the landscaping around the temple is a re-creation of the miniature Japanese garden found originally on the site when it was the mission office. Plants from those grounds, stone Japanese lanterns, and some nicely shaped rocks were preserved for reuse in the temple landscaping, linking the past with the present. Brother Fetzer explained, "As we designed the garden area and fence around the temple, we opened up the heavy stone wall with decorative metal fencing to allow passersby to view the temple and the garden. Even with this change, we have still preserved the possibility of securing the grounds. I think it is a very nice feature of the temple site."

An editorial in the *Church News* discussed the significance of the Tokyo Japan Temple to the Saints in Asia: "The construction and dedication of that sacred temple is both momentous and portentous. It portends a new day for the Orient, an extension of the light of Christ in that region such as never has been known before. . . . This is not just another temple. It is not just another dedication. It is the opening of an era, the extension of a dispensation, the dawning of a day when millions of Oriental people may have access to the Savior and His Atonement through the only ordinances that can save—those of His one and only true Church."

Seattle Washington Temple

The Seattle Washington Temple was built in the suburb of Bellevue on more than twenty-three acres of pristine woodlands. With the exception of the area cleared for the temple and a stake center, the rest of the surrounding forest has been left undisturbed. Visitors to the temple walk on paths among tall trees to enjoy an area known as "the Grove," a secluded nook reminiscent of the Sacred Grove. To make the building harmonious with the surrounding trees, the architect used vertical lines throughout the exterior and interior of the temple.

A temple in the Pacific Northwest had initially been proposed to the First Presidency by a group of stake presidents in 1960 during the administration of President David O. McKay. But no action was taken until 1974, when the First Presidency assigned F. Arthur Kay, then a regional representative, to locate property suitable for a temple. Strict instructions were given to keep the search private. The five-month search for a site covered a broad geographic region and was at times very discouraging.

On the evening of December 23, 1974, Brother Kay and his real estate agent had experienced yet another fruitless day in their search. Disheartened, they drove back toward the real estate office. During the long ride back to Issaquah, deep discouragement overcame Brother Kay, and he silently cried out, "Heavenly Father, will I ever find the land that Thou hast in mind for Thy holy house? Please, Father, wilt Thou lead me to the property and reveal it unto me?" As they approached

19

the parking lot in the East Gate Shopping Center, suddenly the property just behind the real estate office caught Elder Kay's attention. How many weeks had he parked his car in the shadow of that very hillside as he came to meet with the agent? Until that moment, the land had been obscured to his natural eye, but on that late December evening, his eyes were opened and he recognized the hillside for what it was. He recorded in his journal, "My eyes were drawn to it. I noticed immediately that it was situated higher than its surrounding property. It was heavily wooded with fir, hemlock, cedar, madrona, and alder trees. There were flowering cherry and numerous other species of trees and shrubs. I pointed to this beautiful hillside and I remarked to Mr. Cade, 'You know, what we're really looking for is a piece of property just like this one above us, just behind your office!' I was impressed to say, 'Could this property possibly be for sale? Who owns it? What would it be worth?' Mr. Cade didn't know but said he would find out. We drove around the property for the first time. Together we walked over and through and around the property. I knew plainly we had found the temple site. My heart was overcome with gratitude beyond description in knowing that the Lord had heard my prayer."

On November 15, 1975, President Spencer W. Kimball made the announcement that a temple would be built in the Pacific Northwest. Saints in the temple district were excited by the news and eager to contribute to the building fund. One individual donated the money required to purchase eighteen chandeliers. Through individual contributions, Relief Society sisters in the temple district donated sixty thousand dollars to purchase three life-size statues. Part of the Monument to Women series, the statues depict women fulfilling their roles in the home and society.

As the temple progressed, several details were added to beautify and give special symbolic meaning to the sacred edifice. On the exterior walls are high-relief sculptures of stalks of wheat that appear to be growing out of the ground. The wheat pattern can also be clearly seen on the metal ornamentation on the entrance doors. These symbolize how we can find spiritual nourishment in the temple by learning of Christ, who is the "bread of life" (John 6:35). Architect of the Seattle Washington Temple, Emil B. Fetzer, incorporated a flying buttress into the

SITE
23.5 acres

GROUNDBREAKING
May 27, 1978, by Marion G. Romney

DEDICATION
November 17–21, 1980,
by Spencer W. Kimball

EXTERIOR
Reinforced concrete faced with white marble aggregate and cast stone

TOTAL FLOOR AREA
110,000 square feet

DIMENSIONS
Ground level is 141 feet by 193 feet; upper levels are 117 feet by 163 feet; height to square is 70 feet; height to top of angel Moroni is 179 feet

HIDDEN IMAGE
An image of Joseph Smith's First Vision is placed in the grove of trees left of the temple.

design of the temple tower. He also designed the temple three feet wider at the base than at the top. Upon close inspection, the temple's exterior walls dramatically curve outward. This tapered effect provides the appearance of being firmly grounded in the earth while directing the focus heavenward.

Various groups opposing the temple attempted to hinder construction throughout the entire planning and building process. Problems arose even before the Church had formally acquired the property. Initial concerns centered on the effect on trees and wildlife, while others disputed the height of the building. Finally, on August 13, 1976, the Church closed on purchasing the property. F. Arthur Kay, who became the temple's first president, commented on these events: "I felt the influence of the adversary so strongly that it caused the very hairs on the back of my neck to stand straight up. But in time, the spirit of the Lord would prevail and assure me that in the end, all would be well."

Formal approval did not end the bitter opposition to the temple and the Church. When picketers attempted to block the entrance on the first day of the open house, some of them had to be physically removed. Later, on the first day of the temple's dedication, November 17, 1980, protesters attempted to chain themselves to the gates, but their efforts failed, and twenty-one were arrested. While opposition raged outside, President Spencer W. Kimball counseled the Saints gathered within the temple's walls, saying, "Temples are a place of peace and holiness. Let us lay aside the cares and worries of the outside world. We can then center our minds on the things of the Spirit as the great mysteries of life are unfolded to us. Here we learn the answers to those important questions that puzzle all mankind. Where did we come from? Why are we here? Where do we go when this mortal life is finished and over? . . . We are here to receive the word of the Lord."

The tremendous opposition only solidified the Saints' commitment to the temple and the ordinances performed in it. One hundred thousand endowments were performed in under six months after the temple opened—double the number that had been expected by the temple committee. This dedication to the temple and the sacred ordinances that are performed in it demonstrate both the faithfulness and the gratitude of the Saints in the Pacific Northwest for the Seattle Washington Temple.

Jordan River Utah Temple

Even with the dedication of two more temples in Utah in 1972, Church growth and an increase in temple attendance led to overcrowding in the Salt Lake and Provo Utah Temples. Of this circumstance, President Spencer W. Kimball said, "We are gratified that attendance at the Salt Lake, Ogden and Provo temples reached all-time highs during 1977, and the trend is still upward." In 1978, Church leaders announced plans to build another temple in Utah.

The Jordan River Utah Temple is situated on a fifteen-acre site atop a slight hill, making the temple easily seen from many parts of the valley. The property was donated to the Church by the family who had owned the land for nearly one hundred years.

The location and name of the temple have special symbolic meaning. The Jordan River, which connects Utah Lake and the Great Salt Lake, runs past the temple and was named after a river in the Holy Land, which connects the freshwater Sea of Galilee with the salty Dead Sea. When the pioneers arrived in the Salt Lake Valley, they could not help but see the parallels between this land and the land where Christ had ministered and been baptized nearly two thousand years before.

The temple, which faces east, was designed so that it would not appear to have a recognizable front or back. "All four facades of the temple will appear equally well," explained Emil B. Fetzer, Church architect and temple designer. The 153,000-square-foot building would have the largest capacity of any

20

temple in the Church up to that point. The design called for vertical, stained-glass panels adorning each of its four facades and the tower. Architects also planned to place on the single spire of the Jordan River Utah Temple an angel Moroni statue.

After formally acquiring the property for the temple, the Church learned that the temple would straddle two areas with different zoning laws. It was fortunate that the part of the temple in the section with more restrictive regulations for height did not include the tallest parts of the building. There were no height restrictions in the zone where the tower and statue of the angel Moroni would be built. Because the temple met the respective zoning regulations, the architects were spared the difficulty of creating a new set of blueprints.

Church leaders decided that the Jordan River Utah Temple would be funded entirely by contributions from members living in the area. A large fund-raising campaign began in all 122 stakes of the Salt Lake and Jordan River Utah Temple districts. When the fund-raising ended just over a year later, the members had contributed $14.5 million, 110 percent of the original goal.

This vast amount of money came from the sacrifices of thousands of members. A bishop recounted: "A woman with cataracts to the point that she cannot see eight inches from her face had been saving to have an operation to restore her sight. She took all the savings she had accumulated for this operation, emptied the entire account, and gave everything for the temple. As a bishop, what could I say? 'Don't do it?' No, I would never rob her of that blessing. I sat here and wept inside."

One woman in the temple district had been struggling with smoking. She told her bishop in an interview that although she didn't have much she could contribute to the temple fund, she would donate as much as she was spending on her cigarettes. The bishop asked her to promise that she would give up her habit of smoking first and then give the money she would have spent on cigarettes to the temple fund. In that setting, she found the courage to promise that she would quit. With great enthusiasm she knelt in prayer to thank the Lord for His inspiration and help.

Two young brothers, one eight years old and the other nearly ten, were excited to do their part in raising money for the temple. The two walked from door to door down the street, asking neighbors if they would like to buy homemade bread.

SITE
15 acres

GROUNDBREAKING
June 9, 1979, by Spencer W. Kimball

DEDICATION
November 16–20, 1981,
by Marion G. Romney

EXTERIOR
Cast stone containing
white marble chips

TOTAL FLOOR AREA
153,000 square feet

DIMENSIONS
Basement and main floor, 211 feet by 218 feet; two upper levels, 140 by 166 feet; height to square is 58 feet, to top of tower is 219 feet (including a 20-foot statue of the angel Moroni)

HIDDEN IMAGE
Among the clouds is a portrait of Christ watching over His temple.

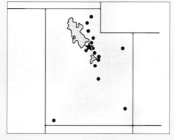

Before long, they had requests for sixteen loaves. The boys hurried home and told their unsuspecting mother that they needed her to bake sixteen loaves of bread right away. Their mother agreed to join in this fund-raising venture, and sixteen hot loaves of bread were delivered. In all, the team sold about thirty loaves for the temple fund.

One man put aside one dollar a day for the temple for the duration of the fund-raising campaign. To do this, the man went without lunch every day of the campaign.

With cloudless blue skies overhead and about 15,000 people attending, ground was broken for the Jordan River Utah Temple on June 9, 1979. In a symbolic gesture, President Spencer W. Kimball departed from the traditional method of groundbreaking. President N. Eldon Tanner, who conducted the service, explained, "You will notice the large power scoop shovel which will be used instead of the traditional-type shovel for such programs. It will be operated by President Kimball in keeping with his oft-quoted counsel to 'lengthen our stride.'" Incredibly, about twenty people who attended the dedication of the Salt Lake Temple in 1893 also attended that of the Jordan River Temple, which took place eighty-eight years later. Among these individuals was Elder LeGrand Richards, a member of the Quorum of the Twelve Apostles.

The powerful image energized members to make full use of the temple. Dedicated November 16, 1981, the Jordan River Utah Temple has been one of the most used temples since its completion.

In December 1981, President Gordon B. Hinckley, then a counselor in the First Presidency, spoke at a fireside. President Hinckley thanked the Jordan River Temple district members for their commitment, saying they were "shining examples of devotion and the spirit of consecration in the work of the Lord. I know that it isn't easy. Some of you arise very early in the morning, some travel very long distances, some of you leave work in order to go to the temple, and then have to make up for it." President Hinckley concluded by encouraging them to find joy in their temple labors. "When you go home so weary that you can scarcely put one foot ahead of the other, may you say to yourselves, 'This is the sweetest weariness I have ever known.'"

The First Presidency has announced the closure of the Jordan River Utah Temple from February 15, 2016, through the latter part of 2017 to undergo extensive renovation.

Atlanta Georgia Temple

The early history of the Church in Atlanta did not foreshadow the great distinction that would come to the city more than one hundred years later when the first temple in the southern United States would be built there. Although missionaries in the Southern States Mission enjoyed some successes in the region, their gains were accompanied by great persecution. In 1957, Elder LeGrand Richards organized Atlanta's first stake. The April 1980 announcement of a temple to be built in Sandy Springs, on the outskirts of Atlanta, was the culmination of years of hard but steady growth.

The southern Saints' enthusiasm for the temple was clearly evidenced on March 7, 1981, when nearly ten thousand members gathered on the site to witness the groundbreaking ceremonies. The crowd erupted into applause as President Spencer W. Kimball turned over the first shovelful of earth. Accompanying President Kimball was Georgia Governor George Busbee, who commented to the crowd, "Frankly, I wish more Georgians placed such importance in the moral aspects of this life, for only through a common responsibility for our neighbor's well-being can we insure that our state will be a better place for our children to live. And we are all taking a big step toward that goal on this beautiful hillside today as we break ground on what will soon be the first Mormon temple in the entire southern United States." The Saints' enthusiasm was also seen in their willingness to make donations. By the end of 1981, nearly $1.4 million had

21

44

been received from contributors worldwide, exceeding the goal of $1.2 million.

Architects planned for the Atlanta Georgia Temple to be the first in a series of smaller temples built throughout the world. The smaller size of the building would keep costs relatively low, and the similar structure of several buildings would make it possible for the Church to produce them quickly. Designers created a layout that was capable of accommodating a large number of patrons in a smaller amount of space.

Among the innovations first used in the Atlanta Georgia Temple was a system that allowed a temple session to be heard in five languages at one time. Using headphones, patrons who did not speak English would receive the words in their own language. Another technological advancement was linking the temple's computer system to the family history library in Utah, allowing for the more efficient transmission of information between the temple and Church headquarters. The temple was also the first to include a video screen beside the temple's baptistry to aid in the reading of names. All of these advancements greatly facilitated temple work and were used in subsequent temples.

One aspect of the new temple plan was not well received by Church members in the Atlanta area, however. This temple was originally designed without any steeple or spire. Two years after the original announcement of the temple, though, it was decided that the temple would have a spire and gold leafed statue of the angel Moroni. President Kimball had reconsidered the design and determined that a steeple would beautify the building and make it a more prominent symbol of the Church.

The statue of the angel Moroni that was eventually placed on the Atlanta Georgia Temple has an interesting history. In the early 1930s, Torlief Knaphus created a statue of the angel Moroni for the steeple of the Washington D.C. Ward chapel. He created it based on the Cyrus Dallin statue atop the Salt Lake Temple. In 1976, the statue was removed from the Washington chapel, and LaVar Wallgren made two castings of it. One was placed on the spire of the Idaho Falls Idaho Temple, and the other on the Atlanta Georgia Temple.

More than sixty thousand people visited the temple during the eighteen-day open house. The first day of the open house

---

SITE
9.6 acres

GROUNDBREAKING
March 7, 1981

DEDICATION
June 1–4, 1983, by
Gordon B. Hinckley

REDEDICATION
May 1, 2011, by Thomas S. Monson

EXTERIOR
Pre-cast stone walls and
a built-up roof

TOTAL FLOOR AREA
34,500 square feet

DIMENSIONS
198 feet by 212 feet; statue of angel
Moroni on top spire, 92 feet high

HIDDEN IMAGE
An image of the Savior is
included among the trees to
the right of the temple.

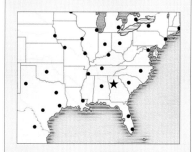

---

was reserved for local leaders in government, education, business, and the military. Among the visitors was Church member and baseball star Dale Murphy of the Atlanta Braves, who had scored the winning run in a game the night before.

Nearly fourteen thousand members of the Atlanta Georgia Temple district attended the eleven dedicatory sessions from June 1 to 4, 1983. The Atlanta Georgia Temple was the first of many temples to be dedicated by President Gordon B. Hinckley, then Second Counselor in the First Presidency. Although President Spencer W. Kimball was not well enough to attend the dedication, Church members who were there were frequently reminded of his love for the southern Saints.

When President Hinckley dedicated the Atlanta Georgia Temple, he promised that the temple's baptistry would someday be enlarged to accommodate more patrons. This promise was fulfilled November 14, 1997, when President Hinckley rededicated a reconstructed portion of the baptistry.

During the temple's first twenty-five years of operation, an estimated 2.5 million Latter-day Saints served within it. After being so well used, the building became "tired and out of date," said temple engineer Mark Romney. The temple was closed July 1, 2009, for extensive renovation. "Before we even closed the building and began the renovation, every last detail was designed in 3-D first, using the latest architectural software," Brother Romney said. "And no finish was allowed into the building unless we had seen a sample first. That meant companies had to send mock-ups of the wood molding, the stonework, the art glass for the windows—everything."

The temple was rededicated by President Thomas S. Monson on May 1, 2011. The night before the dedication, he addressed members in the Atlanta area prior to a cultural celebration. "The magnificent Atlanta temple, in this beautiful part of the country, will be rededicated in the morning," said President Monson to a capacity audience. "It is, of course, the reason for this great celebration. Although . . . its light has been somewhat dimmed for nearly two years, tomorrow that light will return. It will shine as a beacon of righteousness to all who will follow its light."

Apia Samoa Temple

The Church has a long history in the islands of Samoa. Since June 1888, when the first Latter-day Saint missionaries arrived, the Church has enjoyed steady success among the islanders. Church-operated schools were soon built on the islands, giving the Latter-day Saints a center of strength.

At the end of the nineteenth century, this plot of ground, called Pesega, was occupied by a plantation and a large, wood-frame house. This structure was a center for Church activity, where members attended meetings and socials. In 1898, Ah Mu, who owned the property, generously offered to sell the land to the Church for the token price of one dollar. His offer was accepted, and the mission headquarters was moved to Pesega in 1902.

Following a visit by President David O. McKay in 1921, Church membership increased dramatically with mass conversions of entire villages. In 1974, Samoa became the first country entirely covered by stakes. By the end of the twentieth century, Church members made up more than twenty-five percent of the population of Western Samoa and American Samoa.

Announced in 1977, ground was broken for the Apia Samoa Temple in 1981 by President Kimball, who was joined by head of state Malietioa Tunumafili II in turning the first shovelful of soil. Temple construction proceeded with the help of members and missionaries who came from all parts of the country to contribute their time and skills. As the open house

22

approached, workers put in many extra hours to complete the temple in time.

The temple was dedicated by President Gordon B. Hinckley, then a counselor in the First Presidency. The temple featured a modern design with a masonry exterior finish over concrete block and a cedar shake shingle roof.

The building of the Apia Samoa Temple and two other temples in the Pacific Islands provided more temples per capita in these areas than anywhere else in the world. And the Samoan Saints have shown their gratitude by making good use of their temple. The Apia Samoa Temple has consistently functioned beyond its projected capacity.

Although the temple has withstood multiple devastating tropical typhoons, it could not survive the disaster that changed the temple forever on July 9, 2003. Less than one month before the temple's twentieth anniversary was to be celebrated, a fire ravaged the building, leaving it completely unsalvageable. Church member Mika Lolo stepped outside of his nearby home and saw the fire trucks, so he ran to see what was happening. At first Lolo thought the gymnasium or some other school building was on fire, but when he got closer he learned that it was the temple. He could see flames coming from the front part and could feel the heat. "I was just speechless [and] I was crying like a baby," he recalled. Lolo thought of the temple as "the centerpiece of the Church in Samoa." Through his tears he questioned, "Why?"

The night-time sky was lit by the blaze as firefighting efforts were made by three fire trucks, police, and more than 100 volunteers. At least twenty members attempted to put out the flames with hoses and buckets of water. Due to the size of the blaze, nearby airport authority firefighters were also called to assist. Despite these efforts, the entire 14,560-square-foot building was engulfed in flames within forty-five minutes. It was the first time an operational temple had been destroyed by fire.

Although there was concern that the fire would spread to surrounding buildings, no others sustained damage. Temple President Daniel Betham reported that it began to rain quite heavily about thirty minutes after the fire began, which likely preserved the other structures. "We could feel the heat and

SITE
2 acres

GROUNDBREAKING
February 19, 1981

DEDICATION
August 5–6, 1983, by
Gordon B. Hinckley

EXTERIOR
Granite

TOTAL FLOOR AREA
18,691 square feet

DIMENSIONS
108 feet by 197 feet

HIDDEN IMAGE
Among the trees and foliage to the right of the temple is a full-length image of the Savior.

sparks go all over the place, and all of a sudden it rained. We thought it was a miracle," said President Betham.

In the morning's first light, amid the smoldering ashes, warped metal, and blackened debris, the angel Moroni miraculously stood in position. Although resin in fiberglass is highly flammable, the statue remained, still gold, not charred black. Members looked to the angel Moroni as another symbol of hope amid the devastation: "Hope is not gone, because the angel Moroni is still there," said public affairs official Olivia King.

One week later, the First Presidency announced that they would rebuild the temple with a newer design. The many prayers to "quickly rebuild the temple" were answered on October 19, 2003, when thousands gathered at the temple site to break ground for a new Apia Samoa Temple. The congregation of eager and grateful members gathered under cloudy skies to view groundbreaking proceedings. Many government officials attended as special guests of the Area Presidency. President Gordon B. Hinckley sent a letter to be read at the proceedings, saying, "We will rebuild the temple in Samoa . . . These holy words, 'Holiness to the Lord' will again hallow this sacred ground." Those attending were challenged to follow President Howard W. Hunter's counsel that every member be temple worthy and that every adult member would be worthy of and carry a current temple recommend.

With heightened anticipation, the newly built temple in Apia opened its doors for a public open house on August 6, 2005. The majestic new edifice was quickly labeled "The Pearl of the Pacific."

The Samoan members' patience was rewarded when their rebuilt temple was dedicated by Gordon B. Hinckley on September 4, 2005. Attending the dedication was Alema Fitisemanu, who remembers telling folks on the night of the fire, "Watch what the Lord is going to do for Samoa. There will be a beautiful temple, and now we have it."

Grateful to again have a dedicated temple in their midst, a long line of temple-goers lined up outside the temple the day after its dedication, eager to get back to work and partake of temple blessings.

Nuku'alofa Tonga Temple

Tonga is located so close to the International Date Line that it is called "the place where time begins." In the small island nation, nearly one of every two people is a member of The Church of Jesus Christ of Latter-day Saints. The dream of the Tongan Saints to have a temple in their islands was bolstered in 1955, when President David O. McKay stopped in the islands on his way to dedicate the ground for the Hamilton New Zealand Temple. The first Church president to visit Tonga, President McKay announced, "Last night in vision I saw a temple in these islands." For years, members waited for the day when this prophecy would be fulfilled.

In the meantime, the Tongan Saints had to travel great distances to obtain their temple blessings. When the Hamilton New Zealand Temple opened in 1958, Brother Viliami Kongaika and his wife, Lu'isa, desired to be part of the first group of Tongans to travel to the temple, but they did not have enough money. They therefore waited another year while they saved enough money for all family members to go to the temple. To cover the cost of travel, they sold nearly everything they owned, including their house, their stove, Viliami's bicycle (their only means of transportation), Lu'isa's sewing machine, and the family's cows, horses, and pigs. The money garnered from these sales enabled the family to travel to the temple the following year, where they were sealed for eternity. The Kongaikas returned to face the reality of being without a home, job, or food. Soon after their return, a devastating hurricane

23

destroyed almost everything on the island of Ha'pai, including the Kongaikas' newly built hut. Viliami then built from scraps and debris another shelter, in which the family lived for quite some time. Yet the family recognized the Lord's hand in their lives. Viliami said, "It was the Lord prompting me to get rid of my goods for a holy cause, because he was going to take them away from me anyway in the hurricane. I came back from the temple a poor man in terms of worldly goods. But after the hurricane, everyone else was just as poor as we were. The difference between us and them was that we were sealed as an eternal family in the Holy Temple of God."

The Tongan Saints were thrilled to learn in 1980 that three temples planned for the Pacific islands would include one near Tonga's capital city, Nuku'alofa. A five-acre site near the Church-operated Liahona College had been intended for a temple long before Church leaders decided it was time to build one in Tonga. The property owner, Brother Tevita Mahu'inga, had served faithfully in many Church capacities. Just before his death in 1973, he told his son: "There will be a temple built in Tonga someday; and our five-acre piece just next to Liahona I have reserved for a temple site. You give it to the Church at the appropriate time." After several unsuccessful attempts at obtaining property on the island, Church officials approached Brother Mahu'inga's son and acquired the land for the temple. Thus Tevita Mahu'inga's dream was fulfilled seven years after his death.

During its public open house, the temple was enthusiastically toured by more than half of the entire population of Tonga. The first of these visitors was King Taufa'ahau Tupou IV, who had participated in the groundbreaking ceremonies.

Thousands of members journeyed to the capital from the scattered islands of Tonga for the open house and dedication of the temple. In his address, President Gordon B. Hinckley noted that a group of prisoners accompanied by their guards had attended the temple open house. He compared them to the many good Tongans waiting in spirit prison for their ordinances so that they can progress. "I think I can hear in my mind their wardens cry out to the Tongan saints, 'won't you do something to help them?' They are your forebears. All you are and all you

have came through them. The house is here; the keys are here. Unlock the door that these good Tongans may go forward into immortality and eternal life." The Tongan Saints apparently took President Hinckley's admonition to heart, for they have consistently used the temple far beyond its projected capacity.

Members from the island of Vava'u, some two hundred miles from the Nuku'alofa Tonga Temple, epitomize the enthusiasm of the Tongan Saints. Even though the cost of travel to the temple is high, many members save enough money to make two excursions to the temple every year, each lasting two to three weeks. The stake, which encourages temple recommend holders to accomplish forty-eight endowments each year, performs an average of five thousand annually. The temple was closed in June 2006 and significantly remodeled. The completed temple is considered by many to be the most beautiful building and the greatest spiritual symbol in all of Tonga.

Less than a year later, as the open house and dedication approached, 13,200 citizens participated in a massive service effort that swept across Tonga. Knowing thousands of visitors would be arriving to the islands for the open house, the Church initiated a two-month cleanup project to ensure the islands were looking their best.

The successful three-week open house was attended by more than 40,000 people—equivalent to 40% of the total population of the nation. On November 4, 2007, President Russell M. Nelson rededicated the temple and commented on the faithfulness of the Tongan people by saying, "The sweetness of these people almost defies comment, they are so anxious to be like the Lord, anxious to do His work well."

Also attending the temple was Area Seventy Elder Sione M. Fineanganofo who made the wonderful observation: "We are blessed here in Tonga. There is a chapel in almost every village in Tonga. We have the temple. We have a mission. What else do we need? We have everything in Tonga. Now we just need to remember to rededicate ourselves." A large banner hanging across the road in front of the 21,000-square-foot temple expressed that message in bold lettering: "Let's rededicate ourselves."

SITE
1.2 acres

GROUNDBREAKING
February 18, 1981, by
Spencer W. Kimball

DEDICATION
August 9–11, 1983, by
Gordon B. Hinckley

REDEDICATION
November 4, 2007, by
Russell M. Nelson

EXTERIOR
R-wall exterior finish and insulation system on concrete block

TOTAL FLOOR AREA
21,184 square feet

DIMENSIONS
142 feet by 115 feet

HIDDEN IMAGE
An image of the Savior is included among the trees to the right of the temple.

Santiago Chile Temple

In March 1977, at an area conference in Santiago, Chile, Elder Bruce R. McConkie told the seven thousand gathered there that the Church would eventually become the most powerful influence in Chile. This promise of future prosperity must have seemed miraculous to the Saints in Chile, where the Church had established a presence only twenty years earlier. Although Elder Parley P. Pratt traveled to Chile in 1850 to preach the gospel, he soon left due to difficulty learning the language. Not until 1956 did missionaries return to Chile. They found a people prepared to receive the gospel message. Soon the Chile Mission became one of the most productive missions of the Church. It was under these circumstances that Elder McConkie prophesied concerning a future temple: "The day will

come when there will be a temple in Chile. I do not say when, but it surely will be."

On April 2, 1980, President Spencer W. Kimball announced plans to build a temple in Santiago, fulfilling Elder McConkie's prophecy. It would be the first temple built in a Spanish-speaking country and the second in South America. The temple would be built in Santiago, where the Church college building and the presiding bishopric area offices were then located.

In 1970, Gregory Billikopf attended a Catholic school. In religion class one day the priest announced that the school would shortly be sold to the Mormon Church. To help the children understand that many people held religious beliefs different from theirs, the

24

priest assigned the students to write reports on The Church of Jesus Christ of Latter-day Saints. To fulfill the assignment, Gregory went to the mission home, where he received a copy of the Book of Mormon and other information about the Church. He read Moroni's promise, gained a witness that the book was true, and eventually joined the Church. He later wrote, "How was I to know, as a youth in that religion class, that one day, on that very property, I would attend the house of the Lord—the Santiago Chile Temple?"

On May 30, 1981, President Kimball broke ground for the temple. Some six thousand Saints attended the ceremonies. Rodolfo Acevedo Acevedo, Chile area historian, described the importance of the day's events to Church members in Chile: "A heavy rainstorm fell during the day when the ground was to be broken for the Santiago Chile Temple and the site dedicated.

"This occasion brought the hope of the years closer to being realized—a temple was to be constructed in our land. It was to be a house sacred and consecrated to the work of the Lord that transcended our mortal lives.

"The strength of the rain . . . proved the faith of the Saints, who ever since the announcement that a prophet would come and dedicate the temple site, had been preparing to take part in this once-in-a-lifetime experience. Upon arriving at the temple site, I was able to see the faith of my brothers and sisters, many of whom did not have hats or umbrellas. On this torrential May morning, thousands and thousands of them stood waiting for the sublime moment that the site would be dedicated for the temple.

"The rain continued to fall with force. All those present stoically waited for the ceremony to begin. As they waited, a choir sang beautiful hymns in the rainfall. Their clothing was soaked, but none moved from his place, even as the rain increased. We sang and we rejoiced in the experience.

"A great surprise was waiting for the Saints. As President Spencer W. Kimball arose from his seat to address the members, from among the dark clouds came a ray of sunshine, followed by others. Soon the clouds parted and bright sunshine warmed all those present. Two years later, the Santiago Temple, with the statue of the angel Moroni crowning its spire, was completed. Through all these years we remember the hope expressed beneath the rain; it was a true joy, something very special; we

SITE
2.61 acres

GROUNDBREAKING
May 30, 1981, by Spencer W. Kimball

DEDICATION
September 15–17, 1983,
by Gordon B. Hinckley

REDEDICATION
March 12, 2006, by
Gordon B. Hinckley

EXTERIOR
Stucco on brick and
reinforced concrete

TOTAL FLOOR AREA
20,831 square feet

DIMENSIONS
178.6 feet by 112.5 feet;
statue of angel Moroni on
top spire, 76 feet high

HIDDEN IMAGE
An image of the Savior is
included among the trees to
the right of the temple.

felt the presence of the Spirit of the Lord. All were inundated with warmth and happiness inside."

On September 15, 1983, at the first of the ten dedicatory services, President Gordon B. Hinckley stated: "I think I know why this temple is here. I think the Lord said, 'I have weighed the Saints of Chile in the balance, and they have not been found wanting. I have determined that the richest blessings I can bestow should be made available to them—the preservation of the sweetest companionships of all human associations for time and all eternity.'"

Twenty-two years later, the small temple in Santiago's upscale Providencia district was closed for a complete renovation and enlarged by one-third. It now contains two additional sealing rooms, enlarged dressing areas, and offices. The temple features local handcrafted details, from the native Chilean marble and blue lapis lazuli stone in the entryway and baptistry floors to the flower motif of the country's national flower, the copíhue, used on furniture, door handles, and art glass. A notable addition was the baptistry, greatly enlarged and with the font resting on the backs of twelve oxen. Commenting on the extensive renovation, Elder Carl Pratt of the Chile Area Presidency said, "A few of the original walls remaining, and the Angel Moroni, and that's about it. But oh, it's just gorgeous, unbelievably beautiful and in comparison to what we had before, which was lovely, it is way and above."

For three weeks in January and February 2006, more than 62,000 people visited the Santiago Temple during its "puertas abiertas," or "open doors."

Preceding the temple dedication, tens of thousands of Chilean members gathered inside Santiago's Monumental Stadium on March 11, 2006, to listen to the devotional address of President Hinckley. This event was the prophet's first official public appearance anywhere since receiving surgical treatment for cancer. Demonstrating incredible stamina, the ninety-five-year-old President Hinckley said, "I wondered whether I would be able to get here," he said. "I pondered over it. I prayed about it. I decided I would make the effort. I am so grateful that I have done so." After concluding his remarks and as he began to exit, the audience rose and waved their handkerchiefs, turning the 50,000-seat stadium into a sea of white.

Papeete Tahiti Temple

Like other Saints living throughout Polynesia, faithful Tahitian members made great sacrifices to travel to New Zealand, Hawaii, or other locations to receive temple ordinances. The costs of attending the temple were high. Former Papeete Tahiti Stake President Victor Cave said that transportation to the Hamilton New Zealand Temple, the nearest temple, cost about eight hundred dollars per person. But Tahitian families, who often have six or more children, generally make about five hundred dollars per month. Families who saved for years to travel to the temple made the very most of their experience. President Cave said that families who were able to attend the temple would stay a month to get as much work done as they could.

Countless stories tell of faithful Tahitian Saints who saved all they could from their meager incomes for long periods of time and made many sacrifices to travel to the temple. Eighty-four-year-old Tahauri Hutihuti had saved money for thirty years to be able to make one trip to the Hamilton New Zealand Temple. When he returned, he said he was eager to go again someday.

The original plan to build a temple only in Pago Pago, American Samoa, would not have significantly reduced the cost to Tahitian Saints of traveling to the temple because there were no direct airline connections between Tahiti and American Samoa. The Tahitian Saints rejoiced when they learned that the Church had decided to build three temples instead, with one in Papeete.

25

52

The site chosen for the temple was on property where a Church-run elementary school had been located. Local leaders obtained permission from Francis Sanford, the head of the Tahitian government, to build the temple. Although the process was somewhat simplified because the Church already owned the land, leaders worried that they might face opposition similar to what they had dealt with when the Church had built the school. But Sanford, who had visited the Laie Hawaii Temple, the Church College of Hawaii, and the Polynesian Cultural Center, had gained a favorable opinion of the Church and promised them that the government would not oppose the building of a temple in Tahiti. With this approval, President Spencer W. Kimball broke ground for the temple and dedicated the site on February 13, 1981, with two thousand people looking on.

Although somewhat smaller, the temple was similar in design to the temples in Samoa and Tonga. Designers also incorporated both French and Polynesian influences into the plans. Because members in French Polynesia come from a variety of cultures, the temple was equipped to serve patrons speaking French, Tahitian, or English. As construction progressed, the building became something of a landmark and was widely admired for its stately entrance, white walls, and blue tile roof. Members and nonmembers alike responded with great excitement when the Church announced that a spire and a statue of the angel Moroni would be added to the structure.

During the ten-day open house, some 16,500 visitors toured the structure. President Gordon B. Hinckley dedicated the temple on October 27, 1983.

In the years since its dedication, the Papeete Tahiti Temple continued to have a great influence in the lives of members. Former temple president C. Jay Larson commented: "The temple has elevated the spirituality of the members. Since the temple was dedicated, we've had a 50 percent increase in the number of temple marriages. Now a lot of the young people qualify for temple marriage. They prepare for the temple."

In 2005, after twenty-two years of steady temple use, the temple was closed for an extensive renovation and a 2,000-square-foot expansion project. The improvements included a larger baptismal font, larger sealing rooms, an office for the temple engineer, and a youth center for children being sealed to their parents. Lead interior designer Greg Hill has

SITE
1.7 acres

GROUNDBREAKING
February 13, 1981, by
Spencer W. Kimball

DEDICATION
October 27–29, 1983, by
Gordon B. Hinckley

REDEDICATION
November 12, 2006, by L. Tom Perry

EXTERIOR
Painted plaster over stucco
using imported white sand

TOTAL FLOOR AREA
12,150 square feet

DIMENSIONS
125 feet by 105 feet, with
an eight-foot statue of angel
Moroni on a 66-foot spire

HIDDEN IMAGE
Among the drawing's foreground
is Tahiti's national flower, the
gardenia. Among the clouds are
silhouetted the nation's islands.

worked on many of the latter-day temples, including the renovated Papeete Tahiti Temple. Hill works on "everything you see" inside the temple, including the art, furniture, carpet, lighting, glass, and drapes. His inspiration, he said, is always drawn from the culture surrounding the region of the temple he's working on. One of his most meaningful and personal experiences came one evening in Tahiti when he realized the value of the work he was doing. "I walked out about sunset just as the sun was setting over Mo'orea," he said. "The water was shimmering and turned gold. As I took in that scene before me . . . the thought that came at that moment was that Christ, our Savior and older brother, created this earth in such a beautiful way because of His love for us." That evening at a remote Tahitian lagoon, Hill's convictions as a designer were strengthened further: "I knew then that everything beautiful around us is because of Him, and I feel in some way I'm able to use my God-given talents to do the same in His home."

When members of the Manihi Branch, Takaroa Tuamotu District, learned that their temple was being renovated, they immediately began to prepare to attend the rededication. Each ticket for two-day voyage to Papeete cost about $60 U.S. dollars. Considering their modest lifestyle, members had to significantly save to make the trip possible. When the group arrived in Papeete, they were grateful to learn that their boat captain had reduced their fare by two-thirds. During the final days of the open house, the group stood in line and toured the building four times in three days. President Faura said members from Tuamotu were grateful they were able to participate in the temple rededication and attend the temple. They want to gain "more knowledge about the temple, to learn more," he said.

The temple's three-week open house was attended by 36,800 visitors. On November 12, 2006, by assignment from President Gordon B. Hinckley, Elder L. Tom Perry of the Quorum of the Twelve Apostles rededicated the temple. An estimated 10,000 Tahitians from six stakes and three districts participated in the rededication, held during two sessions in the Papeete temple and broadcast to local stake centers. In addition, the meeting was broadcast via the Church satellite system to Salt Lake City, New Caledonia, and the BYU–Hawaii campus in Laie, Hawaii. The temple continues to be for the faithful Saints of French Polynesia a place to begin a new level of discipleship and consecration to the gospel.

Mexico City Mexico Temple

The Mexico City Mexico Temple, the first Latter-day Saint temple to be built in that country, was announced April 3, 1976, a century after Mormon missionaries first arrived there. During a speech given at the Mexico City area conference in 1979, President Spencer W. Kimball told of an impression he had received on a trip to Mexico more than thirty years earlier: "I had great expectation for the Mexican people, and I had a dream about your progress and growth. . . . When I had my dream there was not a single stake or ward in all Mexico. I saw a temple, and I expect to see it full of young men and women."

But many seemingly insurmountable obstacles stood in the way of plans to build the temple in the capital of Mexico. Foreign missionaries were not formally recognized in Mexico, and laws required all buildings to be open to the public. Such stipulations would compromise the sacred nature of dedicated temples. Before long, however, laws regarding religion were changed in ways favorable to the Church, and the necessary building permits were approved in the latter part of 1979.

Another obstacle the Church faced was a federal law that prohibited importation into Mexico of building materials, furnishings, or furniture already available in the country. Because the Church desired to use only materials of the highest quality for the temple, leaders requested exemption from the importation law. They also asked that the government allow them to import those materials, worth some $2.6 million,

26

without tax. In a spirit of fasting and prayer, Elder Richard G. Scott and other Church officials presented their request to government leaders. Miraculously, government leaders approved the request and signed the necessary documents, commenting that they could not understand why they had changed their mind and sided with the Church.

Because the proposed site for the temple had once been covered by a lake, the ground was marshy, and local Saints feared it could not support the weight of a temple. Aware of this concern, President Kimball visited Mexico City before construction began and spent several hours alone on the property. He prayed for guidance regarding the site and received a confirmation that it was the will of the Lord for the temple to be built there. Plans were modified to strengthen the foundation of the temple and make it resistant to the effects of earthquakes, which are prevalent in the area.

When architect Emil B. Fetzer was assigned by President Spencer W. Kimball to design the temple, his thoughts turned to a book on Mayan architecture that Heber Grant Taylor, a grandson of Heber J. Grant, had given him more than ten years before. The book, which had come from President Grant's personal library, was an important heirloom to Brother Taylor, but he had felt that he should give it to Brother Fetzer. As Brother Fetzer prepared the design for the temple in Mexico City, he reread the book and produced a design in harmony with Mayan architecture. He also created four other potential styles for the temple so that Church leaders would have several designs from which to choose. As the First Presidency examined each of the proposed designs, they felt that the one with the Mayan influences was the best.

The result was equally approved of by citizens of Mexico, both members and nonmembers. Considered by many to be one of the most beautiful buildings in the country, the Mexico City Mexico Temple is faced with white cast stone and white marble chips, in what Brother Fetzer called "a modern adaptation of ancient Mayan architecture." The grounds are landscaped with traditional Mexican plants and feature a fountain in front of the temple. Favorable reviews of the structure soon came in from citizens, the mayor of Mexico City, and architecture students at the University of Mexico.

When completed, the 117,133-square-foot temple was the fifth largest temple in the Church and the largest outside

SITE
7 acres

GROUNDBREAKING
November 25, 1979, by
Boyd K. Packer

DEDICATION
December 2–4, 1983, by
Gordon B. Hinckley

EXTERIOR
White cast stone made with ornate adaptations of ancient Mayan designs

TOTAL FLOOR AREA
116,642 square feet

DIMENSIONS
178 feet by 214.5 feet; two upper levels, 119.5 feet by 157 feet; height to square, 70 feet; to top of tower with statue of angel Moroni, 152 feet.

HIDDEN IMAGE
An image of the Savior is included among the foliage right of the temple.

the United States. Each of the four ordinance rooms seats one hundred patrons. The temple features twelve sealing rooms and a three-hundred-seat chapel to serve hundreds of thousands of Saints from all over Mexico and Central America.

Enthusiasm for the temple was evidenced by the more than 100,000 people who toured the temple during its public open house. On December 2, 1983, President Gordon B. Hinckley dedicated the temple, the sixth dedicated that year. An adjacent visitors' center was also dedicated at that time. Twenty-one years after the temple's dedication, the Church in Mexico passed the million-member mark, becoming the first country to reach seven figures outside the United States.

In March 2007, after a quarter century of consistent uninterrupted service, the temple closed its doors for an extensive eighteen-month remodeling project. The long list of improvements included the brightening of the exterior with a new shell of white concrete. Among the interior improvements were new carpeting, paint, stone floor work, ornate glass features, and chandeliers. Structural work was also performed on the temple's foundation to fortify the 35,551-square foot edifice.

The temple's refurbishing project has offered new opportunities for local residents to learn about the Church by attending the open house. Many who, perhaps, passed by the temple each morning and evening were able to walk its halls and learn its eternal, family centered mission for the first time prior to the rededication. Some 91,000 people toured the temple during its open house. Missionaries collected more than 10,000 referrals from people who wanted to learn more. The visitors' center alone received more than 20,000 guests during the first two weeks of being reopened.

President Thomas S. Monson rededicated the temple on November 16, 2008. Following the ceremony, he was asked how members could get the most from the rededicated temple. He responded, "Use it. The best way to appreciate this temple is to use it." The faithful members followed his counsel and did indeed use it—often beyond its capacity. Six years later, the steady use necessitated the need for another extensive renovation closure. On September 13, 2015, the historic Mexico City Mexico Temple was again rededicated, beginning another chapter in the temple's already rich legacy in Mexico.

Boise Idaho Temple

Discussions about building a temple in Boise, Idaho, began decades before the actual announcement. In 1939, when Church leaders expressed interest in building a temple in Idaho, Boise Stake President Ezra Taft Benson invited President Heber J. Grant to visit the state's capital and largest city to look at potential sites. During the visit, some fifteen prominent businessmen from the area offered many available sites for a temple in the Boise area. Despite the generosity of this offer, there were many more Saints in eastern Idaho at the time than in the western part of the state, so President Grant decided to build a temple in Idaho Falls. He did tell the businessmen, however, that when Church membership increased substantially, a temple would be built. At the dedication of the Boise Idaho Temple in 1984, President Benson, then a member of the Quorum of the Twelve Apostles, testified, "Today, we are witnessing the fulfilling of that prophecy made forty-five years ago."

Once the temple was announced, Church members from the Boise area offered land on which the structure could be built. The property eventually chosen, however, was a site owned by a nonmember. Because accessibility was the search committee's most important criterion for a temple site, this property, located near an exit from Interstate 84, was ideal.

This location has made the temple a well-known landmark for travelers along the highway. And, located near the municipal airport, the temple provides a noticeable marker for pilots guiding their planes

27

to the runway. The temple was originally designed with its entryway facing the busy street that runs beside the grounds, but President Spencer W. Kimball asked that the building be turned 180 degrees so the entrance would face west, toward the temple's parking lot.

The Boise Idaho Temple was the first of a series of six-spired temples designed to maximize efficiency and space. These temples could be built at a lower cost in a shorter time, and they were easily adaptable for international construction. The original design did not include a statue of the angel Moroni, but as the plans were being finalized, President Kimball decided to have a statue of Moroni added to the eastern spire. Between 1984 and 1989, fourteen temples around the world were built using adaptations of this original plan.

When construction was completed in the spring of 1984, 70,000 visitors were expected to tour the temple during the nineteen-day open house. Instead, nearly twice that number attended. The open house proved to be a great missionary tool in the area. Two areas of the Idaho Boise Mission reported that thirty people joined the Church during the month following the open house, several of them responding to the feelings and impressions they had received while touring the temple.

During the open house, Church officials worked to obtain an occupancy permit to accommodate the many Saints who wanted to attend dedicatory services, because the number would exceed fire safety codes. Early one morning, architect Ronald W. Thurber called the city's fire chief and invited him to a personally guided tour of the entire temple. An appointment was made for 10:00 a.m. that day. Brother Thurber immediately notified Elder Hugh W. Pinnock of the First Quorum of the Seventy, the General Authority assisting with the temple, who agreed to arrive at the temple half an hour early. As Brother Thurber, Elder Pinnock, and other Church officials gathered in the temple president's office, Elder Pinnock told the others that he had called the First Presidency that morning to make them aware of the challenge, and the First Presidency had put the item on the prayer roll for that day's meeting in the temple. Elder Pinnock explained that they would likely be praying while the tour was taking place.

At 10:00 a.m., the fire chief arrived and was given a private tour of the temple. Afterward, he agreed to grant the temple a permit for unlimited occupancy, as long as a few safety

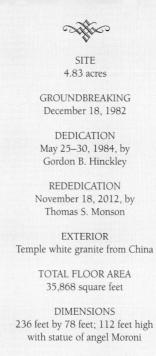

SITE
4.83 acres

GROUNDBREAKING
December 18, 1982

DEDICATION
May 25–30, 1984, by
Gordon B. Hinckley

REDEDICATION
November 18, 2012, by
Thomas S. Monson

EXTERIOR
Temple white granite from China

TOTAL FLOOR AREA
35,868 square feet

DIMENSIONS
236 feet by 78 feet; 112 feet high
with statue of angel Moroni

HIDDEN IMAGE
The Savior's face is softly rendered
on the surface of the temple where
the celestial room is located.

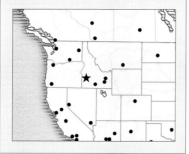

procedures were followed. As the fire chief drove away, Elder Pinnock said, "Brethren, I want you to know that we have just learned a great lesson. Come with me and I will show you." The men followed Elder Pinnock into the president's office. Asking them to kneel, he said, "We often forget to give thanks," and asked Brother Thurber to pray. Brother Thurber later said, "I was in such tears I could hardly pray. The First Presidency had taken a particular issue and solved it by imploring the assistance of Heavenly Father."

The temple was dedicated by President Gordon B. Hinckley on May 25, 1984. President Hinckley spoke at all twenty-four sessions, four sessions a day for six days, each time giving new insights and wisdom concerning the house of the Lord. Not since the dedication of the Salt Lake Temple had so many dedicatory sessions been held for a temple.

Attendance at the temple over the first two years following the dedication was much higher than anticipated, so in October 1986 the temple was closed for significant renovations and additions. Completed in May 1987 were a new baptistry, a cafeteria, additional dressing rooms, and expanded office space.

The temple closed again in July 2011 for an extensive renovation of the grounds and the interior. The temple's darker exterior has been replaced with white granite. The grounds were entirely re-landscaped, and a new maintenance and engineering building was added. A new gold-leafed statue of the angel Moroni was positioned atop the tallest spire. The temple's interior was literally "taken down to the concrete" in most places. The new interior features a syringa flower and tree motif, which can be seen in the art glass and decorative painting. Beautiful grained hardwoods from Africa and the United States give the interior a warm and entirely new look.

The temple's successful open house ushered more than 166,000 through the temple. The evening prior to the rededication, a large youth cultural celebration took place at the arena on Boise State University campus. Nearly 9,000 youth delivered a musical and dance performance with the theme "Treasure of Light." The celebration featured 4,000 dancers, 99 fiddlers, and a choir of more than 1,000 singers.

President Thomas S. Monson rededicated the temple on November 18, 2012. As a dedicated house of the Lord, the temple once again became a beacon of light throughout the "Treasure Valley."

Sydney Australia Temple

After years of growth and gaining experience in the gospel, the Saints in Australia were delighted when President Spencer W. Kimball announced in April 1980 that a temple would be built in Sydney, along with six others throughout the world. These new temples, smaller than previous temples, were to be built in the United States, South America, and several Pacific countries, including Australia.

The search for a suitable location commenced immediately. Within three weeks, five potential properties had been identified in the vicinity of Sydney. Several months were spent settling on a site, meeting legal requirements to begin building, and dealing with opposition from some members of the surrounding community. The location finally chosen, which was

approved by the local government one year after the announcement, was located in the Carlingford section of Sydney, about twelve miles north of the downtown area. The Church retained several school buildings on the site as offices. The beautiful site features eucalyptus trees with lush fields and the grand Blue Mountains in the distance.

Soon after the temple was announced, regional representatives in the area organized a fund-raising project among the Australian Saints. The members responded to the task enthusiastically, achieving their goal of raising nearly one million dollars in just six months. One contribution to the fund came as the result of an institute teacher's object lesson. The teacher had pretended to have received a letter from

28

the stake president calling on his class to raise eight thousand dollars for the temple. His intention was to see how they would react to a difficult challenge, not for them to sacrifice to achieve it. But the class eagerly took on the challenge, deciding that each of the forty students would need to raise two hundred dollars to meet the goal. For the rest of the semester, these young adult students found ways to earn the money, and by the end of the semester the class had earned forty dollars more than their goal.

Elder Bruce R. McConkie broke ground for the temple on August 13, 1982. Following the services, he spoke at a fireside to an audience of more than fifteen hundred. "There could scarcely be a more memorable day in the entire history of this great nation," stated Elder McConkie. "I cannot use language that is too emphatic. There is no way to overemphasize what we are presenting—the fact that a house of the Lord is about to rise in Australia will be the crowning event for the Church here at this time, when the blessings and ordinances are made available."

Elder McConkie went on to say that this was only the beginning of temple work in Australia. "There is no reason why we can't have temples in Adelaide, Melbourne, Brisbane, Perth, or wherever the number of Saints justifies it." Elder McConkie's statement proved prophetic when, eighteen years later, temples were dedicated in Adelaide and Melbourne (both in 2000), and temples were under construction in Brisbane and Perth.

The design of the Sydney Australia Temple is similar to that which had been used in other temples built recently in the South Pacific. Local designers decided to use blue tile for the roof, as had been done with the Papeete Tahiti Temple. A striking azure color, dubbed "Mormon blue," was developed for the temple. More than twenty-five thousand terra cotta tiles were manufactured specifically for the building.

Because President Spencer W. Kimball was not well enough to attend, President Gordon B. Hinckley, then Second Counselor in the First Presidency, conveyed the prophet's love and a special request of the youth of Australia: prepare to serve a mission, get a good education, and marry in the temple. The temple was dedicated on September 20, 1984. In the first of fourteen dedicatory sessions, President Hinckley said, "There will be other temples here as the Church grows in this vast land. . . . As we assemble here, a large audience of unseen eyes is witnessing.

SITE
3.06 acres

GROUNDBREAKING
August 13, 1982, by
Bruce R. McConkie

DEDICATION
September 20–23, 1984,
by Gordon B. Hinckley

EXTERIOR
Precast panels; white quartz
finish; terra cotta roof tiles

TOTAL FLOOR AREA
30,677 square feet

DIMENSIONS
145 feet by 115 feet; statue of
angel Moroni added to top spire

HIDDEN IMAGE
An image of the Savior is included
among the trees to the right of
the temple. Additionally, the
shape of Australia is found among
the foreground shadows.

I believe the God of Heaven smiles on us this day. This temple is part of his plan. I am satisfied that the Prophet Joseph smiles on us."

Since the dedication of the temple, Latter-day Saints have performed faithful service in the Sydney Australia Temple. In 1994, more than forty Australian aboriginal Saints attended a weeklong temple trip, during which they performed ordinances for the entire Larrakee Tribe in the Northern Territory. "The aboriginal people have always been a deeply spiritual people," said Donna Ballangarry, of the Sydney Australia Parramatta Stake, "and the Church provides an opportunity for us to express that spirituality. Our dreamtime legend says that the aboriginal people came to Australia from the waters the same way Lehi sailed to the promised land, and that's one reason why we find it so easy to accept the Book of Mormon."

The dedication of the Australian Saints and their love for the temple are clearly evident in their desire to attend, even if that means traveling great distances under difficult circumstances. In the Busselton Branch, nine of the eleven active adults determined in June 1997 to make the nearly three-thousand-mile trip to the temple the following year.

"Within a month of making that commitment, things happened that might have prevented us from going," said Marilyn Domroe, branch Relief Society president. "In July, one of the sisters in the branch in her mid-seventies suffered a stroke. Later, another sister came down with a serious bout of pneumonia. Then our branch president, Charles Roper, broke his back while surfing, and another sister was stricken with a serious gall bladder condition. Every one of us experienced setbacks that reduced our savings for our intended trip."

Then she noted how blessings came to the branch members as they sought to keep their commitment despite the setbacks. Through medical help, prayers, and healing blessings, those with physical problems, including President Roper, recovered sufficiently to make the trip. In March 1998, the group set out on its journey across the entire continent of Australia. During their four-day visit to the temple, the group participated in three endowment sessions each day as well as in baptisms, initiatory ordinances, and sealings. "It was difficult to leave the temple," Sister Domroe said. "But we will return, and with Heavenly Father's guidance, we will overcome any obstacle that Satan puts in our path to prevent us from honoring our commitment."

Manila Philippines Temple

Although the first official missionaries did not arrive in the Philippines until 1961, the archipelago of more than seven thousand islands off of southeast Asia has seen some of the most dynamic growth in the Church. By 1969, the Philippine Mission was the highest baptizing mission in the Church. As the Church grew in numbers, so the members grew in experience and understanding of the gospel plan. Just twenty years after the Church first became established in the islands, President Spencer W. Kimball announced plans to build the Manila Philippines Temple.

Approximately seventy thousand Saints in the Philippines were overjoyed to hear the news. The expense of traveling to the nearest temple, in Tokyo, Japan, was prohibitively high for most. Not only

would a temple in the Philippines make temple blessings available to a rapidly growing area of the Church, but it also represented an era of stability and maturity in the country. This maturity was reflected in the creation of nine new stakes in the Philippines in 1981 and three more in 1982.

In January 1981, the Church purchased some land in Quezon City, in the metro Manila area, on a street called Zebra Drive, which was later changed to Temple Drive. A fund-raising campaign for the temple was quickly set up among Church members. The Saints sacrificed greatly, but nine months later, they still had reached only sixty-five percent of their goal. Church leaders again encouraged members to give all they could, and the devoted Filipino Saints responded

29

once again, reaching and exceeding the goal in three months' time.

President Gordon B. Hinckley and Elder Marion D. Hanks arrived in August 1982 to break ground for the temple. It was then typhoon season in the Philippines, so there had been a daily downpour of rain for some time. At a meeting with missionaries of the Philippines Manila Mission on the morning of the groundbreaking, President Hinckley asked the missionary assigned to offer the benediction to pray that God would temper the elements for the duration of the ceremony. The elder expressed this plea, and almost immediately the sky began to clear. That afternoon, some twenty-five hundred people attended the groundbreaking. Though the skies were still ominous and the winds still blew, no rain fell on the spectators. As soon as the ceremony ended, however, the rains returned and continued falling well into the next day.

A challenge faced by Church leaders during the construction was that of making temple garments available to the many members who would soon attend the temple for the first time. Because of the Philippine government's strict rules concerning the importing of any clothing, the Church commissioned a local clothing manufacturer to make 28,000 sets of garments. After the garments were manufactured, twenty endowed sisters volunteered to complete the sewing, mark the sizes, and package the garments. Because of these sisters' sacrifice, the process was completed in under three months.

Two powerful typhoons hit the Philippines in the days preceding the temple open house. The second, named Nitang, led to the deaths of more than 1,900 people and caused an estimated $111 million in damage. Because of this natural disaster, many who had planned to attend the VIP day of the open house were unable to travel to the temple. Midway through the open house, a volcano on the island of Luzon erupted, sending ash high into the air. And two days before the dedication, a strong earthquake shook the island.

Despite these powerful displays of nature, some 27,000 people toured the 13,800-square-foot temple during the open house. The first day the temple opened to the public, "a beautiful heavenly spectacle was unfurled over the temple," said Jovencio Ilagan, executive secretary of the temple committee

SITE
3.5 acres

GROUNDBREAKING
August 25, 1982, by
Gordon B. Hinckley

DEDICATION
September 25–27, 1984,
by Gordon B. Hinckley

EXTERIOR
Ceramic tile

TOTAL FLOOR AREA
26,683 square feet

DIMENSIONS
200 feet by 75 feet, six spires; 115
feet high with statue of angel Moroni

HIDDEN IMAGE
An image of the Savior is
included among the clouds.

during its construction. "The sun, in all its brilliance, was seen through a corona of varying colors. . . . At one point, the center spire with the statue of the Angel Moroni was seen at the center of the corona. Almost a hundred people at the temple grounds attest to it. Many were in tears." On September 25, 1984, President Hinckley dedicated the Manila Philippines Temple.

Since its dedication, the Manila Philippines Temple has been a great blessing for the Saints in the Philippines, Indonesia, Malaysia, Thailand, and Singapore. Many of these Saints travel from some of the most remote and isolated places on Earth. The first group of members to serve from the tiny island of Pohnpei, Micronesia, traveled thousands of miles across the Pacific Ocean to the temple in 2006. Not knowing when or if they may ever return, they made a "frantic effort" to perform as much work as possible.

Former temple president Myron F. Francom described the dedication of these members who love the temple and make extreme sacrifices to be there: "These beautiful people come from far, far distances to be sealed as an eternal family in the House of the Lord. They come by boat and by land, by bus, by 'Jeepney' and by tricycle, often traveling two or three days and nights to come to the temple. They come with great faith and a longing desire to become an eternal family. Because many are very poor, it becomes a once-in-a-lifetime experience for some of them to come to the temple. They will give all they have for this wonderful opportunity. They never seem to complain about the trials and hardships they may endure. . . . I will never forget the experience I had when I sealed ten children, all dressed in white, to their parents. As they all looked at me with such childlike faith, I could feel their joy and happiness. We felt very close to our Father in Heaven and the tears filled our eyes. Yes, the temple is an experience of love: our love for our Father in Heaven and His children and His great love for us." In 2007, the temple was named the "Best Lighted Church" in Manila. The award was received because of the annual lighting display created on the temple grounds during the Christmas season. The Church was awarded a cash prize, which was promptly donated to an organization working with the victims of Typhoon Durian.

Dallas Texas Temple

On April 1, 1981, President Spencer W. Kimball announced plans to build nine temples in various parts of the world. These temples were designed to be small, efficient, and more economical to build than earlier temples. One of them, the Dallas Texas Temple, would serve nearly 120,000 members in most of Texas, all of Oklahoma, and parts of Arkansas, Louisiana, and Missouri.

A fund-raising committee was promptly formed after the announcement. Almost immediately, individual members' contributions and money from ward and stake projects began coming in. By collecting and selling aluminum cans, children in one stake raised seven hundred dollars. In another stake, the children raised money through a program they called "Nickels

for Nails." Even members with limited means responded generously. A bishop encouraged one widow, who had a very limited income, to pledge twenty dollars to the fund. Instead she gave him one hundred dollars, saying, "This is money I've been saving to go to the temple in Salt Lake City, but I'll contribute it to the building fund and go to the temple here." The Saints made generous contributions, and by the time ground was broken to begin construction of the temple, they had raised 140 percent of their goal.

Not all contributions were monetary, however. Relief Society sisters in the area were asked to crochet cloths that would cover the altars. To have money to buy the needed thread, one sister and her sick husband went without several meals until they

30

had saved enough. When offered assistance, she refused, saying, "I have never been able to do anything for my Father in Heaven until now. Don't deny this blessing to my ill husband or me."

After considering a variety of sites, the Church chose one in a quiet residential neighborhood twelve miles north of downtown Dallas. The property included an orchard of pecan trees. During a visit to examine the site, Elder Mark E. Petersen of the Quorum of the Twelve Apostles described the location as peaceful and serene and expressed his opinion that this was indeed an appropriate location for a temple.

Before the announcement of the Dallas Texas Temple, the Church had been largely unnoticed by the area's media. But with the announcement, some groups voiced strong opposition to the Church and its teachings. One headline in a major local newspaper read, "Southern Baptists brace for invasion of Mormons," and a story stated, "Southern Baptists, alarmed by a potential influx of Mormons into the South, are putting on their gospel armor and mounting their defenses against an invasion."

Opposition was also voiced in magazine articles and radio and television programs devoted to warning the Christian community about the dangers of Mormonism. Church members had never experienced such an intense opposition from other people in the community. A group opposed to the temple went as far as writing down the license plate numbers in the parking lot during a Latter-day Saint Sunday meeting so they could find out their addresses and encourage them to leave the Church. But such efforts were largely ineffective, and the Saints were strengthened in their beliefs as they renewed their conviction of the truth of the gospel.

During this time, Bishop H. Burke Peterson, of the presiding bishopric, and Elder Ivan L. Hobson, a regional representative, visited the temple site to discuss these problems. While they were speaking, a man approached them and introduced himself as Reverend Pryor. Bishop Peterson asked the reverend what he thought of their plan to build the temple and about the community's reaction. Reverend Pryor explained that although he had been pressured to speak against the temple, he had decided not to take a stand for or against it. He noted that years earlier, when his church had been building the facility

SITE
6 acres

GROUNDBREAKING
January 22, 1983, by
Gordon B. Hinckley

DEDICATION
October 19–24, 1984, by
Gordon B. Hinckley

EXTERIOR
Light-colored marble tile
walls, dark gray slate roof

TOTAL FLOOR AREA
44,207 square feet

DIMENSIONS
236 feet by 78 feet; tower 95 feet;
statue of angel Moroni on top spire

HIDDEN IMAGE
Among the tiles of the temple is
the Good Shepherd cradling one of
His sheep, with His flock scattered
in the clouds and landscaping.

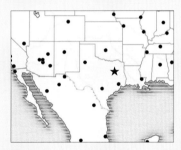

he preached in, his church had received similar opposition. But, he said, once the building was completed, opposition had ceased, and they had not had any further problems.

At the groundbreaking ceremony on January 22, 1983, a prayer was offered asking the Lord to ease animosity toward the temple and help the local people come to appreciate the temple as a beautiful addition to the community. President Gordon B. Hinckley emphasized that "this is the Lord's work; it cannot be stopped, it will not be stopped, it will roll forth. We'll build this temple here, we will build all the others presently scheduled, and there are others yet to come which have been tentatively designated."

Part of the answer to this prayer came when the temple opened its doors in September 1984 and nearly eighty thousand visitors, more than half of whom were nonmembers, came to visit the edifice. On the second day of open house tours, Janet Del Corso visited the temple because she was impressed by its architectural beauty. As she walked its halls, the temporal aspects dwindled, and "eternal truths became the highlight of my visit." Before the nineteen-day open house was over, she was baptized a member of the Church.

On October 19, 1984, the temple was dedicated by President Gordon B. Hinckley before an audience of 1,100 people.

Like the Boise Idaho Temple, which was built according to a similar plan, this temple was remodeled in 1987 to increase its size and make it more functional and efficient. The addition gave the temple 22,749 new square feet of space, an additional ordinance room, a cafeteria, and expanded laundry facilities. It also relocated the baptistry.

Over the years, the Dallas Texas Temple has been used by patrons to receive ordinances for themselves and for the dead. In addition to thousands of family members for whom patrons have acted as proxies, ordinances have been performed for individuals of historical significance in the temple district. For instance, in 1986, work was completed for the men who perished at the Alamo on March 6, 1836, and their families. Work was also performed for the 1,500 Choctaws who were forced to relocate more than 500 miles in the middle of winter. Many of them died in zero-degree temperatures. The route they took has since come to be known as the "Trail of Tears."

Taipei Taiwan Temple

T he people of Taiwan, whose island was once called *Formosa,* meaning "beautiful," were first introduced to the Church when American servicemen were stationed there in the mid-1950s. The printing of the Book of Mormon in Chinese in 1965 was a great boon to the local members, who had waited for years to have the book available in their own language. However, it is the building of the Taipei Taiwan Temple that many Taiwanese Saints see as the greatest development in the history of the Church in their land.

After the announcement of the temple in 1981, Church leaders decided to build on the site of the mission home in the center of Taipei. Although not on a hilltop or in a wooded area, and therefore different from many other temples throughout the world,

the temple is easily accessible to members. Church leaders hoped the beauty of the temple would attract the attention of passersby who would notice the contrast between it and the surrounding secular buildings.

Materials used on the building were scheduled to arrive on site early to facilitate an uninterrupted flow in the construction process. But it was often difficult to find room to store supplies on the limited space at the site. In one instance, additional storage space was provided in an unusual way. When crates containing the baptismal font and its large oxen, as well as the statue of the angel Moroni, arrived in the country, customs authorities declined to release them. LaVar Wallgren, who sculpted the statue and the oxen, described the situation: "The

31

Church authorities were not concerned at all, and they did not push the matter because they did not have any place to put them. When the construction officials finally needed them for the temple, they called up [customs authorities] and said, 'We have some containers that have been on your dock for a long period of time—a month or two.' The person managing the dock was surprised and, after going through his papers, said, 'Get these things off the dock!' The whole thing was a blessing in disguise."

The Taipei Taiwan Temple was completed in 1984, and more than twenty thousand visitors toured it during the open house. The dedication was performed on November 17, 1984 by President Gordon B. Hinckley. Although a typhoon was reportedly headed toward Taiwan on the second day of the dedication, members were undaunted as they stood in line to participate. Five dedicatory sessions were held, four in Mandarin and one in Cantonese. President Hinckley pointed out that the ordinances of the temple were available not only to the living members of the Church but also to the millions of their ancestors who had preceded them in life.

In his dedicatory prayer, President Hinckley expressed gratitude for "the firm foundation on which thy Church is now established in this part of the earth. We thank thee for this day when those who will use this temple may turn their hearts to their fathers, participating in thy holy house in those ordinances which will make it possible for their deceased forebears to move forward on the way that leads to eternal life."

Part of the Church's favorable reception in Taiwan stems from Taiwanese interest in their ancestors and family history. David C. H. Liu, who served as recorder for the Taipei Taiwan Temple, said that he believed the Lord had been preparing the Taiwanese for centuries for the coming of the gospel and temple work to their island. "They love their families and have a good tradition of keeping the family genealogy," he said. Some families in Taiwan have family records dating back two thousand years. Even before the dedication of the temple, some 12,000 names had been submitted for temple work. In a land of many different temples, honoring one's ancestors is part of a long, rich history. Countless traditional temples and shrines provide places where people believe they can connect with

SITE
0.48 acres

GROUNDBREAKING
August 27, 1982, by
Gordon B. Hinckley

DEDICATION
November 17–18, 1984, by
Gordon B. Hinckley

EXTERIOR
Empress white granite

TOTAL FLOOR AREA
9,945 square feet

DIMENSIONS
178 feet by 72 feet, six spires;
statue of angel Moroni rises
to height of 126 feet

HIDDEN IMAGE
The Savior is left of temple
and "Families are forever" is
written in Chinese among
the palm tree shadows.

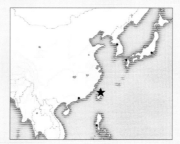

their ancestors. Their traditional emphasis on ancestors makes "turning our hearts to our fathers" a natural part of their culture. While most people use these traditional temples to seek blessings *from* their ancestors, there the ordinances of the restored gospel bring about blessings *for* their ancestors. Over the past thirty-five-plus years, Brother Li Chiun-tsan, a member of the Hu Wei Ward, has dedicated himself to family history and temple work. He and his wife, Li-hsueh, have traced his family line back nearly 5,000 years to the Yellow Emperor, said to be the ancestor of all Han Chinese. They have submitted more than 100,000 names to the temple. In 2014, the temple's thirty-year anniversary was celebrated by members attending temple-themed devotionals in various parts of the temple district. During the devotionals, choirs performed, historical photos were displayed, and messages were shared from former temple presidents and matrons. A blind sister temple worker shared her story at one of the events. Since the temple was dedicated in 1984, she traveled an hour by train to serve in the temple for an entire week every month. Though she cannot see, she is as familiar with every nook and corner of the temple as any other member. In March 1985, after receiving a serious surgical operation, doctors advised her to rest for at least one year before resuming her normal activities. However, she felt an urgent need to serve her deceased ancestors and began serving in the temple immediately after returning from the hospital. Upon returning to the temple, she said, "The spirit of the temple made me feel like I was home again." She has performed over 3,500 endowments for the deceased, and her lifetime goal is to perform 5,000.

Temple attendance has steadily increased over the years. The total number of deceased endowments performed in 2014 was 10.7% higher than 2013—the greatest number since its dedication. Arnie Chen, Taipei Taiwan Temple recorder, observed, "Not only are we witnessing membership growth in Taiwan, we are also seeing an increase in temple attendance of the Lord's faithful children here. Patrons and workers are more willing to serve their deceased ancestors by doing family history work and temple work and are coming in increasing numbers. Stakes have set goals and are doubling, even tripling their attendance. Busloads of Saints attend regularly."

Guatemala City Guatemala Temple

Guatemala City is a pleasant place, with its delightful blend of European and Indian heritage and a tropical climate tempered by its elevation, nearly 5,000 feet above sea level. In a land rich with ancient Mayan pyramids, palaces, and towering temples, the latter-day faithful now have a temple of their own. Many members waited a generation to partake of temple blessings within their nation's borders. For them, the temple means the opportunity at last to partake of eternal blessings.

Latter-day Saint missionaries were first sent to Guatemala in 1947 after John F. O'Donnal, a North American living there, visited Church headquarters in Salt Lake City and reported that there were people in the country ready to hear the gospel. His wife,

Carmen, was the first Guatemalan baptized; Brother O'Donnal would later serve as a mission president and temple president in Guatemala.

Brother O'Donnal also assisted in a vital way prior to the temple's construction. Guatemala City always struggles with water shortages, so Brother O'Donnal suggested drilling a well to supply the needs of the new building. After grinding through two hundred feet of solid rock, the drillers found an abundant supply of pure water. The stately Guatemala City Guatemala Temple is a worthy addition to its location on Vista Hermosa, which means "beautiful view." Faced with white Guatemalan marble and flanked by six elegant spires, the temple

32

stands at the foot of rolling hills in southeastern Guatemala City.

The interior of the temple is equally beautiful, featuring authentic Mayan pieces. Those assigned to select materials for the temple's interior believe they were guided by the Spirit to local marketplaces, where they purchased two beautiful *guipiles* (hand woven, embroidered blouses) that were framed and hung in the temple's foyer.

During the open house, some 24,000 people visited the temple, requiring 179 missionaries from the Guatemala City Mission to work in six-hour shifts with twenty missionaries per shift. About 3,700 copies of the Book of Mormon were distributed. Of these, 3,500 had been donated by Guatemalan Saints, who included their testimonies. A university student who toured the temple described it as a "beautiful pearl" overlooking the capital city.

During the first dedicatory session, President Gordon B. Hinckley noted that the temple was a blessing "for which many generations have prayed behind the veil, descendants of Father Lehi, who have been taught the gospel . . . so they may continue with their journey to eternal life." In the dedicatory prayer, he expressed gratitude that the temple would open "the gates of salvation and eternal life" for "the many generations of our fathers and mothers who suffered so greatly and who walked for so long in darkness." Each session was filled to capacity with about 900 Saints, who came from not only Guatemala City but also from remote rural areas in Guatemala and from neighboring Honduras, El Salvador, and Costa Rica.

The temple's first matron, Sister Carmen O'Donnal, said that having a temple in her native land was the culmination of thirty-six years of work and growth. "It will be a blessing not just for the members," she said, "but for the whole nation, as the people come to know Jesus Christ through this holy and sanctified place."

Adjacent to the temple is the Guatemala Missionary Training Center, evidence of the Church's growth in Central America. At the center's groundbreaking ceremony, Udine Fallabella, a regional representative and the first stake president in Central America, noted, "The Church is growing faster than our steps keep up with it. We must follow the admonition of President Spencer W. Kimball to lengthen our stride."

SITE
About 1.4 acres

GROUNDBREAKING
September 12, 1982, by
Richard G. Scott

DEDICATION
December 14–16, 1984, by
Gordon B. Hinckley

EXTERIOR
Natural white Guatemalan marble

TOTAL FLOOR AREA
11,610 square feet

DIMENSIONS
178 feet by 72 feet, six spires; 127
feet high with statue of angel Moroni

HIDDEN IMAGE
The angel Moroni statue is seen in the
distant hills behind the national flag.

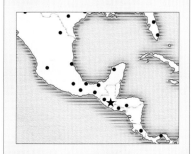

During his service as the temple president, Owen Dean Call wrote: "Since its dedication in 1984, the Guatemala City Temple has blessed the lives of thousands of faithful members. Indeed, the impact and influence of the temple in the lives of the members can be measured in the increasing number of stakes and missions. In 1984 there were eight stakes and two missions in Guatemala. At the end of 1993, there were 24 stakes and four missions in this country.

"We have seen the influence and spiritual impact of the temple as the many indigenous groups come for their sacred ordinances: Mam, Kekchi, Quiche, Pocoman, Cakchiqel, Sutuil, and others who are direct descendants of the ancient Lamanites. One of the most beautiful sights one can enjoy in the temple is to watch these pure Lamanites, indigenous to the country, come to claim the blessings that by royal birthright belong to them. All the temple workers know that they are special; they have such a strong spirit that the temple's atmosphere changes when they walk in. We have never seen people as reverent, humble, and with such spirituality as these 'true Lamanites.' To see them arrive, a little nervous and full of expectations, and after a few hours to see them leave with the brightness of eternity shining in their eyes is the most rewarding feeling one can have working in the temple.

"Two responses demonstrate the impact of these ordinances: 'After being in this holy building, I have been able to better understand the order of things pertaining to eternal life,' said one indigenous brother. 'I have understood that if we desire we can be instruments in the hands of God to bless the lives of others on this or the other side of the veil.' Another patron commented, 'As I ponder the privilege we have, as part of the children of God, to receive through correct channels and from authorized servants the saving ordinances, I cannot go forward without thanking Heavenly Father for the opportunity to partake of them.'

"We are also touched by the great sacrifices made by many of the Saints who come. Saints from Honduras and Nicaragua spend from fourteen to thirty-two hours on a bus to get to the temple. A sister ordinance worker spends two hours or more by bus to get to the temple and takes in washing on other days so she will have the money needed for her bus fare. She seldom misses a day and is always on time."

Freiburg Germany Temple

The Freiberg Germany Temple stands on a beautiful site in Freiberg, a city about 120 miles south of Berlin. Cut off from the West since the end of World War II and under the fist of an oppressive Communist government, the German Saints remained faithful during their years behind the Iron Curtain, despite their isolation. "The war cost us everything," one said, "but there was something they couldn't take—our testimonies." The dedication of the Bern Switzerland Temple in 1955 changed the course of history for Saints living in East Germany. Without its attraction and influence, it is hard to imagine that the Freiberg Germany Temple would have ever been built. Henry J. Burkhardt, who served as president of the Dresden Germany Mission and President of the Freiberg

Germany Temple said, "The commandment to the Saints to attend the temple . . . remained an important but unfulfilled part of the gospel plan . . . hardly anyone had the expectation of attending a temple during their lifetime, despite their faithfulness to the commandments of God. . . . [But] after the temple in Zollikofen [the Bern Switzerland Temple] was dedicated in 1955, the wish burned within many Saints to go there. . . . Nothing was more important to the priesthood leaders of our country than to fulfill this wish for the members."

After visiting the Dresden mission in May 1978, Bishop H. Burke Peterson of the Presiding Bishopric proposed to the First Presidency the possibility of creating an endowment house for Church members

33

in Eastern Germany. The proposed building would have two separate functions: a meetinghouse on one side and an endowment facility on the other. The building would not include a baptistry, and ordinances would be performed for only living persons. The endowment house never came to fruition because to the surprise of Church leaders, on May 31, 1978, top government officials proposed the building of a temple in the German Democratic Republic.

At the temple groundbreaking ceremony on April 23, 1983, officials from the communist government attended and sat on the front row. Conducting the service was President Thomas S. Monson. Before the invocation was offered, he looked the government representatives straight in the eye and said, "When we pray in our church, we fold our arms, bow our heads and close our eyes." As the prayer began, every one of the officials had their arms folded, heads bowed, and eyes closed.

At the conclusion of the event, the county council chairman said, "We've never experienced anything so beautiful as this. If you ever need anything, come to me and I will help you."

After the ceremony, President Monson recorded: "This is a miracle of miracles! I think it all began when we made a final effort with the government to get permission for our faithful couples to go to the Swiss Temple. The [German] minister in their government then said, 'Why not build a temple in our country?' We took him up on his offer, and the building is now under way." The temple was a result of President Monson's nearly twenty-year effort to work with the East German government. Referring to the Communist leaders with whom he worked, President Monson said, "They trusted me, and I trusted them, and the result was marvelous."

There were other miracles, too. Henry J. Burkhardt explained that private ownership of property was not permitted in East Germany, and yet the Church was granted private ownership. The building of a temple had never before been permitted in a Communist nation, but in this case, government officials themselves suggested the building of a temple as an alternative to considering the request that Church members be

SITE
1 acre

GROUNDBREAKING
April 23, 1983, by Thomas S. Monson

DEDICATION
June 29–30, 1985, by
Gordon B. Hinckley

REDEDICATION
September 7, 2002, by
Gordon B. Hinckley

EXTERIOR
White-German stucco plastered over 24-inch thick brick walls and a blue gray slate stone slab roof

TOTAL FLOOR AREA
13,300 square feet

DIMENSIONS
Originally 94 feet by 75 feet; 94 feet by 112 feet after remodeling

HIDDEN IMAGE
An image of the Savior is included among the trees to the left of the temple.

permitted to visit the temple in Switzerland. Allowing the temple to be built was an incredible, unprecedented move for Communist leaders. "All in all, the event [was] miraculous," said President Burkhardt.

Only 4,000 Church members lived in the German Democratic Republic at the time, but nearly 90,000 people went through the open house. President Monson considered that attendance to be an answer to his prayer in 1975, when he had asked Heavenly Father to "instill within the citizenry a curiosity concerning the Church and a desire to learn more of our teachings."

Once dedicated, great concern existed among Church members they would not have access to their sacred temple for long. Therefore, priority during the first few weeks was given to members who had not previously been to the temple. Members came by appointment with their branches to receive their personal ordinances. Therefore, even if the temple became unavailable for use, it would have already accomplished its major purpose. Considering the likelihood that the temple may have had a brief period of use, cost-saving efforts were made on building materials and decor.

President Monson wrote in his journal: "Frequently people will ask, 'How has it been possible for the Church to obtain permission to build a temple behind the Iron Curtain?' My feeling is simply that the faith and devotion of our Latter-day Saints in that area brought forth the help of Almighty God and provided for them the eternal blessings which they so richly deserve."

The temple received a major renovation and expansion starting in July 2001. Improvements included a redesigned baptistry, a non-patrons waiting area, a matron/bride's room, and the addition of an angel Moroni statue. The reconstructed temple is 13,300 square feet, nearly doubling the size of the original temple. Although the temple was significantly enlarged, the building's front appearance remained much the same, a purposeful move by architect Hanno Luschin. He said affection for the temple ran so deeply among the Saints that they chose to not change the look.

Stockholm Sweden Temple

The Stockholm Sweden Temple, reflecting traditional architecture of the "Land of the North," is located in Vasterhaninge, a suburb of Haninge, about thirteen miles southeast of Stockholm. Its six spires rise above the pines in the nearby forest, and a cobblestone path leads to its doors. Near the temple is a Church-owned guesthouse with 120 beds for patrons who have traveled long distances to attend the house of the Lord.

After President Spencer W. Kimball announced that a temple would be built near Stockholm, Sweden, a site-selection committee was formed to consider twenty-eight possible sites. Two were presented to the First Presidency for consideration. The First Presidency chose the community of Haninge

because of its large concentration of Latter-day Saints. City officials and merchants welcomed the temple project, and later the city showed further support by changing the name of the street on which the temple is located to Temple Drive. City officials also renamed the three blocks of the temple site as Temple, Genealogist, and Chapel.

When the local Environmental Party raised concerns, temple president Bo G. Wennerlund, then a regional representative, attended a community meeting to discuss the issues. At first the people seemed hostile, but as the meeting progressed, their feelings changed, and matters were resolved amicably. When the temple architect asked Elder Wennerlund later how he turned

34

the crowd around, Elder Wennerlund told him, "I didn't do it. It was the Lord."

On March 17, 1984, more than four hundred people braved frigid weather to attend the groundbreaking for the first temple in Scandinavia. Heaters had to be used to thaw the icy ground in preparation for the ceremonial first turning of the soil. President Thomas S. Monson, who was presiding, said, "On this cold morning you have warm smiles on your faces and warm feelings in your hearts, for it is a day of thanksgiving." Many Church members described the occasion as a new day in Sweden, a phrase President Monson had used on July 8, 1977, in a prayer dedicating and rededicating the country.

Shortly after temple construction began, an incredible discovery was made at the temple site. The temple site was found to be located on a gravesite dating back over 2,000 years. Temple construction was delayed for three years while seventeen graves of different sizes were excavated. Because of this discovery, many portions of the temple grounds could not be altered. The oldest graves date back to 700 years BC and were located exactly where the temple now stands. In the surrounding area, there are approximately 200 graves, the youngest dating around AD 400.

In the Stockholm Sweden Temple, sessions are routinely conducted in nine languages, with sessions in other languages as needed. Here people from many nations put aside their traditional differences—Estonians, Finns, Russians, Germans, Danes, Swedes, and Norwegians—working together in love. An ordinance worker who fled the second Russian invasion of Estonia at the end of World War II is now glad to see the Russians—coming to the temple.

In 1973, President Spencer W. Kimball asked the Saints to pray that the doors of all nations—including those behind the Iron Curtain—would be opened to missionary work. The Saints responded, praying for years that it might be so. In 1989, the Iron Curtain began to fall. Church members in Russia, Hungary, Poland, and the Baltic States began preparing to go to the temple in Sweden.

On December 10, 1991, the first Russian family was sealed in the Stockholm Sweden Temple. Their trip cost more than most Russians earn in a year. Temple president Reid Johnson

SITE
4.47 acres

GROUNDBREAKING
March 17, 1984, by
Thomas S. Monson

DEDICATION
July 2–4, 1985, by
Gordon B. Hinckley

EXTERIOR
Masonry exterior with copper roof

TOTAL FLOOR AREA
16,366 square feet

DIMENSIONS
178 feet by 71 feet; angel Moroni statue is atop tallest spire at 112 feet

HIDDEN IMAGE
An image of the Savior is found in the trees and sky left of the temple. Among the dense vegetation to the right of the temple is Joseph Smith holding the Book of Mormon.

described their visit: "They have immersed themselves in the ordinances of the temple. All have been 'anxiously engaged' in performing ordinances, receiving the covenants of the endowment, striving to absorb and understand the almost unfathomable depths of the eternal marriage covenant and sealing power. They were more literally immersed in the baptismal font, leaving tears in the water as the names of parents, grandparents and other loved ones were read."

Since then, many other patrons have traveled to the temple from Russia and the Baltic states. Eventually, however, they must return home, a journey of four to six days. "They wave good-bye," said one temple worker. "Some look up at the statue of the angel Moroni and say, 'Good-bye, Moroni, we may never see you again.'" The temple celebrated a historic occasion on August 23, 1995, when President Thomas S. Monson welcomed Their Majesties King Carl XVI Gustaf and Queen Silvia to the temple grounds. Sweden's royal couple visited the temple site in the "Eriksgata" tradition that dates back to the thirteenth century, in which the king traveled through the country to be met by its citizens. As they approached the temple, the king and queen paused to listen to Primary children sing "I Am a Child of God."

In 2000, a fantastic discovery was made on grounds adjacent to the temple site. Remains of an ancient temple built between 400 BC and AD 400 were excavated. The exact distance from the ancient and modern temple is only 165 feet. The octagon-shaped structure was built in a fashion similar to antique temples of Rome. No other find of its kind has ever been made in Sweden or northern Europe.

Resting upon an ancient gravesite, the Stockholm Sweden Temple has been the place where sacred ordinances for millions have occurred. The spirit of Elijah makes an impression on all who visit the temple site, said temple recorder Ingvar Olsson: "Participating in these events [temple work], which are governed by the Lord for the salvation and exaltation of the children of God, leave us in wonderment. We see and feel the grandeur, the love, and mercy of the wonderful work of God, and acknowledge His hands in all things, at all times."

Chicago Illinois Temple

The Chicago Illinois Temple, dedicated in 1985, was the first temple to be built in the Midwestern United States since the Nauvoo Temple, which was begun during the life of Joseph Smith and afterward was destroyed by mobs. The land on which the Chicago Illinois Temple sits is known as "the Grove" and is famous for its wildflowers, birds, and grasslands. This site, in Glenview, Illinois, about twenty miles north of Chicago, was selected after two years of searching and two more years of seeking governmental approvals amid intense opposition by groups concerned about the visual effect the temple would have on the area.

When ground was finally broken and construction of the temple commenced, President Gordon B. Hinckley sought to allay the fears of local residents.

At the groundbreaking ceremony he said, "We promise that what we do here will be beautiful and will enhance rather than diminish the charm of this lovely area." The Church was true to these words, taking measures to preserve the native landscape on the temple grounds and allowing for a 100-foot buffer zone along the southern border of the site. The southern side of the temple roof remains unlighted so as not to disrupt bird migration flyways. Large trees and beautiful lawns surrounded by an ornate brick-and-iron fence beautify the grounds. The site has proven to be a perfect, peaceful setting for a house of the Lord. Elder Robert L. Simpson, a member of the Seventy, commented that the selection of this site was heaven directed.

35

The temple adds to the natural beauty of its setting. As a result of contributions from faithful Saints in the area, both the outside and the inside of the building reflect the love the members have for the temple and the sacrifices they made to beautify it. The landscaping was in part funded with "temple pennies" donated by Primary children in the temple district. Members gave of their time, talents, and money to provide furnishings for the temple. A group of young women made dolls for the temple nursery. Women crocheted and tatted altar cloths for the ordinance and sealing rooms. One of them, a seventy-eight-year-old sister from Indiana, wrote that although her infirmities kept her from attending the temple, she felt blessed to be able to participate by creating something beautiful for the building. Another sister sent her finished cloth and a note offering to make another one if needed. She wept with gratitude after a phone call came accepting her offer.

In addition to preparing the temple for its open house, dedication, and subsequent use for the performing of ordinances, members began preparing themselves to serve in the temple regularly. Home teachers in the Naperville Illinois Stake asked the families they taught to consider the question, "Are you really spiritually prepared to go to the temple?" Members who took this assignment seriously felt a change occur. Robert Ensign, of the Woodridge Ward, said at that time, "People's lives are changing, and we're finding that the closer we draw to the dedication, the more that momentum is building."

Many members volunteered to help with the open house of the temple. During the time it was open to the public, more than one hundred thousand people walked through the halls of the sacred building, marveling at its beauty, learning of its purpose, and feeling the peaceful spirit that is only found in a temple. Visitors made such comments as "an obvious place of devotion," "everyone should feel closer to God in this special place," and "I felt the hand of God."

The dedication of the Chicago Illinois Temple took place on August 9, 1985, nearly 140 years after the dedication of the Nauvoo Temple. "We of this generation remember Nauvoo," remarked President Gordon B. Hinckley. "We think of the sacred edifice which stood high on its hill. We remember with appreciation and gratitude those who built it. We recall their sacrifice when they were driven from it. Knowing they soon would be

SITE
13 acres

GROUNDBREAKING
August 13, 1983, by
Gordon B. Hinckley

DEDICATION
August 9–13, 1985, by
Gordon B. Hinckley

REDEDICATION
October 8, 1989, by Gordon B.
Hinckley (addition only)

EXTERIOR
Gray buff marble and a gray slate roof

TOTAL FLOOR AREA
34,000 square feet

DIMENSIONS
236 feet by 78 feet; seven-foot-tall angel Moroni statue reaches 112 feet high

HIDDEN IMAGE
The Savior's face is seen in the tree left of the temple, and His arms and hands are extended in the foreground flowers.

banished, and with many of their number already gone, they yet chose to complete it."

"I have a feeling that the erection and dedication of this House of the Lord carries something of a redemption of what happened in the past. It brings together the tradition of Nauvoo and the blessings of today," President Hinckley said before the dedication.

"I think there is an unseen audience today. I cannot escape the feeling that God, our Eternal Father, and the Risen Lord today are looking down on us. I am confident Joseph and Hyrum, who gave their lives in testimony of this work—who gave their lives and were buried in the soil of Illinois—are looking down upon us. I am confident that John Taylor looks down upon us.

"I'm grateful for this day when another temple now stands in Illinois, built in an environment of peace, goodwill, appreciation, and respect."

Twenty-four thousand Church members attended the nineteen dedication ceremonies. President Hinckley offered the dedicatory prayer, which referred to the faithful Saints of the past as well as those in the present: "O God, we thank Thee for the inheritance of faith that has come down from that generation. We thank Thee for a new and better day when our people have returned to this area and large numbers have been added to Thy Church in this part of the nation."

After only three years of consistent and faithful use, the Chicago Illinois Temple was closed in September 1988 for renovation and expansion. The remodeling effort more than doubled the size of the temple. The temple's administrative area was expanded, a sealing room and a cafeteria were added, and the baptistry was relocated and beautified. To provide convenience to temple workers, an elevator was added in 1994.

At the conclusion of the dedicatory prayer, the message was of a challenging past and a promising future: "May this holy house, built in peace and dedicated in faith, stand as a testimony that the oppression of the past has faded and that Thy people today enjoy the precious blessings of worshipping Thee according to Thy revelations without fear or molestation. May Thy work move forward to the encompassing glory Thou hast set for it, we humbly pray, as in faith we rededicate ourselves to Thy service, with songs of thanksgiving and praise."

Johannesburg South Africa Temple

The Johannesburg South Africa Temple is a sparkling jewel in a land noted for its diamonds. Located two miles north of Johannesburg, the temple is visible from many parts of the city, its six spires gleaming in the sunlight. At the northeast corner of the one-acre temple site is an area of grass, trees, and massive rock outcroppings that provides a panoramic view of the Johannesburg suburbs. A prominent landmark, the temple attracts thousands of curious visitors.

Once the site of estates built by nineteenth-century mining magnates and financiers, the area around the temple now features hospitals, office buildings, and schools, many of which are housed in mansions from the Victorian era. In an extensive effort to preserve the area's historical value, planners selected indigenous quartzite for the temple's perimeter walls and entrance archways. The gray brick and slate on the temple's exterior are harmonious with the historic buildings nearby. The temple was rotated forty-five degrees in order for the temple grounds to be used most efficiently. Beneath the ground, a parking garage accommodates approximately forty cars.

The temple is a refuge of peace in this land of political strife. Afrikaners and Zulus greet each other warmly; the clicks of Zulu, Sotho, and other African languages mingle with the sounds of Saints whose ancestors came from England, Ireland, Holland, Germany, Portugal, and India. Church members come not only from South Africa but also from Zimbabwe, Lesotho, Swaziland, and Botswana. Temple sessions

36

are conducted in six languages, including English, Afrikaans, French, and Portuguese, to meet the needs of the patrons.

Before the Johannesburg South Africa Temple was erected, Church members in Africa had to travel to London—5,600 miles—to visit the house of the Lord. One family ate next to nothing for some time so they could save money to go to the temple. Another family gave them one hundred dollars to aid in their travel to London, where they spent three weeks doing temple work. When they returned home, the family that had been to the temple saved another hundred dollars, which they gave to still another family who wanted to go to the temple. That family in turn gave to yet another family. And so the tradition continued.

At the laying of the temple's cornerstone, President Gordon B. Hinckley commended the members: "Our witness to you about the temple is that the Lord wanted it built because of the faith of the Saints of South Africa and Zimbabwe. Treasure the blessings of the temple! It houses all of the facilities to do the work required for salvation. God placed you in this land."

Elder Neal A. Maxwell observed, "Families sealed in this temple in South Africa will still be sealed when the pyramids in northern Africa have become nothing but shifting sands."

During the dedication service, President Hinckley noted that the Church now has a temple on every continent but Antarctica. Even so, reaching the temple is no easy matter for many African Saints. Travel costs are high, and air travel can be challenging. Many still find it easier to fly to London than to Johannesburg. Land travel, too, is difficult, because few roads are paved, and bridges are often washed out.

One family, Joseph and Gladys Sitati and their five children, traveled two thousand miles from Nairobi, Kenya, to keep their promise to Heavenly Father that they would be sealed to each other in the Johannesburg South Africa Temple. Elder J. Ballard Washburn, then first counselor in the Africa Area presidency, performed the ordinance. "It was one of the sweetest experiences," Elder Washburn said. "The father and mother had worked hard, and planned a long time. As they

SITE
One acre

GROUNDBREAKING
November 27, 1982, by
Marvin J. Ashton

DEDICATION
August 24–25, 1985, by
Gordon B. Hinckley

EXTERIOR
Masonry exterior with gray slate roof

TOTAL FLOOR AREA
19,184 square feet

DIMENSIONS
178 feet by 71 feet; angel Moroni
statue is atop tallest spire at 112 feet

HIDDEN IMAGE
An image of the Savior
kneeling and looking up is
located left of the temple.

knelt at the altar in fulfillment of their dream, the Spirit of the Lord was there with power."

Brother Sitati said, "With what has happened this one week in the temple and receiving our patriarchal blessings, I would say that our family will never be the same again. The light has been lit and we have something to follow. There is a guide."

Cultural, social, political, and economic circumstances have frequently been a challenge to Latter-day Saints living in South Africa. For Church members, this extreme diversity has been bridged by the gospel of Jesus Christ. Much of the healing that takes place among members seems to happen in the temple. Charles Canfield, former president of the temple, describes an experience he had shortly after assuming his duties: "One day I heard a commotion in the temple and went back to restore some reverence. It so happened that a number of groups from all over South Africa had come that day. What I saw when I entered the room was friends greeting each other—colored people embracing Afrikaners, British members embracing blacks. Where else but in the temple would you find that kind of natural outpouring of love? I learned a good lesson that day. I learned a new definition of reverence."

Members from Madagascar made their first stake temple trip in December 2001 to the Johannesburg South Africa Temple. During the four days of temple sessions for the thirty-three members, nineteen members received their own endowments, eight couples were sealed, and five families were sealed. While in Johannesburg, the members attended a special devotional during which Elder Steven E. Snow of the Seventy and counselor in the Africa Southeast Area presidency addressed them. Stake President Dominique Andriamanantoa said the trip "will have a strong and lasting impact on the Church in Madagascar."

The Johannesburg South Africa Temple rests on a high point of ground in the city and has become a prominent landmark. At night pilots flying into Johannesburg often use its lights as a beacon. The temple is indeed a beacon—a beacon symbolizing the fullness of the gospel to South Africa and the entire African continent.

Seoul South Korea Temple

Located in west central Seoul, the Seoul South Korea Temple was dedicated in 1985 in the "Land of the Morning Calm." Following Eastern tradition, the meticulous temple grounds are groomed as a natural garden. The temple walls feature Korean granite reminiscent of the Salt Lake Temple, its six white pillars drawing the viewer's eyes toward heaven. A traditional, tiled "hundred-year roof" gives the temple a uniquely Korean appearance. Inside, the temple is decorated with delicate brush paintings, intricate wooden molding, silk wall coverings, gold leaf, dome chandeliers, and white lacquer furniture inlaid with mother of pearl.

The first member of the Church in Korea was baptized in 1951, at a time when Korea was in the midst of a civil war with Communist armies from the north. Latter-day Saint servicemen from America taught the gospel through the way they lived. As one convert noted, "Many of these men had come fresh from the front line . . . yet even that did not deter [them] from meeting to honor the Sabbath and to share their testimonies."

In October 1980, Korean Church leaders attended the dedication of the Tokyo Japan Temple. President Spencer W. Kimball encouraged those in the temple district, which included Korea, to attend the temple often. A Korean stake president commented, "I wondered how I could deliver the prophet's message to my people when we had no temple and they were not allowed to leave the country, to be sealed as man and wife." Legal restrictions prevented Korean husbands and

37

wives from leaving the country together or with their children. But during President Kimball's visit to Korea the next week, the government promised to review the restriction. On October 26, 1980, President Kimball paused during his opening address to the Seoul area conference to say, "Before long we hope there will be a temple in Korea." At the time only a hundred Korean members had received their endowments, and only twenty couples had been sealed.

The next year, the Church announced that a temple would be built in Seoul. A local priesthood leader recalled, "I was born in North Korea. I escaped when I was young. My mother died after we crossed the border. I will be able to do her temple work now. Think of all the people whose work can be done now!" When stake patriarch Lee Bum-tae heard the news, tears streamed down his face. He had always promised Church members the blessings of the temple. He declared, "The sounds of [Moroni's trumpet] will now reach my country. From the Paekdu Mountains in the North to Cheju in the South. And because of this, my country, which we love, will be blessed."

Under the direction of Korea Mission President Spencer Palmer, the Church purchased the property in 1967. Originally purchased as a location for a chapel, mission home, and institute building, the site eventually became the location for the new temple.

Obtaining the required building permit to allow construction to begin was difficult. After a year of failed efforts, building permits were granted under the condition that the Church drill on site for water to supply emergency fire protection. This was a difficult task because the temple rests on at least 450 feet of solid granite. Knowing that temple construction could not proceed until water was found, things looked dismal as the first of several drilling attempts proved unsuccessful. Finally, after drilling at the lower portion of the property, a large supply of spring water was discovered. So much water was available that a 165-ton storage tank was installed to hold the large amount of water the spring produced. The water, which is pure and does not need to be boiled, is used in the temple as drinking water. With an abundant supply of water found, construction could begin.

SITE
1 acre

GROUNDBREAKING
May 9, 1983, by Marvin J. Ashton

DEDICATION
December 14–15, 1985, by
Gordon B. Hinckley

EXTERIOR
Granite exterior

TOTAL FLOOR AREA
28,057 square feet

DIMENSIONS
178 feet by 71 feet; angel Moroni
statue is atop tallest spire at 112 feet

HIDDEN IMAGE
"House of the Lord" in Korean is
among the shadows on the temple.

A problem with the importation of the audiovisual equipment threatened the completion of the temple. A trade law prevented the import of electronic equipment if a similar product was available in Korea. Although no products capable of performing the same function existed, the importation of the temple's high-tech equipment was declined. After much negotiation, an exception was made, and the audiovisual system arrived to the temple just in time for its scheduled installation.

The eagerly anticipated temple would not be completed without opposition. The thirteen thousand visitors at the open house were heckled by protesters from as far away as Hawaii. Referring to the opposition, President Gordon B. Hinckley said, "We have been strengthened and we have moved forward under the promise of the Lord, who said, 'I will not suffer that they (the enemy) shall destroy my work: yea I shall show unto them that my wisdom is greater than the cunning of the devil' (D&C 10:43)."

After the dedication, entire sessions were composed of members receiving their own endowments. Ken Jennings, a temple worker from the military servicemen's district, noted, "The unity of our human family was . . . made manifest as we assisted our Korean brothers and sisters to receive these holy ordinances. The differences in appearance, language, and culture vanished, and our common heritage as children of an Eternal Father with an eternal future ahead of us was manifest."

Respect for one's ancestors and the importance of families have long been traditions in Korea. Some families have kept records for hundreds, even thousands, of years. Kim Jung Shik, whose family had kept extensive records, said, "As we learned about the Church family history program, I became even more interested in my personal family records." After the temple's dedication, he submitted his direct line back to his first known ancestor, representing more than fifty generations.

In 1954, Elder Harold B. Lee said, "I feel the Spirit of the Almighty brooding amongst the Korean people and the unfolding of a great work is yet to come." That work is now being fulfilled.

Lima Peru Temple

Religious structures are nothing new to Peruvians. Their country, whose geographical features range from tropical jungles to the towering Andes and whose temperatures span the thermometer, also has numerous cathedrals and the ruins of ancient Incan temples with a history that spans the centuries. Since 1986, the capital city, Lima, has been home to a true house of the Lord, the Lima Peru Temple, which serves one hundred thousand Peruvian Saints.

Members of the South America North Area presidency discussed the Lima Peru Temple during a 1997 meeting, noting the profound influence the temple has had on their communities and nation. The temple was constructed in an undeveloped area, but today beautiful homes and streets surround it.

"Wonderful things also happen inside people's hearts as the influence of the temple reaches them," the presidency said. "Building a new temple is like throwing a stone into a lake: the resulting ripples radiate out and lift everything they touch."

The growth of the Church in Peru has been tremendous since the dedication of the temple in 1986. For example, two years later, in 1988, Elder M. Russell Ballard organized seven new stakes in Lima in a single twenty-eight-hour period. Despite serious economic and political problems in Peru, temple attendance also increased, tripling from 1988 to 1990. The temple has added additional sessions to accommodate the faithful members. On Saturdays and holidays, when the temple is heavily attended, extra chairs are placed in

38

sessions. The temple has no chapel, so patrons often wait in sealing rooms until an ordinance room is available.

For some members, attending the temple is difficult and costly. Saints from Iquitos, in the heart of Peru's jungle, must come to the temple by river or air because there are no roads from this area to Lima. A single plane ticket costs three months' worth of an average worker's salary, making transportation for large families extremely expensive. In February 2001, more than 140 Iquitos members prepared for their temple journey by selling their stoves, sewing machines, furniture, or other personal items to raise money. Temple President J. Marlan Walker said, "The people figured those items could be replaced, but they needed to get to the temple." Making the historic and adventuresome journey was Humberto Vilchez, president of the Iquitos Peru Punchana Stake. "One of the buses was built for 50 passengers and there were 65 people in the group," President Vilchez said. "So people took turns standing and sitting." After six days of treacherous travel, the group celebrated as the house of the Lord came into view.

President Walker remembers watching the weary members step off the bus outside the temple. "The Israelites arriving in the promised land could not have had more euphoric looks on their faces than these people from Iquitos arriving at the temple," he said. Without patron housing facilities, the Iquitos members were lodged in nearby member homes. Sleeping pads were placed in tight rows to accommodate each member. "They were stacked in there like cord wood, but the people did not complain a bit," President Walker said. After three days of diligent service, the faithful members returned safely home to Iquitos rich with the Spirit, strengthened by the temple. "These people will now bring a strength to their units that they've never had before," President Walker said.

A Church member from another outlying area told temple president Isidoro Villanueva: "My family and I met in family home evening and made the commitment to travel to the temple. We found a box in which to save the necessary money for my wife, my two youngest sons, and me to receive our ordinances and be sealed to each other and our deceased ancestors. After the passing of several months we had collected by a united effort, [Peruvian] *sole* by *sole,* the amount of 150 *soles*

SITE
4.5 acres

GROUNDBREAKING
September 11, 1982, by
Boyd K. Packer

DEDICATION
January 10–12, 1986, by
Gordon B. Hinckley

EXTERIOR
Light-colored Peruvian marble

TOTAL FLOOR AREA
9,600 square feet

DIMENSIONS
178 feet by 71 feet; angel Moroni
statue is atop tallest spire at 112 feet

HIDDEN IMAGE
An image of the Savior's face
is included among the trees
to the left of the temple.

(about $55 U.S.). We considered this to be sufficient to purchase our tickets for passage. Then my married daughter visited with the pleasant surprise of a gift to us of 100 *soles* to use for buying our food and temple clothing. We estimated now that we would have enough for food. We were very pleased to receive this help and were excited and ready to begin. However, the trip would be long and difficult, and my health had been deteriorating. As we prepared to buy these tickets, you can imagine our great surprise when our oldest married son told us that such a trip would not be good for my health. He unselfishly went to a travel agency and bought four round-trip airplane tickets for us. This was a blessing of an indescribable nature for us. I feel that the money we have left should be given to our stake president to help the others who are not as fortunate as we."

The temple workers, missionaries, and employees often work more than their scheduled hours at the temple, and operational challenges must be met almost daily. Commercial power outages, for instance, are common, requiring the use of a backup generator. During a power outage on one of the busiest days of the year, the generator stopped, halting work in the temple. Numerous prayers and the quick work of temple engineers soon had it going again. The temple engineers are often required to repair and even manufacture components for mechanical, electrical, and electronic systems. Yet the temple has never had to close for mechanical problems. Former temple president Glen V. Holley credits the ordinance workers, temple missionaries, office staff, security force, and maintenance crew, who keep the temple going.

The dedicatory prayer for the Lima Peru Temple, offered by President Gordon B. Hinckley, included these words: "Surely father Lehi has wept with sorrow over his posterity. Surely he weeps today with gladness." During the service, President Hinckley also said, "The day has arrived. Lehi, Sariah, Nephi, and others in that other sphere are rejoicing. This is the day of salvation for generations."

Pedro Chinchay, financial clerk for the Lima Peru Limatambo Stake, commented, "As it says in the scriptures, the Lamanites will blossom as a rose (see D&C 49:24). For me, the temple is an indication that that day is coming."

Buenos Aires Argentina Temple

When traveling to downtown Buenos Aires, many visitors are struck by the beauty of the Buenos Aires Argentina Temple, which stands near the busy thoroughfare from the airport. This house of the Lord was dedicated in 1986, the third temple to be built in Spanish-speaking South America (the Santiago Chile Temple was the first). Twelve million people—more than a third of Argentina's inhabitants—live in greater Buenos Aires. The cosmopolitan city is the political, economic, and cultural capital of Argentina. With the dedication of the temple, the city has become a focal point for Latter-day Saints as well.

In the early 1920s, Latter-day Saints who emigrated from Germany to Argentina asked the First Presidency to send missionaries to their new country.

On Christmas Day of 1925, Elder Melvin J. Ballard dedicated South America for the preaching of the gospel in a Buenos Aires park. A monument celebrating this historic event is located just a few steps from the Buenos Aires Argentina Temple. Carved on the face of a flat black stone are the words uttered by LDS Apostle Melvin J. Ballard a short time after he dedicated South America for missionary work: "The work will go forth slowly just as the oak grows from an acorn," he said. "[But] the South American Mission will become a power in the Church." That prophecy has been fulfilled to a remarkable degree. Today, millions of South Americans claim Church membership and temples dot the continent in almost every nation.

Ramon B. Paez, then a counselor in the bishopric

39

of the Centro Ward, Mar del Plata Argentina Stake, was chosen as the Argentine architect for the temple. Church leaders asked him to remember that he was working for a "very special client"—the Lord. Brother Paez later said that his work on the temple brought great changes in both his professional and spiritual life.

Although Argentine Saints were generally unable to contribute much money toward building the temple, they contributed in other ways. A group of sisters, for example, crocheted sixty-four altar cloths, although only seven had been requested.

During the temple's eight-day open house in December 1985, more than 29,000 visitors toured the building, some waiting as long as two and a half hours to get in. The temple's influence on these people was profound. One member noted in the guest book, "I have become a bit removed from the Church, and this visit makes me think about many things I could come to lose."

Another person wrote, "Very pretty, and I need to know more. It interests me."

A third visitor, perhaps an investigator, prayed: "Lord, guide me and help me to be baptized. Today I did not deserve this reward of knowing thy temple."

Alfredo Goyeneche, a member of the high council in the Buenos Aires Banfield Stake, and his wife, Marina, take advantage of the temple's proximity by attending regularly. "I tell Marina," Brother Goyeneche said, "that going to the temple weekly will be like vaccinating ourselves against the illnesses of the world."

Near the temple are a missionary training center and a patron housing facility, dedicated in 1994 by Elder Joseph B. Wirthlin. "We see here an example of the Church," Elder Wirthlin said. "It is compacted in these three buildings. The missionary training center is where we train and send out these wonderful missionaries in order to bring many people to the gospel of Jesus Christ. And then, later, as the converts proceed and improve themselves, they will be able to come to the patron housing and then go to the temple."

Youth groups often visit the temple to do baptisms, even

SITE
3.73 acres

GROUNDBREAKING
April 20, 1983

DEDICATION
January 17–19, 1986, by
Thomas S. Monson

REDEDICATION
September 9, 2012, by
Henry B. Eyring

EXTERIOR
Light gray native granite

TOTAL FLOOR AREA
17,683 square feet

HIDDEN IMAGE
An image of the Savior is included
among the palm trees.

though some who live in the city find it difficult to get there—the distances are great in the huge metropolis. Those living closest to the temple perform baptisms once a month. One young woman, Vanesa Ray, commented, "Coming to the temple is wonderful, because I can be baptized in the name of people who have died. They can receive the blessings of the gospel because of me. I can feel the Spirit because I know I am doing something good for the work, and I know my Father in Heaven is going to be happy about it."

After nearly three decades of service, the temple doors were closed in 2009 to allow for a major renovation and expansion. Renovation included building two new wings, which harmoniously complement the temple's original and distinctive design. Prominent throughout the exterior is vertical art glass, with triple-paned insulated glass incorporating the colors of the Argentine flag. Gardeners showed national pride by capturing the same flag color pattern in many of the flower designs. New decorative painting and gold leafing reflect patterns taken from historic architecture in Buenos Aires, and enhanced decorative wood trim and paneling feature Anigre and Makore hardwoods from Africa. An additional building was completed adjacent to the temple to provide housing for temple leadership.

Following a successful open house, which accommodated nearly 100,000 visitors, the temple was rededicated on September 9, 2012. The rededication marked another key moment in Argentine Church history. Scores of Argentine Latter-day Saints attended one of the three rededicatory sessions at the temple. Tens of thousands more viewed the ceremonies in meetinghouses stretched across the South American nation via closed circuit broadcasts.

Without having access to their temple for three years, many members reflected on their own lives and rededicated themselves to temple worship. Although most Argentine members lacked financial resources to attend a temple outside the country, they maintained their temple recommends and never lacked faith or worthiness.

Denver Colorado Temple

The tops of the mountains have long been a place of communion with God. It is fitting, then, that in the Rocky Mountain state of Colorado stands a house of the Lord, located on seven acres in Littleton, about twenty miles south of Denver.

The Church faced intense public opposition while selecting a site for the temple. Two locations were rejected in a four-month period. Joseph H. Barton, chairman of the Denver Temple Committee, recorded: "We didn't realize the forces Satan can muster when he really puts his mind to stopping a project. Literally all hell broke loose when we announced the first two sites to the public. We weren't welcome at those locations. . . . We obtained the third site, the right site, with very little opposition. Had we gone ahead with the site we're at now without

knowing what kind of blockades Satan was setting up for us, we would have failed. I bear testimony we have the right site and the Lord helped us to get it by diverting our attention elsewhere until we learned the proper procedures to get approval."

This third site, known as the "Four Lakes" site, was a hilltop that had once featured a nine-hole golf course and country club. President Barton described his first impressions of the place: "I'd never set foot on the land until that time, but as I stood for the first time on the spot where the clubhouse used to be, and where the temple is now, I was awed by the gorgeous, unobstructed view. I had the strongest feeling that this was the right site."

The Denver temple was originally proposed to be patterned after the six-spired Boise Idaho Temple.

40

During the first two site acquisition attempts, the proposed "Boise plan" had proved to be a major deterrent in gaining approval. Local architects and city planners noted that the A-frame design featured similarities to a mountain lodge or relatively inexpensive construction. Additionally, the proposed six spires were of major concern for a residential environment.

In March 1983, President Gordon B. Hinckley and President Ezra Taft Benson arrived to the Four Lakes site to make a final site inspection. Accompanying President Hinckley and President Benson was local temple architect Bobby Thomas. Brother Thomas recorded the following: "I stood off the side while the Presidents conferred among themselves . . . then President Hinckley came over and said, 'Well, Mr. Architect, what do you think?' We discussed the pros and cons and then we got in our cars and headed to the airport. As we dropped Presidents Hinckley and Benson at the airport, President Benson took hold of my arm and told me that they would pray and confer, but that the Four Lakes site was definitely the best and that he preferred the design of the Atlanta over the standard plan for the Four Lakes site. He would see to it that we would have the larger plan to fit this larger site. At that moment I knew that we finally had a site and a building scope and program."

"The First Presidency feels temples should reflect the highest expression of man's talents. . . . What is used in the temple must be of the highest quality and appropriate to the building and its purposes," explained Lawrence Wyss, the temple's interior designer. Attention to detail is a hallmark of this beautiful building. Hundreds of feet of hand-carved woodwork adorn the interior, along with hand-painted designs on the walls and ceilings. The temple also features more than 600 square feet of specially designed stained-glass windows. The fountain near the entrance has moldings patterned after designs on the temple. The seven-foot angel Moroni statue required about 1,750 three-inch squares of gold leafing—each so thin it could float on water.

Several times during the construction of the temple, three white doves were noticed circling it. They appeared again when the statue of the angel Moroni was set in place. Temple architect Bobby Thomas wrote in his journal, "The ceremony was complete and most of the spectators had dispersed. Then, just above Moroni, President Joseph Barton saw three white birds

SITE
7.5 acres

GROUNDBREAKING
May 19, 1984, by Gordon B. Hinckley

DEDICATION
October 24–28, 1986, by
Ezra Taft Benson

EXTERIOR
Precast stone walls and a built-up roof

TOTAL FLOOR AREA
29,117 square feet

DIMENSIONS
184 feet by 192 feet; single
90-foot spire capped with
statue of angel Moroni

HIDDEN IMAGE
Among the trees and landscaping is an
image of the Savior leading a couple
to the temple with His left hand and
gently offering support with His right.

circling above the angel and pointed them out to me. I then related the seeming approval or blessing that was in process and the three previous [dove sightings] which I had witnessed."

A year later, when the temple open house began, dozens of seagulls circled the angel Moroni statue. Media representatives caught the birds on video, and one of the seagulls was featured in a photo that appeared in the *Denver Post*. A woman who was investigating the Church called the stake missionaries to say, "Every seagull in Colorado must have been there. Surely there must be some spiritual significance. I want to know more." Approximately 140,000 visitors toured the newly completed temple during its three-week open house. More than half of all visitors viewed the missionary exhibits that were housed in a separate building, and over 17,000 copies of the Book of Mormon were distributed.

Thousands of members in the Denver Colorado Temple district contributed to building and beautifying the Lord's house. Nineteen sisters spent hours tatting altar cloths. Primary children earned and donated nearly ten thousand dollars for three stone "bride's benches" at the rear of the building. Young men and women spent a thousand hours building an ornate dollhouse for the temple's youth center. More than 600 members volunteered to clean the temple before the open house. During the open house, missionaries received 14,000 referrals, resulting in at least fifty baptisms within a few months.

In 1997, eleven years after the dedication of the temple, 22,000 people gathered to celebrate the one-hundredth anniversary of the first permanent branch of the Church in Denver. President Gordon B. Hinckley was the featured speaker, and during the celebration he and Sister Hinckley were presented with two Colorado blue spruce trees. Commenting that he loved Colorado blue spruce but didn't have a way to get the trees home, President Hinckley gave them to temple president Russell C. Taylor and said, "If you want to call them the Hinckley trees, it's all right with me." The trees now stand on the grounds of the Denver Colorado Temple.

Described by President Ezra Taft Benson as "a refuge from the evil and turmoil of the world," the Denver Colorado Temple stands as a haven to the Saints of the Rocky Mountains.

Frankfurt Germany Temple

In the center of the old Huguenot city of Friedrichsdorf, Germany, nine miles north of Frankfurt, stands the Frankfurt Germany Temple. The town lies in a mountainous region removed from cities and major industry. The temple site was originally occupied by two five-story noodle factories, which hid the area's natural beauty. Nevertheless, Church leaders chose the site because of its accessible location.

The proposal to build a temple in Friedrichsdorf brought intense opposition from local religious leaders, who fought the idea in town meetings and newspapers and characterized the battle as a "religious war." A letter in one paper claimed that the Church would "turn [the] town into a Mormon city." A minister warned the city council, "They will attempt to win the citizenry over to their sect." Latter-day Saint leaders tried to overcome misconceptions and stereotypes by providing correct information about the Church. They also offered to provide beautifully landscaped temple grounds that the public could enjoy. City leaders imposed expensive conditions on the construction of the temple, hoping to make costs so high that the Church would withdraw its request. The list of conditions was long and intended to provoke and, to some extent, humiliate Church leaders.

After the temple was approved, Friedrichsdorf officials placed restrictions on the temple's appearance, insisting that their skyline not be "stamped with a Mormon symbol." They ruled that the temple's spire could not be higher than the tower on

41

the nearby Protestant church. Brother Peter Mourik, who played a key role in securing approval for the temple, wrote about the process: "Looking back over the last two years, it is a miracle that the project finalized against so much opposition of the prince of darkness. But the Prince of Peace won the victory—a major one. Many people said that a temple never would be built in Friedrichsdorf."

The temple's first president, F. Enzio Busche, arrived at the temple grounds as it was nearing completion and reflected on the miracle of how the temple was built amid such hostile opposition. "As I stood and looked at the almost-finished temple, I was overcome with emotion. It was like the Lord's birth all over again. The Lord wanted to come to His world and the world did not want Him. There was no place in the inn. As I saw the dimension of that rejection, it hurt me. Church leaders in Germany had the grace to endure all of the needles thrust into their flesh. I was awed by the graciousness of the leaders of the church in accepting all of the demands and insults in order to establish the Lord's house."

In addition to building the temple, the Church also purchased and restored a historic villa located on the property. Once restored to its original 1890 beauty, the villa was utilized as living quarters for the temple president and several missionary couples. At the building's entry is an original cast-iron ornament on which are the initials of the first owner and his wife: *HLT.* Those initials are the German equivalent of "LDS." *Latter-day Saints* in German is *Heilige der Letzten Tage.* Regarding the initials, President Busche commented, "Could there be any doubt that the Lord had known it all along?"

During the construction of the temple, Friedrichsdorf celebrated the anniversary of its founding three hundred years before when settlers had come from France seeking refuge from religious persecution. Known as Huguenots by their persecutors, they were threatened, "Change your beliefs or you will be driven out." Living true to their ideal "to obey God more than man," thousands of these people were granted sanctuary in Germany on March 13, 1687, by Count Friedrich II. The town was named for him as an expression of gratitude. The people built a chapel, which they called a temple, hoping for greater fulfillment in their quest for truth. The old white church neighboring the temple site features inscriptions on

SITE
5.2 acres

GROUNDBREAKING
July 1, 1985, by Gordon B. Hinckley

DEDICATION
August 28–30, 1987, by
Ezra Taft Benson

EXTERIOR
Bethel white granite from
northern Vermont; copper roof

TOTAL FLOOR AREA
24,170 square feet

DIMENSIONS
93 feet by 232 feet; statue of angel
Moroni on top spire, 82 feet

HIDDEN IMAGE
An image of the Savior is
included in the motion of
welcoming all to His temple.

its walls, in German and in French, written in the spirit of Moroni's Title of Liberty: "For our liberty, our wives, our children" (see Alma 46:11–13). During the temple's open house, Friedrichsdorf Mayor Gerd Schmidt characterized the temple as "a modern version of religious tolerance that should prevail among mankind."

In 1987, Rudi W. B. Mueller was set apart as a counselor in the temple presidency, and his wife, Erika F. Mueller, was set apart as assistant matron. Researching the town's history, Sister Mueller pondered the similarities between the Huguenots and the Mormon pioneers. She developed a love for the Huguenots and began searching for their records. Eventually she met a man who gave her a book about Friedrichsdorf's founders. The book was organized by families and contained names, dates, and locations for all of the town's births, marriages, and deaths from 1687 to 1900! She said that as she held the book, "the Spirit bore witness . . . that many of these men and women, now on the other side of the veil, had prayed that their names would be found and that their temple work would be performed." Three hundred years after they had established their city of refuge, the Huguenots' prayers were answered. In all, 1,666 family group sheets were completed, 5,002 endowments performed, and 1,651 marriages sealed.

Visitors to the Frankfurt Germany Temple come from many lands. During French Week, patrons and workers come from the stakes in France. Many other visitors come during German Week and Dutch Week. Church members mark their calendars months and even years in advance, arranging for vacation time to serve for a week in the temple. E. Lionel Brady, who served in the Frankfurt Germany Temple presidency, described a typical prayer meeting on the last day of one of these temple weeks: "Tears come to the eyes of temple workers and patrons as we sing 'God Be with You Till We Meet Again.' Each one sings in his own language, but the same message comes to all through the Spirit. As we say auf wiedersehen, or au revoir, or tot ziens, or good-bye, we know that we really will see one another again, if not in the Frankfurt temple, then in another place where friends who are united in the gospel will meet and continue to work together as participants in the great plan of eternal salvation and exaltation."

Portland Oregon Temple

In the 1960s, the Church purchased land in Oregon for a junior college, but two decades later the property became the site for the Portland Oregon Temple. Elder James H. Bean, vice chairman of the temple committee, said, "I've watched the things that have happened on this property for 20 years. I have felt the whisperings of the Spirit, that it was intended to be preserved for special purposes, and I've seen the Lord soften the hearts of people . . . to the point that the work is going forward uninhibited."

This does not mean, however, that the process of building the temple began without opposition. "Whenever temples are built," commented Elder Bean, "there are challenges that come. The Saints are tested; it is almost as though the Lord wants the members to know how much they want a temple. It really isn't easy." The process of getting the property approved for the temple included at least twenty-seven public hearings, eight lawsuits, and four petition drives intended to stop development. Local feelings seemed to change, however, when the initial opposition subsided and plans for a temple became a reality.

When the temple was completed, one of the architects observed, "There's been a change of attitude in the community. People appreciate the quality of the building. They pull over on the highway to look at it." Elder W. Craig Zwick of the Seventy, who worked twenty years in the construction industry, served as general contractor on the Portland Oregon Temple.

42

Elder Zwick said, "We were delighted that every man working on this project understood the sacred nature of this building and of the sacred site upon which it was built." For three years after ground was broken on September 20, 1986, there was rain, rain, and more rain, causing the soil to be supersaturated. Working through each challenge was worth it because nothing is too good for the Lord, said Elder Zwick: "Anything of value requires overcoming adversity and prevailing over any hardships."

Once completed, the temple was a stunning sight, with six white spires contrasted against a backdrop of deep green in the daylight and interior lights glowing through walls of translucent marble at night. The white marble exterior is accented with green marble trim and topped with a green slate roof. The temple is equally stunning on the inside, where trees and flowers fill a skylit atrium in the foyer and Honduras mahogany woodwork runs through all the rooms. The mahogany was purchased in advance and stored due to limited availability. No windows are visible on the outside, but sunlight enters many parts of the building through white marble. The beauty of the Portland Oregon Temple impressed President Thomas S. Monson, who said, "You won't find a better example of beautiful craftsmanship combined with the beautiful craftsmanship of the Lord—the lovely trees and vegetation—than here at the Portland temple. . . . I've seen none more beautiful."

The appearance of the Portland Oregon Temple has more to offer than visual appeal, however. As with all temples, certain features both inside and out are symbolic of the higher meaning the temple holds. The spires are symbolic of priesthood authority on earth; the east spires represent the Melchizedek Priesthood and the west spires represent the Aaronic Priesthood. The celestial bodies depicted on the temple—sun, moon, and earth—represent the varying kingdoms of glory. The celestial room features different levels, with the highest tier opening to a hallway where the sealing rooms are located. This arrangement shows that celestial marriage is essential to exaltation in the highest heaven. Symbols such as these add deeper meaning to the solemn beauty of the building.

In preparation for the temple's open house, the temple committee was determined to do everything possible to prevent disruptive protests similar to what occurred at the Seattle

SITE
7.3 acres

GROUNDBREAKING
September 20, 1986, by
Gordon B. Hinckley

DEDICATION
August 19–21, 1989, by
Gordon B. Hinckley

EXTERIOR
White Vermont marble walls
with green Vermont slate roof

TOTAL FLOOR AREA
80,500 square feet

DIMENSIONS
267 feet by 180 feet, four towers
124 feet tall; statue of angel Moroni
on east spire reaches 181 feet tall

HIDDEN IMAGE
A full-length image of the Savior
is included among the trees
to the left of the temple.

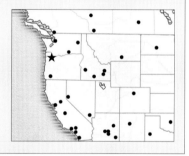

Temple. The committee felt this type of hostile behavior could be prevented by proactively providing information about the Church to the public and by extending an invitation to attend the open house. In April 1987, with the temple still under construction, 174,000 homes received a full-color, eight-page newspaper insert that discussed Christ's life. Seven months later, 700,000 inserts of "Another Witness of Jesus Christ" were distributed in all major newspapers in the state of Oregon and southwest Washington.

When the temple was opened to the public during its twenty-three-day open house, more than 300,000 people walked through its halls and entered its rooms. 2,500 visitors walked through an hour, with many waiting up to forty-five minutes in lines that stretched a quarter of a mile. More than 240 pictures of the Savior displayed in the temple emphasized that Christ is the center of Latter-day Saint worship. Those in charge of the open house estimated that more than half of the visitors were not Latter-day Saints, and many of the Church members who attended were less active. Hearts were softened as visitors felt the influence of the temple. One member commented, "I've been away from the Church for several years now. I haven't felt the Spirit in all that time. This experience today has convinced me that I must come back—I'll see you in church tomorrow." A man who was handing out anti-Mormon literature decided to tour the temple before continuing his task. When he came out of the temple, he chose to stop distributing the materials and destroy them.

Following the successful open house was the dedication of the Portland Oregon Temple. It was pronounced "a place of peace and holiness, a refuge from storms of life." President Ezra Taft Benson, who had recently celebrated his ninetieth birthday, presided over three of the eleven dedicatory sessions.

In 2012, a visitors' center was completed on the temple site. "This beautiful facility will be a great blessing to the surrounding community," said Mark Lusvardi, director of public programs for the Church's Missionary Department. "It creates an opportunity for visitors to learn more about the temple and the basic beliefs of members of the Church." A commissioned painting depicting a sunrise over a local area provides an indigenous background for Bertel Thorvaldsen's statue of the *Christus*.

Las Vegas Nevada Temple

Although Las Vegas has a reputation as a tourist mecca dedicated solely to entertainment and escape, there is another side to this world-renowned metropolis. It is a community of committed citizens, including numerous devoted Latter-day Saints striving to live in the service of the Lord. In fact, before the neon signs and busy streets, before the casinos and high-rise hotels, and before the sprawling suburbs, Las Vegas was a little fort founded by Mormon pioneers in 1855. A few years later a small branch of the Church was formed. As the city of Las Vegas grew into a booming tourist attraction, local membership of the Church also grew.

In 1987, two years before the Las Vegas Nevada Temple was completed, 15,000 Latter-day Saints gathered for the first multiregional conference ever held in Nevada. President Gordon B. Hinckley spoke of the temple and made a challenge and a promise to the Saints: "As the years pass, you will never miss a dollar you have contributed to the construction of the temple. And, as the years pass, there will grow in your heart a sense of gratitude you were able to do so." The members in the area accepted his challenge and contributed $11 million, and the Las Vegas Nevada Temple now stands as a beacon on a hill overlooking the lights of Babylon below.

Located near the mountains on the east side of the city, the temple overlooks downtown and can be seen at night from almost every part of the Las Vegas Valley. The statue of the angel Moroni stands on the central eastern spire, facing away from the city and

43

toward the eastern mountains. The copper roof and white, cast-stone towers have made the temple a recognizable landmark in the city's scenery.

Peace is almost tangible in the interior of the temple, which is decorated in soft colors such as rust and dusty rose to reflect the Southwest's desert landscape. The open courtyard, with trees and a fountain, lets natural light into the entranceway. One interior designer who worked on the temple explained that the design helps temple patrons enter the proper frame of mind for worship. "We have tried to use not only the depth of colors but the light and dark values and the intensity of light and its warmth," he said. "We have used a little brass, silver, polished marble, and soft fabric. All of this creates a wonderfully human interior that becomes restful, serene, and peaceful."

The highlight of the temple is the celestial room, with prism-cut glass in the windows casting small rainbows on the soft curve of the walls. This kaleidoscope of colors rotates slowly, following the rotation of the earth. Two large, elegant chandeliers with thousands of pieces of cut crystal hang from the ceiling. The narrow windows at the sides of the celestial room each contain a transparent cut star. All of these elements combine to create an interior unique to this temple and a peaceful atmosphere that harmonizes perfectly with the spirit felt in every temple.

Architects and workers paid great attention to every detail of the temple during construction. Before the windows were installed, one section of glass was sent back to California to be reworked. While the glass was in the shop, a large earthquake shook the San Francisco area, destroying much of the delicate glasswork in the building. The glass for the temple window was spared, however, as it swayed in the sling where it had been suspended. The glass was finished and returned safely to the temple, where it now takes its place in the flawless design.

As the temple's architect and later a stake president, stake patriarch, and temple sealer in Las Vegas, President George Tate developed a unique appreciation for the Las Vegas Nevada Temple. He said, "As I am within the temple and my eyes look around and I notice certain details, I remember the picture of some craftsman working on that specific area. Those pictures keep coming back to me because those scenes are lost now, and the members who use the temple today maybe do not have

SITE
10.3 acres

GROUNDBREAKING
November 30, 1985, by
Gordon B. Hinckley

DEDICATION
December 16–18, 1989, by
Gordon B. Hinckley

EXTERIOR
White precast stone walls and
copper roof and detailing

TOTAL FLOOR AREA
80,350 square feet

DIMENSIONS
195 feet by 260 feet; statue
of angel Moroni on top spire
reaches 137 feet high

HIDDEN IMAGE
Referencing temple marriage, among
the clouds is a man's hand sliding a
ring on the finger of his bride. The
statue of angel Moroni is the ring.

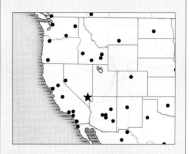

that appreciation of the skill, precision, time, and effort that went into every detail on the temple. I notice the small details that are overlooked by many. Eleven years after its completion, I am still amazed at the quality that went into the temple."

That quality is seen in every detail of the structure, including a symbol unique to the Las Vegas Nevada Temple—a stylized desert lily. It is found on the edges of all six spires and in various locations within the temple. President Tate explained why he found that flower a particularly appropriate symbol of what the temple represents: "When our children were small, we used to explore the desert. One thing that I remember noticing is that in the valleys along the sides of the roads there were dark green leafy plants with a beautiful large white lily flower. I was impressed that even in such an arid climate, the plant was able to produce a beautiful blossom. We used the desert lily on the temple because just as the beautiful lily stood out amidst the barren desert, the temple stands out with great contrast from the world."

Las Vegas is a mecca for tourists, industry conventions, and sporting events. These events provide opportunities for members visiting the city to also serve in the temple. The temple's first president, Boyad M. Tanner, noted that he could often tell what was happening in the city by those visiting the temple. For example, temple workers always knew when the annual National Finals Rodeo was in town due to the increased number of cowboy boots entering the doors. President Tanner observed, "You would not believe the number of cowboys from that rodeo who had temple recommends and came to the temple."

The love and commitment local members have for their temple was clearly demonstrated on September 12, 1998. The day before, a series of severe thunderstorms swept through southern Nevada, causing widespread flooding and damage. The storm produced high winds, hail, a tornado, and rain. Waves of flooding deposited tons of debris throughout the temple parking lot and temple grounds. During the night, the temple presidency made an emergency petition to five local stakes for helping hands. Before daybreak the next day, over 200 Church members had gathered on the grounds armed with shovels, wheelbarrows, and even a backhoe. Without interrupting the sacred work inside the temple, another kind of faithful temple work proceeded on the outside.

Toronto Ontario Temple

At the time of the dedication of the Toronto Ontario Temple, which is located in a suburb twenty miles west of downtown Toronto and just north of Lake Ontario, the temple district included Latter-day Saints living in an enormous geographic area that has been called "the cradle of Mormonism." Covering six Canadian provinces and parts of five American states, this district included such Church history sites as Sharon, Vermont, where the Prophet Joseph Smith was born; the Sacred Grove and the Hill Cumorah near Palmyra, New York; and Kirtland, Ohio, where the Church was headquartered in the early and mid-1830s. The district also covered an area in Canada where the Church sent the first missionaries outside the United States. Early converts baptized in Toronto included John Taylor, the third President of the Church. Everett S. Pallin, who collected histories and artifacts for the cornerstone box of the temple, described the significance of the site with these words: "From the location of the statue of Moroni on the temple, I assume we could see Cumorah—the birthplace of the Restoration. . . . And Moroni looks east toward home, Cumorah."

President Thomas S. Monson and Elder M. Russell Ballard, each of whom had served as mission president in Toronto, officiated at the groundbreaking for the Toronto Ontario Temple in 1987. During the ceremony, President Monson told the congregation of the question President Gordon B. Hinckley had asked during a discussion about building a temple

44

in Toronto. Turning to President Monson and Elder Ballard, President Hinckley had asked, "Can you guarantee we'll have enough members in Ontario to keep a temple busy?"

President Monson replied, "Brother Hinckley, we'll have more than enough members in the city of Toronto, without considering Ontario. I'll guarantee it, and Brother Ballard will second the matter."

Members in the area followed through on President Monson's guarantee from the very beginning. As the final touches were being put on the temple construction, a labor strike was called that involved workers at the temple site. Church leaders were concerned that the work would not be completed in time for the scheduled open house, but union leaders allowed a few union members to do finishing work inside the temple on a voluntary basis. The project manager, Jerry D. Sears, was "working night and day" to finish the work.

During the thirteen-day open house, more than 2,600 members from across the temple district volunteered to help in such activities as hosting and cleaning, donating more than 64,000 hours of service. Members also volunteered to clean the temple between dedicatory sessions. After the last session, they completed in just two-and-a-half hours the cleaning and furniture moving that had been scheduled to last through the night.

The interior reflects the great care that goes into designing, building, and generally maintaining a temple. The walls are decorated with off-white and pastel colors and accented with fine woodwork and wall coverings. Beautiful stained glass windows and paintings of the Savior are found throughout. The celestial room features white tones with crystal candelabra and gold accents adorning the walls. An elegant chandelier hangs from the center of the vaulted ceiling. These details all contribute to the tranquil feeling inside the temple.

As visitors walked through the building during the open house, they were awed by what they saw and felt. More than 61,000 people came to the open house, and the response was overwhelmingly positive. As evidence of the community's admiration of the temple, the city of Brampton gave the temple an award of excellence. The award is given every two years to honor a quality development that enhances the city. Of thirty-six submissions, the temple won one of only two awards given.

More than 17,000 members of the temple district—from

SITE
14 acres

GROUNDBREAKING
October 10, 1987, by
Thomas S. Monson

DEDICATION
August 25–27, 1990, by
Gordon B. Hinckley

EXTERIOR
White cast stone

TOTAL FLOOR AREA
57,982 square feet

DIMENSIONS
154 feet by 208 feet; spire,
171 feet high with 11-foot
statue of angel Moroni

HIDDEN IMAGE
An image of the Savior is
included among the trees to
the right of the temple.

two countries and a number of different cultures—attended the dedicatory sessions of the Toronto Ontario Temple. The dedicatory prayer, which was read in each session, mentioned the cultural diversity of the temple district: "This nation has become a gathering place for people from scores of other lands. In their veins flows the blood of Israel." The dedication was translated into French, one of the official languages of Canada, as well as Spanish, Portuguese, Mandarin, Cantonese, and Korean. The inscription on the outside of the temple—Holiness to the Lord, The House of the Lord—is etched in both English and French, hinting at the diversity of the members served by this particular temple.

The members of the Toronto Ontario Temple district do more than just attend often. They have continued to show their appreciation by sacrificing time and means to keep the temple clean and beautiful. Ten years after the dedication, a group of nearly 200 young single adults gathered to paint the fence surrounding the temple grounds. They purchased paint and brushes, coveralls and paint trays, and went to work, demonstrating their love for the temple and their understanding of the importance of the work that takes place inside.

At the dedication of the Toronto Ontario Temple, Elder Marvin J. Ashton reflected: "The temple is not a destination. I prefer to refer to the temple as a starting point where we not only prepare ourselves but we help prepare others, even those who have gone ahead, for the important events and occasions that are available and so necessary for all of us." The temple in Toronto has made it possible for local members to take this teaching to heart and return many times, bringing blessings upon themselves and countless others.

The splendid beauty of the temple grounds has become a photo shoot destination even for brides who were not married inside. Saturday afternoons often feature long lines of bridal parties who wait their turn to capture their memories amid the spectacular display of flowers, shrubs, trees, and other natural backdrops. The renowned Toronto Temple gardens have helped their community win multiple "Communities in Bloom" awards. Opening the grounds to the public and participating in the community's beautification efforts are making a splendid impact for the Church in the community and region.

San Diego California Temple

With twin spires rising majestically into the warm blue air of Southern California, the breathtaking San Diego California Temple shines in white splendor. Ground was broken for the temple in February 1988, and construction took nearly five years to complete.

The visual marvel of the San Diego California Temple was achieved by design architect William S. Lewis Jr. The exterior is matched by a stunning interior design. Dennis and Shelly Hyndman, members of the design team, said they "wanted to create a vertical scheme to symbolize an ascension toward heaven." They accomplished this in part by using "darker colors on the lower levels and lighten[ing] the wall and carpet colors on the higher levels." Dennis added that the design for the temple was inspired by the Salt Lake and Washington D.C. Temples. Although the Hyndmans, who are Roman Catholics, were unable to visit the interior of those temples, they toured the Las Vegas Nevada Temple before its dedication. Even during the first year of temple construction, the unique structure was already generating heightened curiosity. With four years of construction remaining, Clyde Romney, who served as chairman of the open house committee, said, "We talked about it becoming a San Diego landmark eventually, but in reality it's already become a landmark. In San Diego, when you consider distinctive structures, there's the Hotel del Coronado, the Coronado-Bay Bridge, (and) the Mission de Alcala—it's a small list. Now we're on the list." Former San Diego city architect Mike

45

Stepner said, "The temple has given image-conscious San Diego what it has long wanted and needed: A signature building on its northern border along the much-traveled corridor from Orange County and Los Angeles."

As are other temples, the San Diego California Temple is surrounded by beautiful landscaping and gardens that help to create a reverent setting for the house of the Lord. As plans were made for the temple's construction and surrounding grounds, many members sought ways to give of their time and talent to its completion. Primary children were even able to contribute, as youngsters from 180 different wards and branches in the temple district were given charge to water and care for some of the flowers that would be used to decorate for the dedication. After the dedication, the potted flowers were planted in the beds around the flagpole.

Children in northern Mexico also wanted to participate but had to come up with a different idea because border restrictions would not allow them to bring plants across. They designed and made a handcrafted rug for the First Presidency to stand on as they laid the cornerstone for the temple. A microfiche with the names of the Primary children in the temple district was later placed in the cornerstone.

Before the dedication, a six-week open house was held to allow the public to walk through and tour the temple. Church officials anticipated half a million guests would tour the temple. Temple open house records were broken, with the number of visitors exceeding 720,000. The success of the open house was noticed nationwide. The Public Relations Society of America presented the Church's Public Affairs Department with the prestigious *Silver Anvil Award.* According to the PRSA website, the award acknowledges the "highest levels of exemplary professional skill, creativity and resourcefulness" in the field of public relations.

Thousands of volunteers helped beautify and prepare the grounds for the open house. Ron Andersen was hoisted above the temple to work on the angel Moroni perched atop the two-hundred-foot spire. On January 18, 1993, the spire had been struck by lightning, and some of the gold leaf on the statue had been damaged. So Andersen, who did the original gold leafing on the statue, was lifted by crane to clean and repair the statue in time for the open house.

SITE
7.2 acres

GROUNDBREAKING
February 27, 1988, by
Ezra Taft Benson

DEDICATION
April 25–30, 1993, by
Gordon B. Hinckley

EXTERIOR
Marble chips in plaster

TOTAL FLOOR AREA
72,000 square feet

DIMENSIONS
165 feet by 194 feet; roof 62 feet
high; statue of angel Moroni on
top spire reaches 200 feet high

HIDDEN IMAGE
Among the foreground shadows
is an image of the Savior kneeling
and looking up at the temple.

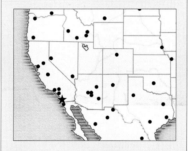

Almost two thousand volunteers pitched in to help clean the temple for the open house and dedication in March and April 1993. Sister Jo Ann Autenrieb, who coordinated the cleaning efforts, noted that while the work was hard, "the volunteers worked with a sweet spirit and harmony, with patience and consideration. Sometimes the work was especially dusty and dirty, and sometimes the workers had to wait for equipment or there was a shortage of supplies, yet I have received many letters from volunteers saying that this was one of the best experiences of their lives."

Even the Saints who lived in Mexico were able to be involved, many of them traveling great distances to participate. Sister Autenrieb was touched at their sacrifice and dedication: "Some came through the floods to clean the temple. . . . About 20 members came from Colorado del Rios, driving 4 hours in the night to arrive in time to clean one morning."

Sister Autenrieb also shared a story about a group of sisters who traveled from Ensenada. They wore white clothes and carried with them white cloths they had bought especially to clean with. When told there were rags already available for cleaning, the sisters answered that they would like to use the ones they had brought, because they were planning to take them home and wash them and then embroider and frame them as decorations in their homes.

The overwhelmingly positive impact the temple had on the community was noticed by the San Diego Press Club. The temple was selected as Headliner of the Year for 1993 in the landmark category. The award was accepted "on behalf of the thousands of members of the Mormon Church in this area who worked so hard to share [the temple] with the community during the public tours last year."

In one of the temple's dedicatory sessions, President Hinckley addressed the issue of craftsmanship in the building of temples. "We have been criticized," he said, "for spending so much on the building of temples and asked why not spend the money taking care of the poor. Nothing is too good for the Lord. Temples don't have to be ostentatious, but they do have to be of high quality. We wouldn't want to give a shabby kind of building to the Lord, whom we love."

Orlando Florida Temple

Before the dedication of the Orlando Florida Temple in 1994, Saints in Florida had to travel as far as Salt Lake City and Mesa Arizona to attend the temple. These distances shortened with the building of the Washington D.C. and Atlanta Georgia Temples, but Floridian Saints had long looked forward to having a temple in their own area.

The search for a temple site began in 1982, and the city of Orlando was selected because of its central location in Florida and its popularity as a tourist destination. Several potential locations had been identified by the time the temple was announced in 1990. The selected location is described as one of Florida's most beautiful areas and was chosen by President Gordon B. Hinckley. When he first saw it, he exclaimed, "That's it!"

The temple site, just south of Orlando, is located on a knoll a few miles north of Universal Studios. Of the site, which sits on the highest elevation in Orange County, President Ezra Taft Benson said, "A more beautiful site could not have been chosen."

Because the site is in an environmentally sensitive area, many neighboring citizens opposed the building. In response to these community voices, local Church members organized a petition drive, going door to door to collect signatures in support of having the temple built. After two weeks, the members delivered to the county commission nearly 11,000 signatures in favor of the temple; more than two-thirds of them were from nonmembers. All local TV and radio stations covered the decisive county hearing. Nearly two-thirds

46

of the 300 in attendance were members of the Church wearing a blue-and-white button displaying a silhouette of the angel Moroni and emblazoned with the words, "For the temple." Many of the members attended the meeting fasting and praying for divine assistance. Considering the provided signatures and clear evidence of community support, the tide eventually turned in favor of the Church. The commissioners voted six to one to allow the temple to be built. The Saints felt that the Lord had intervened to make their dream become a reality.

On June 20, 1992, President James E. Faust broke ground for the Orlando Florida Temple. In his remarks he recalled the many temples that had been built in ancient times. He noted that the temple of Herod in Jerusalem had been built so meticulously that each stone was marked with a signature. Of this grand temple in the meridian of time, he said, "This is the temple to which the Savior went. Now, when the Savior comes to Florida, surely He will come to this house that will be at this spot."

Evan D. Porter Jr., former president of the Orlando Florida Stake, handled most of the negotiations and legal procedures for the temple. Many of those who strongly opposed the temple did so based upon the assumption that the temple would become a tourist attraction and dramatically increase traffic flow. False information, rumors, and unsubstantiated fears fueled the opposition and resulted in several zoning setbacks and time delays. The opposition gained momentum, and at times the hope to get the project approved seemed bleak. During the groundbreaking ceremony, President Porter told of the many struggles he had faced over ten years as he had tried to locate and purchase land and receive permission to build the temple. "On several occasions I found it was impossible to move forward without the Lord's intervention," he said. "I came to realize that He does not want this to move forward without His intervention. This is His will." The temple reached a milestone on May 1, 1993 when the angel Moroni statue was hoisted on top of the 167-foot spire. About a year later during a severe thunderstorm, the statue was blackened by multiple lightning strikes. Three days were required to clean the statue and apply new gold leafing and a larger lightning rod.

Surrounding the temple, a tropical ambiance is created through many tropical flowers, plants, and palm trees. Further

SITE
13 acres

GROUNDBREAKING
June 20, 1992, by James E. Faust

DEDICATION
October 9–11, 1994, by
Howard W. Hunter

EXTERIOR
White precast concrete
with marble chips

TOTAL FLOOR AREA
70,000 square feet

DIMENSIONS
216 feet by 252 feet; tower with statue
of angel Moroni is 165 feet high

HIDDEN IMAGE
In the clouds is an image
of the Savior inviting all to
partake of temple blessings.

enhancing the grounds are twenty-four massive Canary Island date palms. These palms were purchased from private residences throughout the state of Florida. The temple's brilliant white exterior, beautiful stained-glass windows, and carefully tended grounds make the building at once imposing and beautiful to observers. The structure, with walls twelve inches thick, is capable of withstanding a major hurricane or earthquake. Inside, the temple's most impressive room is the celestial room, with its contemporary furniture and a stained-glass dome in the ceiling. Interior walls, ceilings, and design features were further enhanced by utilizing 16,500 feet of 23-karat gold leaf.

During the temple's three-week open house, 90,000 people witnessed the beauty of the structure's interior. Local news media reporting on the open house soon began calling the site "Temple Hill." Many of those who had toured the structure were impressed by its simple beauty and significance. One member led his blind father-in-law through the temple. Feeling the delicate molding and woodwork throughout the temple, the father-in-law, who had been a carpenter by trade, was deeply impressed by the quality of the workmanship. A Catholic clergyman who toured the temple later said publicly, "It is very impressive. The structure is magnificent, and the people were very hospitable and welcoming. It is obvious the temple was built for the Lord."

When the sun rose Sunday, October 9, 1994, more than a thousand people had already lined up to take part in the cornerstone and dedication ceremony. The occasion was made particularly memorable by the presence of all three members of the First Presidency. It had been six years since the entire First Presidency had officiated together at a temple dedication.

Local Saints placed various objects and statements of their faith and commitment to the temple inside the cornerstone. Among the items were pledges signed by the young men, young women, and single adults from the temple district, all of whom planned to be married in the temple someday. A letter stated: "We feel that this pledge will encourage our young people to be more involved in the temple and look forward to the day when they will be married for time and all eternity. It will increase their faith. Each time they come to the temple to perform baptisms or simply to visit, they will know that their names and promises are inside their temple."

Bountiful Utah Temple

Plans to build the Bountiful Utah Temple, the eighth temple constructed in Utah, were first announced in May 1988. Earlier that month, the Church purchased a nine-acre site on Bountiful's east bench. The site, high above Davis County, offers a stunning view of the Great Salt Lake and the bustling communities that lie along the Wasatch Front.

The known history of the temple site began in 1897, when John Haven Barlow Sr. purchased a forty-acre plot from the United States government that included the future temple site. Because of a lack of water and the steep terrain, little could be done with the land. In 1947, portions of the north acreage were cleared, and an orchard of four hundred apricot trees was planted. In the spring of 1983, flash flooding from Holbrook

Canyon caused a great deal of damage in Bountiful, resulting in the decision to build an earthen dam across the canyon to limit the flow of water during heavy rainstorms. The city requested use of the soil from the future temple site. Construction crews removed some 200,000 cubic yards of soil from the site, leaving an ideal plateau on which the temple would later be built.

The Church had considered several sites before making a final decision about the temple's location. On April 3, 1988, the entire First Presidency traveled to the site, and President Ezra Taft Benson said, "This will be a beautiful site for the House of the Lord." President Thomas S. Monson later recalled the spiritual affirmation he felt as President Benson spoke these words. Upon their decision, the site earned the

47

distinction of being the only temple site chosen with the entire First Presidency present. It is also the only temple site personally chosen by President Ezra Taft Benson.

Approximately four years later, President Benson, at age ninety-two, turned the first shovelful of soil at the groundbreaking ceremony on May 2, 1992. More than 8,000 people attended the ceremony.

The Bountiful Utah Temple was intended to be both figuratively and literally a light on a hill. Architectural plans called for the structure to stand prominently on the hill, where it could be seen from many miles away. At night, under bright floodlights, the temple is the most visible landmark in the valley.

Symbols traditional to temple architecture are featured in the design of the Bountiful Utah Temple. The most prominent symbol is the angel Moroni statue. Other notable symbols include the keystone (representing Christ), earth stones, and design elements representing the sun, moon, and stars. The temple also features twelve round windows, six in the celestial room and six in the chapel, which represent the Quorum of the Twelve Apostles. The Bethel white exterior granite used on the temple was quarried near Sharon, Vermont, about fifteen minutes away from Joseph Smith's birthplace.

Equally important is the symbolism in the temple's interior. As patrons progress through the ordinances of the temple, they ascend toward the sealing rooms, which represent the highest degree of the celestial kingdom and are one step higher than the celestial room. Light also plays an important role in the interior design of the temple, with the light increasing as one progresses upward. The brightest rooms in the temple are the eight sealing rooms.

Another feature of the building that adds both beauty and symbolic significance is the art glass. The temple has forty windows totaling approximately 4,000 square feet of art glass. "There is an ascending feel to the glass," said Allen B. Erekson, projects administrator for the Church's temples and special projects. Brother Erekson explained: "It is more open as you go up . . . , with more clear glass higher that allows more light to come in and still gives privacy to the building." The windows follow a motif of Jacob's ladder, as recorded in the book Genesis, and increase in detail as they rise, representing man's progression toward heaven.

SITE
9 acres

GROUNDBREAKING
May 2, 1992

DEDICATION
January 8–14, 1995, by
Howard W. Hunter

EXTERIOR
Bethel white granite

TOTAL FLOOR AREA
104,000 square feet

DIMENSIONS
145 feet by 98 feet; statue of angel
Moroni on top spire, 176 feet high

HIDDEN IMAGE
Christ is placed standing on the
rock in the midst of a multitude
of Nephites near the temple
located in the land of Bountiful.

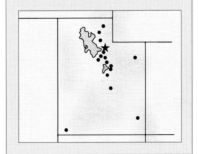

Of the design, Brother Erekson said, "What we are trying to accomplish in the Bountiful Utah Temple is to have a level of elegance that doesn't distract from the Spirit." Perhaps this is best achieved in the celestial room, which, with its thirty-four-foot ceiling and its spectacular chandelier, represents the glory and sublimity of heaven. The fifteen-foot-tall chandelier, created in the Czech Republic, is one of the artistic highlights of the entire building.

Even before the temple was dedicated, its beauty and place in the community was honored. The Bountiful City Council formally recognized the temple as the city's most beautiful building and landmark. An award was presented to the temple's first president, Harold C. Yancey.

When the temple was opened for public tours from November 5 through December 17, 1994, 870,000 people toured the edifice. One day during the event, a violent snowstorm blanketed the Bountiful area. The temple's mountainside location received so much snow that roads to and from the temple became impassable. Several thousand visitors were stranded inside the building. Using specially equipped vehicles, visitors were shuttled down the mountain in limited numbers. Those waiting in the temple were made comfortable in the chapel or cafeteria.

The Bountiful Utah Temple was the first of two temples to be dedicated by President Howard W. Hunter. On January 8, 1995, before the dedicatory service, a brief cornerstone-laying ceremony was held outside the temple in the bitter cold of the predawn hour. Members were grateful for the new temple and quickly began using it. Twelve weddings were held the day after the dedication. Some 900 temple workers were called to fill the great demand, and the temple became the first to operate for a full day on Saturdays.

Since the temple's dedication, grounds supervisor Bruce Bennett has lovingly created spectacular gardens that enhance and compliment the building. Considering the temple's high elevation of 5,000 feet, special attention is given to only select specimens that will survive and flourish. Each year, 17,000 bulbs and 10,000 pansies are planted. Brother Bennett works a year in advance to design, budget, and purchase planting stock. The Bountiful Temple gardens, along with the ground's breathtaking views, provide a wonderful atmosphere to all who visit the temple.

Hong Kong China Temple

In 1992, President Gordon B. Hinckley announced plans to build the Hong Kong China Temple. President Hinckley, who had visited Asia in 1960 to oversee the Church's activities there, said to a group of missionaries the day before the temple dedication in Hong Kong, "This temple represents one of the great dreams of my life."

Beginning in the 1840s, Hong Kong was ruled by the British. In 1898, England signed a ninety-nine-year lease of Hong Kong that was to expire on July 1, 1997. At that time, Hong Kong would revert to the control of the government of mainland China. President Hinckley commented in a 1996 interview: "This is a time of uncertainty in this land, but it is going to come, everyone faces it, and we face it with faith. We

do not know what will happen. No one knows, but we have faith that everything will work out and go forward."

Church leaders showed faith that the government of communist China would allow the Church to function after the government of Hong Kong was reunited with that of the mainland. Therefore, all involved moved forward with a sense of urgency and were determined to find a location where the temple could be built and dedicated before July 1.

In the spring of 1991, the First Presidency asked the Asia Area Presidency to discreetly begin searching for a site for a temple in Hong Kong. Throughout 1991, possible sites were identified, considered, and eventually found inadequate. When President Hinckley traveled to Hong Kong on July 25, 1992

48

to consider additional temple locations, he felt unsatisfied with all of them. "We looked at one after another after another. I became very discouraged," he later said. "The sites were so tiny in some respects and the cost of real estate is so high, many millions of dollars for a little piece of ground."

One night, he retired with no clear understanding of how he should proceed on his assignment to find a location for the temple, but in the middle of the night, he awoke with an impression to have the temple built on the site of the mission home and chapel. "To me it was inspiration," he said. "I drew [the temple] out, and I still have the little drawing that I made . . . in my journal. [This drawing] is essentially the plan which we had for this temple."

Early the next morning at 6:45 a.m., President Hinckley called Asia Area Presidency members Elder Monte J. Brough and John K. Carmack. He asked them to come to his hotel room at 8:00 a.m. Once gathered President Hinckley shared his little drawing of the new temple. Of the event, Elder Brough wrote, "After briefly reviewing the plan, President Hinckley asked us to join in prayer. He asked if it would be all right if he offered the prayer. He then discussed the whole matter with the Lord. He talked of the need for a temple in China to bless the people in that area of the world. The prayer was powerful and compelling, evidencing his love for all the people of Asia." At the conclusion of the early morning meeting, all present visited the proposed temple location to walk through the area, check the neighborhood, and view the site from all aspects.

President Hinckley's drawing called for a temple plan unlike any other. Of the temple, Elder Rulon G. Craven of the Seventy said, "The cost of land in Hong Kong is very expensive, and therefore, instead of spreading out to build, we had to build up." The six-story building was designed to not only house a temple but also a chapel, mission offices, and living quarters for the temple president, mission president, and several missionaries. The ordinance rooms, celestial room, and sealing rooms are in the top three floors of the building, and the baptistry is in the basement. The other purposes of the building are carried out on the three floors in between. The

SITE
0.3 acres

GROUNDBREAKING
January 22, 1994, by
John K. Carmack

DEDICATION
May 26–27, 1996, by
Gordon B. Hinckley

EXTERIOR
Polished granite

TOTAL FLOOR AREA
21,744 square feet

DIMENSIONS
70 feet by 92 feet; angel Moroni
statue is 135 feet above main floor

HIDDEN IMAGE
To the left of temple is the
phrase "Families are together
forever" in Chinese.

building has two separate main entrances, one for the temple and the other for the mission offices and chapel.

After returning to Salt Lake City, President Hinckley presented his sketch to the Temple Department, asking that the architects turn the concept into building plans as soon as possible. Department architects created a plan for a larger building—nearly twice the size of President Hinckley's initial concept. This larger plan resulted in the denial of required building permits and subsequently the plans were redone to reflect the concept of President Hinckley's original sketch.

When construction of the building was finished in May 1996, the temple was opened for public tours, which were attended by more than 13,000 people. Guests were impressed that amid the traffic and confusion of Hong Kong, quiet, peace, and tranquility were so easily felt inside the temple. A minister from another religion wrote a letter to Elder Jerry D. Wheat, who was a public affairs missionary heavily involved in the open house, saying, "There is something different about your temple. Hong Kong lacks what you have in your temple—it is reverence." Visitors also expressed feeling something special while touring the building.

At the time of the temple's dedication, President Hinckley described the events that had led to a temple being built in Hong Kong as a miracle: "It is a miracle that we have reached this point of maturity here in Hong Kong. . . . I look upon it as a miracle because of what I have known in the past, the growth I have seen, the stabilization of the work, and the strength of it today, it is a miracle."

President Thomas S. Monson expressed his zeal both for the outcome and the prospect of temple work in Hong Kong's future: "The spirit of the Saints there in the temple was a marvel to behold. They love the temple, and have waited a long time for it. They are very anxious for it to open. With all the great numbers of Chinese people who have gone on in the years past—this being one of the ancient civilizations—surely there is no dearth of names for whom the current Chinese members can officiate."

Mount Timpanogos Utah Temple

In an address at general conference on April 4, 1993, President Gordon B. Hinckley announced that the ninth temple in Utah would be built in American Fork. This temple is one of the few temples not named after a city location. The site chosen was already owned by the Church and had once been part of a Church welfare farm. It sits on top of a rise overlooking the city of American Fork as well as Utah Lake; the majesty of Mount Timpanogos and the Wasatch Mountains rise behind it. At night the brilliant glow of the temple can be seen from Orem to Lehi.

At the groundbreaking ceremony on October 9, 1993, President Hinckley answered questions about the decision to build the temple in American Fork. "People across the Church are asking why build another temple in Utah, when there are so many people without temples. . . . The answer lies in the pressure on the Provo Temple and the Jordan River Temple. The Provo Temple is the busiest temple in the Church." President Hinckley then commended the members of the Church in Utah County for their faithful temple attendance, which essentially created the need for another holy edifice.

Counsel by President Monson for the Saints to sacrifice to build the temple brought many touching experiences and created enduring memories for those who gave of their time and substance to complete the Mount Timpanogos Utah Temple. Howard Ault decided that he and his family could contribute to the temple by donating the sod for the temple grounds

49

from his family's sod farm. In addition to giving the care and time required to grow the sod, the Ault family, including five children, twenty-eight grandchildren, and one great-grandchild, all volunteered to help lay the sod as well. Brother Ault observed that "most of the family have been here every night helping, along with many other volunteers. I think it's a great tie for the children with the temple. This temple will always have a special place in their hearts, since they helped work on it."

Students of the American Fork High School seminary decided that they could use the construction of the temple as motivation to help them improve spiritually. They built a ten-foot model of the temple out of popsicle sticks; students who memorized ten scriptures could put their name on a stick and add it to the model.

The temple's exterior is covered in a beautiful granite facing that represents the strength of the mountains behind it. Numerous stained-glass windows fill the interior of the temple with a radiant display of light and color. The art glass for the windows was created using a patented technique that seals together several matched layers of glass. Not only does this new technique allow for larger windows with better insulation but it also creates windows that maintain their beauty and integrity when viewed under reflected light. This means that the full color and splendor of the windows are visible from the exterior during the day and from the inside at night—an effect not wholly possible with traditional leaded glass.

An interesting event occurred during the construction of the temple on a particularly sunny summer day. In the middle of a committee meeting that was being held in the chapel, a sister sitting on a bench suddenly exclaimed, "My purse is smoking!"

About the same time, the man sitting in front of her felt his hair and added, "My hair is singed!" The large, round window that is a prominent feature of the chapel was focusing sunlight into the room like a giant magnifying glass. Special thermometers were used to measure the temperature of the beam of light,

SITE
16.7 acres; part of a larger parcel of land that was once a welfare farm

GROUNDBREAKING
October 9, 1993, by
Gordon B. Hinckley

DEDICATION
October 13–19, 1996, by
Gordon B. Hinckley

EXTERIOR
Sierra white granite clad temple with art glass windows and bronze doors

TOTAL FLOOR AREA
107,240 square feet

DIMENSIONS
145 feet by 198 feet; 190-foot spire, including statue of angel Moroni

HIDDEN IMAGE
Among the distant mountains, the Good Shepherd is cradling one of His sheep. Dispersed in the clouds and snowcapped mountains is His flock of sheep.

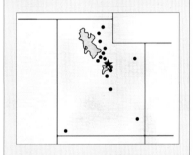

which registered at 165 degrees Fahrenheit. Where the light hit an object, the temperature was as high as 500 degrees Fahrenheit! The glass in the window was immediately sandblasted to help diffuse the light, and all present were grateful that the problem had been discovered before the temple was opened.

Nearly 20,000 people crowded the streets around the temple on July 17, 1995, to watch a crane lift the statue of angel Moroni atop its resting place on the 177-foot spire of the temple. The statue, made of fiberglass and covered in gold leaf, weighed about two hundred pounds and measured thirteen feet, three inches tall. As the statue was fitted into its place, the crowd spontaneously began singing "The Spirit of God." The number in attendance at this event was almost equal to the number of people who had attended the groundbreaking ceremony.

The Mount Timpanogos Utah Temple was dedicated on October 13, 1996, after an open house of several weeks, which permitted nearly 700,000 people to tour the temple. When completed, it was the forty-ninth operating temple of The Church of Jesus Christ of Latter-day Saints. The twenty-seven dedicatory sessions included Church members in the temple and at local stake centers via satellite broadcast, permitting almost 160,000 worthy Church members to attend.

Stephen M. Studdert, who served as vice chairman of the temple committee, commented on the spiritual outpouring during the dedication ceremonies: "It has been a spiritual feast for all who have prepared themselves and come in the spirit of worship and reverence. Each day has been a day of joyous grandeur." Then, adding a personal note, he remarked, "My heart is full of very tender feelings. I think they can be mostly described as feelings of profound gratitude, coupled with feelings of a witness of the divinity of the work of the Master. I have been deeply moved by the outpouring of the Spirit and by the faith and faithfulness of the thousands of Saints who helped prepare this temple. It is clear that the Spirit of the Lord surrounds all that goes on with temples. From the preparation of a temple to the work for kindred dead, the Lord directs it all."

St. Louis Missouri Temple

Partly because of the Church's strong history in the region and partly due to the long distances that had been required for members in the area to attend the temple, Missouri Saints were overjoyed in 1990 at the announcement of the St. Louis Missouri Temple, which would be the fiftieth operating temple in the Church. When members of the First Presidency separately considered the handful of potential sites for the temple, all agreed that the temple should be located on a beautiful site in Town and Country, a community approximately twenty miles west of St. Louis. The site is located atop a prominent hill that overlooks the surrounding region. A wooded area provides a

barrier between the temple and one of the area's busiest highways, with nearly 200,000 cars passing by every day.

Those involved in the nineteen-acre temple property's acquisition recognize how divine intervention played a role in the project from the beginning. The previous owners of the property were enduring financial difficulties, which prompted an immediate need to sell the parcel. It was placed on the market shortly before the decision was made to acquire a site for a temple in St. Louis. This beneficial timing allowed the Church to acquire this highly sought-after property before competing offers could be made. One of the conditions of the sale of the property was that the neighboring Missouri Baptist College had to agree with the transaction—which they did. A few

50

weeks after the transaction was completed, the college hired new administration. The position of the new college president was that he would not have permitted the sale of the property.

A welcoming spirit of friendship was clearly seen when the temple committee sought city approval for the building. One example came at an aldermen's meeting on March 15, 1993. At the meeting, approval for the temple would either be granted or denied. During the course of events an alderman commented, "This seems to be fine but you have not yet shown us what the building is going to look like architecturally." Until then, the temple's architectural rendering had been covered and mounted on a tripod. When the covering was removed, there was an audible sigh of amazement followed by several moments of silence as all in the crowded hall gazed at the beautiful rendering. One leader rose and said, "I am not going to move approval of this project!" After a long pause, he continued, "I move unanimous and enthusiastic approval of this project." The aldermen then cast a unanimous vote in favor of approving the temple, causing the audience to erupt in applause. Additional approval was given for a variance that allowed for additional height to the temple's steeple and exterior fencing. These actions and others required to build the temple all happened without any opposition.

On an unseasonably cold day, October 30, 1993, Church leaders and some five thousand members from the area gathered for the St. Louis Missouri Temple groundbreaking ceremony. Despite the freezing temperatures and snow flurries, members began flocking to the site two hours before the ceremonies began.

In his remarks, President Gordon B. Hinckley reminisced about the Saints' past in the area. "This may sound strange, but I am rather glad it is cold," he said. "I think it brings us to a greater appreciation for the Saints who left the state of Missouri in 1838 under the orders of the then governor; a tragic episode

SITE
19 acres

GROUNDBREAKING
October 30, 1993, by
Gordon B. Hinckley

DEDICATION
June 1–5, 1997, by
Gordon B. Hinckley

EXTERIOR
Cast stone and Bethal white
granite with thermal finish

TOTAL FLOOR AREA
58,749 square feet

DIMENSIONS
88 feet by 190 feet; 150 feet high
including angel Moroni statue

HIDDEN IMAGE
A pioneer man in the distant trees
is mounted on a horse and leading
a covered wagon pulled by a team
of oxen. Above this pioneer is
world-famous Gateway Arch.

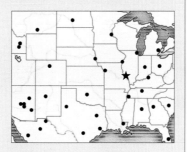

in the history of our people, and I think that it must be so for Missouri."

President Thomas S. Monson, in his address, noted that Charles A. Lindbergh made his famous flight in *The Spirit of St. Louis* in 1927, the year President Monson was born. He said, "I love the name—'The Spirit of St. Louis.' It reflects a pioneer spirit. Those who helped establish the Church in this area and continue to help it grow are real pioneers. I simply say, 'Thanks be to God for a temple, a temple of the Lord, to be erected here.' That will be the true spirit of St. Louis."

Work began immediately on the temple, which was to be completed in three and a half years. The temple, based on the general design of the Nauvoo Temple, included white granite facing and a single, one-hundred-fifty-foot spire with a gold-leafed statue of the angel Moroni. The temple's architects based a few elements on the Salt Lake Temple. These features include tall and narrow arched windows topped with round windows, vertical pilasters, and a cornice along the top of the temple. In designing the structure, the architects had set out to create a structure that would communicate the wholeness and solidarity of the Church and be both recognizable and dignified. Great care was taken with design and materials to ensure the temple would last at least 300 years.

On June 1, 1997, President Gordon B. Hinckley dedicated the St. Louis Missouri Temple. Twenty-three thousand members from throughout the temple district participated in the dedication services despite rain during some of the nineteen sessions. Members of the First Presidency participated in all nineteen sessions.

In a city that once provided early Latter-day Saints with a haven from raging persecution, it is fitting to have a temple dedicated to the Lord. The St. Louis Missouri Temple is a tribute to those who endured the hardships of the past and to the community that gave them refuge. And it is a promise of life everlasting to those who enter its doors in the years to come.

1907 1997

Vernal Utah Temple

In August 1907, President Joseph F. Smith dedicated the recently completed Uintah Stake Tabernacle, one of Ashley Valley's most outstanding landmarks, which was used through the years for such gatherings as quarterly conferences, concerts, baptisms, weddings, and funerals. At the dedication, President Smith said he "would not be surprised if a temple were built here some day." His prophecy was fulfilled ninety years later when the beloved old tabernacle was converted into the beautiful new Vernal Utah Temple.

Although for decades the Uintah Stake Tabernacle had served and unified the Vernal community, by the 1970s the building could no longer be used for Church gatherings. Many in the community feared that it would be condemned and torn down. One group of citizens formed a "Save the Tabernacle Committee" to raise money, write petitions, and do whatever they could to save the tabernacle that their ancestors had labored on and sacrificed to build.

The First Presidency knew of the concerns and the deteriorating state of the tabernacle. President Gordon B. Hinckley and President Thomas S. Monson traveled to Vernal to tour the building. Laird M. Hartman, the stake president who accompanied them on their tour, recorded: "They arrived at ten in the morning. We spent approximately two hours touring the tabernacle. Their purpose was to look at its condition and see if they could feel what the Lord wanted them to do with that beautiful old building. . . . As they left, President Hinckley said, 'I

51

don't know what the Lord wants us to do with the building. We will find out.'" Not long after this visit, the First Presidency invited all the stake presidents from the Vernal area to meet with them in Salt Lake City. There the stake presidents received news that the Brethren felt impressed to convert the tabernacle into a temple. Later an official letter was read to the members, who rejoiced at the news that not only would their tabernacle be saved, but they would have the blessing of a temple close by.

With the beginning of construction in the summer of 1995 came a search throughout the area for high-quality period brick that matched the brick on the tabernacle walls. This brick would be used to replace damaged bricks and to construct a gateway. Satisfactory brick was found on only one house, owned by Nick J. Meagher. He had planned to raze the home but instead agreed to donate it to the Church. The bricks on the old home had the same markings as those used for the tabernacle, suggesting that they came from the same clay pit and kiln as the tabernacle bricks.

More than a thousand volunteers helped dismantle the home, brick by brick. The job took nearly two months of evenings and Saturdays to be completed. Members of all ages throughout the temple district donated their time and service. Small children stacked bricks while adults removed and cleaned them. Even a ninety-year-old man in a wheelchair helped clean bricks. When the project was over, about sixteen thousand bricks had been salvaged and prepared to become a part of the temple.

Making a temple out of the existing tabernacle was no easy feat for the architects and builders. Roger Jackson, the project's chief architect, explained the process: "The walls are four bricks thick. We actually took off the inside layer of brick and did some reinforcing to the entire building and left just the four walls and part of the roof. The original roof was made of hand-sawn, thick, huge, timber trusses. We thought we could save them, so the roof trusses stayed, but the rest of the roof came down, and then we built on to the roof trusses. So basically, we kept the outside and built a new building inside."

To create a lower level and baptistry, ground underneath the tabernacle had to be excavated. To the surprise of

SITE
1.6 acres

GROUNDBREAKING
May 13, 1995, by Gordon B. Hinckley

DEDICATION
November 2–4, 1997, by
Gordon B. Hinckley

EXTERIOR
Face brick

TOTAL FLOOR AREA
33,400 square feet

DIMENSIONS
175 feet by 210 feet

HIDDEN IMAGE
In the clouds is an image
of the Savior inviting all to
partake of temple blessings.

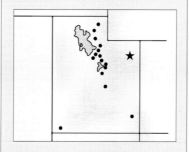

construction workers, an open arch was discovered under the north tabernacle doors. This large gap in the foundation conveniently allowed for heavy equipment and workers to enter. At nine feet wide, the archway was the exact width—to the inch—needed to allow the entrance of a backhoe tractor. Those constructing the temple were grateful that the tabernacle builders allowed for this open space that would, many decades later, greatly assist in the building of the temple.

In addition to the original walls and roof trusses, the temple features many historically significant items. The stained-glass window displayed on the temple's east side was originally made for the Mt. Olivet Methodist Episcopal Church of Hollywood. The oxen under the baptismal font also have a unique history—they were on public display for more than twenty years in the South Visitors' Center on Temple Square in Salt Lake City. Eighteen original pews from the tabernacle were refinished for use in the temple. From the woodwork to the furniture, the interior of the temple was designed to be reminiscent of the early twentieth-century style found inside the original tabernacle.

When construction was completed, the building was again opened to the public for tours, but this time as a temple of the Lord. One young woman at the temple's open house commented that her great-grandfather had been told in a blessing that he would help construct a temple for the Lord. Motivated by that blessing, he traveled to Salt Lake City to receive instruction. He was told to go and use his talents on the Ashley Uintah Stake tabernacle, where he stayed and worked until its completion. Not having built any other building for the Church, he died believing his blessing had been unfulfilled. The dedication of the Vernal Utah Temple on November 2, 1997, marked the fulfillment of the man's blessing.

The dedication of the temple was a spiritual feast for the thousands who attended and participated in the Hosanna Shout. Talks were given, prayers were offered, and hearts were filled with rejoicing as members celebrated the conversion of their beloved tabernacle into a temple of the Lord.

Preston England Temple

In July 1837, Heber C. Kimball, Orson Hyde, and five other elders arrived in Liverpool as the first missionaries of the restored gospel to serve in England. They began their work in Preston, where the first English converts were baptized in the River Ribble. Fifty people were baptized within the week, and despite opposition from local preachers and the press, nearly two thousand people were baptized in the next nine months. The work continued to progress, and thousands of converts gathered to America to join the Saints, but many other faithful members stayed in the British Isles, where there are now seventh-generation Latter-day Saints. The Preston Ward is the world's longest-functioning unit of the Church.

This area rich in Church history became the site for England's second temple. President Gordon B. Hinckley announced the Preston, Lancashire, vicinity as the chosen site on October 19, 1992, during the second day of the rededication of the London England Temple. The First Presidency considered a number of sites for the temple, including Manchester, Liverpool, and Chorley. Both President Monson and President Hinckley visited the Chorley site and confirmed that it was the correct location.

The First Presidency instructed local Church leadership to purchase the property. With the property purchased, Church leaders approached the local council about building a temple and were told that the city wanted to create jobs and new businesses, not a temple! The council was then shown pictures

52

of temples and how the temple would be of the highest quality and become a local landmark. However, they were clearly not impressed, and they said they would reject any application for a temple.

A local task force was organized to rally support from city council members and local residents. A stake fast was organized in which members "called upon the powers of heaven." These efforts were successful, and many sincere prayers were answered. Local temple architect Peter J. Trebilcock represented the Church and made a presentation for the temple at a decisive meeting with city leaders. As he addressed the entirely non-member audience, he asked, "Has anybody here visited one of our temples?" Brother Trebilcock then described what happened next: "One hand went up in the back. I then asked, 'Would you please tell these people what you saw?' He said, 'I have visited a Mormon Temple. It was beautiful, the landscaping superb, and the quality first class.' He continued in a loud, firm voice, 'I firmly support this proposal and hope each of you would too!'—pointing to his neighbors. I then witnessed a miracle. It was as if someone had raised a baton and signaled to every person attending. One by one we heard 'Yes. . . . We will support you, we will not object.' The chairman of the group, who had so energetically led the opposition, was the last person to speak. He looked at me and said 'I'd like to ask you another question, not only will we support you, but what more can we do to help you?'" In the end, the council offered their unanimous support. Brother Trebilcock summarized the historic proceedings by saying, "We were amazed. I was thrilled! My professional colleagues were dumbfounded."

The temple is located at the junction of the M61 motorway, making it highly visible to all who pass by. Ian D. Swanney, former president of the temple, said of its location, "I love the vision that all motorways seem to lead to the temple." This beautiful building is the perfect addition to the surrounding countryside as well as to the lives of Church members in

SITE
15 acres

GROUNDBREAKING
June 12, 1994, by Gordon B. Hinckley

DEDICATION
June 7–10, 1998, by
Gordon B. Hinckley

EXTERIOR
Olympia white granite from Sardinia

TOTAL FLOOR AREA
69,630 square feet

DIMENSIONS
102 feet by 174 feet; 159 feet to
top of angel Moroni statue

HIDDEN IMAGE
Within this drawing is the
Good Shepherd accompanied
by His flock of sheep.

Scotland, Ireland, and the northern part of England.

More than seventy thousand people learned about the beliefs of the Latter-day Saints during the temple's two-week open house. Tour guides led group after group through the rooms and hallways, and missionaries received referrals from many people interested in learning more about the Church. Local members seized the opportunity to share the gospel with their neighbors by talking with them about the temple.

The beautiful grounds, with seven hundred trees and more than one hundred thousand other plants, earned the landscapers a prestigious industry award three years in a row. The temple itself, with its exterior of white granite and zinc roof, has been described as "reminiscent to the old churches built in this land many years ago."

When the Preston England Temple was dedicated, President Hinckley returned to his former mission area to preside over thirteen of the fifteen dedication ceremonies. He addressed the members in attendance, speaking of his memories and his love for England. "I feel as if I've come home," he said. "This is an emotional day. . . . It has been a treasured experience for me to come back to this area of Lancashire where I served as a missionary 65 years ago." After four days of dedicatory sessions, the Saints gratefully began serving in their temple.

The members of the Preston England Temple district take advantage of the proximity of the temple, returning again and again. "When people leave," explained President Swanney, "they express reluctance of having to go back into the world after having been in the temple."

The England Missionary Training Center opened in 1985 and was originally located adjacent to the London England Temple. In 1998, the MTC was relocated to the Preston England Temple complex. This MTC primarily serves the British Isles missions of London, London South, Birmingham, Manchester, Leeds, and Scotland/Ireland.

Monticello Utah Temple

The beautiful Monticello Utah Temple, nestled at the foot of the Abajo Mountains, was the first of a new series of smaller temples announced by President Gordon B. Hinckley in general conference in October 1997. Although smaller than other temples, it is in every way as beautiful, with elegant chandeliers, high-quality marble from Turkey, and stained glass from Germany.

As one of the first three "smaller" temples announced, the Monticello Utah Temple is referred to as a "test" temple. In speaking of Monticello as the site of the first smaller temple, President Hinckley said, "We wanted to build one that we could get to, that we could observe. This is somewhat new ground we were treading, and we wanted to be able to examine it and see how things fit together. We knew of this part of the state, which is isolated and a long ways from a temple. These people had to travel all the way to Manti in the past, more than a four-hour drive each way, so we concluded to put one here in San Juan County. And the determination was made to put it in Monticello."

The land for the temple is in the northwest part of town, next to a chapel, and was donated to the Church by a father and his son. The groundbreaking ceremony took place just six weeks after President Hinckley introduced the idea of small temples. About twenty-six hundred people attended the event, and some had to stand on construction equipment and truck beds to see the proceedings.

53

Elder Neil L. Andersen of the Seventy spoke to the congregation. "Isn't it wonderful," he asked, "to know that the Lord knows and loves you, the people of Monticello? . . . He knows you, He knows your heart, He knows of your testimonies and your goodness. And He has directed His prophet to build for you and for your children a house unto Him, here on this spot."

Construction began quickly following the groundbreaking ceremony. Much care was taken to ensure that the Monticello Utah Temple was as well built and as beautiful as any other temple. The exterior is finished in a marble called Noah's Creme, which was chosen for its color and range of shades. The hue of the temple seems to change with the weather conditions and time of day. Members in the area agree that the color of the marble perfectly complements the color of the local landscape. Some thirteen thousand tiles used on the temple were evaluated carefully to make sure they blended with each other for a uniform effect. The marble on the exterior of the temple is the ideal material for weathering severe sandstorms, which are common in the Four Corners area.

The statue of the angel Moroni originally placed on the spire of the Monticello Utah Temple was six feet tall and made of white fiberglass. It was a new model created especially for use on smaller temples. The statue served its purpose well until the first overcast day, when it seemed to disappear against the cloudy sky. It was also difficult to light properly at night because it was not as bright as the gold-leafed statues. The Brethren considered these observations and decided to use a different style of statue—one covered with 23-karat gold—on the small temples. When the new statue arrived from Salt Lake City, workers discovered that it was two feet taller than the fiberglass statue, which was transported to the Salt Lake City area and stored for future use.

The temple was soon finished and opened for public viewing before the dedication. One morning, a member of the temple committee arrived just before the open house to find thousands of moths covering the grounds and walls of the

SITE
1.33 acres

GROUNDBREAKING
November 17, 1997, by Ben B. Banks

DEDICATION
July 26–27, 1998, by
Gordon B. Hinckley

EXTERIOR
Turkish off-white marble

TOTAL FLOOR AREA
11,225 square feet

DIMENSIONS
79 feet by 108 feet, 66 feet
high to angel Moroni statue

HIDDEN IMAGE
In memory of the faithful pioneers, hidden in the distant Blue Mountains are images of a driver, a team of horses, and two men holding back a wagon.

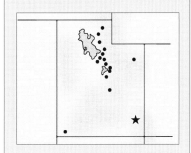

temple. After some unsuccessful attempts to remove the moths, maintenance workers began to scatter them with air blowers. As they did so, starlings that had been building nests nearby swooped down and caught the moths in midair, ridding the temple of most of the insects in about twenty minutes.

"It was just like the crickets and the seagulls in Salt Lake," mused Brother Cooper Jones, referring to the 1848 incident in which seagulls devoured the crickets that threatened to destroy the pioneers' crops.

More than eight thousand members attended the eight dedicatory sessions of the Monticello Utah Temple. President Hinckley told the story of a San Juan Stake conference in 1894, during which Brigham Young Jr., a member of the Quorum of the Twelve Apostles, spoke on vicarious work for the dead and declared, "In the near future a temple will be built in this country."

President Hinckley said, "It's taken a long time to fulfill Brigham Young Jr.'s prophetic statement. I'm glad to be in harmony with Brigham Young Jr. The inspiration of the Spirit is strong, clear and certain that this is where the House of the Lord should be built. . . . No one could be happier than I am."

In the first three months following the temple's dedication, faithful members showed their gratitude by performing nearly fifty-seven thousand ordinances—no small work for a "smaller" temple. Many of the sessions serve those who speak the Navajo language. After four years of consistently high temple attendance, it was determined that the temple needed to be expanded. The temple's first president, Lisle G. Adams, said, "The facilities we had were just not adequate to take care of the work that was being done." After eight months of renovations, the temple was enlarged from 7,000 to 11,225 square feet. A second ordinance room and second sealing room were added. Other areas have been enlarged to accommodate a waiting room, offices for temple workers, and a laundry facility.

President Gordon B. Hinckley rededicated the expanded temple in one session on November 17, 2002. The event took place five years to the day from the date of its groundbreaking.

Anchorage Alaska Temple

The Anchorage Alaska Temple is the northernmost temple in the world and was the second of the Church's smaller temples to be completed. Before the announcement that a temple would be built in Anchorage, the eighteen thousand Saints in Alaska had watched and prayed for the day they would have a temple nearby; they had previously needed to travel well over a thousand miles to attend the Seattle Washington or Cardston Alberta Temple.

The Church had already purchased five acres of land on which to build a stake center to accommodate the growth of Church membership in Anchorage. The land, however, was triangular in shape and was not large enough for a stake center. Though at first the Saints thought a new site would

have to be found, the Church was able to buy some of the adjoining land, making the entire tract rectangular. Today, the chapel and the temple fit perfectly on the property, leaving adequate space for landscaping and parking.

Although Church leaders originally intended the Anchorage Alaska Temple to be the first of the smaller temples, architect Doug Green suggested that the first small temple be built somewhere closer to Salt Lake City, where Church officials could monitor construction more closely and discover any potential problems that might arise in the building of other small temples. President Gordon B. Hinckley agreed and decided to have the prototype for small temples built in Monticello, Utah.

54

During the process of building that first small temple, architects and designers learned many valuable things. Accordingly, Brother Green made nearly three hundred changes to improve plans for the Anchorage Alaska Temple. Design elements that he added to the Anchorage Alaska Temple include a canopy over the entrance and heated stairs to help keep walkways clear of snow and ice.

Speaking of his job as a temple architect, Brother Green said, "You hit your knees and pray. You do have to pray. To me, if you're going to build something for the Lord, you have to ask for his help and inspiration." One challenge Brother Green faced was finding ways to make the temple uniquely Alaskan. He prayed for inspiration, and on a trip to Salt Lake City he noticed something on the Salt Lake Temple that he hadn't seen before: the seven stars of the Big Dipper pointing to the North Star. That symbol is found on the Alaskan flag, and it is now depicted on the west side of the Anchorage Alaska Temple. The Big Dipper and the North Star, which have been used for thousands of years as navigation aids, are appropriate symbols for a temple, which, as Hugh Nibley said, is where we take our "bearings on the universe and in the eternities, both in time and space."

Brother Green also found other ways to make the temple look and feel like it belongs in Alaska. The stained glass is reminiscent of water, and stylized evergreens with patterns resembling native designs are used to adorn interior furnishings. Forget-me-nots, the official flower of Alaska, adorn the walls and carpeting in the sealing room. These elements combine with other features—such as the celestial room chandelier, which is made of exquisite Hungarian crystal and weighs seven hundred pounds—to create the peaceful, elegant atmosphere that prevails in the temple.

The Anchorage Alaska Temple is covered with Sierra white granite that was quarried near Fresno, California. This same granite was also used on the exteriors of the temples in Oakland and Fresno, California. Surrounded by tall trees, the temple is located just off a main freeway. The statue of the angel Moroni faces the Chugach mountain range to the east. During the dark hours of the day the steeple is lit, but in consideration of nearby neighbors, the lights are turned off before midnight.

SITE
5.4 acres (including adjoining meetinghouse)

GROUNDBREAKING
April 17, 1998

DEDICATION
January 9–10, 1999, by
Gordon B. Hinckley

REDEDICATION
February 8, 2004, by
Gordon B. Hinckley

EXTERIOR
Stone-clad Sierra white granite quarried from near Fresno, California

TOTAL FLOOR AREA
11,937 square feet

DIMENSIONS
79 feet by 108 feet

HIDDEN IMAGE
Ursa Major (The Big Dipper) and the North Star are seen among the distant trees and mountain. Also included is the Savior kneeling and looking up at the temple.

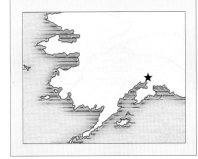

In winter months, the steeple is lit most of the day.

The Church made every effort to be considerate of local residents during all phases of construction. Builders went to great expense to save as much forest as possible during landscaping so neighbors could continue to use the surrounding land for recreation. After requests from people living nearby, designers changed the roof and spire so they wouldn't cast an overwhelming shadow. "We lowered the [profile] as much as we could so it wouldn't loom," Brother Green said.

The dedication of the Anchorage Alaska Temple began early on a freezing January morning. More than six thousand members braved the weather and traveled to the temple to hear the prophet speak. Some came from as far away as the Yukon, a journey of fourteen hours by bus. Outside, the temperature was eighteen degrees with a freezing wind. Snowdrifts were three feet high, and eight-foot icicles hung from the nearby chapel roof. An enclosed, heated walkway sheltered members as they walked from the chapel to the temple.

Members continue to attend and serve in the Anchorage Alaska Temple, seeking and finding the same spiritual warmth they felt there on that cold day of the dedication. Supervisors in the temple's baptistry say that every session is a "journal experience" for them. One day two young men brought eighty-five names to the temple. They were all names of Inupiat Eskimos from St. Lawrence and King Island. The supervisor commented, "It was an incredible experience to watch the baptisms and confirmations performed for these true Alaskans in the first Alaska temple."

To accommodate high use, the temple was enlarged just four years after the dedication from 6,800 to 11,937 square feet to add a second ordinance room. Other enlarged areas of the temple included the men's and women's dressing rooms, a waiting room, offices for temple workers, and a laundry facility. After nearly a year of renovation, the temple was rededicated on February 8, 2004, by President Gordon B. Hinckley. Under a beautiful, full moon, members began to line up hours before the ceremonies, in spite of cold weather. Anxious to again attend the temple, members came from all over the state—from North Pole to Juneau—to take part in the temple's rededication.

Colonia Juárez Temple

The tiny community of Colonia Juárez, Chihuahua, Mexico, is about two hundred miles southwest of El Paso, Texas. On a hill west of town, at the very end of the paved road and overlooking a little valley, sits the first of the smaller temples to be completed outside of the United States.

The Mormon colonies of northern Mexico are an important part of the Church's history. Pioneers arrived there in the mid-1880s and settled the region. They suffered many hardships during the Mexican revolutions of 1912 and 1914, but they built an enduring legacy of faithfulness and Church service that has been passed down to their children and grandchildren. Today those descendants are found in many Spanish-speaking areas throughout the world, passing on the

values of endurance and faith that they learned growing up in a close-knit Mormon colony.

President Gordon B. Hinckley visited the Saints in Colonia Juárez in June 1997 as the guest of honor at the graduation ceremony of Juárez Academy, a Latter-day Saint preparatory school. During the three-and-a-half-hour drive back to the airport in El Paso, Texas, President Hinckley thought about the situation of the members he had just met. He later explained, "As we were riding to El Paso, I reflected on what we could do to help these people in the Church colonies in Mexico." He continued, "I thought of these things and what could be done. The concept of these smaller temples came into my mind. I concluded we didn't need the laundry. We didn't need

55

to rent temple clothing. We didn't need eating facilities. These have been added for the convenience of the people, but are not necessary [for the temple ordinances]." When he was on the airplane, he continued to refine the idea. "I took a piece of paper," he said, "and sketched out the [floor] plan, and turned it over to the architects to refine it." This inspiration was the beginning of the small temples that have come to bless the lives of so many Saints in remote areas of the world.

The groundbreaking ceremony for the temple in Colonia Juárez took place in March 1998. A congregation of about eight hundred people endured the sleet, wind, rain, and snow to participate in the ceremony. President Meredith I. Romney of the Colonia Juárez Stake remembered: "It was cold and snowy all during the prayers and during the singing of the choir. As soon as Elder [Eran A.] Call got up to speak and give the dedicatory prayer, the sun came out and all the time he was speaking it was just like another day. As soon as he sat down, it clouded up and started snowing."

Just as their ancestors had worked together and sacrificed to establish the colonies, members in Colonia Juárez collectively donated their time, goods, and services to make the temple a reality. Sister Nellie Romney and her children donated the land, giving up part of their apple orchard to make room for the temple. As soon as the temple was announced, one member designated a plot on his farm, planted grass, and watered and fertilized it for almost a year. Then he rigged up a sod cutter and took all the sod from his farm and laid it on the temple grounds. The Church members in the area helped with the landscaping. At times nearly four hundred people with their equipment were working on the grounds.

In this small town of only one store, one hamburger restaurant, one school, and many farms, the building of a temple was the center of activity. Often the Church-owned academy let students out early so they could help work on the temple. Local Saints even helped to position the spire and statue of the angel Moroni. It was done without a crane—just lots of rope and people working together. When the temple was completed,

SITE
2.56 acres

GROUNDBREAKING
March 7, 1998, by Eran A. Call

DEDICATION
March 6–7, 1999, by
Gordon B. Hinckley

EXTERIOR
White marble

TOTAL FLOOR AREA
6,800 square feet

DIMENSIONS
102 feet by 76 feet

HIDDEN IMAGE
Within this drawing is the Good
Shepherd to the right of the temple.

an estimated eighty-two thousand work hours had been donated. Elder Richard Skidmore and Sister Bon Adell Skidmore, the temple construction missionaries who served among these Saints and witnessed their contributions, concluded, "This could not have happened anywhere else. It was a community project. It was a huge project for everyone that unified the community in purpose. Their rendered service really has made the temple theirs." The local members working on the temple made a lasting impression on decorative painter Michael Funk from Murray, Utah. "Nowhere could you go and find so many people working to help build a temple," Brother Funk said. "I have seen young—very young—and the old—very old—raking and moving rocks, laying sod, moving dirt to perfection and with no pay in return but giving thanks to their Heavenly Father. Thanks to the people of Colonia Juárez, I know where I am going and what I need to do to get there. I can answer the question: 'What the celestial kingdom is like?' I know what it is like. I have been there. I have been to Colonia Juárez, Mexico."

Temple construction unified not only one small community but also Saints from two different cultures as they worked together to build the temple. For a time, the stakes in El Paso, Texas, belonged to the Colonia Juárez Temple district, and bonds of friendship were formed that reached across the border. After the temple was dedicated, a member's home in Colonia Juárez was destroyed by fire. The Saints in El Paso quickly gathered clothing, food, and money and traveled two hundred miles to rebuild the home. Within twenty-four hours, they had prepared a temporary house for the family to stay in. The house was newly painted, the laundry was done, the beds were made, and they had all they needed to feel comfortable. This service was a direct result of the friendships made during the temple's construction.

The road leading to Colonia Juárez drops down a hill and allows a beautiful view of the peaceful little valley. In the words of President Hinckley, the white marble temple is the "crowning glory to this community."

Madrid Spain Temple

As histories go, the Church's experience in Spain has not been particularly long, and it has been challenging. In 1955, when President Gordon B. Hinckley first passed through the country, the Church had essentially no presence there. In 1967, Spain passed a religious liberty law, allowing for official recognition of The Church of Jesus Christ of Latter-day Saints. The first branch was organized in Madrid one year later, and in May 1969, the first four full-time missionaries entered the country.

The temple is part of a larger building complex that has become known as the Temple Square of Spain. Other buildings on the square include an eight-story building and a shorter building, which combine to offer a family history center,

accommodations for temple administrators and visitors, a missionary training center, a distribution center, and a multi-purpose stake center. The square is surrounded by red brick apartment buildings. Three Spanish-style fountains adorn the 3.1-acre plaza, surrounded by a pleasant Madrid suburb.

Under a sweltering sun, President Gordon B. Hinckley presided over the groundbreaking in June 1996. Although the temperature was a scorching 113 degrees, some 4,500 gathered to witness the historic day. President Hinckley was the first President of the Church to visit Spain. During the groundbreaking ceremony, President Hinckley said, "This is a happy day for me. I came here in 1992 to find a site where this temple

56

SITE
3.5 acres

GROUNDBREAKING
June 11, 1996, by Gordon B. Hinckley

DEDICATION
March 19–21, 1999, by
Gordon B. Hinckley

EXTERIOR
Italian Carrara Marble

TOTAL FLOOR AREA
45,800 square feet

DIMENSIONS
116 feet by 138 feet

HIDDEN IMAGE
Rendered in this drawing is
a Lladró Christus figurine on
the surface of the temple.

may be built. After looking at many areas we felt that this would be an appropriate place.

"I hope we will be good neighbors to those who live around here. I promise you and the officials of Madrid that what is built here will be beautiful. . . . The structure will be beautiful and the grounds will be beautiful. This will be a hallowed and sacred place." At the end of the ceremonies, the prophet waved farewell and began to move toward his car, but then he stopped and returned again to the congregation to repeatedly wave to them. Feeling of his love for them, many wept when he at last left them.

With the temple's exterior clad in brilliant white marble, the architecture is rich in symbolism and Spanish culture. The 45,800-square-foot, modern-classic structure has four ordinance rooms and four sealing rooms. Designs throughout the temple are patterned after Charles IV's royal palace in Madrid, and much of the interior furnishings are Mediterranean in appearance. Temple architect Carlos Langdon said, "I am not a member of the Church but I am very proud of the result. I think it combines very well what the Church wanted with the very honorable traditions in this country."

More than 100,200 people visited the temple in a public open house during February and March 1999. Government representatives visited the temple during its open house and seemed to agree with Madrid's mayor, who stated that the holy edifice "has enriched the tradition of Spanish architecture." Faustino Lopez, an early convert in Spain, shared his feelings about the temple: "When we think about the temple we feel as if it were a dream. Something impossible. It is a miracle of the Lord he has given us. We will try to be faithful to it and be worthy for this wonderful blessing. A temple in Spain means the Lord and the prophet have faith in us."

While President Hinckley was in Spain to dedicate the temple, he visited King Juan Carlos and Queen Sofia at the royal palace. This was his third visit with the royal couple. Following up on his 1992 visit, in which he had presented them with a leather-bound Book of Mormon, he gave them a special gift created by well-known Spanish artists: a Lladró figurine of the

Christus, modeled after the original by Bertel Thorvaldsen and "created in commemoration of the opening of the very first temple in Spain pertaining to The Church of Jesus Christ of Latter-day Saints." Jose Lladró, president of the Lladró company, had personally delivered the first five issues of the figurine to President Hinckley at the Madrid Spain Temple site. One of the five figurines is now on permanent display in the temple's foyer.

Elder Jeffrey R. Holland, who participated in the dedicatory services, commented: "To have a beautiful temple—an exquisitely beautiful temple—in this country with such a Christian tradition and historic influence has been truly inspirational." He continued: "I have been so deeply touched by the love, devotion and emotion of the members here, such as the sisters who served in the cafeteria and volunteers who have cleaned every aspect of the temple grounds, to say nothing of the temple itself. A sweet sister, in the dark on her hands and knees, washed the marble trim at the base of the fountains of the garden plaza. They are all so grateful for this temple and so moved to realize that this magnificent edifice is for them."

President Hinckley was confident that the new temple would be very busy: "We're not building any temples where there is not a need for them," he told local reporters. Indeed, before the construction had even risen above ground level, President Carlos Jesus Somoza Diaz of the Madrid Spain Stake said, "The stake is holding meetings and activities that will motivate members to prepare themselves to attend and serve in the temple. We also have three functioning family history centers, and will soon open a fourth. We are preparing for a great work to be done in Madrid." He explained that the family history centers were so busy there was hardly ever free time.

R. Raymond Barnes, who was president of the first LDS mission in Spain, returned for the dedicatory events. As he toured the temple grounds, he said, "When we came here, we started with one room in a rented place. Seeing this temple is almost like a miracle. I get choked up. This is a spine-tingling sight." That sense of enthusiasm was shared by all of the faithful members living on the Iberian Peninsula.

Bogotá Colombia Temple

In the Niza section of Bogotá, about ten miles from downtown, stands the incredible Bogotá Columbia Temple. It is surrounded by high-rise buildings and a busy freeway, yet it is considered by many to be the most beautiful building in the city, perhaps the most beautiful in all of Colombia. Álvaro Uribe Vélez, former president of Colombia, calls the temple "a magnificent treasure in our city and our nation."

President Spencer W. Kimball announced the Bogotá Colombia Temple in April 1984, but the temple was not dedicated until fifteen long years later. Those years were filled with opposition, legal struggles, and discouragement. Many members made the most of this waiting period by doing family history work so they would have names ready to take to the temple once dedicated. As they waited, stakes continued to contract with bus companies to make the five- or six-day trip each way to the nearest temple—in Lima, Peru.

Elder Jay E. Jensen of the Seventy served as president of the South America North Area during many of the significant events required to take the temple from announcement to actual construction. He later commented on the spiritual support the Saints gave: "The progress on the Bogotá temple is a fulfillment of members' faith and fasting." Members would have countrywide fasts whenever critical moments were reached in the approval process. "In each instance when a particular obstacle was faced, a special focus in fasting and prayer would produce miracles."

57

The temple is a masterful edifice that combines local architectural themes and building materials with beautiful grounds to occupy an entire city block. The temple itself is faced with a silver-gray Brazilian granite that portrays a subtle elegance and reverence on both rainy and sunny days. Some of that light enters through tall, stained-glass windows, designed both functionally and aesthetically to enhance local Colombian craftsmanship.

On the inside, local motifs continue, as evidenced by fixtures displaying a distinct likeness to ancient Incan designs. Marble finishes tastefully preserve the light, whether natural or otherwise, creating an atmosphere conducive to spiritual warmth, enlightenment, and peace, each shade and vein of color within each piece of marble adding interest and natural beauty. One prominent feature of the celestial room is the room's arches, which are made of hollow marble blocks. This preserves the marble's inherent beauty while substantially reducing its weight.

The temple grounds are landscaped with plants indigenous to Colombia, such as flowering eucalyptus trees with beautiful red flowers. The grounds also include housing to accommodate Saints in the temple district who must travel long distances to attend the temple.

Rain, which promotes the area's lush, natural vegetation, is a regular feature in Colombia's climate. During a three-month stretch of temple construction, rain fell every single day. The workers got used to the rain and continued their labors without stopping.

The workers laboring on the temple gave special care to their craft. Built to last for centuries, the temple's foundation includes more than 200 reinforced columns driven fifty meters into the ground. As the temple's construction progressed, even those workers who were not members of the Church began to develop great reverence and respect for the building they were constructing. Temple project manager Jim Aulesita later explained: "There came a time that one particular contractor, who was a Catholic, would not talk aloud to me in the celestial room—he would whisper. All of the workers who entered the celestial room would not talk aloud. Although the temple was

SITE
3.71 acres

GROUNDBREAKING
June 26, 1993

DEDICATION
April 24–26, 1999, by
Gordon B. Hinckley

EXTERIOR
Brazilian granite, Asa Branca

TOTAL FLOOR AREA
53,500 square feet

DIMENSIONS
76 feet by 186 feet; spire,
124 feet high

HIDDEN IMAGE
An image of the Christus statue
is located among the trees.

not completed, it produced a reverence that was felt by many of the workers."

One electrician showed great faith and determination to complete his responsibilities on the temple. While working on the wiring, he was electrocuted so severely that he received third-degree burns on his arms. Brother Aulesita described his thoughts regarding the accident: "I thought that I would never see the man again. Monday morning he was there and I asked him, 'Why are you here?' He responded by saying, 'Because we have not finished our work in the temple.' I was very touched. He is a nonmember and he feels that he needs to complete the job and needs to do it well. I watched him as he went to work with his arms burned, covered with bandages, and in a great deal of pain. I then made the comment that because of his faithfulness that he would not have any problems recovering. A couple of months later his bandages were off and he barely had any scars. He worked to the last minute. Why didn't he just quit? I think it is because he felt the spirit of the temple."

Early one morning during the construction, a man was walking around the grounds recording various measurements. Project managers did not learn the identity of this man until they read a local newspaper article. The article mentioned that a city inspector had visited many construction sites throughout the city, and the Mormon temple was the only project that complied with local building codes in every way.

Church members from throughout Colombia rejoiced at the dedication, grateful that the temple would provide for them a place of refuge in their troubled land. "Many who come are poor economically," says former temple president Roberto Rubio, "but they have a millionaire spirit. A woman who recently came on the bus from Pereira is more than 80 years old and is extremely poor. She sells newspapers and collects and sells old bottles to come to the temple. There are many like her."

This beautiful temple contrasts the peace it brings within its walls with the daily difficulties faced by Latter-day Saints in the region. Given the challenges faced by the country of Colombia, this house of the Lord is indeed a great blessing.

Guayaquil Ecuador Temple

Ecuador is rich in natural resources, but they are largely underdeveloped. Its spiritual resources, however, are quietly increasing day by day. Named for the equator, which passes through it, the country itself is rugged and filled with a variety of beauties. Its lands range from the Pacific coastline, with the fascinating Galapagos Islands lying offshore, to the semi-desert plains in the east. In the middle are two ranges of glacial Andes.

The Church's fifty-eighth operating temple stands prominently on a hill in a quiet section of northern Guayaquil, Ecuador's largest city. Fertile volcanic soil and bounteous rain create a perfect setting for the temple's well-designed landscape. Shrubs, a variety of large palm trees, and colorful native plants enhance the temple's outward appearance.

The Guayaquil Ecuador Temple has four ordinance rooms, three sealing rooms, and a celestial room. Its floor plan is identical to that of the Bogotá Colombia Temple, and its exterior is adorned with the same Brazilian granite. Despite similarities between the two temples, however, the interior decor of the Guayaquil Ecuador Temple has unique qualities. Local wood with a cherry finish accents the flawless quality of workmanship throughout the building. No nails can be seen, joints come together flawlessly, and the grain patterns in the wood match consistently. The temple has been described

58

by members, nonmembers, and the press as "the most beautiful building in Ecuador."

President Spencer W. Kimball announced the temple in 1982, but it took fourteen years to secure the necessary government authorizations. Meanwhile, the Saints in Ecuador continued to travel by bus, often at great sacrifice, to attend the Lima Peru Temple. In 1994, Elder Jay E. Jensen, president of the South America North Area, explained, "Many stakes, if not all, continue to have their excursions to Lima, which take three days one way, and then they spend one day or two in the temple. Then they come back, another three days on the bus. We just marvel at their faith. It almost makes you weep when you see the sacrifices they make in order to go to the temple for their one time. Some will return during their lifetime, but not many."

The announcement of a temple in Ecuador was received with rejoicing by Saints in Ecuador, who would be able to attend more often and at lower expense. Couples such as Santiago León and Raquel Plúas de León exemplify how Latter-day Saints prepared for the Guayaquil Ecuador Temple. Santiago and Raquel were married in the Lima Peru Temple, despite economic difficulties. "Just seeing the temple from outside made me happy," recalls Santiago. "But to be able to go inside and participate in the ordinances there—that was a real blessing." On the wall in the front room of their small home is a photograph of the Washington D.C. Temple. Under it hangs a hand-lettered sign: "Ecuador: Prepare Yourself for Your Temple."

The temple's open house was a resounding success by all accounts. More than one hundred thousand people toured the sacred edifice, demonstrating the support that members and nonmembers alike gave to the arrival of a house of the Lord in their country. After waiting seventeen years, faithful Saints went to great lengths to show their love of the temple. Some, for example, walked six miles at night so they could arrive at the temple by 5:00 a.m. to begin their volunteer work of cleaning the temple. That evening, they walked back to their homes. These same members attended the dedication with similar enthusiasm.

President Gordon B. Hinckley dedicated the Church's fifty-eighth temple before thousands of grateful Saints who had

SITE
6.2 acres

GROUNDBREAKING
August 10, 1996, by Richard G. Scott

DEDICATION
August 1–2, 1999, by
Gordon B. Hinckley

EXTERIOR
Brazilian granite, Asa Branca

TOTAL FLOOR AREA
45,000 square feet

DIMENSIONS
154 feet by 76 feet

HIDDEN IMAGE
An image of the Christus statue is
located above the celestial room.

waited for the temple since President Kimball's announcement seventeen years earlier.

In an interview with the *Church News,* President Hinckley commented on the appreciation of the Church members in Ecuador for the new temple. "I sense a great spirit of gratitude for this new temple in Guayaquil," he said. "The Saints have waited a very, very long time. They contributed generously toward its construction, but for one reason or another, it has been delayed until now at this late date. It is finished and completed and dedicated and they are grateful for this and indicate their gratitude." He noted: "It has been a very interesting thing to see the descendants of Father Lehi in the congregations that have gathered in the temple. So very many of these people have the blood of Lehi in their veins and it is just an intriguing thing to see their tremendous response and their tremendous interest."

Members came from stakes throughout the nation by bus, some traveling for three or four hours. Among those who attended the dedication were the colorful natives of Otavalo, adorned with gold necklaces and long, braided hair. Following the ceremonies, the first ordinance sessions were held for the faithful Saints from Otavalo.

After the dedication, President Russell M. Nelson commented: "The presence of a temple here and the establishment of a people worthy of entrance to the temple will make a great difference to the future of this country and for the nations round about. It is really a very important hinge point in the history of this nation."

The Guayaquil Ecuador Temple is a symbol that the Lord has heard the supplications of the many Latter-day Saints for a temple in their country. Gustavo Maruri, a longtime member of the Church, shared his feelings about the temple: "I like this temple. It is the best in the world because it is in my city. . . . I see the temple every day. I look up early in the morning and see the statue of the Angel Moroni standing way up there, the fulfillment of our faith, our work, our efforts." After the temple's dedication, Guillermo Granja Garcia, vice chairman of the temple committee, summed up the feelings of many: "All Ecuador is blessed today."

Spokane Washington Temple

The Spokane Washington Temple was the fourth small temple built by the Church. With walls covered in speckled, light gray granite, the temple is situated in the Spokane suburb of Opportunity, in a beautiful eastern Washington valley among farmhouses, wheat fields, and pine trees. Alongside the temple is the Spokane Washington East Stake Center, with which it shares an LDS recreational complex. In the 1980s, shade trees were planted on the field and now form a pleasant border between the temple and the recreational complex.

As Church leaders worked to bring a temple to eastern Washington, many people came to recognize the sacred feeling present at the site. For example, when looking for property on which to build, Dick Waide, a Church physical facilities representative, visited the location that was eventually chosen and received the feeling that it was holy ground. Elder Don McGary, a building missionary, walked across the site and "felt that he should take his shoes off" because it was sacred ground.

The morning of October 10, 1998, was rainy and cloudy, but by the time a thousand people had witnessed the temple's groundbreaking, the sun was shining. President Steven N. Holdaway, whose local stake had coordinated the groundbreaking ceremony, later reported: "We had the groundbreaking in the sunshine. By the time the groundbreaking was over, it clouded up again. So the sunshine was just for the period of time of the groundbreaking." Speaking of the joy of

59

having a temple in the area, he added, "The members, of course, are delighted we'll have this. I don't think anyone thought we'd have a temple this soon, but they are very appreciative and thankful for it."

A number of other, smaller temples were being constructed during the same period as the Spokane Washington Temple. The First Presidency subsequently chose to avoid the logistical challenges that would come from dedicating several temples simultaneously and thus moved forward the Spokane temple completion date by two months. Great faith was combined with hard work on the part of the construction workers to meet this tight deadline. One worker observed, "The completion date was made possible due to favorable weather conditions and efficient contractors."

Professional construction workers were not the only ones to manifest their faith by hard work. On May 22, 1999, approximately forty Aaronic Priesthood young men from the Spokane Washington East Stake carried the oxen to the baptismal font area and carefully placed them in position. Even young children helped to the extent that they were able. For example, over the holiday weekend of July 4, little ones brought their toy wheelbarrows and hauled small unwanted rocks from the areas to be landscaped.

Rush Hashie, a truck driver and Latter-day Saint from Albuquerque, New Mexico, delivered a load of cargo to the Spokane Washington Temple. Only after his arrival at the site did he learn that he had just transported the statue of the angel Moroni, the oxen for the baptismal font, and the font itself. Temple historian Mark Bickley records: "Brother Hashie was so overcome with emotion when he learned what his cargo was that he went to the grove of trees just east of the temple and cried."

Another man involved with the temple was Dale Reese of the Spokane Washington East Stake, who served as the building's project manager. For months he worked fourteen- to sixteen-hour days at the temple site. He remembered laying sod in early August before the open house. "The landscaping company that was supposed to do it failed to get the job done sooner," he related. "I and some other members started rolling the grass out and it looked bad. It was basically dead. Look at that grass now. . . . It's gorgeous. All we did was water it and pray. That grass looks like it's been there for five years. You don't even see any seam lines in it. It was all done by members."

SITE
2 acres

GROUNDBREAKING
October 10, 1998, by
F. Melvin Hammond

DEDICATION
August 21–23, 1999, by
Gordon B. Hinckley

EXTERIOR
Granite

TOTAL FLOOR AREA
10,700 square feet

DIMENSIONS
149 feet by 77 feet

HIDDEN IMAGE
An image of the Savior is
included among the trees.

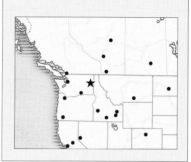

The statue of the angel Moroni was placed atop the temple spire on April 21, 1999. Handlers were required to wear white cotton gloves whenever they touched the statue. Although this event was not publicized, approximately two thousand people attended, some waiting for several hours to see the statue raised and placed. Cars filled the parking lot, found places on adjoining streets, and lined the highway for almost a mile. When the statue was put into position, facing east toward the hills, the afternoon sun broke through the clouds, gleaming on the golden figure.

When the time for the dedication arrived, from August 21 through 23, 1999, President Hinckley spoke to approximately twelve thousand young people and their families in a hockey arena near downtown Spokane. Some of his counsel included encouragement to follow the six "B's": be grateful, be smart, be clean, be true, be humble, and be prayerful.

More than sixteen thousand members attended the eleven dedicatory sessions, watching the proceedings from within the temple or in the stake center by means of closed-circuit television. Another two hundred huddled together in unseasonably cold morning temperatures at the southeast corner of the temple to view the 8:00 a.m. ceremonial sealing of the cornerstone. The morning greeted them with dark clouds, light rain, thunder, and chilling winds, but as President Hinckley exited the temple doors for the cornerstone ceremony, the sun broke through the clouds.

The Spokane Washington Temple opened for ordinance work on August 24, 1999, and was filled to capacity. Having the temple filled to capacity aptly portrays the joy of the Saints in having their own temple—a temple in which they serve with the same relentless faith and dedication exhibited during its construction.

Demonstrating their love for the Prophet Joseph Smith and their temple, members in the Spokane Washington Temple District took advantage of thirty-two continuous hours of service on December 16–17, 2005. The event commemorated the birth of the Prophet Joseph Smith. The special temple service included baptisms, endowments, initiatories, and sealings, with more than 7,300 ordinances performed and more than 4,200 individuals being blessed.

Columbus Ohio Temple

Decades of faith and sacrifice on the part of Ohio Saints reached a culmination in September 1999, when the state's second latter-day temple was dedicated. The Columbus Ohio Temple is located approximately 150 miles south of Kirtland, where the first temple of this dispensation was dedicated in 1836.

On April 25, 1998, nearly seven thousand Ohio Saints assembled to hear President Gordon B. Hinckley speak. Not only did they have occasion that day to hear the words of a prophet, but they were given hope that a temple would soon be in their midst. The following account was taken from the book *The Columbus Ohio Temple*, which was prepared for placement in the temple's cornerstone:

"'What does the Lord expect from us?' asked the prophet, 'To be Latter-day Saints.' He expounded on the great expectations required of members and thanked the Ohio Saints for being faithful in temple attendance. He then asked the question the Saints had long hoped for, 'Do you need a temple here?' A soft but excited 'Yes' was echoed. 'Are you worthy of a temple here?' Again, a little louder and with more determination, the congregation said in unison, 'Yes!' . . .

"The prophet then uttered the most beautiful words: 'I feel impressed to say that when we leave here, we are going to take an hour or so . . . to look around for a place where we might build a small temple in Columbus or in the nearby community, where you will have a temple of your own.'"

60

David W. Martin, who researched the property rights of the land on which the temple stands, observed, "As far as we can tell, good and honest people have always owned the land." Interestingly, the land has historic ties to early Church history through Julia Clapp Murdock, a devoted member of the Church who lived in Kirtland at the time of Joseph Smith. Her uncle Abner Clapp held the first recorded deed to the land. Julia died after giving birth to twins on April 30, 1831, the same day that Emma Smith's twins were born and died. Julia's husband, John Murdock, felt unable to rear the twins and asked the Prophet and Emma to care for them. The request somewhat softened Emma's sorrow.

Architecturally, the Columbus Ohio Temple also has ties to Kirtland and the Church's first temple there. Perhaps most noticeable is the Window Beautiful, a window designed by early Church architect Truman O. Angell for the east side of the upper court in the Kirtland Temple. This distinctive window is characterized by a delicate, running vine, a hand-carved flower keystone, distinctive moldings, and 23-karat gold leafing. When Rich Christensen, a member of the temple construction committee, proposed including elements of the Kirtland Temple, Brent Harris, a member of the Cambridge Branch and a skilled wood craftsman, volunteered to build a replica of the Window Beautiful for the Columbus Ohio Temple.

The Columbus Ohio Temple was built to meet high standards. The foundation is engineered to withstand earthquakes two seismic zones higher than required by local building standards, and the parking lot is made of material durable enough to land an airplane on.

The temple's exterior is covered completely with glistening white "sugar marble" quarried in Danby, Vermont, about forty miles south of the Prophet Joseph's birthplace. This high-quality marble is covered with small, round granules, which look like sugar crystals, thus the name "sugar marble." Installing the marble was tedious work, requiring careful attention to detail. Elder Clyde Stewart, a temple construction missionary, examined and organized each piece of marble according to its different shade and pattern, placing the slabs into stacks that would result in the uniform appearance of the

SITE
1.35 acres

GROUNDBREAKING
September 12, 1998, by
John K. Carmack

DEDICATION
September 4–5, 1999, by
Gordon B. Hinckley

EXTERIOR
Imperial Danby Vermont marble

TOTAL FLOOR AREA
10,700 square feet

DIMENSIONS
149 feet by 77 feet

HIDDEN IMAGE
Among the trees to the left of the
temple is the Prophet Joseph Smith
holding the Book of Mormon.
The Prophet is looking at the new
temple as well as the temple that
he helped construct in Kirtland.

exterior walls. On occasions, Elder Stewart received helpful promptings while in his sleep. Sister Stewart said, "At times, Clyde would wake up at night feeling there was a problem with the construction. He would arise early the next day and would find those errors just as he had felt."

Other members living within the Columbus Ohio Temple district eagerly took part in a variety of special projects. "I could tell countless stories of young people helping," said Neil C. Farr, second counselor in the temple presidency. "One evening, during the open house, we had some young women cleaning the celestial room after tours that day. Gradually, all the young women left except one. When she came out, tears were streaming down her cheeks. She simply said, 'I can't wait to attend the temple.'"

Ed Hammond, who assisted with the operational details of preparing the temple, commented, "This has been a Zion-like project. People would come to the door and say with excitement, 'I'm here to clean. What can I do?' All the way down the line, we had the right people willing to help—like Erik and Lois Mars, who are landscapers. They worked late at night landscaping the grounds while their baby slept in the carriage."

As the dedication date approached, full-time missionaries were given the special nighttime assignments to stand watch over the temple grounds. Every night, four companionships would sleep in cots located strategically at the corners of the temple. They would report hourly to their district leader of any disturbances. One of the missionaries, Elder Moon, recorded, "Here I sit upon sacred ground gazing at the Columbus Ohio Temple. I am far from home but the spirit is still the same. I feel a familiar spiritual sense of my heavenly home as I ponder the splendid awe and power the House of the Lord radiates. I am indeed grateful to have this magnificent opportunity to watch over the temple and its grounds."

Some eleven thousand members from eleven stakes attended six dedicatory sessions for the Columbus Ohio Temple. More than 150 years after the first Saints gathered to dedicate their temple in Ohio, another generation of Church members met together in this great state to welcome the Lord to His house and dedicate their lives in service to Him.

Bismarck North Dakota Temple

Bismarck, the capital of North Dakota, is located in the south-central part of the state and is a port on the Missouri River. The state's flat prairies yield the largest crop of spring and durum wheat in the nation. Built in a residential neighborhood on a double lot adjacent to the local stake center, the Bismarck North Dakota Temple is the first operating temple in the upper Midwest of the United States.

The temple serves about five thousand members scattered throughout a vast area upwards of 200,000 square miles. North Dakota's first stake was organized in Fargo in 1977. One year before the stake was organized, Church officials began searching for a site on which to construct a chapel for the Bismarck Branch and that could accommodate future expansion.

Reed E. Barker, branch president at the time, stated, "We selected a site on the open prairie where we knew there would be expansion in the future. There was only one house in the area at that time." The dimensions of the site were somewhat odd, forming the shape of the letter L. Although the Church acquired the property, some Saints in the area wondered what to do with one leg of the property, which seemed useless. However, President Barker explained that others, including himself, "felt differently about it, without ever having a confirmation of what it was to be used for." Each time they considered selling the land, the district presidency received strong impressions that the land should not be sold, but they did not know why.

When the Bismarck North Dakota Temple was

61

announced, the purpose for preserving this extra piece of land became clear. Unlike the seemingly endless delays and struggles that had been experienced with other temples throughout the world, very little effort was required for this temple to receive approval from the city. When the building permit request was submitted, the city employee simply asked, "You own the property, don't you?" The answer was affirmative. "Then we don't see a problem."

Lowell L. Cheney, a counselor in the stake presidency, shared his thoughts on these events: "Though individually each of these events may not have seemed exceptionally significant, an overview of what has transpired gives profound assurance of the Lord's awareness of His children in this part of His vineyard and the desire for them to receive His choicest blessings. If we will but follow as directed by the Spirit, even though we may not see the whole picture, we can be confident that the work will go forth, for the Lord surely directs His work to completion."

Close to a thousand people attended the groundbreaking ceremony on October 17, 1998. Bishop Keith B. McMullin of the presiding bishopric observed, "Many of Lehi's descendants are here in the Dakotas. We have a sacred obligation to them." There are eleven Native American reservations in the Dakotas, and many children of Lehi live in Canada, directly to the north. Bishop McMullin challenged every Anglo-American visiting the temple to invite two children of Lehi.

Church member Dr. Tyson Williams of Minot, North Dakota, created an acrylic painting of a local landscape that is displayed in the temple. "I consider this as a gift to the Savior and His holy house," Williams said. "I've made this donation as a token of the gratitude of the members of the Church in this region." After working long hours, he completed the painting half an hour before his deadline. "I don't take full credit for the painting," he said. "I thank the Lord for giving me the talent and blessing me with the ability to complete the painting on time."

Another member, Brother Robert Colvin of the Sioux Falls South Dakota Stake, participated in the choir that sang during

SITE
1.6 acres

GROUNDBREAKING
October 17, 1998

DEDICATION
September 19, 1999, by
Gordon B. Hinckley

EXTERIOR
Granite veneer from Québec

TOTAL FLOOR AREA
10,700 square feet

DIMENSIONS
149 feet by 77 feet

HIDDEN IMAGE
The Savior's image is in the sky and across the surface of the temple. Shafts of wheat are found among the foreground shadows.

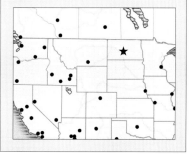

the dedicatory services. He wrote: "Yesterday I had the incredible opportunity to sing in a thirteen-voice choir for the dedication of the temple in Bismarck, North Dakota. The spirit of God truly was burning like a fire in that beautiful celestial room. The prophet Gordon B. Hinckley pronounced some wonderful blessings upon the people and workers of the temple.

"One of the most memorable points of the dedicatory prayer was asking the blessing of safe travel upon those coming to this temple. Living in the Dakotas, winter travel is often dangerous and that should bring peace of mind to Saints traveling to do work in the temple during those months."

President Gordon B. Hinckley had never been to North Dakota until the dedication of the temple in Bismarck. With a touch of humor, the prophet told the Saints gathered for the dedication that if he were governor of the state, he would move the cities closer together.

President Hinckley said, "I love these smaller temples; I am very grateful for them. They are very efficient and exceedingly well built with the best materials." The Bismarck North Dakota Temple is constructed of materials gathered from throughout the world. The marble for the exterior came from Quebec, other marble from Italy, the stained-glass windows from Germany, and the chandeliers in the celestial room and sealing rooms from the Czech Republic.

At the dedication, President Hinckley explained that "even with the temple here, some will still have to travel a very long distance, but it will be much shorter than it was before. There is so much faith on the part of the people in these areas. They're willing to go anywhere to accomplish the temple work."

Former Bismarck North Dakota Temple president Robert B. Dahlgren spoke of one such willing couple, who had retired and were living in an area some distance from Bismarck. He asked them, "Would you be willing to move to Bismarck and work in the temple full time?" The couple agreed and promptly made the arrangements.

Columbia South Carolina Temple

Nestled among native loblolly pine and tall oak trees is the beautiful Columbia South Carolina Temple. Immaculate homes, quaint churches, and dense woods surround the temple site. The grounds themselves are landscaped with a variety of plant species, including crape myrtle (a summer-blooming shrub), large holly, mums, dogwood trees, maples, and oak—all combining to increase the natural beauty of the temple's setting. And though the temple itself is similar in design to many of the smaller temples, its furnishings, grounds, and decor reflect the flavor of the Carolinas and surrounding areas.

Ground was broken for the temple on December 5, 1998, with more than thirty-five hundred people in attendance. Record-breaking temperatures—eighty

degrees Fahrenheit during the first week of December!—made the ceremony particularly memorable. Many of the thousands of Church members in attendance used umbrellas to shade themselves from the hot afternoon sun. Elder Gordon T. Watts, first counselor in the North America Southeast Area, presided over the ceremony and called on members to begin their own spiritual construction. "As the contractors and building people prepare and begin construction, let us also begin a program of personal construction that we will be as exemplary as this beautiful temple when it is completed," he said. "If changes are required in your life to gain entrance into the temple, let them begin now." Elder Watts invited a few Primary children and young men and women to step forward to "represent

62

the young people whose lives [would] be benefited now and in the future as a result of the temple."

Throughout the building process, the Saints in the area were willing to assist in any way. For example, one stake held a youth conference at the park across from the temple. Youth and their leaders beautified the temple property by spreading mulch, building steps, and repairing retaining walls. Groups of members and missionaries planted bushes, flowers, and trees and laid sod around the temple. Adults and youth cleaned the temple during construction. Priests from one ward cleaned the baptismal font and oxen. Young women from the area strung crystals on the chandeliers. Sister Janie Smith, a member of the Caughman Park Ward, described her memory of the event. "They lowered the celestial room chandelier and the girls were sitting in a circle with it almost in their laps. The girls were covered with the strings of lights and sparkling crystal. It was a beautiful sight."

When the temple was ready to be opened to the public, citizens from throughout the community eagerly toured the building. One of them, Rabbi Philip Silverstein, was impressed to find so many references in the temple to the Old Testament. "You are the only Church that cares about the spirit of Elijah," he said. Following a tour for residents in the neighborhood, another citizen, the president of the homeowners association, said, "Call us day or night and we will help with the landscaping or anything else."

The temple was dedicated in six sessions over the weekend of October 16 and 17, 1999. Hurricane Irene, which was assaulting the Florida coast, threatened the proceedings. The heavy rain predicted for both days of the dedicatory services did not materialize, and the moderate rainfall did not detract from the historic event. President Gordon B. Hinckley conducted all six sessions. "The gospel was first preached here 160 years ago," said President Hinckley. "In the generations that have followed, hundreds and thousands of people have joined the Church. We have placed a temple here in Columbia because it's the capital of the state and somewhat in the center of the state."

As President and Sister Hinckley left the temple after the

SITE
3.6 acres

GROUNDBREAKING
December 5, 1998, by
Gordon T. Watts

EXTERIOR
Imperial Danby Vermont marble

TOTAL FLOOR AREA
10,700 square feet

DIMENSIONS
149 feet by 77 feet

HIDDEN IMAGE
An image of the Savior inviting all to partake of temple blessings is included among the trees.

final session, a large group of Church members lined the parking lot and sang "We Thank Thee, O God, for a Prophet." President Hinckley waved to them and then rolled down his window and waved again as the car drove away. Regarding her experience at the dedication, Sister Sigg, a member of the Charlotte North Carolina Stake, said: "I will never for the rest of my life forget the feeling in the celestial room. I will never ever forget that feeling that confirms everything I've been taught since I joined the Church. There is no doubt!"

The temple has been a source of strength and courage for John and Patty Cline, members of the Beaufort South Carolina Ward, who served as ushers for the Columbia South Carolina Temple dedication. "I was overwhelmed with the cornerstone ceremony," Sister Cline said. "Just to be in the presence of the prophet—the Spirit was overwhelming."

The experience was particularly poignant for Brother Cline, who had been diagnosed with terminal cancer just a week before the dedication. "I've got some time, one and a half, two, maybe three years. But I'm still happy," he smiled. "I still feel good, and I've got some good times left." There is yet a twenty percent chance that the cancer could go into remission. Brother and Sister Cline cling to that hope, but they are prepared to accept the will of their Father in Heaven. "I'm the only one in my family who is a member of the Church," he said. "I told my brother, 'If you knew in your heart what I know in mine, you would know that I have absolutely no fear of crossing over. None.'" He said colleagues at work express amazement that he is so positive. "I tell them it's because I know what I know. It's because of the things that we learn in the temple."

Since its dedication, minor additions and renovation efforts have been made to the temple or its grounds. These modifications include an expansion of the parking lot, new interior furnishings, and a power generator. According to temple president Stephen C. Lenker, "Significant storms frequent our area and cause power outages. When the power goes out, the generator immediately turns on and allows us to proceed with the work without interruption."

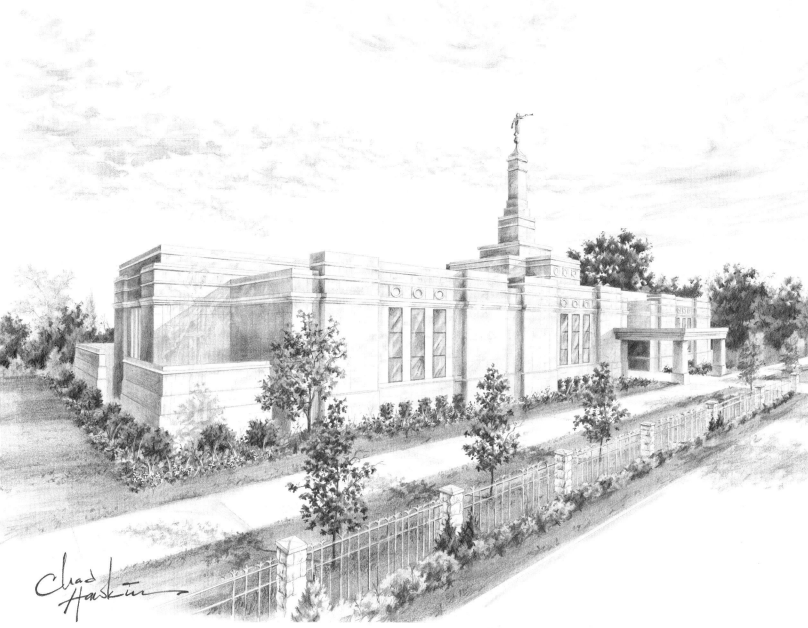

Detroit Michigan Temple

Fifty tons of glistening white Vermont marble form the facade of the Detroit Michigan Temple, which is nestled at the foot of gently rolling hills twenty miles north of Detroit. This beautiful landmark is well suited for the area. While simple in design and thus unobtrusive, it is also easy to access from one of Detroit's major thoroughfares. For the Michigan Saints, the temple is a ready respite from the hustle and bustle of daily life.

The history of the Church in the Detroit area began with Lucy Mack Smith, mother of the Prophet Joseph Smith. In 1831, Lucy traveled to Michigan to visit the family of her brother Colonel Stephen Mack, founder of Pontiac, Michigan. Stephen Mack, the proprietor of a large mercantile establishment in

Detroit, built a turnpike from Detroit to his farm in Pontiac at his own expense. That same road now runs in front of the temple and is known as Woodward Avenue. The Prophet Joseph himself may have stood on the grounds of the temple site during his 1834 visit to Detroit, when he likely traveled this road to his uncle's home.

In 1956, the Church bought nearly eight acres of land for construction of the area's first stake center. The stake center stands on part of this land, and many individuals felt that the Church should sell the remaining acreage. George Romney, the first stake president in Michigan and future governor of the state, felt strongly that the land should not be sold. Decades later, President Thomas C. Bithell, who was in charge

63

of finding a site for the temple, said he looked at the property in question—which was just north of the stake center—but did not pursue the possibility because it was assumed the lot was too small. But then, after reviewing several properties near other chapels, President Bithell looked again at the lot outside his office window in the Bloomfield Hills Stake Center and wondered about the property. It was measured, "and it was just perfect," he said. "The more I looked and contemplated, the more this seemed to be the right location. It was as if this land had been hidden; waiting to be discovered at the right time."

Over the years, the property where the temple now stands had been landscaped with grass and a variety of trees. Members had always kept the grounds free of weeds and litter. Many remember holding various outdoor activities on the property. Sister Bonnie Shurtz reminisced about being a Primary president in the Bloomfield Hills Ward: "We used to have Primary activities right where the temple is, under the trees, and we never realized there was enough land there to build a temple."

On October 10, 1998, more than a thousand people attended the groundbreaking for the Detroit Michigan Temple. During the ceremony, President Bithell observed, "To the best of my knowledge, nothing has ever been built on this property. It is sacred ground, preserved for this very purpose."

With emotion, one member said, "We have prayed to have a temple in Michigan. Today, we are looking at a tangible reply to prayers."

As construction on the temple progressed, the Saints prayed that Michigan's winter weather would be moderated and thus facilitate the work. Workers began pouring concrete for the temple's foundation in January and continued to do so through the cold and snowy months that followed. To allow the concrete to set up properly, it had to be covered and heated for several days until it had properly cured. Temple construction missionary Elder Keith Brown said, "As cold as it was, I do not think that we ever had weather severe enough to interrupt construction." The weather was also tempered on the day that the temple walls were put in place. The walls were assembled

SITE
6.34 acres (including adjacent meetinghouse)

GROUNDBREAKING
October 10, 1998, by Jay E. Jensen

DEDICATION
October 23–24, 1999, by Gordon B. Hinckley

EXTERIOR
Imperial Danby Vermont marble

TOTAL FLOOR AREA
10,700 square feet

DIMENSIONS
149 feet by 77 feet

HIDDEN IMAGE
An image of the Savior is included on the surface of the temple where the celestial room is located.

flat on the ground and then hoisted by a crane into position. Elder Brown described the experience: "The day the crane arrived, the area was experiencing thirty-mile-an-hour winds. But on the building site, it was never too windy to set the walls. Can you imagine a forty-foot wall, twenty feet high, in a thirty-mile-an-hour wind? On the site it was not that windy, and we set all of the walls in one day."

The temple quickly became an important feature in the lives of area Saints, including the Primary children. The Primary room in the meetinghouse nearby has windows that face the temple. During all phases of construction, the children would look toward the temple and sing "I Love to See the Temple." In addition to remembering the temple in their prayers, the children saved their pennies so they could put them into a bank—a hollow wooden replica of the temple. In the end, nearly two hundred dollars were collected and donated to the temple fund.

During a special tour prior to the public open house in October 1999, two local government officials, referring to the statue of the angel Moroni, said, "We are glad to have an angel watching over our city." The open house attracted many visitors of other faiths from Michigan and Canada. Television, radio, and newspapers throughout the state covered the event. One front-page headline read, "Close to God, Closer to Home."

In the temple's first month of service, more than ten thousand ordinances were performed. As a smaller temple, there is minimal staffing to facilitate some of the building's daily operations. Often, those attending are expected to help keep the temple clean. For example, as youth finish with baptisms, they wipe around the baptismal font, help do the laundry, and make sure everything is left in order. The temple becomes even more personal to patrons who help take care it. Some of the cleaning responsibilities may not seem very pleasant. However Michael Oniones, a teacher, expressed his positive attitude by saying it is a privilege, not a chore. "If you clean the bathroom, people may not think that's so great," he said. "But still, you're cleaning the bathroom in the temple, and even to be in the temple is a great thing."

Halifax Nova Scotia Temple

Halifax, the capital of Nova Scotia, Canada, and the largest city in the Canadian Maritime provinces, is a busy port in a harbor inlet of the Atlantic Ocean. In this land known for its lighthouses that protect seafarers from the treacherous shores, a beacon of spiritual light has been erected. That beacon is the Halifax Nova Scotia Temple, located in the Cole Harbour area of the city of Dartmouth, across the harbor from Halifax. The temple serves Church members in a temple district roughly the size of the western United States.

The Church was first organized in Halifax in 1843. Thanks to the commitment and sacrifice of the early Latter-day Saints in the area, Halifax and Dartmouth still stand as the hub of Church activity in the region a century and a half later. And now the temple has become a benchmark of beauty in the area as well as a symbol of spirituality and family togetherness. People are aware of the architectural distinction and religious commitment the temple adds to the community, which, in turn, has brought new respect for the Church. Even some nonmembers have hung distinctive pictures of the temple on the walls of their homes.

The history of the temple location originates in the 1980s, when Church membership increased and a new meetinghouse was needed. An ideal property was located, but the lot size was much larger than the building required. Since the landowner would not sell only a smaller portion, the Church acquired the entire six acres. Rather than selling off the excess

64

property, the Church maintained and used the grounds for picnics, Church activities, and as a neighborhood sledding hill. Over a decade later, President Gordon B. Hinckley identified this extra property as the perfect location for the Halifax Nova Scotia Temple.

President Hinckley said in the October 1997 general conference: "There are many areas of the Church that are remote, where the membership is small and not likely to grow very much in the near future. Are those who live in these places to be denied forever the blessings of temple ordinances? . . . We will construct small temples in some of these areas, buildings with all of the facilities to administer all of the ordinances." For Latter-day Saints living in such areas as the Maritime provinces of Canada, President Hinckley's announcement brought much happiness and gratitude.

For Church members in Maritime Canada, attending the temple had been a major effort. At different times, the area belonged to temple districts ranging from the Cardston Alberta Temple (2,331 miles away) to the Washington D.C. Temple (798 miles away) to the Toronto Ontario Temple (788 miles away).

Like many Saints living in New Brunswick, David and Carol Ray had been driving to the Washington D.C. Temple or Toronto Ontario Temple to attend the house of the Lord. "It's eighteen hours either way," Sister Ray, an institute and seminary teacher in the St. John's New Brunswick Stake, observed. "For other people in Nova Scotia, Newfoundland, and Prince Edward Island, it's even farther, by another four or five hours. It's a big deal [to go to the temple] and very expensive for the people here. [The new temple] will be less than five hours away."

Approximately seven hundred Church members in Maritime Canada spent their Thanksgiving Day on October 12, 1998, participating in the groundbreaking ceremony. Many drove seven hours to attend. James Bailey, branch president in the New Glasgow District, said, "I never thought it would happen in my day. I have driven this road many times, but today was a different feeling."

Unfortunately, heavy rains forced the groundbreaking ceremony indoors to the nearby Dartmouth Stake Center.

SITE
2 acres

GROUNDBREAKING
October 12, 1998, by Jay E. Jensen

DEDICATION
November 14, 1999, by
Gordon B. Hinckley

EXTERIOR
White Bethel granite

TOTAL FLOOR AREA
10,700 square feet

DIMENSIONS
149 feet by 77 feet

HIDDEN IMAGE
The iconic Peggys Point Lighthouse
is seen with its beam of light
leading to the temple.

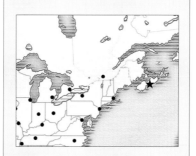

Later, Elder Jay E. Jensen, a member of the Seventy and president of the North America Northeast Area, led a small group of local leaders outdoors to turn over shovelfuls of mud. "Thanksgiving Day in Canada, and what a happy day it is," said Elder Jensen. "Whoever thought that during your mortal life we would really be here doing this? If everything goes well, we could be back here in about a year."

The open house for the Halifax Nova Scotia Temple lasted four days and brought heightened emotion and increased interest in the Church for many of the approximately eight thousand people who attended. Church officials were pleased with the attendance and with the responses of those who came. One elderly man, after completing a tour, tapped the shoulder of a member and said, "I'm so emotional I can hardly speak. God bless you and your people. Please tell your leaders that." And after the last session of the open house, one newspaper reporter said there was no way he could write what he felt in the small space he would be given for the article.

The dedications of the Halifax Nova Scotia Temple and the Regina Saskatchewan Temple on November 14, 1999 marked the first time in Church history that two temples were dedicated on the same day. They are the sixty-fourth and sixty-fifth operating temples, respectively.

The Halifax Nova Scotia Temple was dedicated in three sessions by President Gordon B. Hinckley. Richard Moses, second counselor in the Dartmouth Nova Scotia Stake presidency and chairman of the local temple committee, said, "It is impossible—there are not words—to adequately express our gratitude for this temple." Shortly after its dedication, an enclosed portico was added to the temple's entrance. This functional space allows members to change their clothes and prepare themselves before entering the House of the Lord.

Through the years following the temple's dedication, members have consistently demonstrated their love for temple work. Despite their smaller membership and vast traveling distances, attendance and genealogy work has remained high. This temple is among the few temples that perform ordinances for names almost exclusively submitted by members in the temple district.

Regina Saskatchewan Temple

In the heart of the Canadian prairie, Regina, the provincial capital of Saskatchewan, is home to the legendary Royal Canadian Mounted Police, or "Mounties." It is also the site of the Regina Saskatchewan Temple, which is built in Wascana View, a suburb of Regina. In addition to the temple itself, the site provides ample parking and room for a future meetinghouse to be built. The temple district covers a 252,000-square-mile area in central Canada that has a population of one million people, about forty-five hundred of whom are Church members.

Part of a residential subdivision, the temple is surrounded by beautiful homes with well-maintained and landscaped yards. Near the temple is a community park that contributes to the neighborhood's

peaceful and comfortable atmosphere. Although the property itself is quite flat, the landscape architect ingeniously created a picturesque and varied setting to bring visual interest to the land. Part of the site east of the temple was hollowed out and then landscaped with trees and vegetation. Temple visitors may enjoy the serenity of the area while resting on benches or walking along its paths.

As president of the North America Central Area, Elder Hugh W. Pinnock of the Seventy presided over the groundbreaking service on November 14, 1998. Nearly five hundred people gathered in a meetinghouse nearby for a ninety-minute service before attending the ceremony outside in the cold. In his talk before the ceremony, Elder Pinnock urged the

65

Saints to make the temple the center of their personal lives. He reminded them that it is in the temple where covenants are made and ordinances performed "so we may be with our Heavenly parents . . . and also with our earthly mother and father." He said he had recently talked with a mother who lost a little girl through disease. "Through tear-stained eyes, the mother communicated profound grief but looked to me and said, 'I could not endure the pain of not being able to talk and laugh and tease my daughter except I know we will be together again. We are sealed together!'"

The two-toned granite that adorns the temple's exterior comes from a quarry in Quebec. When it was being placed on the temple, many young people were given a unique opportunity they will never forget. After a stake youth conference, the young men and women gathered at the park across from the temple. Having received permission from Church officials and the temple contractor, they signed their names with the date on the back of the granite pieces, which were then placed on the temple. Construction missionary Sterling L. Burch assisted in the process and told them exactly where each stone was going to be placed. They walked away knowing that their names were going to become a permanent part of the temple.

Elder Burch initiated another project involving the young men and women. Stake leaders offered them the opportunity to record their testimonies and commitments to temple worthiness on paper. These treasured documents were then placed in a capsule crafted by Elder Burch. A young man and a young woman were then selected to help place the capsule in the temple's spire, directly beneath the statue of the angel Moroni. Elder Burch described the event:

"Right after the angel Moroni was placed into position, I took two of the youth up the scaffolding and I had them fasten the capsule right under his [Moroni's] feet. I could have easily done this, but I thought, 'No, this is for the youth; I want them to do it.' All of the stone was not yet attached to the spire, so all

SITE
1 acre

GROUNDBREAKING
November 14, 1998, by
Hugh W. Pinnock

DEDICATION
November 14, 1999, by
Boyd K. Packer

EXTERIOR
Light gray granite

TOTAL FLOOR AREA
10,700 square feet

DIMENSIONS
149 feet by 77 feet

HIDDEN IMAGE
The Savior is kneeling and
looking up at the temple.

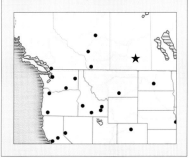

of the youth could look up and see where the box containing their precious feelings, goals, and commitments was permanently placed." This choice experience serves as a constant reminder for the youth to be true to their testimonies and commitments that are now a part of the temple.

During the week between the conclusion of the open house and the official dedication, crews worked around the clock to finish the temple exterior and landscape the grounds. A truckers' strike had delayed the delivery of necessary materials until a few days before the deadline. Granite facing was being set twenty-four hours a day—right up to the night before the dedication. A group of more than one hundred Latter-day Saints—missionaries, youth, and adults—laid eighteen thousand square feet of sod, planted trees, and raised the granite sign in front of the temple just hours before the temple dedication. Two thousand members attended the three dedicatory sessions.

Dedication plans originally called for the Regina Saskatchewan Temple to be dedicated one day after the dedication of the Halifax Nova Scotia Temple. But plans were altered at the last minute when technicians were unable to repair the airplane that was to carry President Gordon B. Hinckley from Salt Lake City to Nova Scotia, causing a one-day delay to the dedication in Halifax. At that point, Church officials decided to hold both on the same day: President Hinckley would dedicate the Halifax Nova Scotia Temple, and President Boyd K. Packer, acting President of the Quorum of the Twelve Apostles, would dedicate the Regina Saskatchewan Temple.

"The only last-minute change we're having to make is getting used to not having President Hinckley here," said Lorin J. Mendenhall, president of the Regina Saskatchewan Temple. "We're looking forward to being here with President Packer. We're definitely excited about the temple being here. We're thrilled to share this day with Halifax. It's kind of a historic event in that respect, having two temples dedicated on the same day."

Billings Montana Temple

Late in August 1996, the First Presidency announced plans to build a temple in Montana's largest city, Billings. The ninth western state to become home to a house of the Lord, Montana is known for its breathtaking scenery and wide-open spaces. Before this temple was completed, Latter-day Saints in the area performed sacred ordinances at the Idaho Falls Idaho and Cardston Alberta Temples.

President Gordon B. Hinckley arrived in Billings to select a temple site without previously making his intentions known. Edward E. Jorden, president of the Billings Montana Stake, accompanied President Hinckley but did not know the purpose of his visit until President Hinckley asked if a new temple should be built in Billings rather than Wyoming. "We then proceeded to prospective sites," said President Jorden. "I may have been a little overzealous as I told him how beautiful this spot would be in the evenings and mornings with the sun and shadows on the Rims [nearby cliffs]. . . . The afternoon was the most memorable and awesome of my life."

Once President Hinckley had chosen the site, the next phase was to secure local approvals for building the temple in that location. To gain access to such services as water, sewer, electric power, and natural gas, it was necessary to ask the Billings city council to make the proposed temple site part of the city. The Billings city council denied the request, surprising the thousand people attending the council meeting.

Church members quickly organized a petition

66

drive to persuade the city council to reconsider the annexation request. Sister Susan Smith, who was given responsibility to organize the drive, recorded: "I sought direction by means of prayer in the work that was about to begin, and the Spirit testified to me how this work was to be done. . . . More than four hundred members of the Church—men, women, teenagers and children—labored with love as they gathered signatures of support from the community. The drive was successful beyond merely gathering thousands of signatures in that it gave Church members a chance to talk with hundreds of people about concerns related to the temple and misconceptions about the LDS Church. . . .

"As more petition signatures came in, cheers of joy erupted and tears were shed. Church members had gathered nearly ten thousand signatures over the weekend. Exhausted, many labored all night and into the morning to complete the recording and get copies of the signatures run off to present to each member of the City Council the next day. We made a presentation and explained our labor of love to many of the City Council members. Some accepted with appreciation and others with doubt, but in our hearts we knew we had accomplished the wishes of our Heavenly Father."

The final approval of the special application ended a fourteen-month process that featured late-night public hearings attended by hundreds of citizens, fierce public debate, and mounds of studies. The approval was accompanied by lighting restrictions and the stipulation that the Church not build a visitors' center or MTC on the temple site. At last, with approvals in place, the groundbreaking was scheduled for March 28, 1998. Despite a spring snowstorm, forty-eight hundred Church members from twelve states and two Canadian provinces attended the event. The day started off cool and cloudy, and by noon, snowflakes had started to fall. Although some tents had been assembled, the seven-hundred-member youth choir and all spectators remained exposed to the elements. Workers even turned metal music stands upside down to push away the snow and ice.

One faithful sister in her sixties had arrived two hours early to ensure she would have a front-row seat. Huddled under a blanket and umbrella, she sat on a lawn chair for more than four hours during the snowstorm. When she moved indoors at the conclusion of the ceremony, the perfectly dry ground

SITE
10 acres

GROUNDBREAKING
March 30, 1998

DEDICATION
November 20–21, 1999, by
Gordon B. Hinckley

EXTERIOR
Wyoming white dolomite
precast concrete

TOTAL FLOOR AREA
33,800 square feet

DIMENSIONS
183 feet by 212 feet

HIDDEN IMAGE
The Good Shepherd is located in
the famous Rimrocks. The Savior is
accompanied by His flock of sheep
in the rims and among the clouds.

beneath her chair was ringed by snow five inches deep.

Later, Church members learned that a large anti-Mormon organization from northern Wyoming had planned to disrupt the groundbreaking ceremonies. Not one protester was able to reach the temple site because of the hazardous weather and traveling conditions.

Construction began soon after the groundbreaking ceremony. The temple site is northeast of the city, near the sandstone cliffs that form a landmark border three to five hundred feet high. Known as the Rimrocks, these cliffs provide a dramatic setting for morning and evening shadows. Temple project leaders located the temple near the base of the cliffs, preserving the Rimrocks' integrity and natural beauty. Throughout the ten-acre temple site are stone-like retaining walls and fence columns made of formed concrete painted to match the Rimrocks. On some Saturdays, as many as three hundred volunteers painted the stones by hand. Many of the Primary children who participated will always remember which stone was "their" stone.

The Rimrocks are not the only Montana beauty the temple reflects. To amplify the sunsets at the Rimrocks, glassmaker Mark Walton and his wife, Susan, designed the windows in the celestial room with cream and amber tones, geometric patterns, and beveled glass. As the sun sets in the west, the sunlight refracts, providing a splendid display of color and brightness. The temple interior also reflects the Montana landscape. The Montana state flower, the bitterroot, is skillfully detailed in the carpet and gold leafing in one of the sealing rooms. The temple includes three sealing rooms, two endowment rooms, a cafeteria, and clothing rental facilities.

Despite all the signatures collected early in the approval process, the temple still faced opposition at the open house. During the open house, one of the temple's major opponents visited the temple, hoping to cause problems. His wife later said that when he entered the temple's lobby and looked through the skylight to the statue of the angel Moroni on the steeple, he was so overwhelmed that he decided not to say one word throughout the tour. When he exited the temple, he said that he had never felt like that before.

At the dedication of the Billings Montana Temple, the Saints' immense gratitude for a temple in their midst matched the magnificence of the big sky country of Montana.

Edmonton Alberta Temple

Edmonton, the capital of Alberta, is on the North Saskatchewan River in the central part of the Canadian province. Edmonton is also the largest metropolitan area in the province and is known as the "Gateway to the North." Reflecting that distinction, the Edmonton Alberta Temple's geographic temple district extends to the North Pole.

Marjorie H. Scully of the Edmonton Bonnie Doon Stake shared her feelings on having a temple in Edmonton: "During President Hinckley's Canadian tour . . . , he talked to us about the temple, but he didn't announce that we were going to get a temple here. Then the official word came. It was so wonderful to know that Edmonton was going to get a temple. We had waited and hoped and prayed for years for this,

and now the dream had come true. Having a temple twenty-two minutes away will change things dramatically.

"To go to the [Cardston] Alberta Temple has been a six-hour trip," Sister Scully continued. "Some of us have to arrange for time off from work as well as for babysitters. Most people don't drive there and back in one day, so sleeping arrangements have to be made as well. Now I can go at least once a month and hopefully more often and increase the number of family names that I can do proxy work for in the temple. What a joy that will be! My heart fills with such love for my Father in Heaven and my Savior Jesus Christ for sending this great blessing to us at this time."

Elder Yoshihiko Kikuchi of the Seventy presided

67

over the groundbreaking for the Edmonton Alberta Temple on February 27, 1999, in a crowded stake center. The proceedings were carried by audio feed to nineteen other locations in northern Alberta and part of British Columbia. "This is a monument of your faith, and Heavenly Father truly has answered your prayers," declared Elder Kikuchi regarding the temple, constructed to the west of the Edmonton Alberta Riverbend Stake Center. An estimated thirty-five hundred people witnessed the service.

After the groundbreaking, construction began. Temple construction missionaries Leo C. Udy and Rhea Udy were two of the workers. "Achieving the highest quality of work was not difficult because the workers wanted to do it right the first time," Elder Udy said. "They understood that if they didn't do it right the first time, they would be back doing it over again. They read the specifications required and did it right the first time."

Elder Udy also remembered a time when the contractors were gathered to discuss an important decision. "We were discussing a few ways that we could solve a problem. One option was to slip by and do it poorly, and the other way would have been the right way. To do it the right way would take a little longer and cost a little more money. Those gathered could not quite come to a decision, so I took my ring off and said, 'See that? What is on there? It says 'CTR,' and that means 'Choose the Right. . . .' ' That was the end of the discussion, and we did it the right way."

The native granite exterior of the temple is supported by laminated lumber, one of the few materials able to support the heavy stone facing. Although the sheer weight of the stone would seem to guarantee the stability of the temple, Robert Bennett, the architect, said he was required to design the building two earthquake-zone categories higher than the usual Edmonton code.

Yet the heavy clay soil of the area would not support the weight of the temple. To support the building and provide enhanced earthquake protection, holes forty-five feet deep and twenty-four inches wide were lined with steel cages and filled with non-corroding concrete. The actual temple floor was built six feet above the concrete foundation, leaving a crawl space

SITE
1 acre

GROUNDBREAKING
February 27, 1999, by
Yoshihiko Kikuchi

DEDICATION
December 11–12, 1999, by
Gordon B. Hinckley

EXTERIOR
Light gray granite veneer
quarried in Quebec

TOTAL FLOOR AREA
10,700 square feet

DIMENSIONS
149 feet by 77 feet

HIDDEN IMAGE
Four oxen are placed beneath the
temple exactly where the actual
baptismal font is positioned.

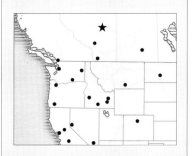

under the temple floor so that the building rests above the ground.

The massive stonework is offset by the use of wild rose patterns throughout the architecture and landscaping. This prominent symbol of Alberta adds a finishing touch to the immovable structure.

As the completion date approached, the president of the Red Deer Stake encouraged members of the stake to prepare for the temple by gathering names to be submitted for ordinance work. They set the goal of preparing seventy-five hundred names by the time of the temple's dedication. When that time arrived, they had prepared information for forty thousand individuals, more than five times their goal.

The temple was dedicated by President Gordon B. Hinckley in seven sessions held December 11 and 12, 1999. "Let Thy providence be felt in this great nation of Canada, that it shall continue to be a land where Thy sons and daughters enjoy the precious boon of freedom of assembly and worship," President Hinckley said in the dedicatory prayer.

After the dedication, when the temple was open to the Saints for ordinances, Elder and Sister Udy watched the members walking in. As they reminisced about their tireless service rendered while building the temple, they thought, "Our work is over here, but their work is just beginning."

After years of faithful use by Church members, it became evident that the temple's entrance would service patrons better if it were expanded. In 2011, the temple was closed for three months to allow for an enclosed portico to be built. Once the portico was complete, the temple reopened, even though the outside stairs and sidewalks were still under construction. For several wintery months, members walked through the construction using a specially marked pathway. During the construction, other improvements were made, including new artwork and replaced tile in the baptistry. In July 2014, the interior received a new look when all of the furniture was replaced with the furnishings from the Montreal Canada Temple. Many of the Edmonton Temple furnishings were then sent to provide the Bismarck North Dakota Temple with a refreshed interior.

Raleigh North Carolina Temple

On November 13, 1998, at a regional conference in Greenville, North Carolina, President Gordon B. Hinckley announced there would be a small temple constructed in the Raleigh area. Church leaders only examined sites that were adjacent to existing or planned meetinghouses. A twelve-acre site in the town of Apex was selected, and city officials approved the project without delay.

As with other temples, volunteerism was a hallmark of construction on the Raleigh North Carolina Temple and its grounds. For example, early in the morning of January 23, 1999, about twelve hundred young Latter-day Saints arrived at the building site to clear it of underbrush and small trees and render it suitable for the groundbreaking ceremony. The young men

and young women worked in a cooperative effort and enjoyed serving the Lord in this way. Although all the weather services predicted a 100 percent chance of heavy rain throughout the day, not until five minutes after the last group prepared to leave did the rain begin to fall.

Another weather miracle occurred near the end of May, when workers were preparing to pour the concrete floor slabs of the temple. When the air temperature is too high, concrete can dry too rapidly, causing it to cure improperly and then crack. Although everything was ready for the pouring and the cement trucks were coming, the weather was still much too hot. Temple construction missionary Alaire Johnson, who kept a history of the project, recorded, "Suddenly, out of a

68

clear blue sky came a dark cloud that hovered over the area, bringing the temperature down about ten degrees." Sister Johnson said that the workers proceeded, and the concrete set up perfectly.

A highlight of the temple construction was placing the statue of the angel Moroni atop the temple. On September 1, 1999, nearly fifteen hundred spectators gathered to witness the placement of both the tower and the statue. Two TV stations were represented, along with reporters from multiple newspapers. The crate was opened in front of the temple so all could see the golden statue inside. A three-year-old girl was featured on the evening news singing "I Love to See the Temple."

Before the statue was lifted from ground level, Agnes D. Creech, who was blind, was escorted to the box holding the statue of Moroni. Wearing soft cotton gloves, Sister Creech slowly reached out, tenderly caressing the form and the trumpet he was holding. She would never see this marvelous golden statue, but she would always remember how large and how smooth it felt.

The Raleigh North Carolina Temple committee assigned a number of women in the local stakes to make altar cloths for the temple's four altars and provided them with specific guidelines for the size, thread, pattern, and durability of the cloths.

Sister Chloe Hodge commented: "I spend twelve to fourteen hours a day on them. It's a tremendous amount of work. It's a great labor of love. It's such an honor and privilege to be able to make something to be used for the Lord's house." Each cloth required about two hundred hours of work. Sister Hodge took four weeks to make one of the large altar cloths.

Primary children in the Raleigh area used the Articles of Faith to contribute financially to the temple. Family members pledged a dime for every one of the thirteen Articles of Faith their children could learn. The children were honored during a special ceremony held in front of the nearly completed temple. They had exceeded their goal of two hundred dollars, raising two hundred and fifty dollars to help pay for stained-glass windows. As a result of their efforts, the names of the Primary children and the youth in the temple district were recorded and sealed in the temple's cornerstone.

SITE
12 acres

GROUNDBREAKING
February 6, 1999, by Loren C. Dunn

DEDICATION
December 18–19, 1999, by
Gordon B. Hinckley

EXTERIOR
Imperial Danby white marble quarried
in Vermont with art glass windows

TOTAL FLOOR AREA
10,700 square feet

DIMENSIONS
149 feet by 77 feet

HIDDEN IMAGE
The distinctive spiral design of the
Cape Hatteras Lighthouse can be seen
among the trees on the left. The Savior
is drawn to the right of the temple.

When Gary Stansbury was confirmed a member of the Church, Bishop Bruce Nay of the Apex Ward commented, "Most people come to the temple by way of the gospel; Gary came to the gospel by way of the temple."

Brother Stansbury, whose expertise is in building such huge projects as $65-million shopping complexes, had planned to spend a year doing that kind of project in St. Louis, Missouri. He was disappointed when the project was delayed and he was asked to build the $5-million temple instead.

"This wasn't what I did. I hadn't built a $5-million job in years," he said. "But I knew I couldn't leave. I didn't want to leave. I do not think it's chance that I'm here," Brother Stansbury said, adding that while studying the Book of Mormon, he had gained a testimony of "building only that which is worth building. I'm doing that. That's what I want to do."

He concluded, "I needed to be here. And thinking back now, it almost seems that I've kind of been led to learn for forty-four years, and now, [joining the Church] is what I'm supposed to do." Brother Stansbury was taught the gospel and baptized by temple missionary Elder Gaylen Johnson. A year after his baptism, Brother Stansbury and his wife were sealed in the temple he had helped build.

In September 1999, category-four Hurricane Floyd raced toward North Carolina, triggering the third largest evacuation in U.S. history. Anticipating the storm, missionaries arrived at the temple construction site to tie everything down and get rid of any rubbish that might become airborne and cause damage. In the words of Elder Johnson, "The Lord was watching over His Temple." Damage in the area was minimal, and only puddles of water surrounded the temple site.

On December 18, 1999, hundreds of faithful members braved the bitter cold morning to participate in the dedicatory services presided over by President Gordon B. Hinckley.

In 2001, the temple received an award from the city of Apex, "Best Appearance—Non-residential Category." A sign acknowledging the designation was posted on the temple grounds, and city officials presented a certificate to the temple presidency.

St. Paul Minnesota Temple

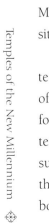

St. Paul is Minnesota's capital city and the state's second larg est city after neighboring Minneapolis; together the two cities form the Twin Cities metropolitan area. The temple itself is actually in Oakdale City, an eastern suburb of St. Paul on the Mississippi River. The eighteen acres that include the temple site are heavily wooded and have several marshy areas.

The Oakdale City administration gave the proposed temple a warm reception, and the St. Paul community offered remarkable support to the Church in its efforts to build it. Longtime neighbors of the stake center voluntarily attended town meetings to speak in support of the temple proposal. They commented that Latter-day Saints are wonderful to have as neighbors. Through the years, the stake center had been

so well maintained that the community welcomed the idea of another building of a similar nature. In fact, around the time of the temple's announcement, the chapel won an award from the city of Oakdale as the city's most attractive building. Not a single known negative comment originated from the neighbors or community during the construction of the temple.

When Elder Thomas A. Holt, Area Seventy and long-time resident of the area, was assigned to find a site for Minnesota's second stake center, he "looked at several sites and felt nothing" until he visited "this beautiful site heavily wooded with oak trees." The Spirit bore witness to him, and he encouraged the Church to purchase additional property beyond what was needed for the stake center. He said "that . . . was to

69

be the place for the St. Paul Stake Center—and now the site for our Minnesota temple. The Lord chose this place." The temple is built on the highest portion of the ground purchased by Elder Holt.

The dedication of the stake center was presided over by Elder Jacob de Jager of the Seventy. During his comments before the dedicatory prayer, he referred to a temple being built nearby. Years later, when the St. Paul Minnesota Temple was announced, members remembered Elder de Jager's talk and felt that his comments had been inspired.

For decades, Minnesota Saints had had to drive for two days to Salt Lake City, Utah, to attend the temple. They were subsequently assigned to the Chicago Illinois Temple district, a seven- to fourteen-hour drive for most. It was even farther for Church members living in the Canadian part of the temple district. According to Mel Hiscock, president of the Ft. Francis Ontario District, Canadian Latter-day Saints paid an average of two hundred dollars in Canadian funds to travel two days each way to the Chicago Illinois Temple. President Hiscock said, "That $200 is a tremendous amount of money to most of these people, who have very limited incomes." He said when they get to the temple they serve nonstop, because they know it will be a long time before they can return. These Church members are now in the St. Paul Minnesota Temple district, and the distance is half what it was to Chicago.

One of these faithful members, who'd had to travel to Cardston, Alberta, Canada, to receive his endowment, promised himself he would create a painting to decorate a temple someday. When the St. Paul Minnesota Temple was announced, the Temple Department chose to display in the temple two paintings from this artist, Wayne M. Howell. The two paintings, *Temperance River* and *Silver Creek,* reflect the beauty of northeastern Minnesota. Brother Howell said the sites in his paintings have a peaceful, temple-like feeling for him. In fact, he said, he felt he was in a temple-like setting while he was painting *Temperance River:*

"I needed a sunny morning [to paint the river], so I prayed for one. At 5:30 a.m. I was in a clearing noticing a long slender opening in a very cloudy sky. I said another prayer, loaded

SITE
7.5-acre site (including adjacent meetinghouse)

GROUNDBREAKING
September 26, 1998, by Hugh W. Pinnock

DEDICATION
January 9, 2000, by Gordon B. Hinckley

EXTERIOR
Light gray granite veneer

TOTAL FLOOR AREA
10,700 square feet

DIMENSIONS
149 feet by 77 feet

HIDDEN IMAGE
Among the trees and foliage is a full-length image of the Savior in the motion of inviting all to receive the blessings of the temple.

the painting and equipment in the car and made the forty-five-minute journey to the Temperance River. As I hiked up the half mile to the top of the cascades, the sun shone brightly against the trees on the far side of the river, exactly the effect I wanted. For the rest of the morning the area was surrounded by clouds, but where I painted it remained sunny until I finished at 11:30 a.m. When I arrived at the car, clouds had closed over me, and it had started raining. During the time I painted I had no visitors or disturbances on a Wednesday morning in a state park. The prayers, the sun, and the serenity gave me a peace that I have often felt in the temple."

Members of the St. Paul Minnesota Temple committee were key figures in developing an advertising campaign for the Church that had an enormous effect on other temples that followed. They refined a newspaper insert that was first used in conjunction with the Billings Montana Temple. The goal of the insert was to increase public awareness of the new temple, provide local history of the Church, encourage attendance at the temple open house, and inform others about basic beliefs of the Church. The sixteen-page insert was distributed to nearly 500,000 homes. This standardized format has since become an important tool for the Church in increasing the world's awareness of the Lord's temples that are beginning to dot the earth.

The temple's open house dates were originally scheduled to take place before the Thanksgiving holiday. Delays caused the open house and dedication to be postponed into December and January. Considering the time of year and the frigid weather in Minnesota, Church leaders created a weather shelter tunnel from the adjacent stake center to the temple. Temple Committee President Richard P. Halverson described the efforts: "We felt it was necessary to heat the entire cornerstone area. We did not want to risk having the prophet exposed to a January day in Minnesota. We also arranged to glass in the entire area."

The St. Paul Minnesota Temple has the distinction of being the last temple to have an open house in 1999 and the first to be dedicated in the year 2000. Thus, the panel on the cornerstone of the temple is engraved "Erected 1999–Dedicated January 2000."

Kona Hawaii Temple

The temple in Kailua-Kona is on Hawaii, the state's largest and southernmost island. White marble walls and orderly rows of royal palms contrast with the island's green hills. The temple itself rests on a hillside flanked by Mount Hualalai to the east and the Pacific Ocean to the west.

As president of the Kona Hawaii Stake, Philip A. Harris prayed to know what the Lord would have him accomplish during his service. He recounted: "One night I dreamt there was to be a temple in Kona. I woke and told my wife. . . . I took my dream to be a direction for me as a stake president that I was to [help] my people to become temple worthy and temple ready."

Knowing the difficult logistics of building a large temple in Kona, President Harris thought that the dream simply meant the people were to be spiritually prepared. Then President Gordon B. Hinckley announced that a number of small temples would be built. And soon, a temple was announced for Kona. "I knew then that in my lifetime I would see the temple here that I had seen in my dream." In 2014, President Harris began serving as temple president of the same temple he had seen in his dream.

Despite the announcement that a temple would be built in Kona, many involved in the process questioned whether the Kailua village planning and design committee would give the Church permission to build the temple. To help the cause, Kona Hawaii Temple architect John Pharis asked President Harris if he could arrange a showing of community

70

142

support. Nearly three hundred faithful Saints and friends showed up at the planning hearing, dressed in their Sunday best. John Pharis described the event: "The place was bursting at the seams. The whole room filled. People were outside the windows looking in. You could barely walk through—the corridor was full, and the sidewalks were packed full of people." It really sent a powerful message of support. The committee members were astonished at the support the proposal had generated. When word got out that the proposal had passed, everyone in attendance cheered.

The temple's structural quality exceeds all local building codes and requirements. Its solid frame goes extra deep into the ground and rests upon solid volcanic bedrock. Since the igneous rock is rough and porous, the poured concrete enters the natural fissures forming a foundation that locks into the rock system. "The temple is a fortress," said architect Pharis.

The temple's structural integrity was tested on October 15, 2006, when a magnitude 6.7 earthquake struck only ten miles northwest of Kona. The massive quake and several aftershocks were felt throughout the islands, causing waves of power outages. At the temple, the only reported damage was to a swaying chandelier.

To protect against floods, the temple was placed just outside the FEMA-designated 500-year flood zone. Additionally, a large floodwall was built behind the temple on the mountainside. Should there ever be excessive flooding from the mountain, water and debris would hit the wall and be diverted around the temple.

Throughout the construction process, many people had incredible spiritual experiences. For example, Myron Lindsey was repositioning a mobile crane one day when the weight it was carrying began to topple the machine. Just when it would have tipped over and possibly killed or injured workers below the crane, it righted itself and became stable. Others felt the influence and presence of those who had gone before. While Mark Kealamakia was working in the baptismal font area, he felt the strong presence of some "very old people." Although he didn't actually see them, he felt they may have been the early settlers of the island, who had never had the fulness of the gospel and wanted their temple ordinances performed for them. These experiences and others made the Hawaiian Saints

SITE
7.02 acres (including
adjacent meetinghouse)

GROUNDBREAKING
March 13, 1999, by John B. Dickson

DEDICATION
January 23–24, 2000, by
Gordon B. Hinckley

EXTERIOR
White marble veneer

TOTAL FLOOR AREA
10,700 square feet

DIMENSIONS
149 feet by 77 feet

HIDDEN IMAGE
A full-length image of the Savior
is included among the trees and
landscaping to the right of the temple.

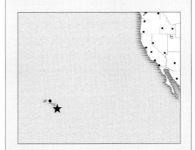

eager to attend the temple and return regularly after its completion.

The fasting and prayers of the Saints helped miracles to happen during the construction of the temple. Construction workers feared that the crane that was available to lift the nine-thousand-pound spire into place was not going to work. They asked all involved to fast and pray that all would go well. As the spire was finally being raised, the crane started to bow. The spire cleared the roof by only a foot, but it was high enough to position the spire and relieve the crane of its burden. After the task was safely completed, the men involved gathered and offered a prayer of gratitude for their Heavenly Father's help.

The beauty of the temple is enhanced by the sugarcane leaf decorations on benches outside and inside the temple. Architect John Pharis was inspired to create these patterns as he was reading the parable of the wheat and the tares. Because wheat is not a native island plant, he felt it would look out of place in the temple. Then he thought of sugarcane and its similarities to wheat, and he incorporated that island plant into his design.

To add vibrant color to the grounds for the temple dedication, hundreds of beautiful red poinsettias, still in their pots, were positioned in front of the temple. President Gordon B. Hinckley dedicated the Kona Hawaii Temple on January 23, 2000. Chad Hawkins was privileged to be in attendance and described the experience: "I will never forget participating in the dedication of the Kona Temple; it was one of the most spiritual experiences of my life. Following the dedicatory prayer and Hosanna Shout, the members in the temple stood and joined in singing the sacred hymn 'The Spirit of God.' I have never heard the hymn sung with such emotion and power. I am certain the temple walls must have been shaking."

After the dedicatory services, more than a thousand Saints gathered in front of the temple to wait for President Hinckley to leave the building. As he made his way from the temple, they began singing reverently, "We Thank Thee, O God, for a Prophet." As the prophet waved before getting into his car, the multitude, as if on cue, began singing the traditional farewell song "Aloha Oe." An unforgettable spirit of gratitude and love embraced all who were there.

Ciudad Juárez Mexico Temple

The Ciudad Juárez Mexico Temple, whose exterior is faced with white marble quarried in Mexico, is a blessing to Latter-day Saints on both sides of the United States–Mexico border. This temple is one of the few smaller temples not built next to a chapel. It is located behind a high school and a public park near downtown Juárez. Ciudad Juárez, Mexico's fourth largest city, is located less than thirty miles from El Paso, Texas, across the Rio Grande River. The temple was built in Ciudad Juárez rather than El Paso because it is relatively easy for citizens of the United States to travel from El Paso into Mexico, but it is very difficult for most Mexican citizens to travel into the United States.

Members living in the Ciudad Juárez stakes had previously been part of the Mexico City Mexico Temple district. When it was announced in May 1998 that Ciudad Juárez would have a temple of its own, many members thought the news too good to be true, believing the announcement to be a publication error. The members thought Ciudad Juárez had been confused with Colonia Juárez, a small Latter-day Saint community located approximately two hundred miles to the south. Leticia Guitiérrez de Orozco, the Ciudad Juárez Temple historian, described her reaction: "At first it was difficult to accept the fact that there was no mistake in the announcement because we never believed a temple here would be possible." She said that when the members were assured that the temple was going to be built in Ciudad Juárez, everyone was overcome with emotion and began to rejoice. Prior

71

to being a temple site, the property was the home of the cherished Church-owned Benito Juarez Primary School. As public schools became generally available, the school was no longer needed. In its place is the glistening white temple. Considering the site's legacy of education, some refer to the temple as "a spiritual university."

From the beginning of the temple construction process, it was noted that the temple would bring together members of two nations and cultures. Presiding at the temple's groundbreaking services on January 9, 1999, Elder Eran A. Call commented, "In this temple district, we have members on both sides of the border. This will bring a uniting and joining of members of both communities. This temple is a great thing for members [in Mexico and] in the United States." The open house, he said, was attended by about 25,438 people. Among those who attended was a business professional who commented, "I don't need to die to see heaven. This is heaven." Another visitor said, "If all the people in this city could come here and feel what I feel, Cuidad Juárez would be a much better city." Approximately 647 referrals were received during the open house.

As the dedication of the temple approached, members of both communities helped to assure that any brothers and sisters in need had temple clothing. Members donated extra or new clothing or loaned their own as needed.

Many of the Mexican members made their own temple clothing. Groups of sisters from El Paso traveled across the border to help the Mexican sisters make temple slippers for themselves in Relief Society. While serving as temple construction missionaries, Elder Richard Skidmore and Sister Bon Adell Skidmore witnessed the loving cooperation of the cultures. "We feel like there has been more than a temple built here. We have

SITE
1.64 acres

GROUNDBREAKING
January 9, 1999, by Eran A. Call

DEDICATION
February 26–27, 2000, by
Gordon B. Hinckley

EXTERIOR
White marble veneer

TOTAL FLOOR AREA
10,700 square feet

DIMENSIONS
77 feet by 149 feet

HIDDEN IMAGE
Oxen are placed beneath the temple
exactly where the actual baptismal
font is positioned within the temple.

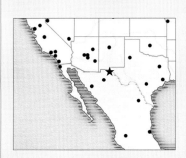

witnessed a mingling of cultures and a sharing of ideas."

As the temple neared completion, some construction supervisors were worried about getting the landscaping finished in the little time that remained. But Elder Skidmore said that he learned a lesson during the temple's construction: "The Lord knew that the temple needed to be finished, and he knew the efforts that everyone had made. A miracle occurred every day, one after another, to get things done on time."

Many Church members assisted in the completion of the landscaping. About forty members from Ciudad Juárez brought their farming equipment and spent an entire day helping with the landscaping. During the final weeks of construction, groups from both the United States and Mexico worked on the temple site daily, cleaning both the interior and exterior of the temple, washing windows, wiping down the exterior walls, and accomplishing last-minute tasks. It was calculated that members donated more than fifty thousand hours on the Ciudad Juárez Mexico Temple.

Following the completion of the temple, a few days before leaving Ciudad Juárez, Elder Skidmore reflected: "The crowning event is watching the members use their new temple. Just to know that now many places in the world have that opportunity to take part in temple blessings without having to go for a week at a time to attend the temple. People who have lived near temples all of their lives may have taken their nearby temples for granted. I think that the thing that impresses me more than anything else is how excited and eager [the members here] are to have a temple within an hour's drive. The humility and eagerness is very unique."

Hermosillo Sonora Mexico Temple

The Hermosillo Sonora Mexico Temple is located in an affluent area in the beautiful town of Pitic, an Indian word that means "where two rivers meet." The word *hermosillo* means "land of beauty." And all who visit the temple in Pitic agree that the temple enhances the land's beauty.

The Church has owned property in Hermosillo, including the temple site, since 1964. The land on which the temple now stands was once home to the Mexico Hermosillo Mission offices. Latter-day Saints living nearby were previously included in the Mexico City Mexico Temple district. For many, making the arduous excursion to Mexico City required up to thirty-six hours each way by car or bus and four hundred thousand pesos (about $400 U.S.) per person. Such

a sum was burdensome to come up with. Even with sufficient funds for the trip, it was often difficult for members to take a week off work to make the journey.

Families desiring to attend the temple together to be sealed had to make great sacrifices to reach that goal. Traveling eight hours north to the Mesa Arizona Temple was a somewhat shorter and less expensive trip, but the expense and difficulty of obtaining passports and visas still prevented many Mexican members from traveling to Arizona.

Moncelo Guerro, a faithful longtime member in Hermosillo shared his feelings about the new temple: "It was hard to raise money to travel to the temple," he said. "Whenever we had things to sell, we sold

72

them. Now, we are full of happiness to have a temple here, and we will be able to visit it."

When President Gordon B. Hinckley visited the city of Hermosillo in March 1998, he told the members that if they would continue to be faithful, they would have a temple in or near their city. During his visit to Hermosillo, President Hinckley personally chose where the temple was to be built. Upon his arrival he visited some of the property that the Church already owned, including the location where the temple now stands. After speaking at a regional conference, President Hinckley asked if he could visit the location again. Local Church leaders were later informed by mail that a temple would be built on this site.

The temple's announcement brought a time of rejoicing. Many of the local members had a great desire to assist in some way in the building of the new temple. Members in Hermosillo donated their time and talents to beautify the unattractive boulevard that ran along the front of the temple. Church architects drew up plans and members implemented the plans, creating beautiful and inviting gardens. Herardo Rivera, Hermosillo Sonora Mexico Temple historian, said, "We would work in the evenings and at night, whenever we could, and we left the spot very precious and beautiful. . . . It has given us great joy to know that we have participated in something that has to do with the temple." The attractive gardens provide a drastic contrast to the previous street conditions. This service beautified the temple's surroundings and was greatly appreciated by the city and the temple's neighbors.

As construction progressed, a brick mason and a carpenter began taking the missionary discussions. By the time the temple was dedicated, the two were converted and baptized. "One of these men said that during the construction, supervisors from Salt Lake would come and say, 'That is not good enough, you have to knock it down; you have to destroy it and return and do it again,'" said Hugo Montoya, a member of the Hermosillo Mexico Pitic Stake. "The men began to realize that they were involved with something very special. They began to be more careful and asked 'Why? What is it that we are building?' They began to ask more questions, then received the missionaries and were converted."

SITE
1.54 acres (including adjacent meetinghouse)

GROUNDBREAKING
December 5, 1998, by Eran A. Call

DEDICATION
February 27, 2000, by Gordon B. Hinckley

EXTERIOR
White marble veneer

TOTAL FLOOR AREA
10,769 square feet

DIMENSIONS
77 feet by 149 feet

HIDDEN IMAGE
The Good Shepherd is seen holding a lamb on the surface of the temple among the palm tree shadows.

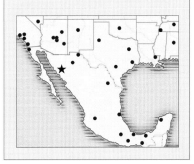

In July 1999, the spire of the Hermosillo Sonora Mexico Temple was carefully placed atop the newly constructed temple. One day, a number of construction workers were on the roof doing work when a severe and quickly moving thunderstorm approached. The workers were hurriedly trying to get off the roof when a lightning bolt hit the spire on the neighboring meetinghouse and burned it to a cinder. Some of the men were in such close proximity to the flash of lightning that they were forced off their feet and stunned by the powerful explosion of electric power. Herardo Rivera, the temple's historian, felt that the event was indeed remarkable: "The height of the temple's metal spire resting on the temple reached sixty-nine feet. The neighboring chapel's spire has a metal spire that reached only twenty feet." News of this wondrous event spread rapidly through the temple district. For generations, members will be able to view the graceful temple spire and remember that by divine intervention, lives were spared.

To accommodate the large numbers of people attending the temple's open house, touring hours were extended until 11:00 p.m. each day. On the final day of the open house, there were so many people wanting to attend that the temple opened early and did not close until midnight. "We noticed many who left the temple had tears on their faces because of the peace that they felt," said Brother Rivera. "We hope and we pray that these people will come closer to the Savior and listen to His words."

The dedication of the temple on February 27, 2000, was an unheralded milestone for President Hinckley. In his long pursuit of promoting temple building and temple worship, that dedicatory service marked the fiftieth temple he had dedicated or rededicated.

Among those who attended the dedication was ninety-two-year-old Purificación Segovia. Sister Segovia was converted and baptized by missionaries in 1961. As a faithful member, she had traveled to the Mesa Arizona Temple every year. To earn money for her annual temple trips, she would go house to house and wash laundry. Referring to the newly dedicated temple in Hermosillo, she said, "There is great joy in my heart today. Now I will be able to return to the temple as often as I want."

Albuquerque New Mexico Temple

Located on the northeast edge of Albuquerque, the Albuquerque New Mexico Temple serves Latter-day Saints in New Mexico, Arizona, and Colorado. From the temple grounds, visitors can see a panoramic view of the metro Albuquerque area, the Rio Grande Valley, and the Sandia Mountains. The temple was dedicated fifteen months after its groundbreaking, on March 5, 2000, becoming the first temple in the Land of Enchantment.

Typically, the first public announcement of a temple comes directly from the Church's First Presidency in a regional or general conference setting. But in an effort to build good public and civic relations, the Church announced plans for a temple in Albuquerque through the local media first and then to the general Church membership a day later.

On a Thursday evening before general conference in April 1997, bishops and stake presidents were informed of the temple announcement and asked not to spread word until 5:30 the following morning. The news media in the region had already been informed of the Church's intention to build a temple in Albuquerque. Media representatives were also asked not to release the information until the following morning. All media outlets honored the Church's request, breaking the Albuquerque temple news simultaneously with local TV and newspaper coverage.

Friday evening, Melchizedek Priesthood holders from three wards located near the temple site were

73

asked to knock on every door in the neighborhood to inform residents about the temple and answer questions. A packet was presented that explained the purpose of temples and how other temples have positively impacted surrounding communities. The neighbors appreciated the personal attention. This proactive approach created a supportive environment for the temple's construction.

The following day, during Saturday morning's session of general conference, President Hinckley informed the general Church membership that property had been obtained in Albuquerque for the building of a temple.

As construction on the temple began, thirty-six-year residents Tony and Ann Knudsen began their temple construction mission. In addition to overseeing the construction of the temple, the Knudsens traveled throughout the temple district speaking about the temple. Unfortunately, Sister Knudsen passed away during her time of service on the temple. Her influence, however, is still felt throughout the area. At the temple open house, a nonmember gave Brother Knudsen a card that praised his wife's service. "It told me how much she affected his life," Brother Knudsen said.

The temple's beautiful exterior is an indigenous color called desert rose. As the desert sun shines on the temple, the color seems to vary depending on the time of day. The upper portion of the temple is formed out of precast concrete. The concrete portions were manufactured in Utah and then trucked to the temple site in Albuquerque. It took more than one hundred trips to transport all of the panels to the site.

Each colored panel is eight inches thick. Exhaustive measures were taken to ensure that the colored panels matched each other perfectly. To take out subtle variations in the installed panels, a crew worked for four months sandblasting the panels and washing them down with acid. Elder Tony Knudsen described the work as "a painstaking process. They washed every one of those things with a sponge." The temple's base is covered with Texas pearl granite, which contrasts beautifully with the lighter-colored upper portion of the edifice.

The temple, the first in the Church of its unique design, brings together members in this area where three cultures meld—American Indian, Hispanic, and Anglo. Native American influence is immediately apparent within the temple. In the entryway are two Navajo tapestries on opposite walls;

SITE
8.5 acres

GROUNDBREAKING
June 20, 1998

DEDICATION
March 5, 2000, by
Gordon B. Hinckley

EXTERIOR
Desert rose pre-cast concrete
trimmed with Texas pearl granite

TOTAL FLOOR AREA
34,245 square feet

HIDDEN IMAGE
Among the distant mountains, the
Good Shepherd is cradling one
of His sheep. A wagon has been
drawn in the lower right corner.

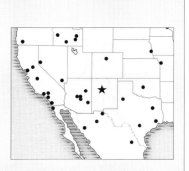

two more are found in the stairways. The longest tapestry measures three feet by ten feet. One of them displays thirty-five vibrant colors that are all derived from natural vegetable dyes. Commissioned by the Church, an elderly Navajo woman made the temple's tapestries by hand. It is such a laborious and complicated task that she was able to complete an average of only three inches per day.

Native American pottery is found throughout the temple. Original oil paintings depict the Rio Grande River and other landscapes typical of the region. The colors in the wallpaper and paint are earth tones.

The temple has ten groups of windows—six on the west, and two on the north and south. Each window has twelve panes. In the center of each pane is a different-colored, diamond-shaped crystal. The small windows in the groupings feature a simple Native American border. Within the windows in the celestial room are six stylized, handwoven baskets.

On the east side of the temple are ordinance rooms, a chapel, sealing rooms, and the celestial room. Contrasted by the darker cherry woods on the west side, all of the woodwork on the east side is painted white. The crown moldings, the decorative molding on the walls, and the doors are painted white.

The beauty of the celestial room is enhanced by its nine-foot-tall, 1,750-pound Austrian crystal chandelier. The ceiling is decorated with a beautifully detailed gold leaf design in 22- and 18-karat gold. It took four artists four days to complete the ceiling decorations.

To accommodate as many members as possible, the dedicatory services were transmitted by satellite to several meetinghouses. Knowing that during the dedicatory broadcast the chapels would be an appendage to the temple, many members prepared their buildings. H. Vern Payne, vice chairman of the local temple committee, stopped by a chapel where the sacred event would be transmitted. He found one hundred people there cleaning. "I have been around that chapel, and I have not seen it gleam and glisten like that since it was new," he said.

In dedicating the temple, President Hinckley prayed, "May [the temple] be a house of quiet contemplation concerning the eternal nature of life and of Thy divine plan for Thy sons and daughters as they walk the road of immortality and eternal life."

Oaxaca Mexico Temple

Most of the state of Oaxaca (pronounced "wah-HAH-kah"), located in southeastern Mexico, includes a mountain range that is home to some of the highest peaks and volcanoes in the country. Below these great mountains lie the Oaxaca Valley and the city of Oaxaca. The temple, widely appreciated as one of the most beautiful buildings in the city, is located on a major boulevard near a university in the Candiani sector of Oaxaca. With more than three million residents, this centuries-old city is known for its colonial architecture and religious traditions.

The archaeologically rich region—known as "land of the temples" because of its many ancient ruins—is situated on the relatively narrow strip of land near the southeastern end of Mexico. Just outside the city of Oaxaca are the ancient Monte Alban ruins; the state of Oaxaca was a center of ancient Mesoamerican cultures.

Because earthquakes are an ever-present possibility in this area of Mexico, the temple was built on pilings to make it as earthquake-proof as possible. Two major earthquakes tested the temple before its construction was even complete. The first, a 6.5-magnitude quake with its epicenter two hundred miles north of Oaxaca, occurred in July 1999 as the temple's footings were being put into place. The next earthquake was much closer and more severe. On September 30, as the temple's exterior walls were nearing completion, a three-minute, 7.6-magnitude earthquake struck.

The temple's project manager, Jay Erekson,

74

described the event: "As we were running out of the temple, the ground was moving up and down six to eight inches. I stood there and watched as the windows went out of square in both directions. The temple's tower was whipping back and forth four or five feet. As I watched it happen, I started to cry because I thought, 'Our temple is ruined.' I thought that we would have to tear it down and start over again."

More than one hundred buildings in the city were destroyed by the quake or damaged to the degree that they were later condemned. After the disaster, instruments were used to check every angle and line of the temple. "When we were through, we discovered that the temple had not moved a millimeter out of square or out of plumb. It was a miracle," said Brother Erekson.

After the building was completed and furnishings and paintings placed throughout, once-irreverent construction workers gained new respect for the temple. "The whole mood in the temple changed," noticed Brother Erekson. "Prior to that time, guys would yell down the hall to each other and run back and forth. But once the furnishings were in, and the workers noticed the paintings of the Savior on the wall, the mood of all the workers changed. Without any instigation, they began to walk, not run, and they would talk only in a whisper. It was something that came from inside of them."

More than ten thousand visitors toured the temple during its open house. One guest commented, "One feels a peace there, a tranquillity. It is heavenly!" A member said, with tears in his eyes, that he knew that "the Lord loves us very much, and having this temple in our city now makes it seem He has come closer to us." Following the open house, full-time missionaries began visiting a thousand people who had requested more information about the gospel.

Although the Oaxaca Mexico Temple has the same architectural design as other smaller temples, many of its decorative features are unique to the area and culture. Temple designers made special efforts to visit the area and become acquainted with its people, customs, and culture. Their research is reflected in the temple's unique Mexican decor. For example, two original oil paintings of local landscapes are prominently displayed

SITE
1.87 acres (including adjacent meetinghouse)

GROUNDBREAKING
March 13, 1999, by Carl B. Pratt

DEDICATION
March 11, 2000, by James E. Faust

EXTERIOR
White marble from Torreón, Mexico

TOTAL FLOOR AREA
10,700 square feet

DIMENSIONS
77 feet by 149 feet

HIDDEN IMAGE
An image of the Christus statue is located among the clouds.

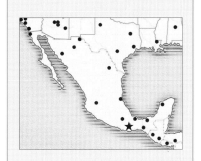

inside. One depicts a nearby lake of historical significance, and the other shows the northern mountains of Oaxaca. A colorful handwoven rug, made with natural dyes, is hung in the temple's foyer.

The Church's seventy-fourth operating temple—Mexico's fifth—was dedicated March 11, 2000, in four sessions by President James E. Faust, second counselor in the First Presidency. It was the first temple dedicated by President Faust. Speaking on behalf of local members, he said in the dedicatory prayer, "We have longed for the day when a house of the Lord would be built nearer to us that we might come here often and worship Thee in spirit and in truth, and receive those ordinances, for both the living and the dead, which lead to immortality and eternal life through the great Atonement wrought by our Redeemer, Thy Beloved Son."

Howard G. Schmidt, who was a temple sealer in the Colonia Juárez Chihuahua Mexico Temple before being called as the Oaxaca Mexico Temple president, said many have volunteered to work in the temple.

One longtime member who serves as a temple worker is Cleotilde Alvarez de Melchor, a widowed mother of thirteen children. She remembers when men, women, and children worked to build the first Oaxaca meetinghouse. Members sold their televisions, watches, jewelry, and food to pay for the building. From that sacrifice, she said, "We have had more blessings than I can enumerate," one of which is the new temple. The faithfulness of Oaxaca members has been characterized by their dedication to travel great distances to partake of temple blessings. Until the temple in Mexico City was built in 1983, Oaxaca Saints sacrificed greatly to travel more than 1,200 miles to the nearest temple in Mesa, Arizona. Ruth Sánchez Velasco, a member of the La Noria Ward, Oaxaca Mexico Atoyac Stake, said, "In 1966, when my husband and I went to the Mesa Arizona Temple to be sealed, I received my patriarchal blessing. In it I was told, 'You will see the day when you will not have to travel far to enter the house of the Lord, . . . and you will enter there many times.' When they built the temple in Mexico City, just five hours away, I thought the promise of my blessing had been fulfilled. But now I realize that that promise has been fulfilled right here in my birthplace of Oaxaca."

Tuxtla Gutiérrez Mexico Temple

Sparkling white marble and crisp, clean lines make the temple a visible landmark in Tuxtla Gutiérrez, the capital city of Mexico's southernmost state, Chiapas, which is bordered on the east by the forests of Guatemala. This region has fascinated archaeologists for generations. Hundreds of ancient ruins and artifacts found in the area indicate that it was home to a highly developed culture between 500 and 300 BC. The city—now home to more than three hundred thousand—is nestled in a valley among the mountains that cover much of Mexico's isthmus. In 1957, on a mountain overlooking the city, President Howard W. Hunter, then of the Quorum of the Twelve Apostles, dedicated the area for the preaching of the gospel.

Local Church members rejoiced when the First Presidency announced in March 1999 that a temple would be built in Tuxtla Gutiérrez. Seven-year-old Ingrid Fabiola Martinez Barredo was so excited that she told everyone she knew. "Temples are where dads and moms can be married for eternity!" she said. "Temples are where families can be sealed together forever!" When Ingrid was five, she and her parents had traveled eighteen hours on a crowded bus to the Mexico City Mexico Temple to be sealed as an eternal family. It is no wonder she rejoiced at the idea of a temple in her own "backyard."

Like Ingrid and her family, members in the area have always been faithful in attending the temple despite inconvenient circumstances. Prior to the dedication of the Mexico City Mexico Temple, members

75

living in Tuxtla would travel some twenty-two hundred miles to the Mesa Arizona Temple to perform ordinance work and be sealed to their families. Enrique Sanchez Casillas, former Tuxtla Gutiérrez Mexico Temple president, served as district president during this time. He recalled, "In order to finance the annual trips to Arizona, members would often sell their possessions, including land, cars, furniture, or typewriters. In those days we could only attend the temple once a year. We had to travel four or five days and nights nonstop to Mesa. All of our children would come along with us. In a bus there may have been forty adults and twenty to forty kids—every one of us had a child. It was a real group effort."

When the Mexico City Mexico Temple was dedicated in 1983, members began making stake temple excursions every three months. With the dedication of the temple in Tuxtla—an hour-long trip for most—members now have the opportunity to visit the house of the Lord as often as they like.

On March 20, 1999, Elder Richard E. Turley Sr. of the Seventy, first counselor in the Mexico South Area presidency, said that "new life in the springtime" had come as ground was broken for the Tuxtla Gutiérrez Mexico Temple. Speaking at the groundbreaking ceremony, Elder Turley observed that "the greatest gift we have received on this earth is the Atonement of the Lord Jesus Christ. But another great gift from the Lord is to have the essential keys to do temple work, which is essential to prepare the world for the Second Coming of the Lord, and to help us gain eternal life with our Heavenly Father." Among the 297 Latter-day Saints attending the groundbreaking, there were many third-generation members of the Church.

When construction began, a group of masonry construction workers arrived from a little town called San Lucas. After working for several weeks, the workers knew they were building a temple but did not understand the significance of it. While working in the temple, these construction workers became acquainted with the full-time missionaries and accepted them into their homes to hear the gospel. Four workers and their families, totaling sixteen people, accepted the gospel and were baptized members of the Church. These families then

SITE
1.77 acres (including adjacent meetinghouse)

GROUNDBREAKING
March 20, 1999, by Richard E. Turley Sr.

DEDICATION
March 12, 2000, by James E. Faust

EXTERIOR
White marble from Torreón, Mexico

TOTAL FLOOR AREA
10,700 square feet

DIMENSIONS
77 feet by 149 feet

HIDDEN IMAGE
Oxen are placed beneath the temple exactly where the actual baptismal font is positioned.

made plans to be sealed in the temple they had helped to construct.

Local members contributed to the temple by helping to landscape the grounds, planting trees and flowers in the area. Indians living in nearby San Cristobal made traditional, hand-embroidered blouses that are displayed on the walls of the temple's entry room. Handmade wool rugs of indigenous colors and patterns are also on display.

When the building was completed, more than eight thousand people attended the open house. As the public left the temple, they used words like "amazing" and "unbelievable" to describe their experience. Many agreed that the white marble temple was the most beautiful building in the entire city, saying, "We need more buildings like this; it is wonderful!" Nearly one thousand referrals were received during the open house, and some four thousand members attended the temple's four dedicatory sessions.

The milestone seventy-fifth temple of the Church was dedicated March 12 in four sessions by President James E. Faust, Second Counselor in the First Presidency. The dedicatory sessions were attended by approximately 3,316 members from five stakes.

President Jose Ernesto Sánchez served as first counselor in the temple's first presidency. He described the reaction of members receiving their endowments: "One of the most beautiful experiences was a youth of eighteen years, a Tzotzil [Indian], a pure Lamanite, who scarcely speaks Spanish, who came to receive his endowments before serving a mission. After receiving his endowments, before leaving, he was filled with emotion to know how much he was loved of the Lord. Afterwards, he felt that his ability to speak other languages increased because of this experience."

President Sánchez said that when couples are sealed, similar emotion is expressed. These families must sacrifice a great deal even to come to a local temple. He described one family's sealing. "This family is very humble, and sustains itself by all the children selling items in the market every day. Despite their situation, they come to the temple every Saturday to do temple work. All the children were sealed to their parents. It was a beautiful experience and a good example to all."

Louisville Kentucky Temple

Located on a forested hill about twelve miles northeast of Louisville, the Louisville Kentucky Temple stands next to the Crestwood Ward chapel. Although the basic design is similar to that of other small temples, the celestial room size was slightly increased, which makes the temple appear larger.

From the earliest stages of construction, it was made clear to contractors that only the best of materials and workmanship would be accepted. As a reminder of the significance of the work they were doing, an image of Jesus Christ was hung in the construction trailer. Beneath the picture were the words, "This is who we are working for; this is the Savior, our Redeemer." As construction progressed and the roof was completed, this picture and message were moved inside the temple lobby.

Elder Marvin Prestridge, a construction missionary, described the effect the picture had on workers: "It set the tone for how we felt about the temple. It made quite an impression on the crew. They understood why we wanted the high quality we did."

In preparation for the temple's concrete foundation, dynamite had to be used to create a hole deep enough for the baptistry. Elder Prestridge related that as the concrete trucks arrived to deposit their heavy loads, a contractor asked, "'If we do it this way will it be appropriate?' I answered him by saying, 'Is that good enough for who it is for?' From then on, that was often my answer when asked if something was done correctly."

Even a city building inspector joked about the

76

high quality of the temple. He said he would never have to worry about the temple, because the Church had much stricter building codes than the city.

The stunning whiteness of the temple's marble exterior is the result of a laborious selection process. As the polished, Danby Vermont marble arrived on site, Elder Prestridge selected only the whitest pieces, rejecting more than forty percent of the incoming stone. Elder Prestridge estimates that he handled 17,000 square feet of marble, totaling just under two hundred thousand pounds.

One faithful and energetic construction worker on the project was not an employee of the general contractor and never received payment for his services. Woodford "Woody" Hatton, a stake patriarch, volunteered his time to work on the temple nearly every day from the time the foundation was poured until the landscaping was completed. The only days he did not work on the site of the Louisville Kentucky Temple were the days he served in the St. Louis Missouri Temple as a sealer. The seventy-five-year-old did anything he was asked to do, including pushing wheelbarrows full of dirt and concrete, sweeping floors, picking up trash, and helping with framing.

Young women from local stakes had a memorable experience hanging crystals on the temple's chandeliers. Working in shifts, the young sisters were awed by what they were doing. As they assembled the chandeliers, they joined in singing songs about the temple. "They had very beautiful, high soprano voices, and it made you think there were groups of angels singing in the temple," said Sister Karla Packer Prestridge, a temple construction missionary and Elder Prestridge's wife. When the chandelier was raised to its permanent position in the celestial room, according to Sister Prestridge, "many of the girls said, 'When I get married in this temple, I can come and say that I helped with the crystals on that chandelier.'"

Valerie Blackwell contributed to the temple project by serving long hours as the temple committee public affairs director. Sister Blackwell recounted how quickly the temple construction was organized and completed. She compared the project to the parable of the ten virgins: "When the announcement

SITE
3 acres (including adjacent meetinghouse)

GROUNDBREAKING
May 29, 1999, by John K. Carmack

DEDICATION
March 19, 2000, by
Thomas S. Monson

EXTERIOR
Imperial Danby white marble
quarried in Vermont

TOTAL FLOOR AREA
10,700 square feet

DIMENSIONS
149 feet by 77 feet

HIDDEN IMAGE
The Savior is kneeling and
looking up at the temple.

[of this new temple] was made, everyone was completely surprised, and the time for preparation was past," she said. "We were either with or without oil in our lamps. We were called into service immediately, without the luxury of a lot of scripture reading or personal preparation. We had to do what we had to do in an incredibly short amount of time—this temple was built in about nine months from the time of its groundbreaking. We now look up at the temple and say to ourselves, 'This is the Lord's work undoubtedly. We are happy to have had even a drop of oil in our lamps so that we could help pull this off.'"

Project superintendent Don Poulsen also felt deeply honored to take part in the temple's construction. "This is absolutely a dream come true. I worked much harder on this than any other project, without question. And I would do it for no one else but the Lord." Although he frequently worked eighteen-hour days, none of it was exhausting, he says. "I haven't been fatigued in any way. I've felt totally sustained by the Lord. Every morning, I was anxious to get to work."

Commenting on blessings that had transpired during construction, Brother Poulsen said, "In this season of temple building, I do not think it is a coincidence that the United States has had one of the warmest winters in recorded history. Call it what you want, but I think the Lord controls it all. From groundbreaking until there was a roof on the temple, we lost fewer than five days to weather." Another blessing came after an adhesive necessary for exterior marble installation was out of stock throughout the East. "I prayed, asking for direction from my Heavenly Father," said Brother Poulsen. "After spending half a day on the phone, I found some. It was shipped overnight, and we only lost one day of construction."

As his calling to assist in the temple's construction came to an end, Elder Prestridge said, "I think that this is true, not just about this temple but about all temples: the Lord built this temple; we just helped. We are just His hands on the earth, but He built the temple. The Spirit was there, right from the very first."

Palmyra

Palmyra New York Temple

The Palmyra New York Temple was the one hundredth temple announced and the seventy-seventh dedicated. Nestled on a hillside, the Palmyra New York Temple overlooks the Sacred Grove. "I regard this temple," President Gordon B. Hinckley said at the spring 1999 groundbreaking, "as perhaps the most significant, in one respect, in the entire Church. This is where it all began. . . . From this place, this work has spread over the earth to more than 160 nations."

On January 22, 1999, President Hinckley arrived at a local airport and traveled to the temple site to personally inspect and approve the location. Due to the muddy conditions, all present put on rubber boots and drove up the hill using four-wheel-drive vehicles. President Hinckley was very animated and

excited. He surveyed the area and personally walked on the grounds. After a short time, he smiled and joyfully said, "This is a good site."

The temple is built within the boundaries of the original one hundred acres purchased by the Smith family in 1818. Preparing the hillside for the temple site required that nearly half a million cubic yards of dirt be excavated from the hill. "We literally moved a small mountain," said the temple architect, David Richards. The hillside had to be leveled without disturbing a rock wall just east of where the temple was to be built. "It is believed that the rock wall was laid up there by the Smiths as they cleared their field," said Brother Richards. "They

77

probably took the rocks out of the dirt and piled them up along their property boundary."

The white granite for the exterior was specifically selected and finished to give the temple its exquisite brightness. It was quarried near Sharon, Vermont, where Joseph Smith was born. "That is why this granite was chosen instead of marble," says Brother Richards.

Brother Richards's architectural design included engraved symbols on the temple exterior. Sun, moon, and star stones detail the exterior temple walls. Stones on the perimeter of the temple depict twenty-one different phases of the moon. These phases begin on the center of the temple's south side, where the date of this moon phase represents April 6, 2000, the date of the temple's dedication. The moonstone found on the center of the temple's west side represents June 27, 1844, the date of the Prophet Joseph's martyrdom. "We oriented the phases so that moonstone would face due west to the Sacred Grove," Brother Richards explained.

The sun and star stones of the temple are on the spire. There are four sunstones, each one facing a cardinal direction. Each sunstone has thirty-three rays of light, representing the number of years of the Savior's mortal existence. Higher on the spire are three stars adorning each of its four sides.

Adding to the beauty and spirit of the Palmyra New York Temple are intricate works of handcrafted, stained-glass art. Equaling the awe-inspiring beauty of the glass are the spiritual messages and stories behind the glass. Tom Holdman and a crew of eight constructed twenty-seven exterior windows, the front doors and side panels, an octagonal baptistry skylight, and a mural window depicting Joseph Smith's First Vision. Adding beauty to the trees depicted in the windows are sixty-five hundred handmade leaves with beveled edges. In all, the glass designs required sixteen thousand individually cut pieces and more than a mile of lead to hold the pieces in place.

Both the architect and President Hinckley agreed that it would be appropriate if the trees in the stained-glass windows gave visitors the impression of being in the Sacred Grove; however, because of the strict budget, a private donor was needed to pay for the windows. The first person Brother Holdman called swiftly replied, "Two weeks ago we were in the celestial room of the Mount Timpanogos Temple and felt impressed that we should donate money for the Palmyra Temple."

SITE
5 acres

GROUNDBREAKING
May 25, 1999, by Gordon B. Hinckley

DEDICATION
April 6, 2000, by Gordon B. Hinckley

EXTERIOR
Bethel white granite

TOTAL FLOOR AREA
10,900 square feet

DIMENSIONS
149 feet by 77 feet

HIDDEN IMAGE
The young Joseph Smith is located in the lower left corner of the image with the Father and the Son in the upper right corner.

The entryway to the temple has two sets of doors, both of which are inlaid with tree designs to give the feeling of entering a forest. Within the front doors is a panel containing a depiction of the tree of knowledge. The baptistry skylight contains twelve trees, symbolic of the twelve tribes of Israel. The leaves on the trees represent the posterity of the twelve tribes.

In the celestial room mural window are seven trees, which represent the seven days of the Creation. One of the trees symbolizes the tree of life, and it contains twelve pieces of clear glass representing the fruit found on the tree. The west side of the temple, which faces the Sacred Grove, has windows with trees that are clear, allowing an unobstructed view of the grove.

Saints within the temple district were given the opportunity to help with the project. Primary children prepared personal inscriptions on small stones that were to be used in the foundation. Youth participated by clearing weeds, vines, and small trees on the grounds. Relief Society sisters crocheted squares that were then connected to form seven cloths for the altars. Three thousand hours of service were required to make these cloths. They "represent each sister's best work, her desire to serve the Lord," said the project supervisor. "As I received each of the squares, I felt the spirit of love that came with each one," she said. "As I washed, shrunk, stretched, blocked, and linked each square to fit the cloth, I sometimes became very emotional. At times I had to walk away, so strongly did I feel the Spirit that came along with each piece."

The Palmyra New York Temple was dedicated April 6, 2000, exactly one hundred seventy years after the Church was organized. Never before in this dispensation have so many members been able to witness the dedication of a temple.

When the dates were announced, it was also announced that the dedication would be broadcast from the temple in Palmyra to the Salt Lake Tabernacle. The response was tremendous. After ticket requests for the broadcast topped two hundred thousand, the First Presidency decided to broadcast the dedication to all stake centers in North America. It was estimated that the total number in attendance at the dedication was 1.5 million.

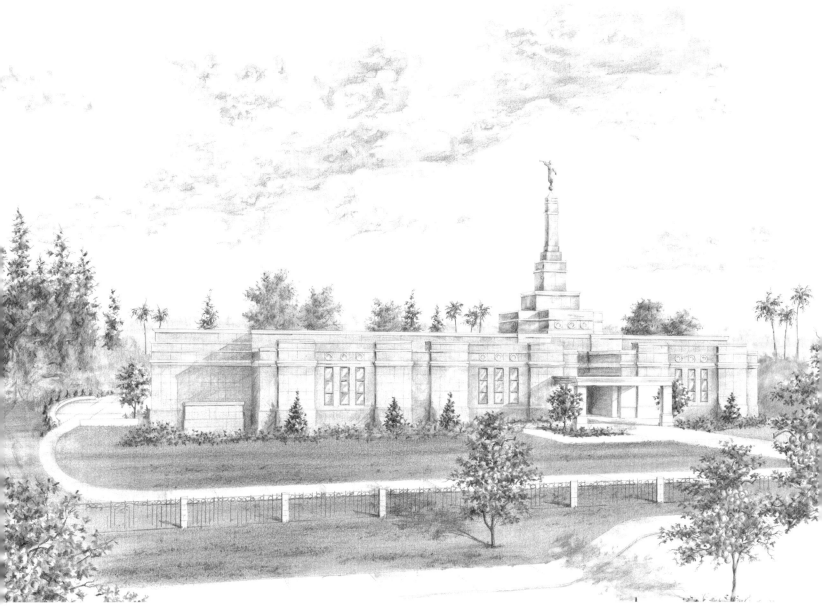

Fresno California Temple

T he Fresno California Temple is on property that was formerly part of twelve thousand acres of fig orchards. In the early 1900s, the area was known as Fig Garden and boasted one of the largest concentrations of figs in the world. Fresno, in central San Joaquin Valley, is one of the largest food-producing regions in the United States.

Preliminary plans for the Fresno California Temple originated in 1997, after President Gordon B. Hinckley announced in October conference the concept of smaller temples. The presidency of the Fresno California West Stake immediately wrote to President Hinckley, suggesting to him the location where the temple now stands. The letter explained how Fresno was ready for a temple: Latter-day Saints in the area

had a longstanding reputation for having the highest temple attendance in the Oakland California Temple district, despite having to travel some two hundred miles to do so.

In the fall of 1998, Church representatives went to Fresno to look into the possibility of building a temple there. Efforts were made to get approval from city planners, local residents, and the city council. According to the director of the Church's temple construction department, this was the fastest approval of a temple from conception to obtaining a building permit in the history of the Church. Much of that success was due to the support of the city and local residents. Years before, people in the area were not nearly as receptive to construction of the stake center near which the temple was

78

built. Because of that, similar opposition was expected with the building of the temple. It never materialized, however, because the presence of the stake center had eventually established a positive precedent of Latter-day Saint influence in the neighborhood.

To ensure continued good public relations, local Church leadership organized a proactive door-to-door approach to address any concerns or questions about the temple from the community. Of the ninety-one residents contacted, eighty-five said they supported the building of the temple. More than nine hundred citizens attended the city council's neighborhood meeting, organized to discuss the proposed temple and its effect on the community. Those attending the hearing voted 935–1 in favor of building the temple. The lone dissenter was eventually won over and even participated in the groundbreaking. The cooperative support furthered the temple's progress without delay. During the 1999 Christmas season, Church youth showed their appreciation to nearly three hundred neighbors living near the temple by going door-to-door caroling.

The temple's groundbreaking was celebrated by additional community service. After the groundbreaking on March 20, 1999, 1,066 Church members converged on the Fresno Chaffee Zoo. At the time, it was the largest volunteer effort ever undertaken in Fresno. Seven months of maintenance items were completed on a single day.

Mature olives trees, chosen both for their Christian symbolism and for their importance as a local agricultural crop, beautify the approach to the front of the temple. The Sierra white granite of the temple exterior was chosen because it is the same as that of the Oakland California Temple. Latter-day Saints in the Fresno area had attended that temple since its dedication in 1964 and had long been familiar with its appearance. It was hoped that the use of the same recognizable granite would quickly make the new temple feel "like home" for Fresno members.

Continuing that impression on the inside, the celestial room was enlarged slightly from the standard plan for smaller temples to accommodate a larger number of anticipated

SITE
2.34 acres

GROUNDBREAKING
March 20, 1999, by John B. Dickson

DEDICATION
April 9, 2000, by Gordon B. Hinckley

EXTERIOR
White Sierra granite quarried
in Raymond, California

TOTAL FLOOR AREA
10,700 square feet

HIDDEN IMAGE
The Savior's portrait is among
the trees left of the temple.

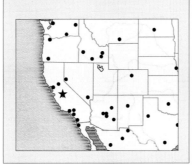

patrons. Two original oil paintings by local artists also beautify the temple's interior. One of these, painted by Mark Gudmundsen, is a scene of nearby Yosemite Valley. As a member of his bishopric, he was sitting on the stand during the sacrament meeting when a member of the stake presidency announced that a temple was going to be built next to his stake center. Of the experience, Brother Gudmundsen explained, "At that very moment, a thought came into my mind that I was supposed to do a painting to hang in it. I could even see the complete painting in my mind—it was an overview of Yosemite Valley from near the Tunnel View." Directly after the meeting, a member of the stake presidency informed him that the temple committee had requested that he create a new painting for the temple. Once completed, the scenic original painting was placed behind the recommend desk.

A second painting, created by David Dalton, depicts several familiar features of the San Joaquin Valley, including oak trees, rolling foothills beneath the Sierra Mountains, and lush vineyards. Brother Dalton's great-grandfather had used his skills as a woodworker to beautify the Cardston Alberta Temple. Remembering his ancestor's contributions, Brother Dalton said, "In a way I felt that I was carrying on a tradition by donating my talents to the temple."

At the open house, tours were planned for leaders of other religious denominations in Fresno. One minister who arrived expressed concern about how much money was spent on the temple. However, after the tour he said, "When I was in that temple, I felt the presence of God. To give people a chance to come somewhere and feel the presence of God has to be something of very great value. While you have spent a lot, what you have acquired with that expenditure is truly worth a great deal." During the eight-day open house, more than fifty-one thousand visitors toured the temple.

The temple was dedicated on April 9, 2000, by President Gordon B. Hinckley. Ten thousand Saints attended the four dedicatory sessions.

Medford Oregon Temple

The Medford Oregon Temple is situated in the community of Central Point in the beautiful Rogue River Valley. Four miles northwest of Medford and thirty-five miles north of the California border, the temple is Oregon's second—the first being in Portland.

In 1924, Elder Melvin J. Ballard of the Quorum of the Twelve Apostles visited the nearby city of Grants Pass to speak at a conference. During his remarks, he promised that someday a temple would be built in the Rogue River Valley. Seventy-six years later the Medford Oregon Temple was dedicated, fulfilling that promise.

Surrounding the temple grounds are farmlands, a creek, and residential neighborhoods. Nearby is the Central Point Stake Center. Years ago, the Church acquired the property on which the stake center is located, intending to build on five acres and sell the remainder. But Bishop Rosecrans, the serving bishop and eventual patriarch of the Central Point Stake, felt strongly that the land should be kept, and it was used for some time as a community garden. That extra acreage now provides an ideal setting for the temple.

A prayer meeting was held every morning before work began during construction. The main petition was that the workers would not become casual about the spirit that existed at the temple site. The result was a strong unity among all who worked there. The daily prayers "truly added a great deal to this experience" said Central Point Stake President Edward Hanson.

79

"It was mentioned by various individuals, 'We are not only building a temple, but we're also building people.'"

Elder Ross Woodward faithfully served as the temple's construction missionary. In 1951, at the age of nineteen, Brother Woodward received his patriarchal blessing, which revealed, "And thou shalt be called to establish the stakes of Zion and help build temples." It was not until the age of sixty-eight and after thirty-five years of construction experience that his blessing was fulfilled as he built the temple in Medford.

During construction, a beautiful painting of a recently completed temple was placed on an easel at the temple's entryway. Along the bottom of the painting was the saying, "May everyone laboring herein feel peace in their lives as they help build this temple to our Father in Heaven and the Savior Jesus Christ." In another area was a small architectural rendering of the Medford Oregon Temple with a statement that read, "Together we are building a temple," reminding workers of their goal.

Because they were building the house of the Lord, the workers tried to be perfect in their labors. One worker was told that everything on the temple had to be as exact as if he were "building a piano."

Building the temple was a particularly significant experience for one construction worker, not a Church member, who said, "I have worked on almost every kind of project in my life, and last year I prayed that someday I could help build a church. This temple is really an answer to prayer."

"Out of the 225 people who worked on the temple," said Corey Vitas, the general contractor, "all of them felt the Spirit here at one time or another. The concrete contractor ripped up the curb after the first time and redid it because it 'wasn't perfect.' And he wasn't even a member. That's the spirit all the workers had about the temple. They would say, this is 'our temple.'"

The Medford Oregon Temple district spans a large area of northern California and southern Oregon. Local leaders wanted each of the nearly twenty-nine thousand Church

SITE
2 acres

GROUNDBREAKING
May 20, 1999, by D. Lee Tobler

DEDICATION
April 16, 2000, by James E. Faust

EXTERIOR
Gray granite quarried from
Mount Airy, North Carolina

TOTAL FLOOR AREA
10,700 square feet

DIMENSIONS
149 feet by 77 feet

HIDDEN IMAGE
Among the trees and landscaping is the Savior with His arm extended to the front door. Additionally, oxen are placed beneath the temple.

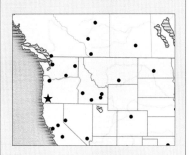

members living in the district to feel invested in the new temple. They knew that when it was completed, much of the Saints' time and effort would be needed to keep it busy, so they used the construction period to motivate members to "lengthen their stride" in Church and temple service.

One project that helped accomplish that goal involved gathering many rounded stones, which Church members cleaned and sealed with varnish. Upon each stone was then written "Lengthening their stride" and the names of the stakes, wards, and branches of the temple district. Before the cement was poured to form the foundation, these special stones were carefully positioned beneath the place where the celestial room would be built.

The entrance to the temple features a water fountain cascading over a one-ton block of granite left over from construction of the Conference Center in Salt Lake City. To keep the building project within its established budget, the water fountain was funded locally and assembled using donated labor.

Nearly forty-six thousand people attended the seven-day open house, triple the number anticipated. The outstanding turnout was largely due to publicity efforts made by the temple committee. Three television networks ran daily updates about the progress being made on the temple. Published in nineteen area newspapers, a sixteen-page insert contained an invitation to the open house, historical and doctrinal information about the Church, and a copy of "The Family: A Proclamation to the World." A quarter of a million inserts were printed and distributed.

Among the contents of the time capsule placed in the temple's cornerstone is the Medford Oregon Temple history, which covers everything from the groundbreaking for the temple to its dedication. Included in this history is an excerpt of a letter written by a local Catholic priest after he attended the open house. "Thank you very much for your kindness and hospitality," read the letter, "and may God bless you and bring all of us—indeed all of His children—into the Father's eternal kingdom."

Memphis Tennessee Temple

The Memphis Tennessee Temple is located northeast of Memphis in the suburb of Bartlett, near the banks of the Mississippi River. The property on which the temple stands was previously used for growing cotton and soybeans. Nearby historical sites, including several homes dating back to the Civil War, give visitors a glimpse into Southern life.

The life of the early Saints in Memphis and the mid-South was marked by persecution and suffering, and yet in spite of that, the Church has continued to grow. Only a month after the Memphis Tennessee Temple was dedicated, the state became home to yet another dedicated temple—in Nashville.

When the temple site near Memphis was first acquired by the Church, it was intended for the building of the Memphis North Stake Center. Only three acres were necessary for the new stake center, but the site totaled more than six acres.

Former Memphis North Stake president David Denton remembered approving the property's purchase. "I was hesitant to purchase the site because of the excess acreage. After pondering for some time on the property acquisition, my counselors and I agreed that the extra property would be a benefit to the new stake center." This extra property eventually became the site for a house of the Lord.

Through the years, Church members in the Memphis area have been assigned to four different temple districts, including Mesa, Arizona; Washington D.C.; Atlanta, Georgia; and St. Louis,

80

Missouri. The long trips to these distant temples were difficult for the Saints.

When the Nashville Tennessee Temple was announced, Latter-day Saints in the Memphis area felt their dreams of having a temple close to home had finally come true. They were overcome when, only a short time later, another announcement was made that a temple would be built right in Memphis. The announcement was received in a letter from the First Presidency dated September 11, 1998. The letter read in part: "We are pleased to announce that one of the new smaller temples will be construction in the Memphis, Tennessee, area. We are confident that this will be a blessing to the many faithful Saints in this and surrounding areas who have had to travel long distances to enjoy the blessings of the temple. We commend the Saints for their devotion and faithfulness and are thankful for the blessings that will come to them through the construction of this new temple."

Church members in some stakes in what would be the new temple district prepared for the temple by focusing on family history research. The Church's Internet genealogy resources and its FamilySearch™ program were explained in family history seminars and then used by members to prepare their ancestors' information for temple work. In 1999, nearly two thousand people used the resources provided, logging more than twenty-five hundred hours on the genealogical computers in these stakes.

Although the Memphis Tennessee Temple uses the same basic design as the other smaller temples, its plans contain more than two hundred revisions. One of the most significant is the lowered and slightly shortened art glass windows. Because of this change, visitors both inside and outside the temple can see the windows in their full splendor. To contrast with them, the windows in the baptistry and celestial room were left at their original height and position.

Every effort was made to construct the temple as quickly as possible. Favorable weather conditions were a tremendous aid in reaching building goals. Sister Trenna Anderson, a temple construction missionary, said: "When the wet weather came, it always seemed to be during the night or on the weekends. I can remember only three days during the six-month construction period that it rained during construction hours. Often the storms would approach the temple from the west, head over the Mississippi River, and then go around us."

SITE
6.35 acres (including adjacent meetinghouse)

GROUNDBREAKING
January 16, 1999, by Gordon T. Watts

DEDICATION
April 23, 2000, by James E. Faust

EXTERIOR
Imperial Danby white marble

TOTAL FLOOR AREA
10,700 square feet

DIMENSIONS
149 feet by 77 feet

HIDDEN IMAGE
An image of the Savior with His arms extended is seen at the temple's entrance. Additionally, oxen are placed beneath the temple.

One memorable milestone was the placement of the statue of the angel Moroni. The statue was positioned on Saturday, November 13, 1999, at 8:00 a.m. All of the workers arriving to help with the statue that day donated their time. About six hundred onlookers gathered along the fence, armed with cameras and video recorders.

The watchers spontaneously joined in singing "The Spirit of God" as the crane hoisted the statue toward the spire. After the statue was successfully placed, the construction worker responsible for raising the statue removed his hard hat in salute.

Detailed beauty can be found in every corner of the temple, from the statue of the angel Moroni and the exterior walls to the warm whites, ivories, and light beige colors throughout the interior.

Adorning the walls are several oil paintings and a framed quilt. Exquisite chairs add grace and ornamentation to the temple's sealing and celestial rooms. On the backs of the chairs are beautifully carved, gold-colored leaves. This pattern on the chairs harmonizes with the leaf pattern repeated on ceilings and in the carpets in the sealing rooms.

One local member who was instrumental in preparing the region for a temple said: "I suppose that it may be difficult for people who have lived in the proximity of a temple all their lives to understand what the temple means to members living in this area of the world. Having a temple so close to home means we now do not have to travel such long distances. So much time has been wasted in travel. Now we can better spend our time doing the work inside the temple. It really is marvelous what has been accomplished for people around the world."

In July 2003, city officials surprised Memphis Tennessee Temple President Boyd Lee when they announced that the temple had won the "America in Bloom" award. Although the temple had never entered the nationwide contest, it still won due to its colorful flowers, beautiful trees, and "planting pride through volunteerism."

The Memphis Temple is the result of the faith that has deep roots in the soil of the South. The temple is a symbol of the faith and growing strength of the Church in the region.

Reno Nevada Temple

Fifteen miles from the California border, the Reno Nevada Temple is the second temple in the Silver State. Surrounding the temple are retaining walls that blend with its environment. Some of the walls are of indigenous stone, and others are made of concrete tinted a desert sand color. For nearby members, this is their temple—far up the hill from a city of glittering lights and neon signs.

In 1997, after President Gordon B. Hinckley announced the concept of building smaller temples, Reno stakes were among the first to request a temple and receive approval.

When local leaders are looking for a suitable location for a smaller temple, they give first consideration to Church-owned property near a stake center.

If no such property is available, they then see if land adjacent to a stake center can be purchased. If neither of these options is viable, they consider other sites that might be appropriate for a house of the Lord.

Because the first two options were not feasible in Reno, a committee was organized to find property suitable for a "stand-alone" temple. Eventually, a peaceful site that provides a panoramic view of the city and valley was obtained.

At the groundbreaking ceremony on July 24, 1999, Elder Rex D. Pinegar of the Seventy encouraged the members to complete the temple in the scheduled six months. Project superintendent Vernon C. Forbush said, "We were able to complete this temple because of the united cooperation of members and

81

nonmembers. Many of the contractors have told me on different occasions that they have felt the spirit of the temple and they know that it is a special place. We found ourselves doing things far above our ability. . . . If there is one thing that needs to be emphasized, it's the spirit of service—that is what got this temple finished in the time in which it was finished."

From the earliest stages of construction, the temple's project superintendent made it clear to all workers that only the highest quality of materials and workmanship was acceptable. He explained to workers, "You are going to do things you never thought you were going to do. We do things almost perfectly." Although speed was a constant factor in the construction, the quality of workmanship was never sacrificed.

In an effort to foster positive relations with the temple's neighbors, Church members were asked to refrain from driving to the temple site during construction and causing congestion in the area. With such overwhelming enthusiasm for the new temple, obeying this counsel was indeed a sacrifice for members.

Local Latter-day Saints willingly donated their time and talents to the temple's construction. For example, members of a small branch installed the site's flagpole; stake presidencies and bishoprics put in the oxen for the baptismal font; and a youth group cleaned the font.

One sister, Dorothy Keele of the Reno 1st Ward, had the distinct honor of hanging the many individual crystals on the celestial room's chandelier. Since she is legally blind, she had to rely solely on her touch and intuition.

Although the Reno Nevada Temple has the same floor plan as most of the other smaller temples, a vestibule was added and the doorway moved to the north. This prevents the constant westerly winds of Reno from entering the temple.

There is also an almost imperceptible difference in the statue of the angel Moroni on this temple. It is not finished with traditional gold leafing. The company that painted the pipes of the organ in the Conference Center in Salt Lake City used the same technology to paint the fiberglass statue a golden color. This method was chosen because of the paint's durability in steady winds.

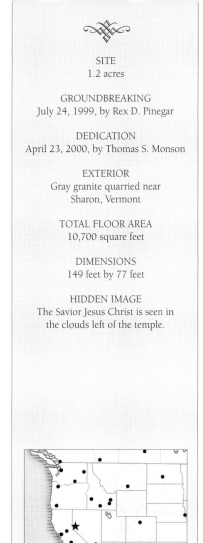

SITE
1.2 acres

GROUNDBREAKING
July 24, 1999, by Rex D. Pinegar

DEDICATION
April 23, 2000, by Thomas S. Monson

EXTERIOR
Gray granite quarried near
Sharon, Vermont

TOTAL FLOOR AREA
10,700 square feet

DIMENSIONS
149 feet by 77 feet

HIDDEN IMAGE
The Savior Jesus Christ is seen in
the clouds left of the temple.

Some opposition is frequently associated with the construction of a temple, and the temple in Reno was no exception. Passionate opposition had to be addressed from the temple's inception to its completion.

During the open house, one temple worker said, "We have had countless examples of resistance to the temple, from groundbreaking until just an hour ago. The adversary does not want temples built, and that has been very obvious on this job."

But Church leaders noted that just as there are influences against the temple's progress, so there are also righteous powers beyond the veil seeing to its successful completion.

Before the dedication of the Reno Nevada Temple, the Saints in the area were part of the Oakland California Temple district. The four-hour journey through the Sierras and Donner Pass could be very treacherous in winter. The unpredictable weather made the months of March through November the only reliably safe time to visit the temple in Oakland. One member commented, "What a unique thing it will be for us to be able to visit the temple throughout the year."

Months before the temple in Reno was dedicated, the blessings of the temple were already touching the lives of many Church members. Members of one stake prepared themselves for the temple by committing to read the Book of Mormon in its entirety by the time the temple was finished. They were asked to mark every verse that referred to the Savior and His mission. During this process, the Saints strengthened their testimonies and gained a better understanding of why the Book of Mormon is called another testament of Jesus Christ.

Near-disaster was averted in July 2003, when an arson fire engulfed the hillside where the temple is located. High winds whipped the fast-moving blaze within feet of the temple. An air tanker was requested when the ten-acre blaze threatened nearby homes. A local resident commented, "It was just the whole mountain on fire. It's kind of scary how quickly it can torch." Thanks to fast-acting firefighters, no injuries or structural damage was reported.

Cochabamba Bolivia Temple

Cochabamba, Bolivia, is in a fairly temperate environment, nearly eight thousand feet above sea level at the base of the Andes. Though Cochabamba has suffered occasional lengthy periods of drought, the coming of a house of the Lord has inundated Church members there with all the blessings that a temple affords.

The temple itself sits on the northern side of the city. On a hill near the temple stands a tall statue of Jesus Christ. The morning and evening sun illuminate this statue, as well as the statue of the angel Moroni atop the temple spire, to create a dramatic presence for residents of Cochabamba. The scene is a daily reminder of the tranquility and stability that the Lord of all offers to a sometimes turbulent country.

On January 21, 1995, Elder Mario Guzman, an Area Seventy, received a telephone call from Elder Julio E. Davila of the South America North Area presidency, inviting him to attend a special meeting. "None of us present had any idea why the meeting had been called," said Elder Guzman. "Elder Davila was very nervous. He kept asking, 'Has the fax come?' Twenty minutes passed; then someone handed him a fax. 'This comes from the First Presidency,' he told us, and read: 'A temple has been approved for Cochabamba, Bolivia.' A profound silence fell. Us? A temple? We had no words to say. We all began to cry."

Soon the news of a temple in Bolivia spread among the members of the Church. The local Church distribution center manager, Rene Cabrerra, echoed

82

the feelings of many when he said, "To have a temple in Cochabamba is to have a temple in the heart of Bolivia, where all the members throughout Bolivia have relatively easy access by bus."

The announcement of a temple for Bolivia took place in January 1995. Just under two years later, on November 10, 1996, President Gordon B. Hinckley arrived to preside over the groundbreaking ceremony. One of Cochabamba's long dry spells was hanging over the area, but the rain finally came just a few hours before he arrived. Latter-day Saints from throughout the country had traveled to attend this momentous ceremony, and they felt it no great sacrifice to stand in the pouring rain for hours to await their prophet to begin construction on a temple of God.

As President Hinckley began his remarks, he faced a throng of umbrellas across a field of mud. The prophet addressed the approximately four thousand attendees by beginning, "My beloved and wet brothers and sisters." The downpour shortened the groundbreaking ceremony, but those who were there said later that neither the rain nor the shortness of the ceremony detracted from the significance of the prophet's visit.

During that somewhat abbreviated and wet groundbreaking ceremony, President Hinckley issued a challenge: "Get a temple recommend now," he said. "Be worthy of a temple recommend now. If you are not worthy, get yourselves worthy. You won't be able to go to the temple here for at least two years. But let that temple recommend be a reminder of that to which you look forward."

Members of the four stakes in Cochabamba became especially dedicated to accepting and obeying that counsel. One ward at a time was invited to tour the temple construction site each Saturday to feel the spirit attendant on the site and to envision the day when they might return worthily to perform ordinances for themselves and their deceased ancestors.

Ivan Gutiérrez, president of the Jaihuayco Bolivia Stake, commented: "We are preparing the people. We encourage them to be ready spiritually. We have a goal to put a picture

SITE
6.67 acres

GROUNDBREAKING
November 10, 1996, by
Gordon B. Hinckley

DEDICATION
April 30, 2000, by
Gordon B. Hinckley

EXTERIOR
Blend of hand-hewn Comanche
granite and plaster

TOTAL FLOOR AREA
33,302 square feet

DIMENSIONS
128 feet by 145 feet

HIDDEN IMAGE
The famous Cristo de la Concordia
statue is featured in this drawing.

of the temple in every home. We have identified those who do not have temple recommends. We visit them and help them set goals for themselves. As a result, great changes are coming into the lives of the people."

Made of granite and plaster, the temple has a sleek, modern design intended to reflect the Bolivian culture. It stands on a 6.67-acre site and has an area of 33,302 square feet. Inside are two ordinance rooms and two sealing rooms.

A two-week open house was scheduled in early April 2000 with the hope that tens of thousands of people would attend before the dedication on April 30. Political unrest, however, was looming, and rebellion was touched off by an increase in utilities prices, causing demonstrations and anxiety throughout the country. Bolivia's president declared a state of emergency on April 8, 2000, and police were sent into the streets with anti-riot gear, tear gas, and rubber bullets to try to quiet things down. Because of obvious safety concerns, the time for the open house was reduced from two weeks to one and the dedication from two days to one. The reduced time allotted for the Saints to take part in these activities created larger groups participating in the remaining open house and dedication ceremonies. Despite the changes, Church officials were pleased with attendance and the 2,232 referrals.

According to Enrique O. Huerta, of the Cochabamba Bolivia Universidad Stake: "We were supposed to be under martial law for ninety days, but it was lifted after thirteen days. We anticipated 50,000 visitors in two weeks of open house, but instead we got 65,570 in one week. Twenty thousand people came in one day. They were lined up for blocks and stayed until midnight."

The family of one Bolivian member has a testimony of temple attendance: "Raising children is much easier now that we have the gospel and temple blessings in our lives," the member stated. "In our home we have a piece of heaven. We have learned that the way to receive blessings—the way to run our home—is to serve the Lord first."

Tampico Mexico Temple

Tampico, Mexico, is an industrial city on central Mexico's Gulf Coast. The temple is built on a hill that many people nearby have long thought of as sacred. It is thus appropriate that a house of the Lord be located there. The temple attracts the attention and respect of many Tampico residents.

The property on which the temple stands was purchased by the Church in the 1950s. The first building to be constructed there was the Tampico Madero Stake Center. Then, in 1967, the Church added a school. Academics were not the only benefits of becoming a student at the school—children attending this highly rated school participated in early-morning seminary at the nearby stake center. The school functioned for

seventeen years before being converted in 1984 into offices for the Mexico Tampico Mission.

After the announcement of a temple for this area, a thorough search for possible locations ensued. Several were identified and considered, but the First Presidency ultimately felt inspired that the temple should be built on the site of the mission offices, which were consequently relocated and the building razed.

For some, the announcement of a temple for this city was the fulfillment of long-felt spiritual inclinations. Nearly twenty years earlier, Church officials had discussed the possibility of selling the property. In the end, the property was retained, in no small measure due to the persuasive beliefs of stake

83

president Roberto de Leon Perales, who humbly witnessed, "One day a temple will be built here."

To involve local leadership in bringing about the successful construction of a temple and its integration into the community, the Church organized a temple committee to assist in various assignments. Roberto Cruz was overwhelmed when asked to serve on that committee as the public affairs director. "I am a humble shoemaker," he said, "and I wondered, 'Why wasn't someone with more experience or more intellect called to this position?' But I have learned from this experience that the Lord qualifies whom He calls, and He has been there to help."

His wife, Ana Bertha, represented their combined commitment and hard work when she said, "We have joined our hearts, souls, and strength together in this work, but it is still humbling to say: 'Lord, this is Thy House.'"

Latter-day Saints living in the Tampico Mexico Temple district are no strangers to committed temple service. Though a trip to the nearest temple—the Mexico City Mexico Temple—was a long twelve hours by bus, most temple recommend holders attended two or three times each year. Their dedication brought great blessings to not only those sacrificing to take these temple trips but also to those who observed them doing so. Many less-active members were influenced by the spirit and enthusiasm for the temple that these faithful members showed, to the extent that they made themselves worthy to join the ranks in receiving temple recommends.

Brother Rodolfo Avalos, project supervisor of the temple construction, commented that the construction crew had to meet two difficult challenges to complete the project successfully. First were the high construction standards required for building a house of the Lord. Labor union workers and contractors struggled to successfully provide adequate building materials and work quality. Many jobs on the temple had to be completed multiple times until acceptable results were achieved. "At times I was not very popular, because if the job was not done right I would say, 'That is not good enough. It has to be done perfectly.'" Once tasks were done correctly, workers began to take pride in their work, improve their skills, and

SITE
3.73 acres (including adjacent meetinghouse)

GROUNDBREAKING
November 28, 1998, by Eran A. Call

DEDICATION
May 20, 2000, by Thomas S. Monson

EXTERIOR
Blanco Guardiano white marble from Torreón, Mexico

TOTAL FLOOR AREA
10,700 square feet

DIMENSIONS
77 feet by 149 feet

HIDDEN IMAGE
Oxen are placed beneath the temple exactly where the actual baptismal font is positioned.

learn to not be satisfied until the job was done right. As attitudes changed, workers began to say, "It has to be done right. This is the House of the Lord."

The second significant challenge was the need to properly translate the building plans, which had been developed in English in Salt Lake City. Fortunately, with the help of the Lord, these challenges were met quite successfully, along with a number of others, such as heavy rains and scorching heat.

On one occasion, the temple committee felt prompted to double night security because of unsafe conditions in a nearby community. That night, very late, ruffians tried to jump the fence, but the additional security forces were able to stop them from entering the temple site. Originally, neighborhood youth would regularly try to play sports on the lawn. As the temple neared completion, they began to respect the area and stay away.

As the walls of the temple grew, so too did the desire for members to help in any way with "their" temple. Brother Avalos said, "Once we started to construct the temple, members began to inquire if they could be of assistance." Although there was not much they could do as the temple was built, members were put to work in preparation for the temple's open house. "We allowed them to clean the grounds and the streets in front of the temple," he said. "We had a constant supply of volunteers for the exterior cleanup crew. Many came at all hours of the day and night to work."

Jose Ponce, patriarch in the Tampico Mexico Bosque Stake, served as branch president outside Tampico fifteen years before the temple was dedicated. He reflected on his calling as the branch president and the growth of the Church in just a generation: "I was so excited that we could fill every teaching position in the branch, only to realize that those callings left us without any students. Now seeing the Church grow to the point where we can build a temple is a joyous blessing."

Even though the Saints in Tampico already had an outstanding temple attendance record, there is no question that having their own temple nearby is making temple blessings more accessible. And that is very important. "The temple is a light," says Manuel Camacho, a member of the Madero stake, "an enormous light for Tampico and the world."

Nashville Tennessee Temple

Franklin, Tennessee, was not the original choice, nor even the second choice, for the site of the temple first announced in 1994, but this is the place where the Nashville Tennessee Temple found its home six years later. This part of the country is known as the Bible Belt, with many considering Nashville the "belt buckle."

In the spring of 1994, President Howard W. Hunter, then President of the Quorum of the Twelve Apostles, felt inspired to consider building a temple in central Tennessee. President Gordon B. Hinckley and President Thomas S. Monson, counselors in the First Presidency, traveled to Nashville in April that year and selected a tentative site in Forest Hills, south of Nashville. When the Church requested that the site

be rezoned for religious use, the city council denied the request. Not all nonmembers, however, were against the notion of a Latter-day Saint temple in their neighborhood. Jacqueline Srouji, for example, wrote in a letter to the editor of a major Tennessee newspaper:

"Although I have never been in one, I have seen Mormon temples during my travels throughout the world. These are structures of unusual spiritual and physical beauty. My only hope is that our Tennessee Mormons will have the same strong character as their pioneer ancestors to withstand whatever opposition is sent until their beautiful temple is finally built." In January 1995, President Thomas S. Monson spoke at a regional conference at the Grand Ole Opry house. During his

84

address, he assured the Saints that the Brethren were praying for their success and that despite the struggle, Nashville would have a temple.

A second site in Forest Hills was selected in July 1995. Although there was newfound support from some local congregations of other faiths and an organized effort to educate residents around the proposed site on what the addition of a temple would mean to their neighborhood, the planning commission once again denied the rezoning request.

In April 1998, the Church announced its plan to build a smaller temple next to the stake center in Franklin. This land, part of a tract owned by the Church, was already zoned for religious purposes. After overcoming minor obstacles in Franklin, the temple project was given permission to proceed. The final temple site is in an immaculate residential and rural area next to a venerable old private high school and two 100-acre horse farms.

On March 13, 1999, approximately fifteen hundred members from central Tennessee and southern Kentucky ignored uncomfortable weather conditions during the temple's groundbreaking ceremony. Drenching rains complicated the ceremonies by requiring officials to hold an umbrella in one hand and a shovel in the other. The muddy shovelfuls of dirt seemed to symbolize five years of struggle.

Hundreds of Laurels who lived in the temple district participated in "crystal parties," in which they assembled the crystal chandeliers for the celestial room and the sealing rooms. For those involved, it was a memorable experience to polish and place the crystals on the chandeliers. After finishing their work, the young women took part in a tour and discussion with Sister Barbara Blake, a temple construction missionary. Sister Blake paused in the brides' room to allow the girls an opportunity to reflect on their own goal of a temple marriage.

Other local Saints also had significant opportunities for service during the construction period. For example, when the decision was made to plant new sod around the neighboring stake center to match the sod of the temple grounds, the assistance of eighty people was requested. Not surprisingly, 140 people came to fill the request, which was done quickly and well. Because their work was finished in less time than anticipated, they stayed to help with other tasks as well. This attitude was typical of the Saints' commitment to their dream of a temple.

SITE
6.86 (including adjacent meetinghouse)

GROUNDBREAKING
March 13, 1999, by John K. Carmack

DEDICATION
May 21, 2000, by James E. Faust

EXTERIOR
Imperial Danby white marble

TOTAL FLOOR AREA
10,700 square feet

DIMENSIONS
149 feet by 77 feet

HIDDEN IMAGE
The Savior's image is drawn to the right of the temple. His face and hands are part of the temple and distant trees.

Though challenges presented themselves almost daily, so too were solutions found—sometimes seemingly at the last minute, but found nonetheless. These challenges ranged from carpet that was improperly installed to chairs that arrived without the bolts necessary to assemble them. The chairs that arrived without bolts were for the endowment rooms and were thus important fixtures in the temple. After searching all over town, temple construction missionary Elder Leo Udy located the necessary hundred specialty bolts and spent half the night painting them to match the chairs. He said, "At the last minute, the Lord provided." Though solving such problems often required faith and significant amounts of hard work and extra hours, the temple was successfully built to the typical high standards.

At times, opposition came not from construction difficulties but from local citizens. The Spirit eventually came to rest on many of those who had raised objections. One outspoken opponent had just such a change of heart. When he was invited to tour the temple during its open house, he responded, "After all the problems I caused you, I never expected to receive such an invitation. I am surprised that you would care or remember me this way. Thank you! I would love to tour your temple."

The temple's first president, Buryl G. McClurg, had been involved with the temple from the beginning. While serving as stake president, he played a key role in purchasing the land now used for the stake center and temple, and he helped get approval from county commissioners to build the temple. He did whatever was needed at the time, whether it was dislodging a large rock that was blocking the stake center sewer line or using steel wool to scrub concrete spatters from the fence surrounding the temple site. When asked to make a statement that would be permanently recorded in the temple's cornerstone, President McClurg responded:

"The gospel is true today; it will be true tomorrow. Although we had some struggles in making this happen, the glory is quite unparalleled in terms of what you can do to make something like this become a reality. . . . As the stone rolls forth, there will be many temples, hundreds and hundreds of temples. . . . Join hands, love the Lord, be true and faithful, never veer from that which is right, because Satan's influence cannot overpower the Lord's Spirit."

Villahermosa Mexico Temple

Villahermosa, the capital of the state of Tabasco, is located in southeastern Mexico. Situated on the Grijalva River, the community has become a regional commercial and manufacturing center. The temple itself, built on a site near the coast of Mexico's isthmus, will someday also have a stake center to the west of it.

The property on which the temple was built had been owned by the Church for many years and was previously the site of a meetinghouse, which had to be removed to make way for the temple. Located in the heart of the city, the site is located in a prestigious area with beautiful rivers nearby.

Ground was broken on January 9, 1999, under the direction of Elder Richard E. Turley Sr. of the

Seventy and first counselor in the Mexico South Area presidency. Only about two hundred people—mostly local leaders and their families—attended the ceremony because there was simply not enough room for more. Elder Turley bore testimony of the Savior and His mission to "bring to pass the immortality and eternal life of man" (Moses 1:39). He reminded the Saints that it is only through the Savior and His Atonement that we can receive exaltation. "This is why," Elder Turley said, "temples are, along with the Atonement, the greatest gift to mankind as well as the greatest tool to prepare the earth for the Second Coming of the Savior." He told the Saints that they "must now develop within their homes a culture of temple attendance and participation. It is our hope that every member home

85

in the temple district will eventually have a picture of the temple to remind them and their children of the opportunities that can be theirs. If you are faithful," he continued, "the spirituality of the members will increase. There will be a measurable impact on the whole community through the faithfulness of the people and the beauty of the temple and its surroundings."

As with other temples built in Mexico, most of the construction was done by hand. Boards were cut, steel was cut and bent, and cement was mixed by hand—often with home-made tools. To make the cement, water was poured into sand and gravel and then mixed on the ground with a shovel. Although a cement pump truck was used to pour the concrete on the roof, most cement was transported to the appropriate area in five-gallon buckets. Workers put in long hours in the sun but remained dedicated to their task. Only when the finishing work on the temple was being completed was a power saw brought on site.

The unforeseen height of the water table caused minor difficulties when the hole was dug for the baptismal font, but an extra pump was installed to prevent any water damage. The climate of the Mexican isthmus does not require any type of heating system, but eight air conditioning units were installed to add to the comfort of the patrons.

The interior colors of the temple, floral arrangements, and commissioned artwork were selected to represent the region. One original painting depicts well-known waterfalls sixty miles from Villahermosa. Another portrays a prominent river south of the city. Adding to the temple's exterior beauty is its Blanco Guardiano marble from Torreón, Mexico.

SITE
1.73 acres

GROUNDBREAKING
January 9, 1999, by
Richard E. Turley Sr.

DEDICATION
May 21, 2000, by Thomas S. Monson

EXTERIOR
Blanco Guardiano white marble
from Torreón, Mexico

TOTAL FLOOR AREA
10,700 square feet

DIMENSIONS
77 feet by 149 feet

HIDDEN IMAGE
A full-length image of the Savior
is included among the trees and
landscaping left of the temple.

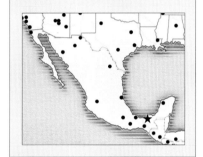

Gracing the grounds of the temple are several ceiba trees, including one tree near the temple's entrance with branches that tower above the building. Ceiba trees are protected by the government so strictly that it is illegal to cut them down in the state of Tabasco. According to Mayan legend, the tree is sacred and symbolizes the need to stay rooted deeply in good Mexican soil while reaching toward the heavens. Embracing this symbolism, the temple's landscaping centers on these important trees.

On May 21, 2000, President Thomas S. Monson dedicated the Villahermosa Mexico Temple in a series of four dedicatory sessions with nearly four thousand Church members in attendance. He was visibly moved by the love and excitement on the faces and in the voices of the local Saints.

Maria Elena Balboa was baptized in 1957 and is reportedly the fifth person to join the Church in Tabasco. "I always wished for a temple in my town, but never really thought it would happen," Sister Balboa said. "Today I'm so happy. I've even been called to work in the temple."

It was a marvelous day of rejoicing and thanksgiving as more than twenty-eight thousand Latter-day Saints in eight stakes and two districts received a temple to call their own. Their feelings were aptly expressed by Samuel Oteo, a longtime member of the Church when he humbly said, "I have prayed often for a temple in this part of Mexico. Today, I am very, very happy and grateful to my Heavenly Father."

Chad/Hawkins ©2015

Montreal Quebec Temple

Montreal, Quebec, which lies on the banks of the St. Lawrence River, is a city of contrasts. Old-world charm mixes comfortably with skyscrapers and hurried businesspeople. Many residents of Montreal are bilingual, speaking both French and English. Building a temple in this Canadian city worked to unite the people, tradition, and future of this beautiful and varied land.

The engraving on the Montreal Quebec Temple's cornerstone reads, "Edifiè en L'an 2000," or "Erected in 2000." But the history of the Church in this part of Canada began long before that historic year.

While serving as president of the Canadian Mission, President Thomas S. Monson sent the first six French-speaking missionaries to Quebec in 1961.

In 1978, the Montreal Quebec Stake, the first French-speaking stake in North America, was created. As these events took place, the hope of a temple grew.

So it was with much rejoicing that the Saints in Montreal greeted President Gordon B. Hinckley's August 6, 1998, announcement that a temple would be built in their city. Seven months later, 450 invited guests took part in the April 9, 1999, groundbreaking for the Montreal Quebec Temple. The services were held in the empty garage of a vacated automobile dealership, which was later demolished to make way for the temple.

A little more than a year later, from May 20 to 27, 2000, the temple's week-long open house attracted nearly ten thousand visitors. The temple

86

was then dedicated in four sessions on June 4, 2000, by President Gordon B. Hinckley. The sixth temple to be built in Canada, the Montreal Quebec Temple serves Church members living in the Canadian provinces of Quebec and Ontario and the state of Vermont in the United States.

The temple's location is a great blessing to local members. For decades, faithful Saints in Quebec traveled great distances to serve in the temple. English-speaking members drove forty-five hours to the Cardston Alberta Temple, and French-speaking members had to travel to the Bern Switzerland Temple to attend a session in their language. The construction of temples in Washington, D.C., and Toronto, Ontario, Canada, brought temple worship closer, but travel even to these locations was long and difficult. Georges Bourget, second counselor in the first Montreal Quebec Temple presidency, explained the members' tradition of temple service and their willingness to sacrifice: "We in this area are a temple-loving people, and we were known for our faithfulness in attending the temple," he said. "I think that's one of the reasons we were able to receive a temple, even though the Church is relatively small here."

This faithfulness was evident in December 1992, when members of the Montreal Quebec Stake showed their commitment to temple service by keeping an appointment to be in the Toronto Ontario Temple despite a heavy snowfall that kept them on the road for twelve hours. On that stormy day, noted a member of the temple presidency, "only members from the Montreal Quebec Stake crossed the white curtain of snow around the temple" to serve in the Lord's house.

The following year, members of the same stake set a goal for temple attendance. Stake president Michel J. Carter, in a 1993 stake priesthood meeting, said, "Brethren, to better prepare for upcoming stake conference, let us as a stake go together to the temple in numbers large enough to perform saving ordinances for an *entire ward* beyond the veil." What President Carter had in mind was to perform all the ordinance work for six hundred individuals. During one three-day visit to the Toronto Ontario Temple, stake members achieved their goal.

But even those who had never experienced nor heard of the Montreal Saints' tradition of temple service felt the excitement of the new temple in their midst. From the time of

SITE
2.4 acres

GROUNDBREAKING
April 9, 1999, by Gary J. Coleman

DEDICATION
June 4, 2000, by Gordon B. Hinckley

EXTERIOR
Bethel white granite from northern Vermont

TOTAL FLOOR AREA
10,700 square feet

DIMENSIONS
149 feet by 77 feet

HIDDEN IMAGE
An image of the Christus statue is located on the surface of the temple.

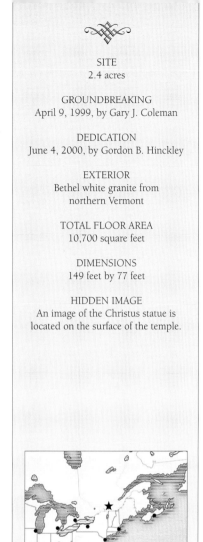

its announcement until its dedication, the temple helped increase public awareness of the Church in Montreal. Local leaders used all avenues of the media and took advantage of every opportunity to explain the importance of temples and to publicize Church beliefs. Montreal stake president Sterling H. Dietze related that during an interview with a local radio station, the interviewer commented, "It's really amazing how attached your Church seems to be to a building—almost like the ancient Jews [to the temple at Jerusalem]." The interview was the perfect chance for President Dietze to explain the heritage and importance of temple worship. He made it clear that although this attachment "is to a building, . . . it's more than the building."

One lifelong resident of Montreal, Jeanne Clement, 91, worked to compile family names back to 1529. In the past she had traveled twelve hours to the Washington D.C. Temple and then later nearly seven hours to the Toronto Ontario Temple to complete the ordinance work for those family members. With the dedication of the Montreal Quebec Temple, her journey was cut to only thirty-five minutes. Sister Clement realized it would be an adjustment for her to have a temple so close. But her commitment to temple work in Montreal is evident: "I wonder what we'll do," she said. "We won't go for a week, just for a day. I hope I will be able to go once a week."

Over the years, extreme weather conditions and humidity caused water to penetrate the temple's exterior surfaces. As water seeped within the temple walls, mold began to form and wood rotted. Once the problem was identified, it was soon determined that the temple needed to be closed and renovated. On Monday, June 2, 2014, the Montreal Quebec Temple closed for a complete renovation of the interior and exterior. Much of the wood framing was replaced with steel, and the mold problem was eradicated. The temple's new stone exterior was increased in thickness, and triple-pane-windows were tightly sealed to prevent future problems. During the process, many efforts were made to further beautify and improve the function of the temple. For example, the ordinance rooms were decorated with beautiful landscape murals, a new angel Moroni was installed, and a maple leaf motif was added to the exterior to give the edifice a unique appearance. The temple was completed and rededicated in the fall of 2015.

Chad Hawkins © 2015

San Jose Costa Rica Temple

San Jose is the capital of Costa Rica and the nation's largest city. In one particularly picturesque part of the city stands a landmark that attracts faithful Saints from all over this Central American country and offers much more than just a beautiful view. High above the Costa Rican heartland, near the summit of the active Poas volcano, is a lookout point shrouded in sulfur mist much of the year. Here, the San Jose Costa Rica Temple represents to Latter-day Saints the promise of an eternal vista.

Although the Church is relatively young in this part of Latin America, Costa Rica has proven to be a land ready for gospel growth, as Church membership has grown from thirty-eight hundred in 1977 to thirty-five thousand in 2000. The Church increased

by another 11,000 members in the decade after the temple's dedication.

The two-acre temple site is located in San Antonio de Belén near an expressway that connects San Jose with the international airport. Regular airline passengers know that the temple can be seen from the air when departing from or arriving at the airport. The temple's exact location was originally part of an expansive thirty-acre colonial ranch and coffee plantation. "Belén" is the Spanish word for "Bethlehem."

The angel Moroni statue was elevated into position on February 12, 2000. Many members witnessed the historic event along with hundreds of local neighbors and curious pedestrians. Considering

87

that 71% of the nation is Roman Catholic, those who were not LDS members naturally thought the golden statue depicted a Saint. Many of those attending showed their respect to the event by making the sign of the cross in the Catholic tradition. Since that time, neighbors have respectfully referred to the statue as "Saint Moroni."

As temple construction progressed, neighbors judged the large size of the building would result in loud and distracting worship services. According to Costa Rica Church historian Mario Jimenez, "Neighbors had a wrong impression about the temple and they thought someday they would need to complain about the noise. They thought the temple would be the site of massive religious gatherings, high-decibel sound systems, and live orchestras. As the construction progressed, they were impressed by the beauty of the building and finally realized that members were discreet, respectful, and educated."

Before the completion of the San Jose Costa Rica Temple, Elder Enrique R. Falabella, an Area Seventy, shared his thoughts on the members' sacrifice to attend the nearest temple, at that time the Guatemala City Guatemala Temple: "I believe that Costa Ricans love the temple," he said. "Even though it is expensive to travel to the Guatemala City Temple—often the cost is twice the monthly income—members still make the effort."

The sacrifice referred to by Elder Falabella was evident long before the Guatemala City Guatemala Temple was built. In January 1976, eighty-four Latter-day Saints, including forty-six from Costa Rica, traveled by bus eight thousand miles round-trip to attend the Mesa Arizona Temple. Misael and Maria Alfaro, who had been baptized in 1956, saved their money to make the excursion with all eight of their children.

"A short time before they were to leave, Brother Alfaro lost the money he had saved for the trip. When he told his wife, they wept, then prayed for help to raise the needed money. A shoemaker, Brother Alfaro took all of his handmade shoes to a neighboring town and sold them for whatever he could

SITE
2 acres

GROUNDBREAKING
April 24, 1999, by Lynn G. Robbins

DEDICATION
June 4, 2000, by James E. Faust

EXTERIOR
Blanco Guardiano white marble
from Torreón, Mexico

TOTAL FLOOR AREA
10,700 square feet

DIMENSIONS
149 feet by 77 feet

HIDDEN IMAGE
The Good Shepherd is found
holding a lamb in the palm trees
to the left of the temple.

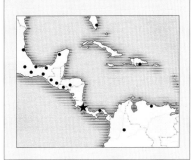

get. When he returned home, still short of the needed amount, he sold his car. 'The blessings of being sealed together in the temple will last forever,' he says. 'It was worth our sacrifice.'"

Such trips were greatly simplified with the dedication of the San Jose Costa Rica Temple on June 4, 2000, by President James E. Faust, Second Counselor in the First Presidency. Heavy rains preceded the dedicatory services, forcing the closure of the airport. But the rains subsided and the sun broke through for the dedicatory services, which some four thousand Saints attended.

Stake president Henry Obando says that another temple in Latin America was simply one more historic step in realizing the eternal blessings promised to Heavenly Father's faithful children. "The temple has already made such a difference in our Church units," he said. "Now there are two kinds of members: those who are ready for the temple, and those who are getting themselves ready for the temple."

The temple's average schedule consists of thirteen sessions per week. Before the construction of additional temples in Central America, members from surrounding countries would plan regular temple visits. During these excursions, a special request is made to Costa Rican members to not use the temple to allow for more room for the international visitors. Members traveling from far distances frequently lodge with local members. This tradition of kindness has resulted in lasting friendships that transcend borders.

During the temple's first decade of history, the sacred edifice has served the members well and has not been closed for major renovation. Although the country has experienced multiple 6.1–7.6-magnitude earthquakes, the temple has not suffered structural damage. In 2009, basic maintenance was performed and new art murals were installed in the endowment room. In 2011, a lightning strike significantly damaged and completely darkened the angel Moroni statue. The damaged statue was promptly replaced with a new "Saint Moroni," as the local neighbors would say.

Fukuoka Japan Temple

Fukuoka, Japan, is located in the northern part of the island of Kyushu. Japan's closest major port to mainland Asia, Fukuoka has a population of 1.3 million. In the midst of one of Japan's largest and busiest centers, the Lord's house provides peace and reverence for those who go within its doors and those who look to it as a landmark.

The Fukuoka Japan Temple is designed much like other small temples, with a few slight variations. In an area where the price of land is exorbitantly high, the temple uses the property's space as efficiently as possible. The gray granite covers the building's lower level, which includes parking space, a mission home, mission offices, and an apartment for the temple president.

The housing of the mission facilities and the temple's highly visible location have prompted many to refer to it as a "Missionary Temple." It is placed on the top of a lush forested hill and positioned in front of the municipal zoo and botanical garden. Thousands of people pass by it every day as they enjoy a wonderful afternoon with their families. As missionaries teach investigators or talk with people in the street, many say they have already seen the temple in front of the zoo.

Japan Fukuoka Mission President C. Samuel Gustafson and his wife, Linda Gustafson, have described having the mission facilities under the temple as a unique opportunity. In the words of Sister Gustafson, "As missionaries, the temple reminds us about our purpose, not just baptizing

88

178

people but guiding them to eternal covenants that can only be done in the temple. The excellent mission office location allows temple visiting members to visit with office missionaries, drop off little gifts, volunteer in the office, or just say 'hi' and thank us for our service. We are extremely grateful for the members and enjoy spending time with them. This is a sacred, beautiful place to live and feel the Spirit. When missionaries first arrive, they feel very much at home here and comment, every time, about the peace and warmth this place has. We are blessed beyond belief to be where we are."

The construction of this unique structure on a relatively small piece of property brought challenges. Workers lacked space to store materials and equipment. A solution was found when workers realized the neighboring zoo was closed on Mondays; they then arranged to use the zoo's parking lot to temporarily store equipment and supplies. Monday subsequently became the busiest and most crucial day of the week during the temple construction.

The temple is also unusual in that its entire two-story structure is made of concrete and steel. "Not a two-by-four was used in the entire building," said temple construction missionary Elder Charles H. Blackburn. Concrete and steel were chosen to make the structure virtually earthquake-proof; these materials also saved on costs because of the high price of wood in the area. The sidewalks, driveways, and parking areas make extensive use of tile.

The land on which the temple is built is of historic significance to Latter-day Saints in Fukuoka. Pioneering Church members remember when the Church obtained the property for a meetinghouse. The site was then "out in the boondocks," said Eugene M. Kitamura, area director of temporal affairs for the Church and a native of Fukuoka. At that time the road to the area was not paved, and those walking to church through the rain were lucky if they didn't lose their shoes in the mud. Later, a mission home also occupied what has become the temple site.

Members rejoiced at the closeness of the temple when ground was broken for the Fukuoka Japan Temple on March 20, 1999. Presiding at the groundbreaking was Elder L. Lionel

SITE
1.25 acres

GROUNDBREAKING
March 20, 1999, by L.
Lionel Kendrick

DEDICATION
June 11, 2000, by Gordon B. Hinckley

EXTERIOR
Empress White and Majestic
Gray granite from China

TOTAL FLOOR AREA
10,700 square feet

DIMENSIONS
149 feet by 77 feet

HIDDEN IMAGE
The Savior's image with clasped
hands is located on surface of
temple among the shadows.

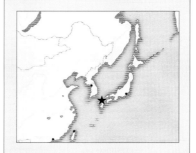

Kendrick of the Seventy and president of the Asia North Area. "When a temple is built in an area it lessens the evil influences of the adversary. It brings blessings to the area and to its people," said Elder Kendrick. "These blessings come not only to the members of the Church but also to all those who live in the bounds of the temple district."

Bringing the Church out of obscurity in Japan has been a difficult task—only one percent of the population is Christian, and Latter-day Saints account for about ten percent of that number. Creating public exposure for the temple and its open house was also a challenge because news media outlets of every kind refused to run stories that could be seen as promoting religious groups.

Members gained strength as they fasted and prayed every month to offer thanks for the temple and to petition for its construction to proceed without difficulty. Construction did proceed according to plan, and a week before the dedication, a three-day open house was attended by more than forty-eight hundred people.

Among the cultural decor items native to Japan are two elegant plates displayed in the celestial room. These handmade traditional ceramic plates were created by local LDS artisan Taiichi Aoba.

Although it took place during the region's rainy season, the dedication of the Fukuoka Japan Temple on June 11, 2000, was warm and dry. President Gordon B. Hinckley dedicated the temple in four sessions. The timing of the dedication of the second temple in Japan was also appropriate, as the year 2000 marked the fiftieth anniversary of the beginning of missionary work in Japan.

Temple construction missionary Elder Charles Blackburn shared his experience in helping to build the temple and his growing love for the Japanese people. He began his mission unable to speak Japanese. This obstacle was overcome with the help of quick pencil sketches, bilingual Church members, and full-time missionaries who acted as interpreters. With these aids, he was able to communicate with the workers, and they and Elder Blackburn developed respect for one another—a respect that helped them achieve their goal of building a house of the Lord.

Adelaide Australia Temple

A modern city situated on the Torrens River and made up of broad streets, large squares, and extensive parks, Adelaide is the capital and chief city of the state of South Australia. The Adelaide Australia Temple is located just a few miles from the Adelaide city center.

When President Gordon B. Hinckley announced that there would be 100 temples throughout the world by the end of the year 2000, the Australian Area Presidency was assigned to find a suitable temple location in Adelaide. With the assistance of three stake presidents, the Marden location was selected.

On March 17, 1999, the Adelaide Australia Temple was announced. An example of the wonderful surprise that accompanied the news is captured by the words of senior missionary Elder Arthur Evans. Of the experience, he wrote, "A message came through the mission office fax machine. I casually walked over and picked it up and started to read—and read and then re-read. I could not believe my eyes. I shouted, 'We are going to have a temple here in Adelaide!' I am known in the office for my joking ways and the staff thought I was not serious. What excitement there was when they finally knew it was true."

On May 29, 1999, five hundred people gathered for the groundbreaking of the Adelaide Australia Temple. In the midst of black clouds and heavy rain, the ceremonial beginning of the temple began. In the comfort of the neighboring chapel, Elder Vaughn J. Featherstone of the Seventy gave credit to

89

the Church members in Adelaide for faithfully serving the Lord as they awaited the day in which a temple would be closer to home. He talked of the Saints who had traveled between fifteen and twenty hours each way to attend the temple in Sydney. For their efforts, he said, "They surely merit a temple in their midst." At the conclusion of the service, the congregation proceeded to the temple site, and as they did, the rain stopped. Dark, ominous clouds gave way to clear skies, and Church leaders broke ground.

The site for the Adelaide Australia Temple was once a productive farm and orchard. Later, the site featured a small college and cricket field.

As workers labored on the temple, many were continually surprised by the high quality specifications. For example, the temple has more structural galvanized steel than a traditional building three times its size. A foreman approached temple construction missionary Elder R. Dean Titensor and said, "There is a tremendous amount of re-bar under this building. It should last forever."

Elder Titensor responded, "That's exactly what is planned."

On the evening of May 9, 2000, several young women and their leaders from the Golden Grove Ward came to the temple. They helped to install the crystal on the large chandelier in the celestial room and the two smaller chandeliers in the sealing rooms.

While working with the temple tradesmen, temple construction missionaries and Elder and Sister Titensor had many opportunities to answer questions about the Church and the purpose of the temple. "The workers are as excited about their work as we are, and they recognize that this building is very special to us," Elder Titensor said. "They feel the Spirit. We have had several other requests for the Book of Mormon from the workers. At Christmas time we prepared our testimony and gave each of the office construction staff a copy. We do it with the faith that it may be read sometime and that the Spirit can touch their lives. They are all very good people."

The temple was officially handed over to Church leaders

SITE
6.94 acres

GROUNDBREAKING
May 29, 1999

DEDICATION
June 15, 2000, by Gordon B. Hinckley

EXTERIOR
Snow white granite

TOTAL FLOOR AREA
10,700 square feet

DIMENSIONS
149 feet by 77 feet

HIDDEN IMAGE
An image of the Christus statue is located on the surface of the temple.

by the construction company on June 1, 2000. The temple was ready to welcome all to the well-planned open house. Many Church members considered the open house to be a historical turning point for the Church. It marked the beginning of recognition by the community that The Church of Jesus Christ of Latter-day Saints was coming of age in Adelaide.

Many were affected by the construction of the new temple. The entire community was intrigued by the temple after substantial media coverage made local citizens aware of its presence. As a result of extensive publicity as well as personal invitations from Church members, many people were prepared to tour the temple; nearly fifty thousand took advantage of the opportunity. The number was remarkably high considering the relatively small number—twelve thousand—of Church members in the temple district. In total, the number of people attending the temple open house represented almost five percent of the total population of South Australia.

The dedication of the Adelaide and Melbourne Australia Temples and the planned construction of two more in Perth and Brisbane were fulfillments of many years of preparation by Australian Latter-day Saints. "Formerly, many of our members had to overcome Australia's famed 'tyranny of distance' to attend the Sydney temple," remarked Elder Bruce C. Hafen, who served as president of the Australia–New Zealand Area. "Where previously a temple visit was just an occasional encounter, now the Saints throughout Australia will have an opportunity for a lifetime of temple experiences."

The temple's first president, Robert J. Wilmott, was given the assignment to write the preface of the temple's historical compilation that would be placed in the cornerstone. Within the preface he wrote, "The Church today has come out of obscurity and is respected by most people. Our chapels have been a blessing to us, and now we have the greatest blessing which we could ever wish for, a temple. A temple, a House of the Lord, at our door steps."

Melbourne Australia Temple

Before the Melbourne Australia Temple was built, local Saints faithfully visited the Sydney Australia Temple. Members making this ten- or twelve-hour journey would often leave Friday evening and travel all night, arriving at the temple by six o'clock Saturday morning. After serving for the entire day in the temple, they would leave in the evening, arriving home early Sunday morning in time to sleep a few hours before attending their church meetings.

"For sixteen years we have traveled the 1,500 miles round trip to the Sydney temple, and before that many members of the Church here had to sacrifice—sometimes their house, car, and other possessions—so they could afford to make the journey to the New Zealand Temple," said Melbourne Australia Pakenham Stake president Murray Lobley at the temple's dedication. "We are now no longer enslaved by the tyranny of distance. We have been truly blessed to have a temple built in Melbourne."

The first efforts to find a suitable spot for a temple in Melbourne, a city in southeastern Australia and the capital of the state of Victoria, were made in 1997 when President Gordon B. Hinckley announced that he was planning a trip to Australia and New Zealand to visit the Saints. Before President Hinckley's arrival, Elder Bruce C. Hafen of the Seventy, then first counselor in the Australia–New Zealand Area presidency, was asked to identify locations in Melbourne and Brisbane as possible temple sites. It was not until after President

90

Hinckley's visit to Australia that he outlined the program to build smaller temples.

The nearly four hundred participants at the groundbreaking service, held on March 20, 1999, also greeted the temple's formal beginning with joy. "It's no surprise that we are commencing a temple here, at this time," said Elder P. Bruce Mitchell, an Area Seventy and second counselor in the Australia–New Zealand Area presidency. Elder Mitchell assured members that their faithfulness in attending the Sydney Australia Temple had not gone unnoticed by the Lord. He honored those who had so many times made the long trip to Sydney.

When Sister Edna Ord of Melbourne's Northcote Ward heard the announcement of the temple, her response was one of joy, but not surprise. "Oh, yes, isn't it marvelous?" she said. "When I heard the announcement, I said, 'Oh, Elder McConkie, you were right.'"

Eighty-four-year-old Sister Ord had served for eighteen years as secretary to the mission presidents in Melbourne. She remembered when Elder Bruce R. McConkie, later a member of the Quorum of the Twelve Apostles, was mission president in Australia and had said to her, "I promise you, Edna, you will have a temple in Melbourne."

A temple in Melbourne was foreseen at least forty years earlier by President Spencer W. Kimball, then of the Quorum of the Twelve Apostles. When the Melbourne Australia Stake was formed in October 1960, President Kimball ordained local member Frank Davenport a Seventy. Elder Kimball blessed Brother Davenport that he "would have his temple in Melbourne."

Sixteen years later, in 1976, as part of a high council assignment, Brother Davenport was given the task of finding suitable land on which to build a stake center. His initial site selections were met with stiff opposition from residents. In a meeting with a city council, Brother Davenport felt impressed to invite them to propose a location for the new Church building. Within hours, the council contacted him with an invitation to meet with them again. They offered a beautiful orchard property, and Church leaders gladly accepted. The stake center and, many years later, the Melbourne Australia Temple were built on that orchard site.

When construction on the temple began, workers ran into a few unexpected challenges. The actual position of the temple

SITE
5.98 acres (including adjacent meetinghouse)

GROUNDBREAKING
March 20, 1999, by P. Bruce Mitchell

DEDICATION
June 16, 2000, by Gordon B. Hinckley

EXTERIOR
Snow white granite

TOTAL FLOOR AREA
10,700 square feet

DIMENSIONS
149 feet by 77 feet

HIDDEN IMAGE
Among the trees left of the temple is the Savior. Additionally, the shape of Australia is found among the trees to the right of the temple.

had been the location of an old dam. This resulted in difficulties creating a solid foundation. The solution was to remove massive amounts of existing soil and replace the soil with over twenty-four tons of special gravel from a nearby quarry. During this excavation process, several old chemical drums were uncovered. This discovery caused concern that some of the soil might be contaminated and therefore unsafe. Excavation was halted until experts could test soil samples, but it was ultimately determined that the soil was not hazardous.

Another interesting development helped workers make up lost time. On several occasions, the building union called a strike that affected the locations of the contractor's other projects but not the area where the temple site was. Under those conditions, the contractor reassigned workers from the affected sites to the temple project without causing any difficulty with the union. The extra workers helped keep the temple project on its tight schedule.

The more than twenty-eight thousand visitors to the temple's week-long open house admired the temple's exterior, which is an attractive light gray Italian granite, as well as the beauty and peace of the temple's interior. The grounds feature sweeping lawns and a rose garden.

Temple construction missionaries Neil and Beverly Ann Langley oversaw the temple's construction and had a profound influence on most of the workers. Their experience in the construction trade and their willingness to help were a great benefit to the project. As Christmas approached in 1999, Elder and Sister Langley carefully gift wrapped forty copies of the Book of Mormon and presented them to the workers before the holiday break. The books were appreciated by the recipients.

The Melbourne Australia Temple was dedicated by President Gordon B. Hinckley on June 16, 2000. "The number of friends we are making in the community because of the temple is just overwhelming," said Pakenham Stake president Murray Lobley. "The lives of tens of thousands within the Church and without will continue to be touched by the temple—here in Melbourne."

This temple—and the others in Australia—are a tangible sign and a direct result of the growth of the Church in that nation. The last national census in Australia identified The Church of Jesus Christ of Latter-day Saints as the fastest growing Christian faith in the country.

Suva Fiji Temple

In October 1997, President Gordon B. Hinckley visited Fiji, an independent republic in the southern Pacific Ocean composed of more than three hundred islands, one hundred of which are inhabited. At a meeting of the Saints during that visit, President Hinckley asked everyone in the congregation who desired a temple in Fiji to raise his or her hand. Every hand shot into the air. Excitement was even greater not long afterward when, during April 1998 general conference, President Hinckley officially announced the Suva Fiji Temple.

Before the completion of the Suva Fiji Temple, Saints in the temple district traveled to Tonga, Samoa, or New Zealand to attend the temple. These trips were long and expensive, and many Saints had limited resources. One family sold their home to raise the funds so they could travel to New Zealand to be sealed. Other faithful Church members likewise sacrificed whatever was necessary to receive their temple ordinances.

Members in the temple district may now attend much more conveniently. Their beautiful temple is located at one of the highest points in Suva, the capital of Fiji, and overlooks the Pacific Ocean on three sides. The granite exterior walls create a striking contrast to the lush green vegetation that surrounds the building.

The site was identified by President Hinckley in October 1997 as the preferred location for the temple. The owners of the property were originally willing to sell it but later took it off the market. Though Church leaders made several attempts to acquire it, it was no

91

longer available. Eventually, leaders identified three other possible sites and were about to take them to the General Authorities for approval. Elder Quentin L. Cook, then a member of the Quorum of the Seventy and president of the Pacific Islands Area, explained, "The original owner called and said that the property would be sold to the Church and at a very reasonable price."

During the dedicatory services, Elder Cook explained that once the site was obtained and construction had begun, workers discovered several underground concrete bunkers. Elder Cook read from a history of the area written by Elder Allen Christensen, who had served as the executive secretary for the Pacific Islands Area presidency, that the bunkers "had been erected during World War II for the defense of Suva." Elder Cook declared, "Where once stood structures erected to resist [invasion] will now stand a fortress of faith, a House of the Lord . . . where the blessings of eternity can be given to the faithful."

The peaceful setting of the temple belies the unwanted excitement that surrounded the temple's opening. On May 19, 2000, a few weeks before the planned open house and dedication, amid ethnic tensions, armed rebels took several government officials hostage. Because of safety concerns in the volatile political climate, the temple open house received limited publicity. Even then, the six-day event brought more than sixteen thousand members of the public and three hundred community leaders to tour the temple.

Temple guides noticed that attending the open house often brought visible relief to the worried citizens of Fiji. "As we took them through the temple, we saw the cares of the world melt away and, by the time they reached the celestial room, you could tell that they were experiencing something very special," said Elder Cook, who conducted tours for community leaders.

One organizer of the open house shared a particularly touching experience: "Three high-ranking military men came through and were very quiet and reserved when they viewed the introductory video. I spoke with the second-in-command and asked how he felt when he looked in the reflections in the mirrors in the celestial room. He said he had studied eternal life for many years and had never understood it, but when he looked in the mirrors it all came clear to him and he was excited." The senior officer asked if it would be possible to bring the full military council to tour the temple. "Because of the strife in Fiji,"

SITE
10 acres

GROUNDBREAKING
May 8, 1999, by Earl M. Monson

DEDICATION
June 18, 2000, by Gordon B. Hinckley

EXTERIOR
Snow white granite

TOTAL FLOOR AREA
10,700 square feet

DIMENSIONS
149 feet by 77 feet

HIDDEN IMAGE
Profile shapes of the Fiji
islands are in the clouds.

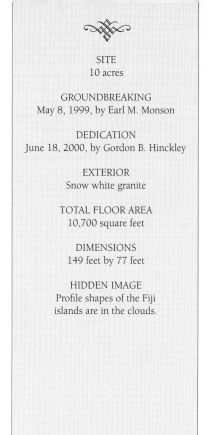

Sister Adams explained, "he felt that the temple was a place they could come and close out the outside world . . . and find peace."

Despite the political unrest, President Gordon B. Hinckley dedicated the Suva Fiji Temple on June 18, 2000. Believing that holding the usual four dedicatory services might be unwise, the First Presidency decided on one small dedicatory session attended mostly by members of the local temple committee and their families. Mindful of the difficulties in the land, President Hinckley petitioned for peace in the temple's dedicatory prayer. "We pray, dear Father," he said, "that these beautiful islands may be blessed with peace, that there shall be no abridgment of the great freedom of worship afforded by the government of this land."

President Hinckley described his feelings after this unusual dedication. "There was a great outpouring of the Spirit," he said, "matched by the feeling of good fellowship among those in attendance." Others commented that the unity of Church members greatly outweighed the political and ethnic division in the country, as evidenced by the love shown by Saints of all ethnic groups at the temple dedication.

The dedication of the Suva Fiji Temple also represented a historical Church event. For the first time, four temples were ready for dedication almost simultaneously. On an extended trip that included meetings with the Saints and other events in addition to the temple dedications, President Gordon B. Hinckley dedicated the Fukuoka Japan Temple on June 11, 2000, the Adelaide Australia Temple on June 15, 2000, the Melbourne Australia Temple on June 16, 2000, and the Suva Fiji Temple on June 18, 2000.

Almost a year following the temple's dedication, President Hinckley returned to Fiji to meet and share a message with Latter-day Saints. His visit was especially meaningful because members were not invited to the temple dedication due to civil unrest. With only about twelve hours' notice, members gathered from throughout the island for a meeting, during which many were moved to tears at seeing and listening to the prophet. Speaking of political unrest that plagued the island country in June 2000, President Hinckley said, "I hope that after the trouble of the coup that there is a more settled feeling here, and that peace will reign in this land, and that the Lord will smile with favor upon you and increase your blessings."

Mérida Mexico Temple

Latter-day Saints living in Mérida, Mexico, capital of the state of Yucatán, are acutely aware of current archaeological research. The history of Mérida, located in the center of Mesoamerica and home to important archaeological sites, may date back to Book of Mormon times. "We love the Book of Mormon; we can *feel* the Book of Mormon," said a branch president in Ticul, a town sixty miles from Mérida.

Mérida is part of the Yucatán Peninsula, which projects into the Atlantic Ocean and separates the Gulf of Mexico from the Caribbean Sea. Founded by the Spanish in 1542, Mérida sits atop an ancient Mayan city. A good number of Church members in this peninsula rich in history meet in dozens of chapels and now flock to a temple of the Lord.

In an area near the famous Uxmal and Chichen Itza Mayan ruins on the Yucatán Peninsula, Elder Carl B. Pratt of the Seventy presided at the ceremonial groundbreaking for the temple on January 16, 1999. Elder Pratt told the more than five hundred members who had gathered for the event: "We want to establish a culture of temple attendance. From sacrifice comes blessings. I know that the construction of this temple will add to the strength of the home; it will add to the love of husbands and wives; it will add to the peace in the Yucatán Peninsula."

The time they now spend to care for their temple is indeed a blessing, not a sacrifice, to these faithful Saints who used to make long, expensive excursions to the temple in Mexico City. The temple in

92

Guatemala City, Guatemala, is actually closer geographically for these Saints, but to reach it, they had to cross an international border, a jungle, and several mountain ranges. These obstacles made the one-thousand-mile trip to the Mexico City Mexico Temple an easier option.

Yet that journey was very costly, and many sacrificed for years to pay their travel expenses. They did so because they know that temple blessings are priceless. Some longtime members even gratefully endured two-week trips to the Mesa Arizona Temple. "Many sacrifices marked those temple trips to Mesa," said Jose Andres Parra, a pioneer Church member in Mérida. "Sometimes it would take four days to travel to the temple. Then we would spend four days in the temple and another four days to return to our homes."

Another pioneer Church member in the area, Celia Carrillo, who was baptized in 1959, described a journey to the temple in Mexico City on a train infested with mice that "scurried across [her] feet as [they] traveled." On a later temple trip, Sister Carrillo was with a group of Saints on a rented bus when the driver lost control on an isolated section of highway and the bus ended up in a gully.

"I didn't want to open my eyes for fear some of the members had been killed," Sister Carrillo said. Fortunately, the passengers' injuries were minor, but as they climbed out of the bus, they were confronted with robbers preparing to get whatever they could from the stranded bus riders. Suddenly, and without explanation for their change of mind, the robbers quickly left the scene. Nearby villagers offered assistance and medical care. "We talked then about returning to Mérida and forgetting about the temple, but we all said, 'Let's continue on,'" Sister Carrillo shared.

Although many of these hardships are now in the past, they will never be forgotten. Remembering these sacrifices increases the Saints' gratitude for their temple.

The Mérida Mexico Temple is located in the old section of the city, where the roads are narrow and the history of the area has been preserved. When Church leaders proposed building a temple there, city planners required that aesthetic and historic consistency be maintained, so designers included a wall

SITE
1.53 acres

GROUNDBREAKING
January 16, 1999, by Carl B. Pratt

DEDICATION
July 8, 2000, by Thomas S. Monson

EXTERIOR
Blanco Guardiano white marble
from Torreón, Mexico

TOTAL FLOOR AREA
10,700 square feet

DIMENSIONS
77 feet by 149 feet

HIDDEN IMAGE
The shape of the Yucatán Peninsula
is found in the left main bush.
The famous Mesoamerican
pyramid of Chichen Itza is
located in the right main bush.

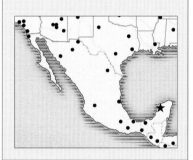

in front of the temple that harmonizes with existing structures. But the old did give way to the new when the stake center, mission office, and seminary building on the temple site were removed. The future of the Church is manifest here: the remaining property is large enough for a stake center to be built when the time is right.

The Mérida Mexico Temple was dedicated in four sessions on July 8, 2000, by President Thomas S. Monson. For Domingo Renan Perez Maldonado, then president of the Mérida Mexico Itzimna Stake, the event was a fulfillment of prophecy. He had been hoping for a temple to be built near his home ever since he served as an interpreter to Elder David B. Haight of the Quorum of the Twelve Apostles during a 1979 visit to the Yucatán Peninsula.

"The Apostle told us a temple would be built here someday," he said. "This temple will be a place of spiritual light for everybody." Since its dedication, it has become known as the "Temple for Mayans." Groups of members of Mayan descent frequently travel together to the temple to enjoy the spirit of the house of the Lord in their own language. Living among an abundance of ancient ruins, they form rural communities and derive their living by cultivating the land. When arriving at the temple, they are welcomed by Mayan-speaking workers, who officiate in the sessions. "It is marvelous to see them arrive in their colorful native dresses, anxious to feel the Spirit that surrounds this holy place," said Sister Enriqueta Pia Gomez, former temple matron. Former temple president Fernando Gomez said, "It is a great testimony for all of us to see these people, descendants of Father Lehi, and in their humble conditions, participate in temple work and be an example us all."

In 2002, the love and respect members have for their temple was demonstrated when members descended upon properties adjacent to the temple. Arriving early in the morning, hardworking volunteers chopped through jungle brush, picked weeds, and gathered trash. Working with enthusiasm, members collected a massive five hundred cubic feet of debris. Members made a commitment to maintain the area in the future to ensure temple patrons will have a more fruitful experience as they visit the holy temple.

Veracruz Mexico Temple

On January 28, 1996, President Gordon B. Hinckley spoke to nine thousand Church members gathered for a regional conference in Veracruz, Mexico. He reminded listeners of a visit he had made to Veracruz in 1978, when there was only one stake of the Church there. "The Church has grown substantially in the intervening years," he remarked; the large crowd gathered to hear him speak that day was evidence of that growth. Through an interpreter, he told the congregation, "The more often you go [to the temple], the more certainly you will know of the truth of this great work in the house of the Lord." In an earlier meeting, with more than one thousand local priesthood leaders in attendance, President Hinckley reminded leaders of their stewardship over the spiritual

growth of their brothers and sisters in the gospel. "You have responsibility for the work of the Lord in this great area," he said. "It will stand or move forward according to what you do. . . . We are all in this together, to build the kingdom of God in the earth; and if we work together, nothing can stop us."

Nothing has stopped them. Their efforts resulted in the announcement of the Veracruz Mexico Temple on April 14, 1999, three short years after President Hinckley's counsel to members in Veracruz.

On May 29, 1999, many of those same stake and ward leaders and their families attended the groundbreaking for the new temple. The temple is located in a beautiful part of the city and positioned only 1,200 feet from popular sandy beaches. Services were held

93

at the temple site outside Veracruz, an important seaport in eastern Mexico dating back to the sixteenth century. Elder Carl B. Pratt of the Seventy presided at the occasion, and during his remarks he acknowledged the early Saints in Veracruz, who had faithfully sacrificed to travel to the temple in Mesa, Arizona. Their example prepared the members for this day of building a temple nearby, Elder Pratt said. "We are preparing the earth for the Second Coming," he continued, "and with the temple we will be better prepared to do so."

The members may have been prepared for the temple's construction, but there was still work to be done among government officials and citizens of Veracruz. Under pressure from the public, city officials hesitated to give the temple project supervisors a license to begin construction. For months, Church leaders made unsuccessful weekly attempts to acquire the license. Finally, Rodolfo "Rudy" Avalos, the project supervisor, met with the mayor. With the mayor's support, city officials finally granted the license, and construction on the temple began.

The construction of the temple was not completed without difficulty, but again the Lord's guiding hand was evident. On one occasion, workers were digging a seven-foot-deep trench to accommodate a sewer line. During the digging, the trench unexpectedly caved in and completely buried two men. "We could not find them for a few seconds," Brother Avalos explained. "We were finally able to uncover their heads, which allowed them to breathe while we dug them out. It was a blessing no one was killed." All who were present that day realized that a fatal accident had been prevented, and they acknowledged the Lord's blessings upon their work.

A watchful heavenly eye also helped workers the day the angel Moroni statue was placed atop the temple. Workers and Church leaders were concerned about the weather. "It had been raining heavily, and I asked the workers and bishops to pray that the rain would cease," Brother Avalos explained. "It is extremely dangerous to place the angel on the metal spire when it is raining because of electrical currents." He continued, "As we prepared to raise the angel, it immediately stopped raining. Once the statue was in position, the rain began to fall again." Workers were able to complete this task on time and maintain their tight construction schedule.

SITE
3.39 acres (including adjacent meetinghouse site)

GROUNDBREAKING
May 29, 1999, by Carl B. Pratt

DEDICATION
July 9, 2000, by Thomas S. Monson

EXTERIOR
Blanco Guardiano white marble from Torreón, Mexico

DIMENSIONS
77 feet by 149 feet

TOTAL FLOOR AREA
10,700 square feet

HIDDEN IMAGE
The Pyramid of the Niches located at the El Tajin pre-Columbian archeological site near Veracruz is rendered near the temple's entrance beneath the flag.

With the construction completed, the dedication of the Veracruz temple was scheduled for July 9, 2000. Shortly before the dedication, Church officials learned of a large all-terrain vehicle and motorcycle rally scheduled to take place near the temple on the morning of the dedicatory services. That event, with its crowds and loud engines, was planned for a location less than fifty yards from the temple grounds. Both it and the temple cornerstone ceremony were to begin at 9:00 a.m. Dedication organizers were concerned and wondered how to maintain the reverent feeling appropriate for placing the cornerstone of a house of the Lord. But Sunday morning arrived with rain showers significant enough to cancel all the scheduled off-road vehicle events. Ron Weekes, media specialist for the dedication, observed, "I know that the hand of the Lord was involved with what transpired."

In his opening comments during the first of the four sessions, President Thomas S. Monson, who presided and gave the dedicatory prayer, acknowledged the hand of the Lord in making sure the dedication of the Veracruz Mexico Temple could be carried out in the spirit it deserved.

Latter-day Saints in Mexico may forever recall the year 2000 as the year of Mexican temples. Two temples were operating in Mexico when the year began, and eight new temples were dedicated in that country during 2000. Two more temples have since been announced—in Guadalajara and Monterrey. This phenomenal increase has made it possible for almost every Church member in Mexico to reach a temple within a four-hour drive.

The great increase in temple building has not gone unnoticed by the citizens of Mexico. Many citizens consider the temples to be the most beautiful buildings in their cities. And after years of sacrifice to attend the temple, grateful Church members are showing their appreciation by being a temple-attending and a temple-loving people. Rodolfo Avalos, project supervisor for the Veracruz Mexico Temple, summed up the feelings of many: "It is a very wonderful process to prepare temples for the Lord. I am grateful for these opportunities. I have grown from all I have experienced."

Baton Rouge Louisiana Temple

The Baton Rouge Temple sits partially in a swamp at the base of a small hill and is only sixteen feet above sea level. Despite its big-city setting, visitors to the temple are impressed by its natural and picturesque surroundings. Members rejoiced in this fulfillment of a dream on May 8, 1999, when ground was broken for the temple. Although a hot and typically humid Louisiana day, approximately twenty-five hundred people gathered to witness the historic event.

When the marble veneer for the temple's exterior walls was shipped to the construction site from Vermont, one of the eighteen-wheel delivery trucks arrived after the construction crew had left. Only the foreman, Max Quayle, was still on site to receive the shipment of ten crates of marble, each weighing

three-quarters of a ton. Brother Quayle unloaded two crates, and then a hydraulic line on the forklift broke.

The truck driver needed to get back on the road quickly, so the only solution seemed to be to unload the truck by hand. A few phone calls were made, and within fifteen minutes, twenty-five young Latter-day Saints were there, ready to assist with the seemingly insurmountable task. They unloaded the remaining eight crates, approximately fifteen thousand pounds of marble. The young men went the extra mile by placing the marble, piece by piece, around the temple where workers could use it as it was needed. Although it was a night of very hard labor, it was work that made the Baton Rouge Louisiana

94

Temple even more of a blessing to the young men who participated.

The final chapter in the building of the temple occurred on July 16, 2000, when President Gordon B. Hinckley dedicated the temple.

In 2005, the Atlantic hurricane season proved to be the most active in recorded history. Category 5 Hurricane Katrina was the costliest natural disaster in the history of the United States. President D. Gregory Brumfield and Sister Alicia Brumfield served as the temple's first president and matron (2000–2005). Hurricane Katrina, which occurred only months prior to their release, would become the most dramatic experience of their five years of service. Of the experience, Sister Brumfield related the following: "The president and I knew the storm was coming, so we went to the temple to lock it up and make sure everything was secure. Before we left, we said a prayer. . . . You know if there is something large in a river, the river goes around the object on both sides . . . that is exactly what happened at the temple. The hurricane went around the temple on both sides, and we sustained very little damage.

"After being closed for a couple of days we opened the temple. We only had a couple of temple workers, but we knew we needed to be open for those who wanted to come to the temple. Our policy was, 'The Lord will provide and He will take care of us. We just need to move forward.'

"As the temple matron, I watched my brothers and sisters come to the temple looking like zombies. Their home was gone, their neighbors were gone, their food storage is gone, their genealogy is gone. . . . They only had the clothes on their backs and nothing more. They had lost their facial expression. Think of someone who is disoriented but somehow knew where they needed to be. The temple was their refuge. Honestly, they had just lost everything and their state of mind was so overwhelmed. . . . They were in shock. As the matron, I would welcome them and give them a hug."

Jeanne Christensen, living in Utah County at the time of the hurricane, called the temple to offer assistance. After learning

SITE
6.3 acres (including adjoining meetinghouse)

GROUNDBREAKING
May 8, 1999

DEDICATION
July 16, 2000, by Gordon B. Hinckley

EXTERIOR
Imperial Danby white marble from Vermont

TOTAL FLOOR AREA
10,700 square feet

DIMENSIONS
149 feet by 77 feet

HIDDEN IMAGE
Among the trees and foliage is a full-length image of the Savior.

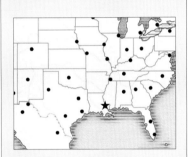

of the situation, she immediately spread the word in her ward and stake that members attending the Baton Rouge Temple had lost their temple clothing. Sister Christensen said, "Within days and weeks we had received an overwhelming amount of packets and new temple clothing for men and women of all sizes. We organized all shoes, dresses, and clothing by size and sealed them in plastic containers and sent them to the temple. In the end, over a hundred packets were sent. Included in every package, hidden in pockets of pants or dresses, were handwritten notes of encouragement, which included sentiments like 'We are praying for you,' 'We love you,' and 'We are here for you.'"

In 2008, category 4 Hurricane Gustav's devastation had an indirect impact on the temple. In the immediate aftermath of the hurricane, thousands of member volunteers from the southern states descended upon the temple grounds to gather, pitch tents, and prepare to serve the Baton Rouge community. The adjoining stake center served as a command center for the hurricane rescue and cleanup operation for the 2,000+ service requests. As volunteers pitched their tents on the temple property, they purposefully positioned their tent "door towards the temple" (see Mosiah 2:6).

On a Sabbath morning, the number of gathered volunteers required that sacrament meeting be held outdoors on the temple grounds. Stake President Randall Bluth described the special experience: "It really was a remarkable event to look at the sea of yellow 'Helping Hands' T-shirts gathered on the hill around the temple. We didn't have enough sacrament trays, so we used huge cookie sheets for the bread and water cups. Following the brief sacrament meeting, we all went out into the community and worked where needed.

"It was powerful. It is hard to describe in words what kind of an event that was. . . . It just felt like the heavens opened as we were there to serve people after a disaster. . . . And then to look over at the temple and realize that there is an eternal purpose for all that we do—it was unforgettable."

Oklahoma City Oklahoma Temple

In March 1999, Church members in Oklahoma City learned that a temple would be constructed next to their meetinghouse. Stake president Gary J. Newman asked in a sacrament meeting, "Would any of you mind giving up your baseball field for a temple?"

Years earlier, when the Church had purchased the property for that meetinghouse, the sellers had donated an additional parcel of land. A meetinghouse was built on the property, and members often enjoyed a baseball game on the donated portion. With gratitude for the Lord's blessings, they rejoiced in the proposal to put the land to another, more sacred use.

Invitations to the groundbreaking ceremonies on July 3, 1999, were kept to a minimum to avoid disrupting the surrounding neighborhood. It was a clear and hot Oklahoma summer day, occasionally punctuated with a cooling breeze. During the groundbreaking, David L. Lawton, president of the Oklahoma City Oklahoma South Stake, spoke of a tornado that had devastated much of their stake just two months earlier. "I feel, in looking back, that there was a great purpose of the Lord in the tornado: (1) it strengthened us—helped us all remember how temporary the things of this world are. [They are] not to be relied on. (2) It . . . temper[ed] opposition to our temple. More than 100,000 Latter-day Saint hours of volunteer labor were given in behalf of those whose homes and businesses and schools and churches were ravaged. The 8,000 members giving a helping hand in the

95

192

community made others view the Mormons in a different light."

Elder Rex D. Pinegar of the Seventy also referred to the tornado disaster during his address: "As we drove through the area of its swath, we saw signs on top of the rubble. . . . 'We've been crushed but we're not out,' 'Temporarily out of service.' . . . As we scanned the area, we saw nothing standing but the people. A sign on a demolished home read, 'In God we trust.'" These signs, Elder Pinegar said, displayed the character of the members and the community living in the vicinity of the planned Oklahoma City temple.

Although it was devastating, many local Latter-day Saints agreed that the tornado helped prepare the way for the temple. The Church's aid in cleanup and relief efforts had a dramatic effect on the community's perception of the faith. Leaders and workers were able to proceed with their building plans because there was no substantial obstacle or notable opposition over building the temple.

The design for the temple did have to be altered slightly for the temple to fit the selected site, however. Architects adjusted the floor plan of the Oklahoma City Oklahoma Temple by mirroring the original plan. Instead of entering toward the right end of the building, patrons go through an entrance on the left. Once inside, they find the baptistry on the left instead of the right as in most other small temples.

Local Church members were always ready to assist with the temple. One day a landscaping contractor did not keep his commitments by laying the sod. A bishop made some phone calls, and within an hour, more than 150 members were on the site laying sod. One member with a tractor graded the site until 2:00 a.m.

As the temple neared completion, member service was utilized in the celestial room. On the evening of June 23rd, a "Crystal Party" was held with forty-one members. Those in attendance had the unique experience of hanging crystals one by one on the chandeliers in both sealing rooms, the celestial room, and the bride's room. This was an exciting time of sharing and service by members who in the future will always remember their unique contribution to the temple.

The temple's fourteen-day open house was attended by more than forty thousand visitors. The open house itself differed in its approach from previous ones. Organizers

SITE
1 acre

GROUNDBREAKING
July 3, 1999, by Rex D. Pinegar

DEDICATION
July 30, 2000, by James E. Faust

EXTERIOR
White marble quarried in Vermont

TOTAL FLOOR AREA
10,769 square feet

DIMENSIONS
149 feet by 77 feet

HIDDEN IMAGE
The Savior is depicted on the surface of the temple.

experimented with replacing the traditional self-guided, silent tours with tours in which a guide explained the rooms. At first, half the tours were self-guided and half were not. But the guided tours were clearly more successful, and organizers soon arranged for all the remaining tours to include assistance from a guide. In the end, the open house resulted in the placing of fifteen hundred copies of the Book of Mormon and receiving thirty-eight missionary referrals. The guided tours were so successful that they were adopted for use in open houses at other temples.

The completed white marble Oklahoma City Oklahoma Temple complements its country atmosphere, standing among tall green trees near a golf course and a quiet residential area in northwest Oklahoma City. At night, the temple can be seen from great distances.

The building's peaceful and dramatic beauty has impressed many in the temple district, which encompasses an area once known as Indian Territory. In the 1840s, thousands of Native Americans were forced from their homes in the cold of winter. They found refuge in Oklahoma. Their march, called the "Trail of Tears," was filled with sickness and death. Former Oklahoma City Temple president H. Jerrel Chesney described the emotional significance of having a temple in this part of the country: "After being driven and suffering as they did, the government then designated this as the official home of the Lamanite people. Now the gospel is here for them with the full benefits." Many members living in the temple district are descendants of those who were forced here and live on the same land as their ancestors.

The temple was dedicated on July 30, 2000, by President James E. Faust, Second Counselor in the First Presidency. Anne Pemberton, a Latter-day Saint and a member of the Delaware tribe, commented: "It's home. . . . [The temple] is sacred and on sacred ground. Our ancestors have waited. They rejoice in this day."

A major tornado outbreak occurred on February 10 and 11, 2009. Tornadoes ripped through parts of Oklahoma, killing nine people and injuring fifty others, with more than 29,000 homes losing power. Church members and missionaries in the affected Oklahoma areas were safe. However, several exterior lights and cars on the Oklahoma City Oklahoma Temple grounds suffered serious damage from hail. It was a blessing that the temple was spared other significant structural damage.

Caracas Venezuela Temple

Venezuela's varied geography ranges from Amazon rain forests to high mountain peaks to balmy beaches. Caracas, its capital, is located twenty-seven hundred feet above sea level and is blessed with temperatures at a nearly constant seventy degrees Fahrenheit.

On November 2, 1966, Elder Marion G. Romney of the Quorum of the Twelve Apostles dedicated the country for the preaching of the gospel. Within weeks, four missionaries from the Costa Rica mission were sent to Venezuela. They found the work hard and the growth slow in the beginning.

Nonetheless, strong individuals and families began entering the waters of baptism. In under eight years, Church membership in this beautiful land had grown to nearly four thousand.

In 1974, the first Latter-day Saint meetinghouse was constructed in the nation. In the mid-1980s, twenty years after the entrance of missionaries into the country, Church membership had reached nearly twenty-five thousand.

In a session of general conference on September 30, 1995, President Gordon B. Hinckley announced plans to construct a temple in Venezuela. Immediately after this announcement, the search for an appropriate building site began. Several properties were identified and considered over the next eighteen months. But because of circumstances ranging from extremely high prices to zoning restrictions that would not allow religious use of the land, no suitable location was found.

Despite discouraging setbacks, the prophet did not lose sight of the goal. On April 5, 1997, President

96

Hinckley again stated in general conference, "The search for a suitable property continues in Venezuela."

When President Hinckley announced the concept of smaller temples, new options opened up in Venezuela, and representatives of the Church reexamined existing holdings in the country. The decision was made to build a house of the Lord in the city of Caracas on a lot the Church had owned since 1977.

Groundbreaking ceremonies were held Sunday, January 10, 1999, with approximately three hundred people crowded into the Caurimare Ward chapel in Caracas to hear their leaders speak at the services. Construction began soon thereafter.

Several unforeseen obstructions blocked progress on the temple construction. For example, when digging the foundation, excavators discovered an underground spring. Once the water was diverted, excavation could continue. The digging, however, caused two landslides. Both occurred after working hours when there were no workers in harm's way, but the second landslide did cause some damage—eight tons of earth and materials were shifted in the slide.

Construction supervisor Duane Cheney stated: "In all my experience as a builder, never have I had the problems that I have seen in temple construction, but besides the fact that the adversary works with power and strength, the feeling that fills me is that all will work out well.

"In fact the Lord, Jesus Christ Himself, directs this project and has helped us and will continue doing so."

The design of the Caracas Venezuela Temple follows the general plan for small temples with the model number "S-240," which means a small temple with two endowment rooms and seating for forty in each room. However, the topography of the building site required a few changes that actually increased the total square footage. To ensure that the baptismal font was lower than other parts of the temple, a second floor was added. The consequent rearrangement of the floor plan allowed for a more spacious and accommodating entry and lobby. The Caracas temple became the first larger small temple in the world, known in the Church archives as model number "S-240 Caracas."

The interior design and decor of the Caracas Venezuela Temple is the result of loving service by local Saints. The lamps

SITE
0.5 acres

GROUNDBREAKING
January 10, 1999

DEDICATION
August 20, 2000, by
Gordon B. Hinckley

EXTERIOR
Granite

TOTAL FLOOR AREA
15,332 square feet

DIMENSIONS
78 feet by 115 feet

HIDDEN IMAGE
The Savior is depicted in the landscaping near the temple's entrance. Oxen are included in the landscaping beneath the temple.

and chandeliers, chosen for their beauty and luminosity and imported from Spain, were assembled in part by volunteers. Nine young women and their mothers and grandmothers carefully placed nearly five thousand crystal pieces in the lamps and chandeliers for the sealing rooms and the celestial room.

Two sisters who are artists created paintings for the temple that represent the country of Venezuela.

The exterior of the temple is granite, imported from Spain and cut and polished in Venezuela. The polished surface gleams almost like a mirror in the sunshine.

Nearly six thousand Latter-day Saints from the temple district attended the four dedicatory sessions presided over by President Gordon B. Hinckley. Perhaps the most important counsel he gave the Saints was never to let a day pass without holding a current temple recommend. Members were obviously deeply moved by the presence and counsel of the living prophet.

At the conclusion of the day's events, President Hinckley, his wife, Sister Marjorie Hinckley, and others in their party climbed into the waiting cars. As they drove from the temple grounds, thousands of Venezuelan Saints saluted the procession, waving white handkerchiefs and singing in their own language, "We Thank Thee, O God, for a Prophet."

President Ruiz of the Caracas Venezuela Stake summed up the feeling among the Saints toward this new house of the Lord as he reminded the people that temples bring blessings—and new responsibilities: "The Venezuelan temple will leave our people spiritually refined," he said. "Our people are going to change. Venezuela is going to change."

Despite political and economic challenges, Church leaders in Venezuela work hard to maintain unity within their congregations while political divisiveness rages outside the walls of their chapels. In 2003, amid government strikes, revolts, and shortages of food and fuel, members tried to remain positive and have gospel unity among those split by political opinion. While the government and banks were shut down and schools closed, the temple doors remained open for those seeking peace from the world's oppressive cares. President Ruiz said, "We have talked about ways to become closer to God and feel peace inside [the Church], even when there is no peace outside."

Houston Texas Temple

Houston, Texas, the fourth largest city in the United States, is home to the ninety-seventh temple of The Church of Jesus Christ of Latter-day Saints. The Church members who live in this area know that it was only through the Spirit of the Lord, combined with years of preparation on the part of local members, that the pathway was made clear for the construction of a house of the Lord.

On January 9, 1997, President Gordon B. Hinckley recorded in his journal: "We are moving forward on the construction of new temples. I made a suggestion to the Council of the Twelve that we . . . proceed to secure ground for a temple in Houston, Texas. President Monson, President Faust, and the

Twelve approved this, and I discussed it in the Temple Sites Committee today."

On February 19, 1997, the search for a temple site began. Houston realtor Steve Cook, a member of the Church who had assisted Church representatives in purchasing real estate in the past, was asked to help find the site. Several potential sites were located, but Brother Cook's top choice belonged to a prominent real estate developer who had no desire to sell. The developer replied, "There's no amount of money that would interest me in selling that property." He had, in fact, received offers from other parties but was holding that prime location in reserve for a project of his own. Brother Cook worked to build a trusting relationship with this developer and

97

maintained an interest in the site. A different religious organization had previously treated the developer dishonestly, and he was extremely cautious as a result.

Brother Cook continued to meet with the property owner and, in time, the owner realized he could trust the Church. This developer had faced financial ruin in the 1980s and had humbly knelt in prayer, asking for God's intervention. Circumstances changed, and he survived the challenge. In an effort to show gratitude for that answered prayer, he decided that he should sell the land for the "Mormon cathedral." Not surprisingly, this soul-searching decision happened on the same weekend that President Gordon B. Hinckley chose this site from among the several possibilities proposed to him.

The Houston Texas Temple was originally intended to resemble the temple in Billings, Montana, but the plans were altered to provide an architectural design and plan more harmonious with local buildings. The final approved design was closely patterned after the exterior of a historic Washington D.C. chapel.

Brother Steve Cook shared some thoughts about his involvement with the temple: "It was astounding to me to witness the miracles that continually occurred in achieving the Lord's purposes and seeing people's hearts changed. Additionally, it was humbling to see the Lord exercise His influence in such a pragmatic way; He moves and touches men's hearts to accomplish His purposes."

Construction on the temple required specifications of "zero tolerance" for disrespect. The high standard was not the requirement only for construction crews. Every worker on site was under contractual obligation to exhibit honest, clean, and respectful behavior. Swearing or improper behavior was grounds for immediate removal.

Even the temple's landscaping was a testimony of the spiritual preparation of the Saints in the area. Several months before the temple was announced, Brother Richard Gieseke, a local nursery owner, had a very vivid dream of gardens surrounding a beautiful temple. Because of the power and detail of the dream, Brother Gieseke felt impressed to begin collecting plants and trees and growing them for the temple. Soon, miraculous events began occurring in his business that allowed him to purchase and grow plants and trees of outstanding quality and beauty. In August 1998, for example, he received a call from a construction foreman offering him thirty large crape myrtles

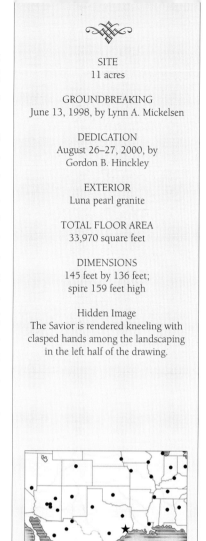

SITE
11 acres

GROUNDBREAKING
June 13, 1998, by Lynn A. Mickelsen

DEDICATION
August 26–27, 2000, by
Gordon B. Hinckley

EXTERIOR
Luna pearl granite

TOTAL FLOOR AREA
33,970 square feet

DIMENSIONS
145 feet by 136 feet;
spire 159 feet high

Hidden Image
The Savior is rendered kneeling with clasped hands among the landscaping in the left half of the drawing.

that were about to be destroyed by a bulldozer. In one-hundred-degree heat, four twenty-five-foot myrtles in ground as hard as concrete were carefully excavated. These myrtles now stand at the front of the temple's entryway, their unusual white flowers contrasting beautifully with the temple's gray granite exterior.

Crape myrtles also surround a beautiful garden on the north side of the temple. The garden has a fountain and benches as well as a meandering brick walkway that leads along the edge of the natural foliage. As the walkway moves closer to the temple, the plants become more formal.

When Brother Gieseke heard the announcement for the Houston Texas Temple, he immediately contacted his stake president about donating plants for the landscaping. Members of the temple committee were delighted with the beauty and quality of the plants and trees offered by Brother Gieseke and used them to create elegant and unique gardens for the temple.

Geometric designs form the basis of many elements created for the Houston Texas Temple, including the grounds, the exterior, and the interior. Of all the geometric forms used, the circle—which has no beginning or end—is perhaps the most prominent.

The temple has a total of 120 stained-glass windows, all imported from Germany. They range in size from small ovals to the multi-paneled window in the celestial room, which measures more than thirty feet in height. Each first-level window contains almost two hundred individual pieces of stained glass held in place by a polished, highly reflective, silver-toned lead.

Fearing that the work of placing the statue of the angel Moroni might damage the finished granite exterior of the temple if the wind blew or the crane operator made an error, contractors planned to position the sculpture early in the construction process. On June 16, 1999, at 11:00 am, a large crowd gathered to witness the placement of the statue of Moroni. As the angel ascended, an organized Primary choir, dressed in their Sunday best, sang "I Love to See the Temple." At 11:45, the statue was placed into position. Joyful onlookers applauded and the Primary choir sang "Families Can Be Together Forever."

The Houston Texas Temple was dedicated on August 26, 2000, and serves a temple district that encompasses the southern half of Texas.

Birmingham Alabama Temple

In early September 2000, Alabama became home to the ninety-eighth temple of The Church of Jesus Christ of Latter-day Saints. The Birmingham Alabama Temple, which took just eleven months to go from groundbreaking to dedication, is located in the Birmingham suburb of Gardendale, where it sits on a heavily wooded hill across the street from the Gardendale Branch meetinghouse. Interestingly, the name of the street where the temple is located is Mount Olive Boulevard.

In December 1998, the Church announced that it would like to build a temple next to the meeting-house in Indian Springs, Alabama. A groundbreaking date was even set. However, tests on the site revealed that the earth there was too unstable to permit the construction. Additionally, the community did not

react favorably toward the proposition. Another site was located and investigated, but again obstacles arose that prevented the project from beginning. Finally, in April 1999, the First Presidency of the Church approved a site in Gardendale. The Church had actually purchased the property in the early 1990s and had promptly constructed a small meetinghouse on it. The remaining property was large enough to accommodate a temple and allowed it to face east. Although there were many options on how to situate the temple on the grounds, its final location was chosen by President Gordon B. Hinckley.

Gardendale is a conservative, family-oriented area. The residents oppose such potentially negative influences, and they have thus far prevented those

98

types of businesses from encroaching into the community. Town leaders welcomed the temple project, however, believing that the Church, its values, and a beautiful temple would be assets to the community.

Before construction on the temple could begin, a building permit was required. To obtain the permit, the Church had to ensure that the temple's sewer line could be attached to an existing county sewer line. This was a challenge because the sewer line was on the other side of two major roadways. Both state and county permits had to be granted before the Church could dig beneath the two roads. Applications were made, impact fees paid, and the Church received all of the required building permits.

Temple construction missionary Dale L. Arave was a key figure in acquiring the permits. He recalled: "As we were going down the road one day, I had just about given up on getting a sewer permit when I thought, 'Let's go over to the courthouse one more time and perhaps we can work something out.' I went to the courthouse and spoke with the man that I needed to talk to, and I found him in a friendly mood. He said, 'If you give me your plans I will stamp them and we will get it done.' I happened to have the plans in my car and got them stamped. And with that approval I was able to get the building permit the same day. It was miraculous the way it happened, and that is one of the reasons why we believe that the Lord wants the temple in Gardendale." Digging the tunnels was challenging because located under the highway were large fiber optic cables, which if broken would cost millions of dollars to repair. Although a difficult task, the job was completed without a problem. Elder Arave said, "We have felt the hand of the Lord helping us to accomplish the things that were done."

On October 9, 1999, the heavens seemed to open up for the twenty-three hundred Latter-day Saints attending the groundbreaking ceremony. Those in attendance huddled under umbrellas and said the heavens "wept for joy." In his remarks,

SITE
5.6 acres (including adjoining meetinghouse)

GROUNDBREAKING
October 9, 1999

DEDICATION
September 3, 2000, by
Gordon B. Hinckley

EXTERIOR
Imperial Danby white marble
quarried in Vermont

TOTAL FLOOR AREA
10,700 square feet

DIMENSIONS
149 feet by 77 feet

HIDDEN IMAGE
A full-length image of the Savior
is positioned overlooking the
temple's celestial room.

Elder Stephen A. West told those huddled under the multitude of umbrellas: "When we drove in about an hour before this meeting was to start, we saw already hundreds of people here, umbrellas up. And my wife and I started to cry. We were touched by your faith." Elder West said that life takes sacrifice. "You are sacrificing here as you come today, as you sit in the rain. And it will take sacrifice to come to the temple. It will take commitment and it will take belief. It will require of each of us that we live worthy of having a temple recommend. . . . Yet it really is not a sacrifice—it really is a blessing."

The golden angel Moroni statue was hoisted into position on March 30, 2000. Due to the lack of space, the event was not publicized, and fewer than 100 people were present. As the temple neared completion, there was heightened anticipation in the community to attend the open house. More than twenty-one thousand visitors toured the temple during the week-long open house.

Less than a year after the groundbreaking, on September 3, 2000, President Gordon B. Hinckley presided at all four dedicatory sessions and the traditional cornerstone ceremony. As he had in so many places in recent months, President Hinckley approached the cornerstone of the temple with a trowel and a small amount of mortar.

"I'll take a little mud here and try to move this along now so you don't have to stand too long out in the Alabama sun," said the prophet. And when others, including children, were invited to follow his lead in sealing the cornerstone with additional mortar, he quipped, "Just like making a cake, except put more on the crack and less on the floor."

Alabama's first temple serves twenty thousand Latter-day Saints in Alabama and Florida. As with most temples, it has not come without years of commitment and faith preparing the way. The same spirit of commitment and faith fills the hearts of worthy members who come here to serve and partake of the blessings of the temple.

Santo Domingo Dominican Republic Temple

Located in the southern part of the Dominican Republic, Santo Domingo is the country's largest city, chief seaport, and capital. Founded in 1496 by Bartholomew Columbus, brother of Christopher Columbus, the city is the oldest European settlement existing in the New World. The temple is located on a rise in the western part of Santo Domingo beside a park for the National Music Conservatory. Overlooking the waters of the Caribbean Sea, the Santo Domingo Dominican Republic Temple is fast becoming a beacon of strength for members throughout the Caribbean.

On December 7, 1978, Elder M. Russell Ballard of the First Quorum of the Seventy dedicated the Dominican Republic for the preaching of the gospel.

In 1979, more than three hundred fifty people were baptized. In 1981, the first mission was organized, and the LDS population reached twenty-five hundred members. In 1998, Church membership had reached more than sixty thousand, making the nation ripe for a house of the Lord.

As with many regions of the world, financial struggles in the Caribbean made it difficult for many families to go to the temple. Although several Dominican families had visited temples in the United States, most had attended temples in Guatemala, Peru, or elsewhere in South America. Before the temple in Santo Domingo was built, only five percent of families in the Church there had been able to receive the ordinances of the temple. Although few could go, they still maintained a vision

99

of eternity, participated in temple seminars, and hoped for a temple of their own someday.

The humble prayers of the faithful were answered when ground was broken for the first temple in the Caribbean area on August 18, 1996, by Elder Richard G. Scott of the Quorum of the Twelve Apostles. Some four thousand members attended the ceremony. The difficult task of excavation was overcome through patience and hard work. The task was largely accomplished by jackhammers and hand labor after attempts with bulldozers and other equipment proved futile in the hard coral rock.

In 1997, President Jose Castro of the Santo Domingo Dominican Republic Stake explained how local members were preparing for service in the temple. He said: "We are working in the area of obtaining family history information for temple work. Members are to receive help from stake family history specialists. Our goal is to have at least 170,000 names available when the temple doors open." In preparation for the temple, he noted: "In the year 1996, we took 10 excursions to the Lima Peru Temple. Also, another group traveled to the Orlando Florida Temple. In 1997, we have made plans and will take nine trips to Peru and other trips to other temples. The members who are preparing themselves for the temple are serving as missionaries and look forward to being temple workers. Their enthusiasm is very, very great."

The temple district serves thirty five stakes, including seven stakes spread throughout the Caribbean area. The temple has four ordinance rooms and four sealing rooms and was built according to the Church's customary high standards for materials and workmanship. But more than that, the temple serves as a source of strength to a rising generation of youth who are striving to live a high moral standard.

Many who recall once praying for the country's first chapel are now rejoicing for their own temple. Thousands of Dominicans and their neighbors from Haiti and Puerto Rico gathered to witness the temple dedication on September 17, 2000. President Gordon B. Hinckley presided over the four

SITE
6.42 acres

GROUNDBREAKING
August 18, 1996, by Richard G. Scott

DEDICATION
September 17, 2000, by
Gordon B. Hinckley

EXTERIOR
Regina white granite

TOTAL FLOOR AREA
67,000 square feet

DIMENSIONS
88 feet by 190 feet

HIDDEN IMAGE
An image of the Christus statue is
located among the palm trees.

sessions. Members who were not able to attend in person were able to participate at stake centers via satellite transmission.

The excitement of the new temple extends beyond Dominican borders. For the first time, Haitian members will now be able to drive to a temple. Although there are deep-set cultural, political, and economic differences between the two nations, the gospel of Jesus Christ brings the members together. "There has been a history of trouble between our two countries, but when we are in the celestial room of this temple there will be no Dominicans, no Haitians—only daughters and sons of our Heavenly Father," said Haitian member Marie Berpetue Robert.

During October and November of 2007, Hurricane Noel ravaged much of the Caribbean, leaving death and disaster in its wake. The storm brought six days of continual rainfall to much of the Dominican Republic, resulting in heavy flooding, eighty-five deaths, and 75,000 displaced people. Many people are still missing. "We really got hit—a 100-year storm," said Kay Briggs, the Church's temporal affairs director in the Dominican Republic. The Santo Domingo Dominican Republic Temple, which was built on a rise in the capital city, suffered no water damage. In fact, electrical power was never interrupted inside the edifice, thanks to internal generators. "The temple stood like a beacon," Brother Briggs said.

The temple in Santo Domingo blesses the lives of Church members throughout the Caribbean. In 2011, the young men and women of Jamaica were able to take part in a "For the Strength of Youth" conference. Before making the journey, families identified and prepared thousands of names for the temple. For three days, 127 youth and 51 adults served in the temple. The trip culminated with eighteen families being sealed and 1,016 baptisms being performed. This remarkable trip was the largest trip ever from Jamaica and was achieved through months of preparation and individual sacrifice. Royce Britton, who helped organize the event, said it "was truly an incredible and amazing experience. It felt like we were in Zion."

Boston Massachusetts Temple

B oston, Massachusetts, a city rich in American history, is home to the Church's one-hundredth temple, which stands as a beacon of truth and spiritual freedom on Belmont Hill.

The construction of a house of the Lord at this location was not easy. The story began in 1995, when the Church announced that a location for a temple in the Hartford, Connecticut, area was being sought. After a day of unsuccessful searching, President Gordon B. Hinckley finally visited a piece of property that the Church already owned. Later that evening he recorded what happened when he walked about the property: "As I stood there I had an electric feeling that this is the place, that the Lord inspired its acquisition and its retention. Very few seemed to know anything about

it. . . . I think I know why I have had such a very difficult time determining the situation concerning Hartford. I have prayed about it. I have come here three or four times. I have studied maps and tables of membership. With all of this I have not had a strong confirmation. I felt a confirmation as I stood in Belmont on this property this afternoon. This is the place for a House of the Lord in the New England area."

Despite the prophet having received a confirming witness that this was the place to build the Lord's temple, challenges plagued the Church's efforts for more than four years. To accommodate earlier requirements and community wishes, the Church reduced the temple's size by fifty percent; more than a third of the remaining area is built below ground level. Despite the array of white steeples and belfries that dot the New England landscape, individuals who live in the neighborhood of the temple challenged the Church's right to build the structure as planned. Originally designed to have six spires, the temple has only one.

On October 8, 1996, Mitt Romney spoke to the zoning board of Belmont, Massachusetts, in favor of allowing the Church to proceed with plans for building a temple spire. In his introductory comments, he said: "Hi, I'm Mitt Romney. I live in Belmont. I stand, and I'd also speak, in favor of a tall steeple, steeples for my church. And in the future I'm going to stand in this room for any steeple of any church that wants to be built in this town, because I believe this town and this state, this commonwealth, and this nation needs more steeples, not less steeples, pointing symbolically to heaven, where I think the source of our blessings and the source of many of our questions come from."

With legal cases pending, the Church proceeded to build the temple. Grant Bennett, a local member who represented the Church during the heated public hearings, shared his thoughts on this vital decision. "In my opinion, [the decision was] both inspired and absolutely essential to the successful outcome. The decision was consistent with the general Church posture of politely but firmly moving forward to exercise its own rights as a landowner and religious institution in the face of opposition while fully respecting and honoring the rights of opponents to pursue every possible avenue to stop the temple."

As the temple walls rose, good-faith efforts were made to build trust and a positive feeling in the community. For example, a sound-proofing box was constructed and hoisted by crane over the jackhammer as the granite was drilled for the temple's footings. Large earthen walls were created to block the wind from blowing dust into neighboring yards. Construction trucks were washed before leaving the site to prevent them from scattering rocks and debris on public streets. Trees were planted on the grounds to block the light that neighbors complained would bother them. All of these efforts aided in softening many skeptical hearts in the community.

"The Church is deeply committed to being a good neighbor," said Brother Bennett. "Our attitude was to do more than

SITE
8 acres

GROUNDBREAKING
June 13, 1997

DEDICATION
October 1, 2000, by
Gordon B. Hinckley

EXTERIOR
Olympia white granite

TOTAL FLOOR AREA
69,600 square feet

DIMENSIONS
90 feet by 190 feet

HIDDEN IMAGE
A full-length image of the Savior
is positioned overlooking the
temple's celestial room.

was requested. We'd listen to the extreme claims that were made during public hearings then ask what more we could do."

Rumors and fears over almost every logistical aspect of the temple spread like wildfire throughout the community. Residents feared property values would plummet, traffic would become unbearable, and the temple spire would reign over the landscape. Opponents sought resolution in the state and federal legal system. A state judge banned the construction of the steeple, citing that the spire was not "necessary" to the function of the building. The decision was ultimately unanimously overturned by the state Supreme Court to the benefit of all religions in Massachusetts—it is the religion itself that decides what is religiously significant.

The open house, which began even before construction was completed, was held August 29 through September 23, 2000, and was attended by more than eighty-two thousand people. At the dedicatory services, President Hinckley commented: "It's time we had a temple in Boston. We're so glad it's here. We wish the steeple were on it. I regret that it isn't. But we can get along without it while awaiting the outcome of the legal action. In the meantime, we'll go forward performing the ordinance work of this sacred house." At the introduction of the temple's dedicatory prayer, President Gordon B. Hinckley said, "We are assembled to dedicate this thy holy house. It is a special occasion. This temple becomes the 100th operating temple of thy Church. We have looked forward to this occasion. We have prayed for this day."

Years following the temple's completion, Brother Grant Bennett observed that ultimately, the high-profile controversy served the Church well, simply because it forced LDS officials in both Massachusetts and Salt Lake City to explain the specifics of their faith in what ultimately became a widespread public education campaign. He noted that a decade after the controversy began, the state had an LDS governor in Mitt Romney; two LDS top administrators at Harvard; and former BYU basketball star Danny Ainge became an executive with the Boston Celtics. "We take government, education and sports very seriously," he said, implying that Massachusetts citizens are now more conversant about and comfortable with the LDS Church and its members.

Temples of the New Millennium

203

Recife Brazil Temple

Located on the Atlantic coast, Recife is one of the Brazil's eastern most cities. The Recife Brazil Temple is a dominating landmark positioned along a well-traveled highway. Missionaries in the area often meet people who know nothing about the Church but are familiar with the temple. The highly visible temple site is located only 600 feet from the Capibaribe River, which flows through the heart of Recife. Ocean breezes from the nearby Atlantic are ever present among the tall palms and sky-covering mango trees.

Located at the delta of the Capibaribe River, the property has a very high water table. The soft, swampy soil deterred other prospective buyers. The land seemed to be hidden to everyone until the Church purchased it and started construction of the temple. To prepare the soft land for construction, more than 1,000 pilings, or *stakes*, were driven to stabilize the land. The stakes supporting the temple have become a metaphor to local members of how their wards and stakes support the temple.

For generations, the property was an old, family-operated plantation. Growing on the plantation were mango, açaí, and cashew trees. Some of these old-growth trees remain on the temple site to beautify and to offer respect to the site's history. In the dedicatory prayer, President Gordon B. Hinckley referenced these trees: "We dedicate this beautiful site, the ground on which Thy temple stands with its trees and shrubs, grass and flowers. May they beautify this stately structure that it may be appreciated by the millions who pass this way."

101

Following a successful three-week temple open house that attracted 78,386 visitors, the temple was dedicated on December 15, 2000. Even in a torrential downpour, more than 7,000 members attended the temple dedication. The temple was the first to be completed in Brazil since the São Paulo Temple was dedicated twenty-two years previously. At the time of its dedication, the São Paulo Temple temple served 137,500 members in thirty-nine stakes and five districts in northern Brazil. Many of these members had not been able to make the cost-prohibitive, seventy-two-hour trip to Sao Paulo.

The temple complex includes housing for visiting patrons and temple missionaries. Former Recife Temple President Frederick G. Williams (2009–2012) shared his memories of the temple visitors: "When visitors come to the temple, they serve all day every day in the temple. Young children are sealed to their families, the youth serve in the baptistry, and adults take turns either watching the children or serving in the temple."

Sister Carol Y. Williams served as temple matron from 2009–2012. One evening after dark, Sister Williams was in the parking lot and noticed some trash. As she cleaned up the area, she tripped over a protruding reflector. In an effort to reduce the impact of her fall, she extended her arms and broke both of her wrists. After three painful months of medical care, she began to slowly regain the use of her hands. President Williams explained, "Although she lost partial use of her thumbs and was in constant pain, she was so grateful to be able to use her hands again that she wanted to show her gratitude. She began using her hands to make elegant white dresses for sisters in which to be sealed to their husbands and lovely dresses for daughters to be sealed to their parents.

Some of the members living in the most distant locations from the temple are also among the most dedicated. Located 350 miles off the coast of Western Africa, Saints living in the small nine-island country of Cape Verde are always saving and planning for their next temple trip. The distance to the temple is 1,800 miles across the central Atlantic Ocean. The nation's limited economy results in members being dependent partially on the Temple Patron Assistance Program. In 2014, over 142 members traveled to the Recife Temple to receive their temple blessings. Brother Holden Duarte, who works for Church Travel Services, shared the story of a faithful Cape Verdean. He said: "One sister named Rosa Varela is fifty years old and broke rocks for twenty years to save enough money to travel to the temple. Some people in Cape Verde break big rocks with a hammer and turn them into small rocks and sell the small rocks. The small rocks are used in construction. A small hand hammer is used to break the rocks. After attending the temple, she said her testimony was strengthened. Indeed, no sacrifice is too great to enter the temple."

Describing his own journey to the temple, Brother Duarte said, "My wife and I were married on September 3, 2012. We made a goal to go to the temple the same month. We had saved the exact amount needed to travel to the temple. However, the week we were to leave, our gas stove broke and we had no money to replace it. We would not touch our travel money. With faith in our hearts, we decided to travel to the temple, knowing that God would provide for us a new gas stove. After returning from the temple, we received a letter from one of our friends in the USA, and inside was twenty dollars. That was the exact amount we needed to purchase a new gas stove. We are so grateful for the opportunity that we had to enter the holy temple. We know that God lives. Our testimonies were strengthened. We know from the bottom of our heart that the Church of Jesus Christ is true. Being in the temple was an experience that will stay with me for my whole life and eternity."

SITE
5.59 acres

GROUNDBREAKING
November 11, 1996, by
Gordon B. Hinckley

DEDICATION
December 15, 2000, by
Gordon B. Hinckley

EXTERIOR
Asa branca granite from the
Brazilian state of Ceara

TOTAL FLOOR AREA
37,200 square feet

DIMENSIONS
114 feet by 158 feet

HIDDEN IMAGE
A full-length image of the Savior
is positioned among shadows
behind the palm trees.

Porto Alegre Brazil Temple

The beautiful temple in Porto Alegre is Brazil's southern-most and smallest temple. The city is located about sixty miles west of the ocean and on the northern end of a large coastal lagoon. Centrally located in the metropolis of 1.5 million, the temple is easily accessible from downtown and a nearby airport. The temple's beautifully landscaped two-acre grounds perfectly complement the neighborhood's name, Vila Jardim (Village Garden).

In general priesthood meeting on October 4, 1997, President Gordon B. Hinckley shared his inspired plans to construct small temples in remote areas of the Church. This historic announcement directly blessed the Saints in the vicinity of Porto Alegre. "There are many areas of the Church that are remote, where the membership is small and not likely to grow very much in the near future," President Hinckley said as he made the announcement. "Are those who live in these places to be denied forever the blessings of the temple ordinances?"

After breaking ground for the Campinas Brazil Temple on May 1, 1998, President James E. Faust, Second Counselor in the First Presidency, broke ground the next day for the temple in Porto Alegre. More than 3,500 people gathered on a hillside overlooking this southern Brazil city to witness the ceremonial beginning of construction.

The Porto Alegre temple is located at the apex of a gradual hill, which offers a beautiful view to the north. The sloping lawn and retaining walls provide multiple picturesque locations for newly

102

married couples to take treasured photographs. Construction of the temple was completed with high standards, said Andre Belo de Faria, temple architect: "I have worked for 20 years on various construction projects but I have never worked on a project of this quality; there is not another one like it in Brazil."

The temple's interior features two original oil paintings. A large oil painting by Frank Magleby, titled "Panorama of Iguacu," hangs over the sofa in the main lobby. Iguacu Falls is a world-renowned natural wonder on the border of Brazil and Argentina. Also included in the temple is an artistic masterpiece created by Valoy Eaton titled "Near Pelotas Brazil."

When the temple opened its doors to the public, over 25,000 visitors seemed very impressed. Elder Yatyr Moreira Cesar, Area Authority Seventy, described the open house as being very successful. "The neighbors love the temple," he said. "Many came to the open house, expressing their gratitude and pleasure that this extraordinary edifice is part of their community. The impact of the open house on missionary work is also extraordinary," continued Elder Cesar. "We received more than 1,000 referrals, written by visitors requesting missionaries, and many wanting to know if they can be baptized. We saw people who were hearing of the Church for the first time, shedding tears as they walked through the temple learning about eternal families."

President Gordon B. Hinckley's ambitious goal in 1997 was to have one hundred temples dedicated by the end of the century. The subsequent years resulted in the greatest period of temple expansion in Church history. As temples were rapidly built and then dedicated, a season of rejoicing unfolded for Heavenly Father's children on both sides of the veil. The achievements of that year in which temples were completed in eleven nations and fourteen U.S. states continue to stand as a miracle.

The Porto Alegre temple was the Church's 102nd temple, and the thirty-fourth and final one to be dedicated during a remarkable year of temples. On December 17, President Hinckley dedicated the temple and thus exceeded his announced goal to

SITE
2 acres

GROUNDBREAKING
May 2, 1998, by James E. Faust

DEDICATION
December 17, 2000, by
Gordon B. Hinckley

EXTERIOR
Cotton white granite
from Ceara, Brazil

TOTAL FLOOR AREA
10,700 square feet

DIMENSIONS
149 feet by 77 feet

HIDDEN IMAGE
The angel Moroni statue is seen
to the right of the temple in
the landscaping and flag

have at least one hundred temples operating by the end of the year 2000. The concluding dedication in Porto Alegre placed an exclamation mark on a year never to be forgotten.

Once dedicated, members began flocking to the temple, coming from locations within a temple district larger than the state of Texas. As of 2015, the temple serves thirty stakes and districts, 202 wards and branches, 76,000 adult members, and 9,000 youth. Prior to the temple's dedication, Saints from the Porto Alegre vicinity had to travel eighteen hours each way to Sao Paulo.

Twelve years after the temple's dedication, a beautiful patron housing building was added to the grounds. The attractive building has provisions to house the temple presidency, temple missionaries, and over sixty visitors. Unfortunately, there were problems receiving the needed occupancy permits from the city, and therefore the completed structure remained vacant for several years. In early 2015, permits were obtained and the building was opened for use.

Prior to the opening of the housing facility, temple patrons living in distant locations would travel by bus, leaving in the early hours on Saturday, and arrive at the temple by seven in the morning. After serving all day, they would repeat the lengthy bus journey home. For a minimal fee, patrons can use the housing and serve for multiple days while remaining alert and refreshed. Additionally, when large youth groups serve for extended hours, they can eat in the building's dining facilities.

The temple has weathered the elements and frequent torrential downpours well. However, during one violent storm, the angel Moroni statue was struck and damaged by lightning. The blackened statue was replaced in 2003.

The love members have for their temple is demonstrated by their faithful example of temple attendance. Although the Porto Alegre Temple is about one-third the size of all other Brazilian temples, almost as many ordinances are performed here annually as in many of the larger ones.

Montevideo Uruguay Temple

Montevideo, Uruguay, gathers all the qualities of a great capital city, from colonial charm to modern urban appearance. This flourishing city has consistently been rated as having the highest quality of life of any city in Latin America. Now it is also home to the spiritual focal point for the nation's Latter-day Saints—the holy temple.

The temple stands in a beautiful residential district of Carrasco, located a few miles east of the city center and less than a mile north of the area's most beautiful ocean beaches. The neighborhood features a wide range of architectural styles, affluent housing, and highly educated citizens. The dignified neighborhood provides a peaceful, beautiful setting for the temple.

The site has been owned by the Church since 1960 and also houses two mission homes, a distribution center, and a regional Church service center. This hub of member activity has become known by locals as the "Mormon Grounds."

On November 2, 1998, President Gordon B. Hinckley officially announced the construction of the Montevideo Uruguay Temple in letters to local priesthood leaders.

On April 27, 1999, a new era for Uruguay began with the historic groundbreaking ceremonies for the temple. Elder Richard G. Scott of the Quorum of the Twelve Apostles (and former missionary in Uruguay) presided over the ceremonies. Some 900 people attended, including Church and community leaders and members. While addressing those in attendance, Elder Scott said, "When the House of the Lord is

103

completed, it will have an impact on all the nation. I have seen it in other nations, where members have eagerly attended the temple. The Spirit that comes affects not just the members, but all of the nation. This is a day of tremendous importance for Uruguay." After the ceremonial groundbreaking, site work promptly began the next day.

During the years of temple construction, Uruguay struggled through a season of recession and increased unemployment. A series of transportation and general union strikes paralyzed the nation. These gripping challenges led to construction delays and prevented the temple from being completed on time. Because of this, it was impossible for construction managers to forecast when the temple would be completed, which led the Church to postpone the originally planned open house and dedication dates.

Nearly 25,000 people attended the February 28–March 10 open house. Among those attending was the President of Uruguay, Jorge Batlle. Following his tour, he spoke about his experience by saying, "All around the world, people are searching for these principles; these principles should be embraced by these people, by their societies and by their leaders."

On March 18, 2001, prayers of the faithful were answered. After decades of perseverance, Uruguayan Saints rejoiced when President Gordon B. Hinckley dedicated the Montevideo Uruguay Temple, the eleventh in South America. At the time of its dedication, the temple served 73,000 Uruguayan members from fifteen stakes, six districts, and two missions. "Dear Father, wilt Thou accept this temple as the gift of Thy sons and daughters," President Hinckley said in the dedicatory prayer. "It has come through the faithful payment of tithing by Thy Saints across the world. May it grace this land. May the nation of Uruguay be blessed because of its presence on this soil. May it stand as a testimony to the world of the knowledge of Thy people concerning the eternal things of God."

Some 7,655 members attended the four dedicatory sessions. For Samuel Piriz, a counselor in the bishopric of the Pueblo Nuevo Ward, being able to attend was a manifestation of the Lord's blessings, and his story was not unique. A relatively new convert, Brother Piriz had been struggling to find employment for a year. Despite the trial, he prayed and had

SITE
1.59 acres

GROUNDBREAKING
April 27, 1999, by Richard G. Scott

DEDICATION
March 18, 2001, by
Gordon B. Hinckley

EXTERIOR
Asa Branca granite

TOTAL FLOOR AREA
10,700 square feet

DIMENSIONS
149 feet by 77 feet

HIDDEN IMAGE
The Good Shepherd is holding
a lamb and shepherd's staff on
the surface of the temple.

faith that somehow he and his family would be able to attend the dedication. He was blessed to find a job a month before the ceremony and was able to pay the bus fare for his family to make the journey to and from Montevideo. He showed his gratitude by paying the fare for two other ward members who otherwise could not have gone.

As members eagerly prepared to serve in their new temple with vigor, they often reminisced of the long temple trips and the sacrifices that had been required to make them possible. Six-hour chartered bus rides to the Buenos Aires Temple would no longer be required. Members have faith that as more and more Uruguayan Saints receive the blessings and ordinances of the temple, they will be blessed individually and Zion will prosper.

The Uruguayan Saints will never forget the fateful outcome of one temple trip in 1999. Seven Church members were killed in a tragic accident while traveling from Uruguay to the Buenos Aires Temple. This experience is still vividly recalled by the members whose tears of sorrow were transformed to tears of peace and faith. The completion of the Montevideo Uruguay Temple has provided an eternal perspective and a place of healing for family members of the victims. President Huber Chineppe of the Rivera Uruguay Stake, who lost his fifteen-year-old son, Matias, said that upon "entering the celestial room, our feelings were very close to our loved ones who are not with us now in life; we will not forget them this day."

The Duarte family had been members of the Church for one year and were traveling to the temple for the first time. In the accident, their daughter Ana Gabriela, fourteen, died, and her brother Julio Cesar was gravely injured. Sister Mirta Da Rosa de Duarte said, "It was a very hard trial for us, but later we felt the spirit of the Comforter many times and we were strengthened by it. Today, we are in the temple at last, and this has been a sweet experience, and we have had an opportunity to be close to President Hinckley and feel that he is a representative of the Savior on this earth." Her husband, Hugo I. Duarte, added, "We feel gratitude for the blessings we have; we feel that we will be an eternal family and that our daughter is waiting on the other side of the veil, where she is doing the work of the Lord."

Winter Quarters Nebraska Temple

The Church's legacy in Winter Quarters began when the Saints were driven from Nauvoo in February 1846. After traveling 300 miles west, the Saints decided to settle in an area west of the Missouri River, now known as Florence. Before Winter Quarters was left as a ghost settlement, more than 60,000 pioneers had passed through the area in wagons, pulling handcarts, or on foot.

The temple is located adjacent to the Mormon Pioneer Cemetery and across from Mormon Trail Center at Historic Winter Quarters. The cemetery is the resting place of more than 325 people who perished in 1846, having been weakened and exposed to disease due to the hasty and forced exodus from Nauvoo. Most of their graves are unmarked. Years after the

Saints abandoned Winter Quarters, the cemetery came under the control of the city of Florence, and residents were allowed to bury their loved ones in the cemetery for free.

Featured prominently in the cemetery is Avard Fairbanks's famous statue *Tragedy at Winter Quarters*, depicting a grieving father and mother standing before the open grave of their child. Until April 1, 1999, the cemetery had been leased to the Church for a dollar a year, at which time the city conveyed the deed to the Church. That action made it possible to proceed with building the Winter Quarters Temple.

Prior to the temple's groundbreaking, the Church spent six months researching who was buried in the Winter Quarters cemetery and where the graves

104

were located. Remote sensors were used to detect unmarked graves. Following the study, Church officials asked a Douglas County judge for permission to move at least five graves. The five graves were believed to contain remains of Florence residents who died in the 1800s. Once approved, plans proceeded under the careful guidance of a licensed funeral director, the Nebraska Historical Society, and other experts. The Church made every effort to contact the descendants of the individuals whose graves were moved. The five graves were relocated within the original boundaries of the cemetery.

Although similar to the generation of temples built in the season of rapid temple expansion of 1998 through 2000, the Winter Quarters Temple is significantly larger, featuring 16,000 square feet of interior space, a second story, and a chapel. Alterations in the design were necessitated by the slope of the historic burial ground that the temple adjoins.

The temple's stained-glass windows include edifying art-glass scenes depicting themes of the latter-day Restoration and the plan of salvation. The stained glass appropriately enhances the purpose of the temple while inviting the temple patron to reflect with gratitude on those who aided in the establishment of Zion. In the baptistry, windows are bordered with quilt patterns, a log cabin, and a crown of thorns. These designs were chosen to be reminiscent of the pioneers who wrapped the bodies of their departed loved ones in quilts before burial.

Other artistic contributions are displayed in the temple's collection of original paintings depicting Chimney Rock located in western Nebraska and an impressive scene of old Winter Quarters at night. The temple is beautified further by a handmade quilt of authentic period design and a painting depicting the nearby Missouri River. Other special features include a brass entry door and handcrafted, period-style furniture, furthering the pioneer ambiance. Antiques garnish the interior, invoking thoughts of an earlier time.

One of the workers who shared his skill to build the temple was Lance Bailey. Lance worked as a stone mason and was preparing to serve a two-year mission. Having pioneer

SITE
1.92 acres

GROUNDBREAKING
28 November 1999 by
Hugh W. Pinnock

DEDICATION
22 April 2001 by Gordon B. Hinckley

EXTERIOR
Bethel white granite

TOTAL FLOOR AREA
16,000 square feet

DIMENSIONS
149 feet by 77 feet; 86 feet high

HIDDEN IMAGE
The Avard Fairbanks sculpture Tragedy at Winter Quarters is drawn on the cemetery side of the temple. An image of the Savior is posed near the temple's entrance.

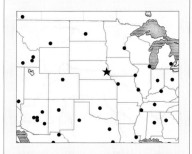

ancestors made his opportunity to build the Lord's house at Winter Quarters significant and meaningful. While attending to his labors on August 17, 2000, Lance prepared to hand a heavy slab to a coworker. In the process, the board he was standing on gave way, causing him to fall headfirst, still holding the slab. His thirty-foot fall was broken by rungs of the scaffolding, but he landed hard. Workers heard him say, "Help me. I'm dying." When his father, Randy, received the call at home, he dropped to his knees. At the hospital, Randy and Lance's grandfather placed their hands on Lance and gave him a priesthood blessing. Lance said he was scared. He had broken two ribs and a shoulder blade, had ruptured his spleen, and was bleeding internally. He received more than 100 stitches on his head. As he recovered, his dad; mom, Debra; and four siblings stood around his bed and sang "Count Your Many Blessings." Said his father: "There's no question in my mind whatsoever that God does grant miracles. Lance had guardian angels with him that day."

The temple's open house concluded on April 14, 2001, 154 years after Brigham Young and the advance company of pioneer Saints departed from Winter Quarters in 1847. The open house attracted some 61,000 people.

On April 22, 2001, hundreds assembled to watch President Gordon B. Hinckley conduct the traditional cornerstone ceremony and dedicate the temple. Performing at the ceremony was acclaimed vocal soloist Ariel Bybee. Attesting to the historic significance of this temple, the first session was videotaped and transmitted by satellite for viewing by members in selected meetinghouses throughout North America. It was only the second time that such a satellite transmission of a temple dedication had been made.

The first temple in Nebraska makes the statement that the Latter-day Saint exodus from Winter Quarters in Omaha to Utah was not a one-way trip. "We are here to stay," said E. Louis Butler, former president of the Papillion Stake. "We're not on our way to Salt Lake anymore."

Guadalajara Mexico Temple

Guadalajara, Mexico, is the capital of the state of Jalisco and is located in the heart of Mexico. It is a major hub of culture, natural resources, and traditional Mexican history. Many of the characteristic traits of the Mexican culture originate from this city. The massive metropolis is the second largest city in Mexico and home to the three professional *futbol* teams, mariachi music, and perhaps the country's most beautiful cathedral.

The pleasant people from the city call themselves "Tapatíos," and they use the term with pride. The Guadalajara Mexico Temple provides local Tapatío members and Church members living in the region with their own place to spiritually grow as they take part in the ultimate form of worship and receive the ultimate in blessings.

The first stake in Guadalajara was created in 1975, and a mission was created there that same year. Missionary work proceeded more slowly in Guadalajara than in some other cities, but it has grown at a steady pace.

Two months after the temple was formally announced, the sun-scorched ground was broken for the temple on June 12, 1999. A heavy rainstorm the previous evening settled the dust and freshened the air for the ceremony. Adding to the spirit of the event was a choir from area stakes. The temple's location is among commercial businesses in the southwest region of this massive city of four million residents.

105

Elder Eran A. Call of the Seventy presided, spoke, and broke ground at the ceremony that was attended by some 470 members. Within days of the groundbreaking, the site was being prepared and construction was under way. Elder Call described the Guadalajara Temple as being among the temples to fulfill President Lorenzo Snow's prophecy: "The time will come when there will be temples established over every portion of the land, and we will go into these temples and work for our kindred dead night and day, that the work of the Lord may be speedily accomplished, that Jesus may come and present the kingdom to His Father." In addition, plans were made to build a beautiful stake center at the site adjacent to the temple.

The building of Mexico's eleventh temple strengthened the nation's momentum of temple building, which began in 1999 with the dedication of the Colonia Juárez Temple. In a period of only twenty-five months, Mexico went from having a single temple to having eleven dedicated temples in all regions of the land. This monumental chapter in Church history continued with the dedication of the Monterrey Mexico Temple being dedicated in April 2002.

"An absolutely marvelous year, no doubt about it," said Elder Call, who presided over the Mexico South Area. When President Hinckley announced in 1998 that the Church would build thirty temples, many hoped a Mexican city or two would be included in his plan. Elder Call remembers feeling "blown away" when he learned a third of the new edifices would be found in Mexico. The members, he adds, were even more excited. "The members here have generally been faithful temple goers," Elder Call said, recalling the efforts of thousands of Mexican Saints who had sacrificed much to participate in costly and sometimes risky trips to the Mexico City or Mesa Arizona temples. "This has been a spiritual 'watershed' year in Mexico," said Elder Lynn A. Mickelsen of the Seventy and president of the Mexico North Area. "The stake presidents and bishops have seen in part the vision of President Hinckley and

SITE
2.69 acres

GROUNDBREAKING
June 12, 1999, by Eran A. Call

DEDICATION
April 29, 2001, by
Gordon B. Hinckley

EXTERIOR
Blanco Guardiano white marble
from Torreón, Mexico

TOTAL FLOOR AREA
10,700 square feet

DIMENSIONS
149 feet by 77 feet

HIDDEN IMAGE
An image of the Christus statue
is located among the clouds.

are working strenuously to prepare the Saints for the temple."

Within only a few years of these temples being dedicated, Mexico became the first country outside the United States to reach the significant membership milestone of 1,000,000 Latter-day Saints. The temples' influence in Mexico was felt beyond the LDS population as open house visits improved the Church's image among government officials and other religions.

The highly anticipated open house tours were held in April 2001 and gleaned 840 missionary referrals, which quickly produced six baptisms. President Ruben Torres of the Guadalajara Mexico Mission described the temple open house as being a fantastic missionary tool. "Many investigators went through the temple open house then came out crying," President Torres said. "The people would hug and express their love to one another. They recognized the temple as a special place where they felt something they have never before felt."

The temple was dedicated in four sessions on Sunday, April 29, 2001. Members traveled hundreds of miles to participate in the day's historic events, gathering in the temple or within the neighboring stake center. They were uplifted by listening to counsel from President Gordon B. Hinckley, Elder Henry B. Eyring, then of the Quorum of the Twelve, and other General Authorities. At the conclusion of the day, hundreds of handkerchief-waving members lined the temple grounds in a reverent display of gratitude and love for their prophet and departing leaders.

In addition to being a historic day for the Mexican Saints, Church members were honored to share a special occasion with the prophet and his wife. On the day of the temple dedication, President and Sister Hinckley celebrated their sixty-fourth wedding anniversary. The prophet expressed his love for his wife and reminded the Mexican members of how families can be blessed through temple service.

Perth Australia Temple

Perth, Australia, is referred to as *the end of the earth* and is the most isolated capital city on the planet. This remote corner of the world is home to tenacious Latter-day Saints who have a long tradition of faithful temple attendance.

On June 11, 1999, the First Presidency announced the Perth Australia Temple in a letter to local priesthood leaders. Shortly after the temple's announcement, President Gordon B. Hinckley visited Perth and selected the Dianella Stake Center property for the site of the future temple. The temple is located fifteen minutes from downtown Perth.

The Church purchased this property for a meetinghouse many years prior, in 1960. The property featured two street frontages and plenty of extra ground around the meetinghouse. Soon after the acquisition, the city designated the expansive property directly across the street as recreation parklands. These three factors were divinely orchestrated, as they proved to be advantageous to the temple that would be built at the site forty years later.

For years preceding the temple announcement, the Church's public affairs department worked diligently to build relationships with religious, civic, and business leaders in the community. This history of establishing trusted relationships proved to soften hearts and assist in bringing the temple to Perth. This benefit was clearly demonstrated when the Stirling City Council gathered to vote on the temple's building permit. Director of Public Affairs Philip A. Baker was in

106

214

attendance and described the event: "Prior to the meeting, the mayor said to me, 'Phil, why do you look so nervous? I have phoned all the City Councilors and they have given the okay.' Sure enough, full approval was given. The path to the house of the Lord had been paved beforehand, by friends of the Church! This was a testimony to me of the value of developing strong relationships of trust with community leaders."

Community leaders joined more than 700 Church members on November 20, 1999, for the temple's groundbreaking. At the conclusion of the service, all three Perth stake presidents, along with members from the community, pioneer members, youth, and children, were invited to turn the soil with gold-painted shovels.

Located two miles south of the temple site is the beautiful Swan River. This historic river flows through downtown Perth and is the habitat of the regal black swan. This large species of bird is so important to the region that it is featured on Western Australia's emblem and state flag. The swan is also represented inside the temple. According to temple construction missionary John Turner, "We could not have a black swan in the temple, so white swans were used." Swans are subtly placed in the sealing room on the chairs. Another beautiful feature inside the temple is the unique use of plaster domes. These domes are located in a variety of locations including hallways, sealing rooms, the baptistry, and the celestial room.

Considering Perth's intimate connection with the ocean, interior designer Greg Hill thought it appropriate to include artwork featuring the sea. After a lengthy search among local art galleries, he finally found the perfect painting. As soon as he saw it, he said, "That's it! That is exactly what we are looking for." The oil painting, created by famed Australian artist Larry Mitchell, depicts a seascape and lighthouse from the nearby tourist location Rottnest Island. The painting's aqua colors blend in perfectly with the colors of the furniture below the art.

The exterior surface of the temple is Olympia white granite from Italy with art glass windows from California. Behind the temple is a picturesque area featuring a water fountain with a

SITE
2.76 acres (with meetinghouse)

GROUNDBREAKING
November 20, 1999, by
Kenneth Johnson

DEDICATION
May 20, 2001, by Gordon B. Hinckley

EXTERIOR
Italian Olympia white granite

TOTAL FLOOR AREA
10,700 square feet

DIMENSIONS
149 feet by 77 feet

HIDDEN IMAGE
Among the foliage to the right of the temple is the Good Shepherd cradling one of His sheep.

smooth stone ball that spins on the water. The angel Moroni statue was hoisted into position on September 21, 2000, to mark the 177th anniversary of Moroni's first appearance to the young Joseph Smith.

In preparation for the open house, statements of support and respect were collected from religious, civic, and political leaders and used to help introduce the temple to the public. Among these comments was the following from the Premier (Governor) of Western Australia, Geoff Gallop: "I am delighted to send my congratulations to The Church of Jesus Christ of Latter-day Saints in celebration of the historic dedication of the Perth Temple. I am sure the Perth Temple will bring much joy to your community and will become a special and beautiful symbol of the role of the Church within Western Australia."

An estimated 37,000 people attended the open house from April 28 to May 12, 2001. At the conclusion of the open house, Chairman of the Temple Organizing Committee Donald W. Cummings thought his duties as chairman were coming to a close. He said he was "looking forward to enjoying some time off and a holiday." His plans changed on the 4th of May at 5:50 a.m., when President Gordon B. Hinckley called to invite Brother and Sister Cummings to be the first temple president and matron of the Perth Australia Temple. Brother Cummings had previously served as temple president of the Sydney Australia Temple. After accepting the call, he became one of the few to have ever served twice as temple president.

President Hinckley dedicated the temple on Sunday, May 20, 2001. More than 2,773 Church members attended the four dedication sessions for the temple, which at the time served 12,000 of Australia's approximately 104,000 Church members. Elder Jeffrey R. Holland of the Quorum of the Twelve Apostles, who participated in the dedication with President Hinckley, called the events in Perth a major milestone in the history of the Church. "With the dedication of this temple on the other side of the earth from Salt Lake City, we are seeing fulfilled the oft-stated prophecy of Church leaders over centuries that temples would eventually circle the globe," he said.

Columbia River Washington Temple

The Columbia River Washington Temple is of exceptional significance for the faithful Saints living throughout the vast Columbia River Basin. For these faithful members, the announcement of the Tri-Cities temple came as a wonderful surprise. "A lot of people were hoping that it would come," said former Pasco Stake President Ferris Naef. "There was a real thrill among the members. People were calling to donate property and everything else."

Even the Temple Department of the Church expressed some shock after learning of the announcement. The department had recommended future temple locations to President Hinckley, and the Tri-Cities location was at the bottom of their list of sixty-six potential locations.

After the temple's announcement, the exact location was not revealed until all necessary building permits and legal issues were resolved and a groundbreaking date set. The delayed announcement combined with good public relations and regular Church community service paved the way for the temple to be accepted into the community without opposition.

Although members had offered to donate many sites to the Church, the temple was built in Richland, adjacent to the Kennewick Washington Stake Center. The previous owner of the property had received multiple offers to purchase his land. However, he had been reluctant to sell because he wanted something nice built there. He was willing to sell to the Church

107

because he knew the Church would build something that "would look nice."

Throughout the temple's construction process, the highest level of craftsmanship was maintained. As the walls went up, a large painting of the Savior was placed in the entryway for all the construction workers to see. The picture was framed with two-by-fours that were painted white and was fixed to an unfinished wall about fifteen feet above the floor. The picture served as a constant reminder of the temple's spiritual significance and whose house it was.

Temple Construction General Contractor Corey E. Vitus and Project Manager Ross Woodward shared their testimonies and construction abilities and blessed the lives of the members in the temple district by creatively involving them in the construction process. Sample granite squares from the temple's exterior were cut and distributed to most of the member families within the temple district. On the stone pieces was printed "Families can be together forever."

The temple's exterior walls and spire are entirely surfaced with a brilliant white Bethel Vermont granite. This granite is considered to be the whitest granite quarried in the United States. Quarried near Joseph Smith's birthplace, the granite was cut into 125-pound 4' x 2' x 1.25" slabs. The lower four feet of the temple and the bands at the eight- and twelve-foot levels are polished granite. The remaining unpolished stone provides texture and color to the temple's exterior walls.

Beautiful art glass from Germany is featured in the tall, narrow windows of the spire. The temple's main entrance is lavishly adorned with cherry wood paneling, a forty-foot domed ceiling, and art glass windows. The floors are covered with granite or marble floor tiles or with warm, plush carpeting. Two original paintings highlight local scenes of the Columbia River. The celestial room is adorned with an elegant chandelier and a high domed ceiling that rises majestically above three impressive art glass windows. The largest chandelier glistens with 6,000 pieces of crystal lit by 224 light bulbs. The unique acoustics within the celestial room allow the subtlest of whispers to

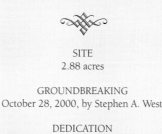

SITE
2.88 acres

GROUNDBREAKING
October 28, 2000, by Stephen A. West

DEDICATION
November 18, 2001, by
Gordon B. Hinckley

EXTERIOR
Bethel white granite from
Vermont and Italy

TOTAL FLOOR AREA
16,880 square feet

DIMENSIONS
196 feet by 196 feet

HIDDEN IMAGE
In the distant mountains the Good Shepherd is cradling one of His sheep. Dispersed in the clouds and landscaping is His flock.

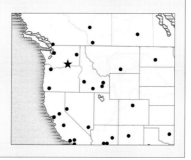

be magnified and heard across the room. The temple presidency was informed of this phenomenon to pacify temple patrons who may wonder why they are "hearing voices" in the celestial room.

On the first day of the open house, there was still much landscaping work needing to be done. Within a few hours, a local member organized member volunteers to finish the job. Demonstrating their gratitude for their new temple, volunteers lined up around the temple almost shoulder to shoulder planting flowers. The small army of members used their shovels and wheelbarrows to haul landscaping bark and bedding plants. The last flowers were planted and plant pots removed about thirty minutes before the first tour began.

In under two weeks, 64,634 visitors toured the temple during its open house. Preparation for such a large event required a dedicated staff of volunteers working months in advance. A food committee provided refreshments for all of the temple guests. A member who owned six Subway sandwich restaurants in the area provided the cookies and use of the ovens at a low cost. Volunteers arrived at the restaurants daily to assist in baking over 6,000 cookies a day.

On November 18, 2001, President Gordon B. Hinckley conducted all four dedicatory sessions as well as the cornerstone ceremony. The sacred words of the dedicatory prayer included the following petition: "Bless our own land in these perilous times. Bless those who serve as trustees of this government formed under an inspired Constitution, the principles of which have come from Thee. May peace replace conflict, we implore Thee." These inspiring and patriotic words take on a solemn significance considering this temple was the first to be dedicated after 9/11, just two months after the terrorist attacks on the United States.

The temple's first president, Allan D. Alder, summarized the feelings of so many members when he said, "I still can't believe we have a temple here. I always knew it would happen, but I never expected to see it occur in my lifetime."

Snowflake Arizona Temple

The site for the Snowflake Arizona Temple is situated on the west end of town on top of a piñon-covered bluff that has become known as "Temple Hill." The temple stands as a culmination of a legacy established by pioneer families whose tradition of faith and obedience has been passed on through the generations.

While serving as an Apostle, Wilford Woodruff visited the little valley where poverty, hunger, and epidemics as well as the rigors of pioneer life took their toll. In February 1880, while speaking at a conference, he prophesied that someday a temple "would be erected here." The dedication of the Snowflake Arizona Temple on March 3, 2002, fulfilled that prophecy, 122 years later.

The prayers and faith that Snowflake would someday have a temple never ceased after that initial prophecy. For several decades, stake presidents made formal appeals to the First Presidency requesting a temple be built in Snowflake. Snowflake Stake President Stephen A. Reidhead visited the town's historical Main Street Chapel one evening in the spring of 1998. There he pondered the possibility of Arizona receiving another temple. He recorded that while in sincere prayer, "the Spirit came upon me until I was bathed in tears and the Lord told me not to worry, that the temple was going to be in Snowflake. My feelings of love, adoration and praise were overwhelming. It was some time before I was able to gain control of my emotions. I was so grateful for the knowledge

108

218

of where the temple would be built, but I did not know when."

President Reidhead first received notice that Snowflake might be considered as a location for a future temple in an official letter from President Gordon B. Hinckley dated January 20, 2000. On March 4 of that year, President Reidhead greeted President Hinckley at a local airport. On the way to dedicate the Albuquerque New Mexico Temple, the prophet visited the Snowflake area long enough to view a few possible temple sites. Approaching the final site, the prophet asked to get out of the car. While many in the accompanying group engaged in conversation, the prophet quietly walked toward the east. As President Reidhead approached, the prophet asked, "What's that hill?"

"That's Pinhead Hill," Reidhead answered.

President Hinckley then asked, "Is there enough room up on top?"

"I don't know and I don't know how much room is needed," Reidhead answered.

"Why don't you find out if we can cut that hill down, and I'll find out how much room we actually need," President Hinckley said.

It was quickly decided that the area would qualify for a small temple. The site was surveyed, and the owners of the property promptly donated the required six acres to the Church. The city of Snowflake cooperated by allowing the modification of a neighboring golf course to accommodate the temple's entryway.

Approximately sixteen feet was removed from the top of the knoll to accommodate the two-level temple, patterned after the Winter Quarters Nebraska Temple, with the lower level partially set into the knoll.

Temple construction missionary Elder Leo Udy's skill, dedication, and love for the Lord gave him a clear understanding of the high standard of quality required to build a temple. He would encourage those building the temple by saying, "When you leave this temple, you will have gained a knowledge of what quality work is. You will have achieved a level that you have never obtained before."

In front of the temple's entry canopy is a beautifully

SITE
7.5 acres

GROUNDBREAKING
September 23, 2000,
by Rex D. Pinegar

DEDICATION
March 3, 2002, by
Gordon B. Hinckley

EXTERIOR
Two tons of imported, polished
granite quarried in China

TOTAL FLOOR AREA
18,621 square feet

DIMENSIONS
91 feet by 149 feet

HIDDEN IMAGE
The Savior is kneeling and looking
up at the temple. Additionally, a
wagon wheel is placed in the lower
right corner of the drawing.

designed water feature. All of the rocks utilized within the feature were excavated from the hill in preparation for the temple. The largest of these rocks weighs seventeen tons.

With the temple atop a windswept hill, temple designers chose granite to surface its exterior rather than marble. Granite's hard and durable qualities offered the ideal solution to prevent erosion. The Chinese rose-tinted granite blends harmoniously with the color of the native soil.

An exquisite set of stained-glass windows that once graced the walls of a Catholic Church in Boston have a new home within the Snowflake Temple. The colorful three-paneled windows depict Christ instructing a circle of children and adults. The stained-glass windows were discovered at a Boston-based auction house, purchased by the Deseret Foundation, and then donated to the Church. After their purchase, the artistic panels were meticulously cleaned and restored.

To accommodate local fire codes, the celestial room was rotated ninety degrees from the original plan. Adding to the room's splendor is a softly painted domed ceiling. The Snowflake Arizona Temple was the first temple of its kind to feature a dome ceiling in the celestial room.

Following the temple's seventeen-month construction period, the temple was ready for its thirteen-day open house. Snowflake, a community of 5,000 in the White Mountains of northeast central Arizona, hosted 91,146 people during this period. Following the open house tours, all visitors were offered refreshments consisting of punch and cookies. The eleven stakes within the temple district worked countless hours to provide over 100,000 freshly baked cookies for temple guests.

On March 3, 2002, President Gordon B. Hinckley presided over four dedication ceremonies that were attended or viewed by 11,000 people. Following the temple's dedication, the "Honeymoon Trail," which had once guided faithful members on long and precarious journeys from Snowflake to St. George and later to Mesa, became a paved and well-groomed road leading to Snowflake's Temple Hill.

Lubbock Texas Temple

Amid the windy and isolated plains of west Texas, the city of Lubbock is central to hundreds of square miles of flat, wide-open farmland. The high plains and prairies of west Texas, where the horizon is unbroken by mountains or skyscrapers, feature a graceful spire adorned by the golden symbol of the restoration.

Plans for a temple in Lubbock began three years prior to its announcement. On October 5, 1997, President Hinckley announced the concept of smaller temples. Following the historic announcement, Lubbock Stake President Jay B. Jensen felt impressed to propose to the First Presidency that a temple be built in Lubbock. Within a month, President Jensen prepared

and submitted a ten-page document supporting the need for a temple in Lubbock.

The temple is built on property that was acquired in the late 1980s for the building of the Lubbock Texas Stake Center. The purchased parcel was much larger than needed for the stake center, and after the building's dedication in 1989, efforts were made to sell off the excess property. The sale of the property never transpired because the acreage lacked street access. This apparent failure developed into a blessing when in the spring of 2000, the ground was deemed to be the prime location for a temple.

From the temple's foundation to its graceful spire, every part of the temple is made with exceptional quality. The temple's exterior walls' superior

109

strength originates from solid, 12" concrete blocks, reinforced steel, and increased pier depths. Although the Lubbock area is not considered to be in danger of earthquakes, the sturdy walls were designed to meet a seismic zone 2 rating, two levels above the area requirement. Even the temple's ten-ton, fifty-foot tower was designed to withstand extreme wind speeds. Referring to the temple's excellence, project manager Leon Rowley said, "This is my seventh [temple] and one of my favorites. As a builder, I enjoy the quality building using the best materials and the best craftsmen. At every temple site, the engineering always surpasses the standard for the area."

The temple was built using 13,000 pieces of Empress white with accents of majestic gray granite quarried in China. Artisans were brought to Lubbock from Italy to assemble the massive stone puzzle. Because of the tremendous amount of stone and the intricacies of the shapes, the temple was actually built around the stone rather than the stone being cut to fit the building.

Donations to the temple include a 100-year-old framed piece of needlework that is traced back to an Amarillo member's great-great-grandmother. This treasured heirloom adds to the delicate ornamentation of the bride's room. Another prominent donation placed in the reception area is an original oil painting depicting an area below the cap rock rendered by Utah artist Valoy Eaton.

A monumental aspect of building such an elaborate structure was coordinating the complex schedule of materials arriving from all over the world: polished granite from China, Pennsylvania cherry wood, custom-crafted millwork from Utah, art glass from England, marble flooring from Italy and Portugal, alabaster from Germany, door hardware from Lithuania, and an elaborate woven carpet from Thailand. As obstacles were overcome through dedication and teamwork, those who labored on the temple were successful in coming as close to perfection as humanly possible. The quality of the temple was noticed and lauded by industry professionals. The temple was awarded *Texas Construction* magazine's prestigious 2002 Best of Texas Award—Private Building Projects.

The construction history is highlighted by many small

SITE
2.7 acres (shared with adjacent stake center)

GROUNDBREAKING
November 4, 2000, by Rex D. Pinegar

DEDICATION
April 21, 2002, by
Gordon B. Hinckley

EXTERIOR
Empress white and majestic gray granite quarried in China

TOTAL FLOOR AREA
16,498 square feet

DIMENSIONS
188 feet by 98 feet

HIDDEN IMAGE
Five oxen are hidden in the landscape shrubbery beneath the baptistry room of the temple.

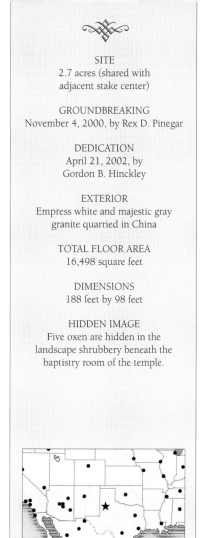

miracles. For example, when the artwork arrived, there were some pieces with damaged frames. Two local non-member men whose business is that of framing made themselves immediately available to assist in any way. They expertly repaired the broken frames within days, allowing the art to be displayed for the open house. Another miraculous event transpired a few days prior to the open house. A six-foot, handcrafted Venetian mirror for the bride's room arrived from Italy broken into many fragments. Immediately, temple interior designer Greg Hill called the mirror vendor to report the situation. A few days later, a new mirror arrived without any breakage. The new mirror was much better in its overall design and size than the original mirror. The new mirror "seemed to compliment the art glass window so perfectly and was of better proportions," said Hill. "The Lord knew what He wanted, even if we didn't."

When furnishings were being unpacked and brought into the temple, it was discovered that a beautiful crystal vase shipped from Salt Lake City was broken in several pieces. This specific imported Italian vase had been ordered months earlier and was available only by special order. As efforts were made to order a replacement, the company reported that an individual in Salt Lake City had recently ordered the exact same vase. This person had determined the piece was too large and had returned it. This vase was shipped from Salt Lake City and arrived the next afternoon in perfect condition.

As the temple's construction approached completion, members within the temple district began to focus on the open house. The temple opened its doors to the public March 23 through 30, 2002, attracting 21,560 people. On April 21, 2002, President Gordon B. Hinckley conducted all four dedicatory sessions and the cornerstone ceremony.

Having served as stake president before the temple was built, President Jensen said he now sees the temple strengthening every individual who takes the opportunity to worship in the house of the Lord. Those who visit the temple frequently are gaining spiritual reinforcement against the debilitating influences of the world. Because of the temple, he adds, "I have a sense that the community is better, and better favored in the Lord's eyes."

Monterrey Mexico Temple

Monterrey is located in northeast Mexico at the foothills of the scenic Sierra Madre Oriental mountain range. These mountains provide a dramatic backdrop for the Monterrey Mexico Temple. Resting on a hill, the temple's prominent position next to the National Highway makes it impossible to pass without noting the majesty of the building and its lush setting.

In 1920, the Church established itself in Monterrey when the first missionaries arrived. For decades, one of the great sources of strength for members was the Mesa Arizona Temple. Members demonstrated their commitment to temple service by making annual trips to the Mesa Arizona Temple (1,180 miles away) and later to the Mexico City Temple (558 miles away). These road trips required great commitment from the

members as they saved their money to travel along hot country roads in rented buses. The faithful members desperately wanted to more regularly claim their temple blessings and fulfill family history commitments.

Announced in 1995, the Monterrey Mexico Temple was to become Mexico's second temple. However, due to extended protests and ensuing legal battles, the temple ended up becoming the twelfth dedicated temple in the nation. The Church originally selected a site for the temple adjacent to Colegio Labastida, a historic Catholic school in San Pedro. According to a Religious News Service report, "Thousands of Catholics gathered signatures and purchased advertisements in newspapers protesting the temple construction." Although the

110

Church won the ensuing three-year legal dispute, Church officials elected to build the temple in another location. This new Valle Alto location allowed for the temple architectural design to change to a larger temple, increase green space, and increase parking capacity. The final location is surrounded by greenery and aggrandized by dramatic mountain peaks and hills.

The lengthy time period from announcement to groundbreaking required faith and patience for the Latter-day Saints. Church members spent years watching temples being built and dedicated throughout Mexico while little progress was being made on their own temple. The temple's first president, Eran A. Call, said that through the years of opposition, there were members who could testify they saw the temple in dreams and knew it would be there.

On Sunday, April 28, 2002, President Hinckley dedicated Mexico's twelfth temple in four sessions. The event marked the seventy-fifth time President Hinckley dedicated a temple. Soon after the temple's dedication, members arranged their lives to allow for frequent temple attendance. Early morning sessions were added to the temple's schedule to accommodate those who want to visit the temple before work. According to Elder Richard H. Winkel of the Seventy, "We have people coming almost on a daily basis, which would have been totally impossible before. Those who at great sacrifice were going once or twice a year are now going monthly, and some even weekly."

Elder Eran A. Call was called to serve as the temple's first president. Having been born in Mexico and dedicated himself to a lifetime of faithful service, he and his wife, Katherine, were well qualified for the responsibility of being the temple's first president and matron. At the conclusion of their service, Elder Call reflected on their calling and shared the following: "Kay and I loved our experience in the beautiful Monterrey Mexico Temple. As we prepare for our release, we both felt it was the crown jewel of our Church service. . . . We would have anywhere from five to thirteen busses arrive on any given Saturday, causing a beehive of activities within the hallowed temple walls."

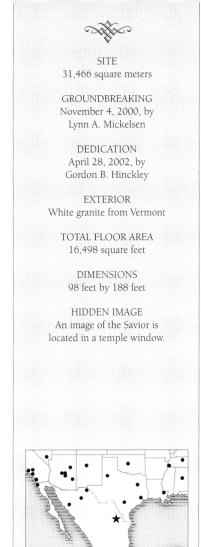

SITE
31,466 square meters

GROUNDBREAKING
November 4, 2000, by
Lynn A. Mickelsen

DEDICATION
April 28, 2002, by
Gordon B. Hinckley

EXTERIOR
White granite from Vermont

TOTAL FLOOR AREA
16,498 square feet

DIMENSIONS
98 feet by 188 feet

HIDDEN IMAGE
An image of the Savior is
located in a temple window.

A tragedy occurred inside the temple on October 16, 2003. Late in the evening when the temple was closed and empty, an intruder broke a window with a hammer and entered the temple. The broken glass caused an alarm to sound, and a security guard notified a member of the temple presidency, Jesús Santos Montes. As the guard stood watch outside the temple, President Santos entered the temple to investigate. Without warning, the intruder severely beat President Santos on the head and arm with his hammer. A biography of President Call recorded the event:

"Two strikes to his head were most damaging, one on the crown that pushed a section of his skull down into his brain. A second blow hit just beneath his left ear. President Santos fell to the floor, blood gushing from his wounds. He offered a silent prayer: *O God, I am in your humble service in your holy temple. Bless me.*

"Even as he thought through the words of his prayer, President Santos felt a strength come into his body—from his feet to the top of his head. He stood up and staggered to the restroom in President Call's office. Taking a white towel, he managed to make a turban over the crown of his head. He then put the phone to his ear and called both his son and the other counselor.

"The intruder meanwhile had done his dark deed. Sensing the need to escape, he jumped out the window and over the security fence. He had successfully escaped into the dark of night."

When President Call arrived at the temple, President Santos was lying in the front seat of his car. President Call administered to him, and he was rushed to the hospital. He was in surgery for four hours, and the doctor expressed that it was impossible for him to still be alive. The doctor felt that it was a miracle that he had not been killed by such heavy blows to the head, shoulders, and arm.

Of the tragic event, President Call expressed, "President Santos was preserved to continue his labors in mortality. He is a wonderful spiritual giant and a faithful servant." Following the release of President Call, Jesús Santos Montes was called to be the Monterrey Mexico Temple's second temple president.

Campinas Brazil Temple

Campinas is located in southeastern Brazil in the interior portion of the state of Sao Paulo, about sixty miles from the city of Sao Paulo. Campinas means *grass fields* in Portuguese and has long served as a major agricultural center. The city retains a strong European influence from its early settlers and is a fast-growing city of about 2.6 million people. The temple site is on the northeast side of the city near three major highways, making it readily accessible to faithful members traveling from the interior portions of Brazil. It was the third temple announced in Brazil and was placed in a city with a large number of members, "where the need is so great."

The first five members of the Church in Campinas were baptized as teenagers when they met the missionaries in 1939. Among these early members was Flavia Garcia Erbolato. She described meeting the missionaries as follows: "The missionaries were so clean and so nice that everybody liked them, and we believed what they told us. At our sacrament meetings, there were about ten to fourteen people in attendance, including four to six missionaries." Shortly after the Brazilian teens were baptized, the missionaries were withdrawn due to World War II. After the war, more conversions came, and in the mid-1950s, the Church began to grow rapidly in Campinas.

Sister Erbolato and the Saints in Campinas received a thrilling surprise in April 1997 when President Gordon B. Hinckley announced a temple would be constructed in Campinas. Sister Erbolato

111

was at home watching general conference on television when the temple was announced for her home city. "I screamed when the temple was announced," she said. "It was exciting!" the great number of temple-attending members in Brazil, a temple in Campinas was needed to relieve the heavy workload of the Sao Paulo Brazil Temple, which has occasionally functioned on a twenty-four-hour schedule.

The first known financial contribution to the Campinas Brazil Temple came from early missionaries to the area. Among these missionaries was Wayne M. Beck. In 1946, to show his faith in the local members, he and his wife, Evelyn, donated the first $20 to go toward a temple in Campinas.

President James E. Faust, Second Counselor in the First Presidency, presided at the groundbreaking ceremonies for the Campinas Brazil and Porto Alegre Brazil Temples. The highly anticipated event in Campinas took place on May 1, 1998, and was attended by about 3,000 people. During the proceedings, President Faust remarked, "None of us will ever forget how we feel today because of the Spirit of the Lord that is present."

Craig Zwick of the Seventy remarked that as the group with President Faust approached, "It was heartwarming to see about 50 buses that had been used to transport the people, and to see the people assembled on the hill; it was a multitude of faithful Saints. The whole experience felt Pentecostal."

President Gordon B. Hinckley selected the temple's ideal location. It is perched above a major highway linking Campinas to Sao Paulo and Rio de Janeiro, which allows the temple to be seen by thousands of motorists every day. The white gleaming edifice is visible from most parts of the city and is especially impressive when lit up at night. The site's panoramic vistas overlook the downtown area of Campinas and several outlying areas. Interestingly, near the temple is the Atibaia River. In this river, the area's earliest converts to the Church were baptized.

Campinas Mayor Antonio da Costa Santos, an architect and historian, toured the construction site of the Campinas Brazil Temple in 2001 and told Church leaders he was impressed by the quality of workmanship. Mayor Santos said he was impressed by the good taste shown and the attention to

SITE
6.18 acres

GROUNDBREAKING
May 1, 1998

DEDICATION
May 17, 2002, by Gordon B. Hinckley

EXTERIOR
Light gray Asa Branca granite
from the state of Ceara

TOTAL FLOOR AREA
48,100 square feet

DIMENSIONS
142 feet by 163 feet

HIDDEN IMAGE
The Good Shepherd holding
a lamb is illustrated on the
surface of the temple.

detail in the building. After receiving an overview on the importance and sacred purpose of temples, Mayor Santos said he felt honored to visit the site.

The entire community celebrated the temple during its three-and-a-half-week open house, which took place in April and May 2002. The successful event attracted 75,000 visitors. Among these visitors, some 3,000 requested more information about the Church and a visit from the missionaries.

On the first day of the open house, the city's new mayor, Izalene Tiene, visited the temple and expressed, "The city is in need at this time of precisely this kind of spiritual refuge." She asked for permission to, at times, leave her office and come to the temple and sit at the fountain for moments of reflection and peace. Mayor Tiene also recognized the temple as one of the most beautiful edifices in the city, known for its magnificent architecture and its prominent location.

The beautiful morning of May 17, 2002, brought the dedication of the Campinas Brazil Temple. President Hinckley dedicated the temple in four sessions. President James E. Faust also attended the dedication. "It is brilliant," said Nei Tobias Garcia Jr., son of the city's first stake president. "Its light in the dark night serves as a teaching that proclaims the truth."

In the dedicatory prayer, President Hinckley invoked the blessings of the Lord for the Saints in Brazil. "Here we will honor Thee in carrying forward the great work of salvation and exaltation made possible through the atoning sacrifice of Thy Beloved Son, our precious Lord," said President Hinckley. "Bless Thy Saints in this great nation of Brazil. As they walk in obedience before Thee, open the windows of heaven and shower down blessings upon them." More than 8,500 people attended the dedication services.

Six years after the temple's dedication, the city of Campinas bestowed an honor on a beloved Latter-day Saint Church leader who had dedicated much of his life to serve the members in Brazil. The street on the north side of the temple was named after President James E. Faust. The mayor of Campinas, Dr. Helio de Oliveira Santos, unveiled the street "Rua James Esdras Faust" in 2008.

Asunción Paraguay Temple

Paraguay's capital city of Asunción is positioned on a bend in the Paraguay River that separates the country from Argentina. Asunción is a vibrant place with soccer-rabid fans, multiple universities, and people who are proud of their indigenous Guarani heritage. Centrally located in this city of 2.3 million is a house of the Lord. For Paraguayan members, the temple is a symbol of dramatic growth of the Church in their beloved country.

The Church was officially recognized in Paraguay in 1950. At that time, ninety-nine percent of the country was Catholic, and only the Catholic Church enjoyed official status in Paraguay. With the official recognition of the LDS faith, the Church was allowed to send its missionaries throughout the country.

Missionary work proceeded slowly, but the restored gospel began to establish its first roots. The earliest converts were immediately put to work and were made strong through service. There was no time to adjust to life in a small branch or district, says longtime member Maria Elena Samaniego. "I was called to be a seminary teacher two weeks after being baptized," said Sister Samaniego, who joined the Church in 1974. "I asked how I was supposed to teach things I didn't even know yet, but the missionaries told me the Lord knows I can do it."

Spring general conference in 2000 was a historic experience for the Saints in Paraguay for two wonderful reasons. First, it marked the first time members could gather in stake centers to participate in

112

general conference via satellite. And second, the timing of this historic broadcast was perfect because it allowed thousands of members throughout the country to hear President Gordon B. Hinckley announce the Asunción Paraguay Temple.

When the Saints heard the news, they literally shouted for joy. President Craig S. Cheney of the Paraguay Asunción Mission stated: "With the announcement of the Asunción Temple, the reaction of the members of the Church was tremendous. Thousands of members were watching general conference live for the first time. Spontaneously, many shouted 'with one voice,' others stood, hugged each other, and many wept."

The joyous reaction was the same across the country. "When we heard the news that a temple was to be built in Paraguay, we clapped and jumped and hollered. We wanted the Lord to know how happy we were," says Abilio Samaniego, former counselor in the Asunción Temple presidency. "The Lord has shown us much love, and I am grateful." The righteous joy felt by the members is reminiscent of the Saints referred to in Mosiah 18:11: "When the people had heard these words, they clapped their hands for joy, and exclaimed: This is the desire of our hearts."

Torrential rains helped cool high temperatures on February 3, 2001, as faithful and saturated members gathered for the temple's groundbreaking ceremony. While the rain poured, a multi-stake choir sang joyfully, allowing everyone gathered at the ceremony to feel the Spirit.

The temple property has a long history and affectionate connection with Church members throughout the country. The property was home to the nation's first LDS chapel, which was dedicated in 1962. For nearly forty years, the well-worn "Moroni Chapel" served as a gathering place for the Saints. Many were surprised and a little saddened when the Church announced the demolition of the chapel to make way for the temple. Longtime members chose to honor their building in their memories and take comfort that they would soon receive a house of the Lord. A new "Moroni Chapel" was built on the property adjacent to the temple.

SITE
7 acres, including stake center

GROUNDBREAKING
February 3, 2001

DEDICATION
May 19, 2002, by Gordon B. Hinckley

EXTERIOR
Light gray Asa Branca Brazilian granite

TOTAL FLOOR AREA
10,700 square feet

DIMENSIONS
149 feet by 77 feet

HIDDEN IMAGE
The Savior is kneeling with clasped hands looking up at the temple.

The temple grounds occupy a city block that features high exposure and visibility in all directions. Building the nation's first temple was a project that demanded the cooperative teamwork of construction workers, architects, and engineers, said temple architect Humberto Canete. "Everyone is working together to make sure the work is up to Church standards," Brother Canete said. "The temple is a structure that blends wells with the culture and surroundings of the region." Brother Canete described the completed temple as a secure edifice of beauty. The granite that forms the temple exterior was quarried and cut in Brazil.

The temple's exterior gray Branca Brazilian granite adds to the building's majesty. Doors and interior trims feature high-quality cedar. A tranquil water feature adorns the garden in front of the temple. The well-manicured gardens abound with colorful flowers and mature palm trees, all complementing the heavenly spirit of the temple.

More than 4,000 people attended the first day of the open house, and by the end of the week, 22,482 visitors had walked the halls. Among these guests was the First Lady of Paraguay, Susana Galli de Gonzalez Macchi. Mrs. Gonzalez expressed her respect for the Church and the temple by saying, "I wish to thank you for the opportunity to visit this beautiful place that now adorns our city. And more than seeing its beauty from outside, we were able to feel the beauty that you have created inside."

Just two days after dedicating the Campinas temple, President Hinckley traveled to Asunción to dedicate the temple on May 19, 2002. Four dedicatory sessions accommodated members of the Church in the area. With the dedication, every Spanish-speaking and Portuguese-speaking nation in South America now had a temple. "May this temple stand as a crowning jewel to Thy work in this nation," President Hinckley said in his dedicatory prayer. "May Thy Saints throughout the land look to this Thy holy house as a sanctuary to which they may come to make sacred covenants with Thee and partake of the great blessings which Thou hast prepared for Thy faithful children."

Nauvoo Illinois Temple

Once again, a temple in Nauvoo stands overlooking the Mississippi, a holy house where today's Latter-day Saints can serve their God. Today's Latter-day Saints have the privilege of serving in a temple that is visually similar to the one the pioneers left behind in 1846. Remembering those early pioneers, who consecrated their all to build the City Beautiful, makes the eternal blessings found within the Nauvoo Illinois Temple even sweeter.

Mirroring the original temple as closely as possible required thorough research, which included examination of photographs, written descriptions, and drawings. "Piecing everything together, we think the outside of the new temple is as close as humanly possible to the original," said Keith Stepan, managing director of the Temple Construction Department. When researching minute details, principal architect Roger Jackson explained, "In some of the fine points, like the shape of a molding or how this piece abutted to that piece, it wasn't clear from the photographs, so we studied other buildings of the time . . . we feel good that we are 99%."

One of the greatest assets to accurately rebuild the temple was William Weeks's original architectural drawings for the Nauvoo Temple. In 1948, two missionaries serving in the California Mojave Desert knocked on the door of a Mr. Griffin, who was the grandson of William Weeks. After developing a friendship with the missionaries, Mr. Griffin gave one of them his grandfather's original temple drawings.

113

The missionary received strict instructions to personally deliver the precious plans to Church headquarters. The manner in which the Nauvoo Temple was reconstructed would not have been possible without these original plans.

The stone on the outside of the new temple was carefully chosen to have, as nearly as possible, the same color and texture as the limestone of the original temple. The original quarry used was mostly underwater, having been flooded when the Keokuk Dam was built. Carvers in Salt Lake City received the Alabama limestone and used custom tools to create the basket-weave pattern found on stones from the original temple. Specialized molds were created from the original sunstones and moonstones to ensure accurate replicas. Despite using modern tools, today's stone carvers required about the same amount of time as the original craftsmen. This is due to the personalized artistry that was given to each unique handcrafted stone.

Architect Steve Goodwin said the reconstruction was a balancing act between authenticity and the inevitable touch of technology. "It's the idea behind it. We're trying to replicate what it looked like," he said. "There are some things where we've married the old and the new together." Prime examples of old world craftsmanship are the temple's 134 windows. They were all built near the temple site by Nauvoo resident Charles Allen, who has worked on specialized restorations around the country. Each window casing was built using a thirty-step method originating in the 1840s. Allen used more than 2,400 hand-carved square wooden pegs to hold the windows' joints together. All wooden frames received five coats of high-quality Dutch paint with the customized color "Nauvoo Temple White."

The temple's interior is a combination of the needs and benefits of modern temples and the precise accuracy of the original period. The baptismal font on the lower level resembles the one in the original temple. Lighting levels in the temple are somewhat lower than in other temples, reminiscent of the earlier temple's reliance on candlelight. Attention to detail is also found on the temple grounds, where concrete sidewalks give way to early period stone and granite walkways.

SITE
3.3 acres

GROUNDBREAKING
October 24, 1999, by
Gordon B. Hinckley

DEDICATION
June 27–30, 2002, by
Gordon B. Hinckley

EXTERIOR
Limestone block quarried
in Russellville, Alabama

TOTAL FLOOR AREA
54,000 square feet

DIMENSIONS
128 feet by 88 feet; 150 feet high

HIDDEN IMAGE
The upper body of Joseph Smith
is seen to the right of the temple
holding the Book of Mormon.

The building itself isn't the only reminder of the Nauvoo Temple's early days. Furnishings were selected from the "American Empire" time period, from 1790 to 1840. According to the temple's interior designer, Bruce Finlinson, the furniture reproductions are "clean and honest furniture, not overdone." Continuing with the interior's period authenticity is the temple's hand-blown glass, made using an 800-year-old process. Highly skilled French artisans worked with molten glass to produce about 6,000 square feet of blown glass for the temple. The sum total of the efforts by temple builders allows temple patrons to almost experience the year 1845 in a temple built in 2002.

On June 27, 2002, Nauvoo's remarkable and sacred place in Church history came full circle. As President Gordon B. Hinckley participated in the sealing of the temple's cornerstone, he noted the special date: "What a great occasion this is, the 27th of June, 2002, when we solemnly and reverently memorialize the death of the Prophet Joseph Smith and his brother, Hyrum, on this date in 1844." President Hinckley then provided one final reminder of the significance of the Nauvoo Temple: "This is Joseph's temple. He began it in 1841, the original. It was completed in 1846 and then left. And now, beginning again, we have reconstructed it. It is a magnificent building."

The first of thirteen dedicatory sessions began at 6:00 p.m. Central Daylight Time, which President Hinckley noted would have been 5:00 p.m. in Joseph Smith's day. "At this hour 158 years ago in Carthage the murderous mob climbed the stairs, fired their pistols, and forced the door to the jail room," said President Hinckley.

Reflecting on why the Nauvoo Illinois Temple means so much to the Latter-day Saint culture, temple architect Roger Jackson provided the following meaningful insight: "We've had the culture in the Church of having this temple lost to us. Every few years in the back of a Church magazine, they publish one of these fuzzy, old daguerreotype images. You see a list of all the temples, and you see Nauvoo, which is gone. For President Hinckley to have the vision to say, 'Let's rebuild our temple,' has really caught the imagination of the Church, because what is lost is now found."

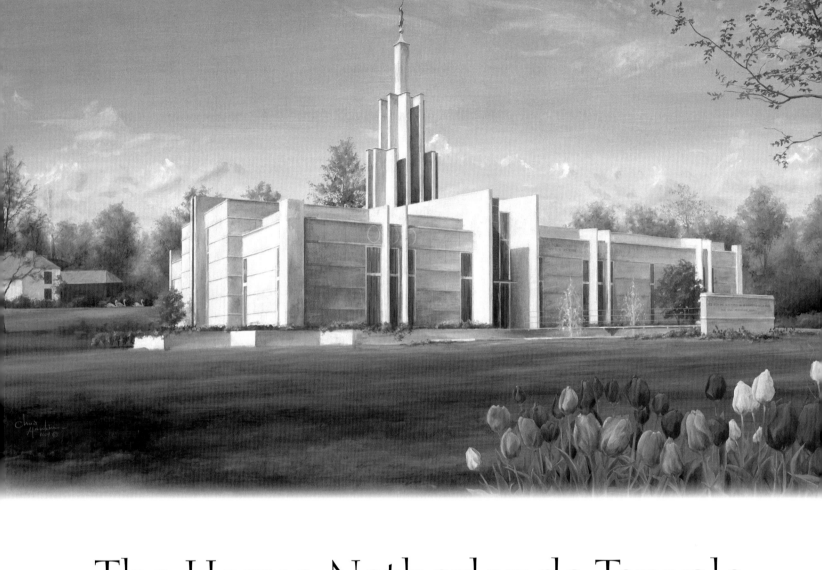

The Hague Netherlands Temple

The restored gospel first had a presence in the Netherlands in 1841, when Elder Orson Hyde arrived to preach the gospel for more than a week in Rotterdam and Amsterdam. After over 160 years of missionary effort, finally in the Dutch language read the revered words, "De Here Gewijd; Het Huis Des Heren" or in English, "Holiness to the Lord, the House of the Lord."

A landmark event for the Church in Holland occurred in August 1955, when after almost twenty years of petitioning, the Church received formal recognition and legal status. This major breakthrough provided public credibility and allowed the Church to own property. The Church overcame another obstacle decades later: although Dutch law prohibits the construction of a building that is closed to the public, the government granted the temple to have exemption from the law.

The temple was formally announced on August 16, 1999, in a letter to priesthood leaders. The temple is located in Zoetermeer, a city on the outskirts of the Hague. The history of the Church owning the temple property traces back to when a permanent meetinghouse for the expanding Zoetermeer branch was needed. Rather than building a new structure, the Church purchased an existing church from the Dutch Reformed Church. About a month after The Church of Jesus Christ of Latter-day Saints purchased the building, a wealthy widow belonging to the Dutch Reformed Church died and left nearly one million Dutch Guilders to her congregation. This

114

donated money would have been sufficient for the Dutch Reformed Church to own and maintain their building for another ten years and would have prevented the sale of their building. After being used by the Zoetermeer branch for many years, the existing thirty-year-old meetinghouse was torn down, allowing the temple to be built in its place.

Like much of the Netherlands, Zoetermeer sits below sea level. Seashells found in the soil during construction served as evidence of a time when the location was underneath the not-so-distant sea. Therefore, stable building foundations were achieved by draining excess water and using sturdy pylons. On December 16, 2000, the earth began to shake as the mayor of Zoetermeer activated the large machine that pounded the steel pylons about sixty feet into the ground. Many of the construction workers dressed that day in white overcoats out of respect for the sanctity of the temple.

Those who labored to build the temple recognized their task to be a once-in-a-life-time opportunity. Dutch architect Albert van Eerde, though not a member, noted the unique feelings of the temple: "From the start, over three years ago, I felt this project was more than just a job. I am very proud and honored that I was part of a process that led to this magnificent building, but also to a home for all of you. Every time I enter the celestial room I feel the serenity and peace we are all looking for at certain times. Thank you very much for giving me the opportunity of establishing this building, which will probably be the best I will ever build." When the temple reached its highest point of construction, workers celebrated in traditional Dutch fashion "het hoogste punt" (the highest point). This construction milestone is observed by workers climbing the scaffolding in their traditional wooden shoes.

Located twenty-three feet below sea level, The Hague Temple holds the distinction of being the temple with the lowest elevation. This fact is emphasized by a small canal located a few hundred feet behind the temple, which flows several feet higher than the temple's foundation. It is a common site to see

SITE
1 acre

GROUNDBREAKING
August 26, 2000, by John K. Carmack

DEDICATION
September 8, 2002, by
Gordon B. Hinckley

EXTERIOR
Polished granite

TOTAL FLOOR AREA
10,500 square feet

DIMENSIONS
81 feet by 154 feet

HIDDEN IMAGE
Among the distant trees is a
Dutch windmill. The presence
of a canal behind the temple is
evidenced by three swans.

a small water vessel floating nearby above the temple grounds.

The use of water at the temple's entrance is the first indication that this temple was truly designed for the Dutch. Temple visitors step across a bridge spanning a pool of water as they approach the temple door. Water was used in the temple's landscaping, reflecting the abundance of water in Holland and the legacy of the Dutch reclaiming land from the sea. Even the temple's underground parking garage features aspects of the Dutch culture. The parking area has accommodations for the parking of as many bicycles as cars.

Familiar Dutch symbols are found throughout the temple's interior. Beautifully carved in the carpet of the bride's, sealing, and celestial rooms are traditional Dutch tulips. The wall murals in the endowment room feature a Dutch landscape, including a windmill painted softly in the distance. The two prominent colors found in all the temple windows are yellow and blue. These two colors represent the official colors of Zoetermeer.

The temple's doors were opened to the public for two weeks in August 2002. Government and city officials were among the 32,819 guests to receive a guided tour during the open house. The Hague's first temple president, Anne Hulleman, shared an experience of another special guest: "An elderly lady slowly made her way back to the temple after having already gone through the open house. When asked if she wanted to go through the temple again, she said, 'No thank you, I am just coming back for my walker. After having gone through the first time, I was so impressed that I forgot my walker and went all the way home without it.'"

A day after rededicating the newly remodeled temple in Freiberg Germany, President Hinckley presided over the dedication of The Hague Netherlands Temple on September 8, 2002. For members living in the temple district, the temple is literally a *sweet* blessing. Local members often purposely mention that there is a temple in Salt Lake City and now there is a temple in "Sweet Lake City," the translation of Zoetermeer.

Brisbane Australia Temple

The Brisbane Australia Temple is in the heart of the city and is poised on the Kangaroo Point peninsula. From its clifftop perch, it has an unobstructed view overlooking the Brisbane River, Captain Cook Bridge, botanic gardens, and the beautiful city center skyline. The spire and golden Moroni statue are visible by thousands of daily travelers on the nearby Pacific Motorway. The beautiful granite building sits adjacent to a lovely meetinghouse that was built concurrently with the temple.

Patience and perseverance were essential for the Brisbane Saints during the long wait for the construction of their new temple. President Hinckley announced the Brisbane temple in 1998. Although it was the first smaller Australian temple

to be announced, it was the last of the four to be dedicated. Opposition from local community groups and individuals resulted in delays to the project. Negotiations over the height of the temple and adjacent meetinghouse, nighttime flood lighting, highly polished stone surface, and traffic concerns created significant delays. The Church complied with requests to reduce the roof pitch of the meetinghouse and to lower the temple platform. Legal action was narrowly averted after Brisbane City Council, residents, and the Church reached a last-minute compromise. Church public affairs director Grant Pitman said all the issues had been resolved "down to the finest of detail." Plans for the temple and adjacent meetinghouse received final approval in February 2001.

115

Almost three years after the temple's announcement, the site for Australia's fifth temple was dedicated at a groundbreaking service on May 26, 2001. More than 400 invited guests witnessed the ceremony at which Church and community leaders turned the soil with gold-painted shovels following a brief outdoor service.

Area President Kenneth Johnson presided at the event and spoke of the lengthy delays preceding the groundbreaking. He said, "Though you have waited here since 1998 for this to begin, I know you have not been impatient. You have enjoyed the experience of preparing for the temple to be built. The building that will rise on this site will be the house of the Lord," he continued, "a sacred sanctuary for those who seek to find Him. The Lord bless you that you might sense the magic of this moment. This is history in the making."

The temple site was originally the home of an Anglican university college. Then the Church acquired the property and built the historic "Kangaroo chapel" in 1956. The chapel needed to be razed to accommodate the temple and new meetinghouse. For forty-three years, the building served as the spiritual center of the Church in Brisbane. Additionally, it was the location of memorable cultural, sporting, and social events. Local members described their chapel as a light on the cliff. With the building of the temple, they looked forward to again having a light on the cliff, "a bigger, brighter light." The final worship services at the Kangaroo Point chapel occurred on Sunday, May 27, 2001, the day after the temple's groundbreaking. The next week, the entire building was razed so work on the temple could begin.

After supervising all aspects of temple construction, temple operations manager Chris Evans shared his strong opinions on the quality of the building's construction: "We set a goal to build the finest quality building in Queensland. Some eighteen months later in construction, and some quarter of a million man hours later, we're confident we've done just that. And we're, as I say, immensely proud of the outcome that we have here today. Buildings like this are seldom built in this day and age, I think it's fair to say, and we certainly had many people

SITE
.86 acres

GROUNDBREAKING
May 26, 2001

DEDICATION
June 15, 2003, by Gordon B. Hinckley

EXTERIOR
Light gray granite

TOTAL FLOOR AREA
10,700 square feet

DIMENSIONS
149 feet by 72 feet; statue of angel
Moroni on top spire; 71 feet high

HIDDEN IMAGE
The Savior is located above the temple
sign with His left hand outstretched.

within the industry questioning just where we would find the capabilities to build to this level of quality, and I think it's a great testament to the construction industry and the trade base in Queensland that to the very large and vast extent, these skills have been found within the workforce of Queensland."

This high quality of work was recognized in June 2003, when the temple was awarded the prestigious title of Project of the Year by the Queensland Master Builders Association. The annual award was judged by peers from within the building industry as well as from the general public. In addition to being the overall winner, the Brisbane Temple also won the category of Community Service Facilities.

The temple and the chapel sit on a thick concrete slab that acts as the roof of a 130-space underground parking lot. Surrounding the temple are stunning, stepped gardens with palm trees, water fountains, and grassed areas. A painting in the temple foyer by Queensland artist Ken Wenzel shows Mt. Mitchell near the Queensland border with New South Wales. The first ordinance room features a mural on three walls painted by Utah artist Linda Curly-Christensen. The scene shows the Glasshouse Mountains, a panoramic part of Queensland in the hinterland north of Brisbane.

In preparation for the open house, statements of support and respect were collected from high-profile religious, civic, and political leaders and used to help introduce the temple to the public. Among these comments was a sincere endorsement from the Honorable John Howard, then Prime Minister of Australia. Most media coverage was positive and invited Brisbane residents to take a "sticky-beak" (curious look). More than 55,000 community members took public tours during the Brisbane Temple open house May 10 through June 7, 2003.

The Brisbane temple was dedicated in four sessions attended by more than 6,500 Saints. The sessions were broadcast via closed-circuit satellite transmissions to local stake centers. Located about 600 miles north of Sydney in Queensland's capital city, the temple serves more than 23,000 Saints living in Queensland and the northern areas of New South Wales.

Redlands California Temple

The Redlands California Temple is located in a city known for its architectural beauty, friendly communities, and flourishing citrus groves. Named for the color of its adobe soil, Redlands has earned the reputation of being the "Jewel of the Inland Empire." This area of the state is at the base of the scenic San Bernardino Mountains and has deep roots in the history of the Church.

In the fall of 1851, members of the Mormon Battalion and settling Church members purchased the 35,000-acre Rancho San Bernardino. Land maps and historical documents confirmed the temple site to be well within the original pioneer holdings. "The pioneers made contributions important to this day," said Redlands city mayor and Church member Kasey

Haws. "They built houses, opened businesses, laid out streets, and greatly expanded irrigation and farming, so for the temple to be built here is something of a coming-home experience."

One feature in the temple's design was made at the request of President Gordon B. Hinckley. When visiting the region, he was impressed with the traditional bell towers featured in local architecture. Prominent examples include the bell tower on the University of Redlands campus and the historic Mission Inn in Riverside. Although the temple does not have a bell, it does have an open bell tower.

Jerry and Libby Quinn served as the temple's construction missionaries and initiated a program that made Tuesdays the favorite day of the week for the construction workers. For seventy-two

116

consecutive Tuesdays, members made and served wonderful meals demonstrating their gratitude for those who were laboring to build "their" temple. "It was such a blessing and opportunity to serve those who are providing a temple for us," a participating member explained. "We felt we were a part of the temple history here as we helped in a very small way."

The building's exquisite quality and craftsmanship is not limited to only what is visible. Many underlying components make the temple a masterpiece of both beauty and structure. For example, to ensure the stability of the temple in an area frequented by earthquakes, fourteen large cement trucks poured 135 cubic yards of concrete for the foundation supporting the temple's tower. "From an engineering standpoint, the base for the tower is something amazing," said Elder Quinn. "The massive reinforced concrete foundation and walls create a building with a seismic rating designed to withstand two levels above the largest earthquake ever recorded in California. There has never been a recorded earthquake in California that would even touch this structure. Redlands's city inspectors were so impressed with our building that they used photos and data from this building to show other contractors how they should build."

Covering the enormous concrete building with granite was another massive task. The granite pieces arrived pre-numbered according to their exact placement on the temple. The granite was of such superior quality that whenever a rare blemish was found, it was always smaller than a dime. The granite at the base of the entire temple is buffed and polished, giving a high-gloss appearance, with the remaining upper portion less polished and shiny. Typical granite panels weigh seventy-five pounds; the large moon stones in the celestial room weigh 700 pounds and the ornate urns weigh 2,500 pounds each. The 12,211 pieces of granite weigh an estimated 2.7 million pounds.

August 2003 marked the end of temple construction and the beginning of the much-anticipated public open house.

SITE
4.6 acres

GROUNDBREAKING
December 1, 2001, by
Dieter F. Uchtdorf

DEDICATION
September 14, 2003, by
Gordon B. Hinckley

EXTERIOR
Light gray granite

TOTAL FLOOR AREA
17,300 square feet

DIMENSIONS
200 feet by 98 feet

HIDDEN IMAGE
The figures depicted in this drawing are patterned after the First Vision portrayed beautifully in stained glass within the temple.

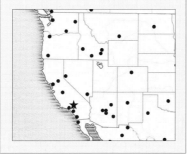

Over 140,000 visitors from the Inland Empire and beyond visited the temple during its four-week open house.

The temple is buffered on the north and west sides by navel orange trees, which are reminiscent of the hundreds of orange trees growing on the location in years past. One of the palm trees on the north side is unique because it is estimated at being a hundred years old and was donated by a local member family.

The Redlands Temple features many unique design and decorative items exclusive to this temple. One example is a back-lit, stained-glass depiction of the First Vision. This large art glass window was created in 1933 for the first chapel built in San Bernardino. The art glass was treasured by the members who had sacrificed for the chapel and its windows during the difficult Depression years. The glasswork remained in the building even after it was sold to a Protestant congregation in 1960. After multiple requests, the work of art was sold back to the Church and subsequently restored in 1978. In its new pristine condition, it was unveiled in the Pacific Avenue building in San Bernardino in 1979. This colorful masterpiece has found its final home within the Redlands Temple. Its illuminating colors and spiritual meaning now inspire visitors to the temple and provide a link to the early beginnings of the Church.

Three murals in the first ordinance room display a vast landscape as viewed from a high vista. Wild animals integrated into the painting include a mountain lion, coyote, bears, deer, and hawks. According to the artist, the depicted sunset suggests "the absolute intense beauty of this world and all that God created."

After the successful open house, members prepared themselves for the temple's dedication. On Sunday, September 14, 2003, nearly 23,000 Church members participated in the four dedicatory ceremonies. "You'll remember this day all of your lives," President Hinckley said toward the end of the ceremony, adding, "It was worth getting up for, wasn't it?"

Accra Ghana Temple

On August 24, 1985, a new era in the Lord's work dawned when Africa's first temple was dedicated in Johannesburg, South Africa. Nineteen years later and 2,902 miles away, the first West African temple was dedicated in Accra, Ghana. In this nation's capital city stands a house of the Lord as an elegant and spiritual landmark. This highly visible edifice makes an appropriate contribution to the architecture of the city and provides evidence of the Church's commitment to West Africa.

Careful political maneuvering and patience were required prior to the Church receiving permission from the government to proceed with the temple. In 1989, the government expelled LDS missionaries and expatriate leaders and shut down the Church's buildings, claiming the faith was challenging the government. Some members were jailed, some left the Church, and others continued to meet in small groups in members' homes. Many of those who endured this eighteen-month time period, known as "the freeze," became stalwart Church leaders. In 1998, eight years after the Church was permitted to resume its activities, President Gordon B. Hinckley visited with Ghana's president, Jerry Rawlings. The Ghanaian president gave his assurance that any issues between his country and the Church had been resolved and that the future looked bright. Within hours of this meeting, President Hinckley announced to more than 6,000 members the purchase of land for a temple on Accra's prominent Independence Avenue. The members were so

117

shocked and delighted by the announcement that they broke into spontaneous applause.

For approximately three years after the temple was announced, official permission to begin construction was impossible to receive. Temple building permits were delayed, altered, and occasionally threatened to be completely denied. On one occasion, Ghanaian authorities denied building proposals for the temple and surrounding buildings because they were not large or tall enough. New plans were submitted that included a two-story stake center and four-story offices and patron housing. Africa West Area President Glenn L. Pace described this period of optimism and subsequent disappointment as "the temple approval roller coaster."

On November 16, 2001, the day of the temple's long-awaited groundbreaking arrived. In a country where most building materials are unavailable and machinery is nearly impossible to procure, the temple had to be built with construction ingenuity. The building's structural integrity, modern technology, and artistic elegance set a new benchmark of excellence in Ghana and the surrounding region. Introducing "temple quality" construction guidelines to those building the temple was a challenge for project leaders. There was not another building in the country with an equivalent building standard. Consequently, a few key individuals were brought to Salt Lake to better understand "temple quality" and how it was to be achieved. During the last phases of construction, when highly technical and fine work was needed, international specialists were brought in.

Working on the temple presented unique challenges for contractors from Ireland and the U.K. who installed the temple's security system, communications system, and air conditioning. Directing the installations was Francis Jennings, who described some challenges: "One of the problems was that because we weren't members of the Mormon Church, we weren't allowed into the building once it had been consecrated. So everything had to be 100% defect free, operating perfectly, the first time." Their workmanship earned them the overall Best Practice Award at the UK Building Services Awards.

The speed and efficiency of the temple's construction was noticed by the casual passersby, city leaders, and political officials. Six months prior to the temple's dedication, Mary Cartin Yates, U.S. Ambassador to Ghana, toured the construction site

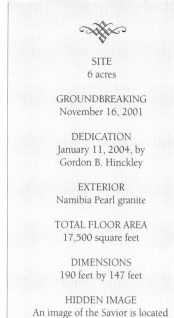

SITE
6 acres

GROUNDBREAKING
November 16, 2001

DEDICATION
January 11, 2004, by
Gordon B. Hinckley

EXTERIOR
Namibia Pearl granite

TOTAL FLOOR AREA
17,500 square feet

DIMENSIONS
190 feet by 147 feet

HIDDEN IMAGE
An image of the Savior is located
at the doors of the temple.

accompanied by Elder Sheldon H. Child of the Seventy. The ambassador commented that she had "never seen anything so complex go up so quickly here in Ghana."

The temple provides a visual oasis on the main avenue that runs through the nation's capital. The entire campus is beautifully perched upon a gently rising hill in the center of the city. Built by Africans with materials indigenous to the continent, the temple was built for African Saints. The result is a landmark all Africans can be proud of.

Starting with the walls, the temple is a monument of remarkable African workmanship and materials. The temple's exterior is clad with Namibian pearl granite quarried among the dunes of the Kalahari Desert. Intricately crafted African granite was used for the floors, and native makore wood was used for all the moldings. Chairs and tables are sculpted to look like lions' feet or elephant tusks. Art windows display a stylized "tree of life" theme taken from the Book of Mormon. Carved carpets, beautiful murals of the Ghanaian countryside, handcrafted furniture, and subtle tree outlines in the wallpaper all reflect an African influence. "This temple has more custom designs than most other temples," said Bengt Erlandsson, interior designer. To get his designs, he spent two weeks in Ghana visiting the markets and studied African culture and design for nearly two years. Although ancient tribal designs are visually referenced, special effort was given to ensure that the designs did not belong exclusively to any one tribe.

A new day dawned in Ghana on January 11, 2004. As the seasonal winds carried red-tinted silt from the Sahara, the temple was dedicated by President Gordon B. Hinckley during three sessions. The Sahara dust obscured the sun, providing some relief from equatorial heat for the Saints as they exited the temple with broad smiles.

Latter-day Saint faith and prayers called down the powers of heaven and allowed enormous obstacles to be overcome. Elder Glenn L. Pace described the impact of the dedicated temple: "Like an atomic bomb has been dropped right in the middle of Satan's stronghold in West Africa. It will be the most significant thing that has affected West Africa since the atonement and resurrection of Jesus Christ. It will be the beginning of the end of Satan's hold on these countries."

Copenhagen Denmark Temple

Denmark is a Scandinavian country that has had a tremendous influence on the history of The Church of Jesus Christ of Latter-day Saints. From converts to the artistic contributions of Bertel Thorvaldsen and Carl Bloch, Denmark has an enduring tradition of building and strengthening the kingdom of God in the latter days. Danish was the first language the Book of Mormon was translated into after English. Denmark was truly a white field ready to harvest during the early years of the Church. Thousands of converts emigrated to the United States, where they gathered to help build Zion. When the Copenhagen Denmark Temple was announced, Saints gathered and united their efforts to build Zion in Denmark.

The building of the Copenhagen Denmark

Temple was announced on March 17, 1999. Much like the Vernal Utah Temple, the temple in Copenhagen involved extensive renovation of an already existing building, the Priorvej Chapel. This chapel's original neo-classical building plans were created by Joseph Don Carlos Young, the son of Brigham Young. Ejnar Thuien was the local Danish architect for the building. The Priorvej Chapel was completed in 1930 and dedicated by Elder John A. Widtsoe of the Quorum of the Twelve Apostles on June 14, 1931, "to be a place where Thy truth, the eternal gospel of Thy Son, Jesus Christ, shall be taught, both by precept and example, and where the introductory ordinances, which belong to this Church, can be performed." The date of the chapel's dedication was the eighty-first

118

anniversary of when missionaries first arrived in Denmark.

During World War II, the chapel was used as a public bomb shelter. Copenhagen Temple Historian Lis Billeskov Jansen said, "When people heard the sirens and alarms, they would run into the church."

On April 24, 1999, nearly 700 Latter-day Saints from Denmark and western Sweden met in the Priorvej Chapel in downtown Copenhagen to attend dedicatory services commencing construction of the Copenhagen Denmark Temple. Part of the restoration involved raising the entire roof and extending the height of the walls. This required extra brick, which was obtained by disassembling the brick villa that once stood on the property. The brick was cleaned and then used on the temple, providing a seamless and perfect match.

The temple reached a building milestone when the final rafter was installed into position. In Denmark, this special occasion, known as "rejsegilde" (topping out ceremony), is traditionally celebrated with a feast of Danish hot dogs and beer. Church builders modified this tradition for the workers by providing a wonderful buffet feast.

Another milestone was reached on August 15, 2004, when the angel Moroni statue was placed on the spire. Many of the construction workers were aware of the event and chose to wear white hats, sweaters, and pants for the occasion. Although the event was not publicized, word leaked to a few members, who then told others, which resulted in a seemingly instantaneous gathering of members.

The temple's baptistry is not located directly beneath the temple; rather, it is strategically placed beneath the reflecting pool on the temple grounds. Beneath the water in the shallow reflecting pool are windows that let light into the underground baptismal room. The light that shines through the rippling water and into the baptistry often provides unique, subtle reflections of the water ripples from above.

The completed temple opened its doors to the public from April 29 to May 15, 2004. The temple's district covers a vast geographic region including Iceland, the Faroe Islands, and a

SITE
Less than 1 acre

GROUNDBREAKING
April 24, 1999, by Spencer J. Condie

DEDICATION
May 23, 2004, by Gordon B. Hinckley

EXTERIOR
Original brick and columns

TOTAL FLOOR AREA
25,000 square feet

DIMENSIONS
45 feet by 120 feet

HIDDEN IMAGE
To the right of the temple is an image of the Christus statue. The original Bertel Thorvaldsen statue stands just a few minutes away in downtown Copenhagen.

portion of Sweden. Saints travel from these distant lands by plane, bus, train, and ferry. Church groups traveling by bus often sing hymns along the way and then cheer when the temple finally comes in sight.

The generous financial donations from members in the United States and Denmark facilitated a valuable marketing opportunity for the temple's open house. Beautifully designed full-color circulars inviting the public to the open house were created and distributed. Messages inside the circular included the Church's fundamental beliefs, the history of the Church in Denmark, and the purpose of temples. Approximately 50,000 circulars were dispersed in newspapers or delivered in person by missionaries and members.

The temple's facade retained the old chapel's original columns. Five long windows on each side feature colored art glass from England, and above them the roof is made of copper, with a copper-clad dome. A brick wall encloses a private garden, paved with granite and including raised planter boxes filled with blossoming trees, bushes, and spring flowers. Materials used in the interior of the temple are distinctly Danish and Swedish. The temple also features murals containing seventy different animals, including moose from Sweden.

On a sunny morning, May 23, 2004, more than 3,400 members participated in person or via satellite as President Gordon B. Hinckley dedicated the Copenhagen Denmark Temple in four sessions. Acknowledging the history of the Priorvej Chapel, President Hinckley said, "It has served very well through these years. It was deemed advisable that we should convert it to a temple. It is all new inside. It is in a good location, and we had the land, which is almost impossible to get in Copenhagen. A miracle has been wrought."

In the dedicatory prayer, President Hinckley remembered the early members who left Denmark more than 150 years ago to join the Saints in Zion. "Now Thy people are urged to remain and build Zion in this good land. That they might have every blessing, and that they might extend these blessings to those beyond the veil of death, this beautiful temple has been constructed in their midst."

Manhattan New York Temple

Amid the honking of horns, the noise of crowds, and the rumble of subways stands the Empire State's second temple. Surrounded by sky-high, steel-girded towers is a silent oasis of calm and respite from the world. The Church's dynamic growth in membership, the timely acquisition of the temple's prime location, and the multiple conversions during the temple's open house are among the many evidences of temple-related divine intervention. Acknowledging this, New York Church members affectionately refer to the temple as "The Miracle in Manhattan."

Less than a year after the New York City skyline was decimated by terrorism, the Church was planning a temple only four miles north of Ground Zero. In the months following September 11, 2001, New York New York Stake President Brent J. Belnap realized the possibility of Church members leaving the city. He explained, "Rather than people leaving the city in droves, people with a pioneering desire have just committed more firmly than ever before to build the kingdom here. We're flourishing back here. I guess that's one of the paradoxes," the coexistence of times of "incredible sadness and turmoil and yet incredible blessings."

Many members found peace and comfort in having a temple in their city following the September 11th terrorist attacks. Soon after the temple's announcement, Kim Stewart, a longtime resident of New York, shared her thoughts on a having a temple so close to home: "Since September 11, you realize

119

that New York City is such a target. And the thought of having a temple here and to know that the Lord is aware of us here—it's just a feeling of protection."

The temple in Manhattan is located on a parcel of land between 65th and 66th streets on Columbus Avenue, purchased by the Church in 1971. Scott Trotter, former public affairs spokesman for the Church in New York, said, "It used to be a rough area. They even filmed 'West Side Story' here. Then the Lincoln Center went up, the Church came in and the neighborhood started changing after that. It's an upscale area now."

After tearing down existing row houses, the Church built a multi-story meeting house in 1975. At the time of the temple announcement, the six-story building was home to eight wards and a branch for deaf members. Rather than building an entirely new structure, the temple was created within the existing shell of the New York New York Stake Center. Following an approach used in the Hong Kong Temple, the stake center was renovated so as to create the temple on the first, second, fifth, and sixth floors, with the chapel, classrooms, basketball court, and administrative offices on the third and fourth floors.

As the temple neared completion, anticipation for the public open house increased. Church officials decided against advertising the open house, fearing they would be inundated with visitors. Still, more than eighty percent of the free tickets were gone days before the month-long open house began. Visitors to the temple included ambassadors, senators, congressmen, and people from fifty-five countries, all ten provinces of Canada, and all fifty states of the United States.

More than 53,000 people attended the forty-minute tour. The ripple effect of the temple's open house in a major news capital like New York reached across the United States and the world. The first sentence of a *USA Today* article stated, "One of the hottest tickets in New York right now is just off Broadway: a tour of a new Mormon temple."

Throughout the temple, the atmosphere is bright and airy despite its lack of natural light. Synthetic Venetian stained-glass windows are backlit by lights inserted between the inner and outer walls, creating the illusion of continuous daylight.

Several rooms in the temple have light fixtures depicting an olive motif. The rooms' stained-glass windows portray vines with bunches of grapes.

One of the temple's unique features is enjoyed throughout the building, not by being seen, but by being heard. Although city noise never stops, it cannot be heard within the walls of the temple. Extensive design and construction techniques were implemented to create a building within a building. Interior walls were built with two layers of sheetrock plus twelve inches of dense insulation. The soundproofed inner shell creates a quiet, serene atmosphere where members can enjoy peaceful reflection, unique in New York City.

On June 12, 2004, President Hinckley met with members of the fourteen stakes in the Manhattan temple district. Reading an entry from his journal dated March 23, 2002, President Hinckley told the congregation that two years previously he had come to New York to look for a way to bring a temple to the Saints in Manhattan. "We then went to our Lincoln Center property," he said. "I went all through this very carefully with the thought that the upper portion might be converted to a beautiful and serviceable temple. The more I saw of it, the better I felt about it. We would do here what we have done in Hong Kong." After praying about the idea, he recorded in his journal, "I feel enthusiastic." Among the final thoughts he shared with the congregation, he said, "We are here in June. The miracle has occurred. That marvelous thing has come to pass and the house of the Lord has been built within the shell of that great building which we have on Broadway and Columbus."

On June 13, 2004, the temple dedication was broadcast live to sixteen meetinghouses in ten languages.

Although dedicated, the temple was not considered complete until nearly four months later, on October 9. After a two-hour sidewalk public display, a ten-foot, gold-plated statue of the angel Moroni was hoisted into position as hundreds of spectators looked on. The statue's quick ascent was accompanied by enthusiastic applause from below. For the Church members in New York, this moment was the grand finale to the many events preceding the "Miracle in Manhattan."

San Antonio Texas Temple

President Gordon B. Hinckley announced that a temple would be built in San Antonio on Sunday, June 25, 2001, during a fireside at the San Antonio Municipal Auditorium. At 1,221 feet above sea level, the temple rests on the highest point in city limits and can be seen from as far as thirty miles away. The temple majestically stands geographically and symbolically above the fray of the world below.

The foresight of having a temple in San Antonio was first demonstrated in the 1970s by faithful member Addie Smith. Sister Smith remained single throughout her life and provided for herself and her mother by cleaning homes. Prior to her passing, she made arrangements to donate the entire value ($20,000) of her life insurance policy to the Church for the

specific benefit of a future temple in San Antonio. Herbert Turley served as Addie's bishop and said, "She had the faith and knew within herself that there would someday be a temple in San Antonio. We sent the money to Church headquarters, where it was set aside for the temple. The money earned interest for a long time until it could to be used. Consequently, she made a great contribution to the San Antonio Texas Temple."

Temple construction missionaries William and Virginia Mannewitz served faithfully and used their skills to creatively make the temple as beautiful as possible. As heavy equipment hammered deep into the solid flint bedrock, a narrow cavern was discovered. The small cavern featured many well-formed

120

stalactites and stalagmites. County experts were notified and after two months of study, it was determined that the cavern could be filled with concrete and excavation could continue. Prior to doing so, Elder Mannewitz carefully removed each gracefully formed stalactite and stalagmite. With great precision, he cut them into ⅛-inch thin strips, exposing their stunning inner patterns and colors. The delicate pieces were then shipped to the temple's art glass creator, Tom Holdman, to be incorporated into the temple windows. These precious pieces were used to form the wheat kernels located in the perimeter of the celestial room windows. Additional shimmering and colorful rock specimens discovered during excavation were also cut with expertise and used in the window designs.

The temple's adorning angel Moroni statue was placed in its permanent position on September 21, 2004. Considering the size of the temple and the height of the spire, the temple was originally designed to feature a ten-foot statue. However, a thirteen-foot-six-inch statue was delivered and installed, resulting in a larger than normal appearance. The larger statue is appreciated by local members, who frequently quip, "Everything is bigger in Texas."

Among the temple's many highlights are the stunning art and stained-glass windows that are strategically positioned in nearly every room. Natural light from outside shines in and provides colorful life that enhances the purpose of the temple. A portion of the glass used has a connection with the first chapel built by the Church in San Antonio. The chapel was built in the early 1940s and was known for decades as the "Bailey Street Chapel." Although the building was eventually sold and used by other denominations, much of the building's original stained glass was salvaged and stored for nearly thirty years. Once temple construction began, stained glass from the Bailey Street Chapel was cleaned and prepared for use in the temple's glass windows. The vivid amber-yellow colors worked perfectly in the glass sections surrounding the wheat.

The Nauvoo Illinois Temple project made a valuable contribution to the temple in San Antonio. During the construction

SITE
5.5 acres

GROUNDBREAKING
March 29, 2003, by H. Bruce Stucki

DEDICATION
May 22, 2005, by Gordon B. Hinckley

EXTERIOR
Granite

TOTAL FLOOR AREA
16,800 square feet

DIMENSIONS
97 feet by 191 feet; height to the top of angel Moroni statue is 115 feet

HIDDEN IMAGE
An image of the Savior is rendered across the surface of the temple where the celestial room is located.

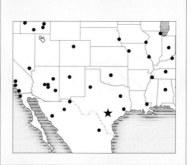

of the Nauvoo Temple, plans for the parking lot were changed, which allowed a large quantity of light gray granite pavers to remain unused. Three years later, these same pavers were used to create the San Antonio Texas Temple's waterfall, crosswalks, and the plaza near the front door. Prior to being installed, members volunteered their time to clean the pavers.

A consistent theme throughout the temple is the traditional quatrefoil symbol. Since ancient times, this geometric shape has been used in art, architecture, and as a traditional Christian symbol. In San Antonio, this recognizable design has been used on some of the area's oldest missions. Since the St. George Temple, variations of the quatrefoil have been used on many temples. The San Antonio Texas Temple features the quatrefoil design in gold leaf on the ceilings of the celestial rooms and sealing rooms. It is also repeated in the windows, on furniture, and carved into the carpet.

While serving in the temple, patrons observe a literal and symbolic progression. For example, the baptistry is eight inches lower and the main portion of the temple and features an extensive amount of wood trim finished in a deep cherry stain. Proceeding through the instruction rooms, the wood colors evolve into lighter tones. Additionally, the ceilings of each room increase in height. Finally, in the celestial room, colors display white brilliance bathed in a splendor of light. The celestial room and the sealing rooms are eight inches higher than the rest of the temple.

The 16,800-square-foot temple attracted some 65,000 visitors during its three-week open house. Encased in an exterior of granite, visitors were greeted by rugged native oaks, mountain laurels, and water features that capture the rugged beauty of south Texas.

The San Antonio Texas Temple became the fourth dedicated temple in the Lone Star State and the 120th in the Church on May 22, 2005. President Gordon B. Hinckley presided over each of the four dedicatory sessions. Following the dedication, one member said, "This is one of the greatest events that has ever happened to San Antonio. I love the fact that the temple is here and it's ours. It's part of San Antonio. Always will be."

Aba Nigeria Temple

Nigeria is often referred to as the "Giant of Africa" due to its large population and economy. With approximately 174 million inhabitants, Nigeria is the most populous country in Africa. Church growth in this "giant" nation has been dramatic and now reigns with the highest membership of any country in Africa. The temple in Aba closed an epic season of worldwide temple expansion. Of the generation of forty-nine smaller temples, it was the last to be dedicated.

To construct the temple complex with its multiple buildings first required the construction of a road to the temple. However, constructing this road leading to the temple first required building a bridge. All was done with government permission and at Church expense. With seemingly endless obstacles,

the Church found a way to build the bridge, road, and temple complex—however long and difficult the process. In a spirit of gratitude, locals now call this "Temple Road." Upon completion, media reported the road as being "without doubt the best in the city of Aba."

The temple is located in the rural Umuchichi Village, where there is an abundance of palm trees and family-operated farms. Longtime resident and village Chief Joseph Ogugua described some of the ways his village directly benefited from the project. He stated, "It must be mentioned that the construction of the road and the temple offered our young men jobs that were hitherto unavailable; it also enhanced the economy of the village tremendously. As soon as

121

the construction of the road and temple took off, investors came and established industries in the area. Land value went up and owners sold their land to investors at an increase of 400% to 500%. With the construction of the road and establishment of the temple complex, new industries and buildings in the area increased. The village is now wearing a new look. In fact, words are inadequate to thank the Church."

The day the angel Moroni statue was hoisted into position was a time to celebrate a symbolic milestone. Before the celebration, however, many challenges had to be overcome. One of the greatest obstacles was getting the crane working long enough to lift the assembled statue and tower into position. Men working on high scaffolding were sweating in intense heat for hours without access to water. "I believe these problems were overcome by priesthood holders closing their eyes in prayer several times during the process. It was very touching and I know there was unseen help from above. No one can know how touching it was to see the Moroni finally placed on top of the temple without first understanding how difficult it was to accomplish the task."

The temple is part of a larger complex that includes a water treatment plant, security gatehouse, reinforced high-security perimeter walls, a power generator house, stake center, temple president apartment, and patron housing. All of these facilities are protected by 10- to 14-foot gates, walls, and fences. Razor-sharp metal is attached to the top of the walls, preventing anyone from successfully climbing over. Twelve powerful cameras survey all angles of the temple complex twenty-four hours a day. These cameras are monitored and controlled within the gate house. Multiple professional security personnel continually staff various positions to protect the temple and secure the safety of temple visitors. Aside

SITE
6.3 acres

GROUNDBREAKING
February 23, 2002

DEDICATION
August 7, 2005, by
Gordon B. Hinckley

EXTERIOR
Namibian pearl granite

TOTAL FLOOR AREA
11,500 square feet

DIMENSIONS
147 feet by 77 feet

HIDDEN IMAGE
The familiar shape of the African continent and a silhouette of Nigeria are located in the clouds.

from the Salt Lake Temple, the Aba Nigeria Temple is likely the most secured temple in the Church.

Due to embargo restrictions, importing furniture was strictly forbidden. Therefore, Nigerian companies were contracted to produce authentic furnishings created by native hands depicting African accents and culture. Highlights of the furniture include chairs with carvings of a "tree of life" motif and chairs for the bride's room that could grace a palace. Company owners and workers who provided the many custom furnishings were not members of the Church. Although not members of the Church, the skilled craftspeople gave their very best to "construct furniture that would please God. Each has been impressed by the fact that they were able to do something for God."

From the moment the Aba Nigeria Temple was announced, members of the Church in that region looked forward to the day they could visit the house of the Lord in their country. Evelyn Momoh and her husband, Wahab, were among those who made a four-hour journey on a crowded bus of members to serve as volunteers at the temple open house. Sister Momoh was expecting a baby at the time, and as their 150-mile journey came to an end, she began having labor pains. The bus driver hurried to the temple complex, and her child was born as soon as they arrived. Born in the temple's parking lot, the Momohs' second son was named "Temple." Although exhausted, Sister Momoh said, "Thanks be to God we made it. I am so happy!" Mother and baby stayed with a local member to recover from the delivery and gain strength for the trip home. On the first day the newly dedicated temple was open, Brother and Sister Momoh returned to receive the endowment and to be sealed as a family. The family was among the first to be sealed in the Aba Nigeria Temple.

Newport Beach California Temple

The Newport Beach California Temple is built on a showcase piece of property in Bonita Canyon situated at the easternmost gateway to Newport Beach. Anciently, the property was an ocean bottom, as demonstrated by whalebones and sea life found during excavation. During the grading process, heavy equipment unearthed Native American arrowheads and pottery. For future generations, the sacred site will bring eternal blessings to faithful members living in Orange County, California.

The temple was built on property shared by a stake center. Originally, the stake center was to be built where the temple now stands. However, anticipating the possibility of a future temple, Church leaders determined the stake center should be positioned farther back on the property.

The temple was announced in a letter dated April 13, 2001. As soon as concept plans for the temple were released, a wave of vocal opposition ensued from local homeowner associations. The *Los Angeles Times* headlined: "Mormons unveil a towering temple." The *Orange County Register* compared the proposed temple height of 125 feet to the Matterhorn at Disneyland.

To appease expressed concerns, Church leaders agreed to modify the exterior color from white to a more natural earth tone, reduce lighting intensity by fifty percent, and turn off lighting after 11:00 p.m. Vocal complaints were still forthcoming regarding

122

the height of the proposed 120-foot spire. Under community and city pressure, the Church agreed to set up a crane for several days in January 2003 to demonstrate the exact height and position of the proposed steeple. A red light was installed on top of the crane so it could be observed all night. This demonstration only fanned the flames of neighbor disapproval. Nonetheless, the city council voted five to one to approve the temple if the Church would reduce the height by twenty-five feet. Church officials agreed to the terms, and then as a demonstration of good faith, offered to lower it an additional ten feet. The opposition accepted the offer and "welcomed the Mormons to the neighborhood." Of the event it was recorded, "A feeling of good will permeated the council chambers as an emotional audience responded with a standing ovation. This long approval order was finally over!"

The temple's architecture was based upon that of the Lubbock Texas Temple. The design was then modified to complement the Southern California region. When the spire height was reduced, the spire was widened to give it more prominence. Architect Lloyd Platt described the temple as if "it could be set in the Holy Land." A mission-style architectural feature that is beautiful from inside and out is the large, copper-clad dome above the celestial room. Brother Platt noted that the royal palms, olive trees, and junipers add to the regional feeling and provide a timeless and classical look. Nearly 400 trees and 54,000 plants were used to enhance the temple grounds. Ensuring the temple will forever have an unobstructed view, about five acres of the temple property was vegetated and set aside as a perpetual nature preserve.

The distinctive salmon color of the temple's granite surface is called "Salisbury Pink." Quarried from North Carolina, much of the stone needed for the temple had already been sent to Italy to be prepared for the construction of a huge palace in the Middle East. One of the side benefits resulting from the long city approval delays was that eventually the palace project stalled out, leaving a large surplus quantity of granite from Italy that the Church was able to acquire at a bargain price.

SITE
8.8 acres

GROUNDBREAKING
August 15, 2003, by Duane B. Gerrard

DEDICATION
August 28, 2005, by
Gordon B. Hinckley

EXTERIOR
Salisbury pink granite
from North Carolina

TOTAL FLOOR AREA
17,800 square feet

DIMENSIONS
200 feet by 98 feet

HIDDEN IMAGE
The Savior and His Apostles are
among the landscaping beneath
the temple's entrance. The clouds
on the left depict the familiar
form of an ocean wave.

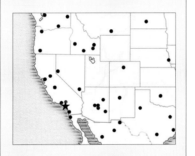

According to Brother Platt, "This temple is built to last. It has solid concrete walls and it far exceeds the standards in the California building code for earthquake safety . . . this building is good to last for a thousand years."

Artist Chris Young created the interior's lifelike murals. He walked early morning hours along the Orange County coast, becoming familiar with the local flora, fauna, and landscape. "I was mesmerized by the ocean and took thousands of photographs." As he immersed himself in the coastal environment, he was fortunate to observe an otter, pelicans, golden eagles, blue herons, and even a whale breaching near the coast. His objective was to depict the particular beauty of "the Lord's handiwork in Orange County." His masterful painting depicts a pristine beach scene with cliffs and water breaking over a rocky coast.

Among those faithfully serving on the temple were construction missionaries Vaughn and Juanee Baird. Although the construction site was a hub of activity, they described the site as a place of "calmness and peace" that construction workers could feel. "There was a security guard that felt the spirit of the temple," Elder Baird explained. "After working on the temple for about two months, walking nightly around the site, he became aware of a special feeling when on the temple grounds. One day the missionaries knocked on the door of his apartment. He opened the door and was soon baptized."

Members of the sixteen Orange County stakes requested and were granted the privilege to completely finance this beautiful house of the Lord. The temple was built entirely from member-donated funds, without any money from tithing funds. On Sunday, February 27, 2005, a letter was sent from the Orange County Temple Committee thanking the Saints and announcing that all of the funds needed to build the temple had been received.

Groundbreaking to completion of construction required just over two years. President Gordon B. Hinckley dedicated the temple on August 28, 2005. The Newport Beach Temple stands as a tribute to Orange County's faithful Latter-day Saints and their firm commitment to the house of the Lord.

Sacramento California Temple

L ocated near the rugged Sierra Nevada Range, California's capital city is rich in Church history. The Sacramento Temple is located close to two of the most famous gold mining sites in American history. In the area that sparked the California gold rush, Church members are grateful to have a temple that is more precious than gold.

The history of the Sacramento California Temple's unique location began in the early 1970s, when the Church acquired a former Aerojet General Corporation recreation facility. At the time, the corporation was downsizing and the Fair Oaks Stake was growing and in desperate of need meetinghouses. Fair Oaks Stake President Harvey Greer was the stake president when the building and land was made available in

September of 1971. President Joseph Fielding Smith recommended the purchase of land and facility, but because there was so much excess land, the members had to pay for it themselves. President Greer said, "When I drove to the top of the hill on the land, I could actually see a temple standing here. I really knew that was the purpose of the land and knowing that gave me the courage to ask the Saints to raise the money and move forward on its purchase."

President Spencer W. Kimball dedicated the land on October 9, 1976. In his comments to the gathered audience he said, "You have a beautiful spot here for a temple. Maybe that would be a wonderful thing. I don't mind talking about temples to the congregations, even far in advance of their need and their

123

readiness for it. Some of the prophets have said there will be hundreds and hundreds of temples—we have only sixteen right now. And it's quite a distance to go. But, brothers and sisters, I just want to say this—that when you are ready, you could have a temple."

The forty-six-acre site included tennis courts, baseball fields, and a large swimming pool. Once purchased, the location became known as the "Mormon Center." The Mormon Center's beautiful grounds and secluded location provided decades of recreational opportunities for Pioneer Day celebrations, roller-skating, festivals, basketball championships, volleyball tournaments, numerous Scouting functions, family reunions, and weddings.

On Sunday, August 23, 2004, Church members rejoiced when President Gordon B. Hinckley broke ground for the new temple. During the proceedings, the prophet said, "We ordinarily don't break ground for a temple on the Sabbath day. I hope the ground is soft, so we don't have to labor on the Sabbath." Previously, President Hinckley chose the exact location where the temple was to be positioned on the property.

Before construction could begin, the approval of the city planning commission was required. When the moment arrived for Church officials to present to the planning commission, Church members arrived early and filled the council chambers. Due to decades of positive LDS efforts in the community, leaders from other religious denominations also arrived to voice their support of the temple. According to Sacramento Temple architect Brian K. Everett, the event transpired as follows: "At the hearing, the religious leaders stood, identified themselves, their faith and voiced their support of the project. The overwhelming support prompted the commission to vote unanimously in favor of the temple. Following the meeting, one of the commissioners commented that it was the largest contingent of interfaith people to come and represent any faith they'd ever seen. The event was tremendous. The spirit that was felt and the things that took place were amazing."

As the temple neared completion, members were given unique opportunities to help the temple prepare for the

SITE
46 acres

GROUNDBREAKING
August 22, 2004, by
Gordon B. Hinckley

DEDICATION
September 3, 2006, by
Gordon B. Hinckley

EXTERIOR
Light gray granite

TOTAL FLOOR AREA
19,500 square feet

DIMENSIONS
220 feet by 120 feet by 131 feet

HIDDEN IMAGE
The Savior's image with arms
outstretched is among the
arched colonnades.

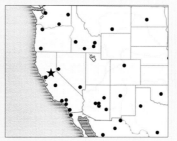

upcoming open house. Due to prolonged significant rains, the landscaping could not be planted on schedule. Once the weather cleared, a call went out to local stakes requesting assistance to prepare the grounds as quickly as possible. Immediately, hundreds of members flocked to the site to plant flowers, plant trees, and lay sod. Working for days in sweltering heat (one day was 113 degrees), the volunteers served without complaining from daybreak until after dark. Within the temple, volunteers served for weeks by cleaning the temple thoroughly. These efforts gave members a sense of ownership and personal connection with their beautiful new temple.

The beautiful hilltop location, known as "Temple Hill," overlooks Lake Natoma on the American River and is blanketed with native oak trees. One of the grandest oak trees is located near the entrance of the temple and is estimated to be over one hundred years old. A water feature is centered at the entrance of the temple with arched colonnades flanking each side of the main entry. There are three compass designs located on the ground at the temple's entrance, symbolizing man's effort to find his way.

The temple's interior features numerous art glass windows, sculpted carpet, and an original mural depicting the Sierra Nevada Mountains. Throughout the temple is a stylized rose and California Poppy motif. These floral designs are seen in the bride's room, floor mosaic, and sealing rooms' carpets. The arched ceiling above the baptismal font is the first of its kind ever built in a baptistry.

The Sacramento Temple architect reflected on his unique experience to design and construct a temple: "When I found out that I had been selected to be the architect of the temple, I knew it would be the highlight of my career," he said. "To see the temple grow out of the blueprints has been amazing."

President Gordon B. Hinckley dedicated California's seventh temple on September 3, 2006. Joining those in the temple, members participated in the dedicatory services via satellite broadcast to meetinghouses in the twenty-one stakes of the temple district. The dedicated temple is the culmination of hopes, dreams, and prayers, and it provides a dawning of a new day for the members in Sacramento.

Helsinki Finland Temple

Rising on a rocky hillside, the Helsinki Finland Temple is nestled in a setting of birch, pine, and coniferous forest. Located in the suburb of Espoo, the majestic temple is approximately seven miles from downtown Helsinki. The temple is a prominent landmark along one of the primary streets traversing the area. At night, the well-lit granite structure transitions smoothly from its imposing granite hillside. This temple is the third temple in the Nordic countries and the first in "The Land of the Midnight Sun."

Although the Church has formally existed in Finland for over 100 years, in ways it remains in its infancy. This is due to the nation being one of the lowest baptizing countries in the world. Church growth in recent years has relied largely on births rather than converts. For these reasons, the 4,500 faithful members are grateful to have a temple that will strengthen their stakes and bless their country.

From the date of the temple's announcement on April 2, 2000, three years were required for obstacles to be overcome and proper building permits secured. Following the groundbreaking on March 29, 2003, it took three more years to construct the temple. A newspaper in Sweden reported the following on the time required to build the temple: "A building this size may normally take only six months. However, noting the level of detail in every corner, visitors to the temple will understand why it has taken three years."

The temple's exterior Italian granite is polished

124

250

to a mirror finish. In the sunlight the walls sparkle, making the entire temple a brilliant source of light. Adding further visual stability to the temple are granite retaining walls featuring recognizable dark Finnish granite. The rockwork is so extraordinary that a popular Finnish magazine printed an eight-page pictorial exclusively on the temple's fine stonework.

Interior designers effectively created the interior to reflect the natural beauty of Finland. Among these designs are snowflakes, tree patterns, vines, and a copper spire. Even the baptismal font is heavily adorned with a stylized tree design.

A Finnish company specializing in ornamentation for exotic yachts and cruise ships created the fine woodwork. Their masterful experience is on full display in dark cherry woods contrasted with light birch. The craftsmanship is so fine that a single finishing nail will not be found. The result is a temple graced with Finnish motifs without distracting from the temple's sacred purpose. Public Affairs Missionaries G. Blaine Davis and Annemarie Davis describe the temple as an "exquisite work of art."

The temple in Helsinki has a unique connection with the Cardston Albert Temple. The murals featured in the baptistry originate from the interior of the temple in Cardston. Premier Utah landscape artist LeConte Stewart painted these murals around 1920. The reproduced artwork marks the first time the unique Cardston artwork has been placed in another temple.

A superior level of workmanship was maintained in all areas of the temple's construction. Much of the quality is so fine that it can hardly be appreciated without precise measuring tools. For instance, the width of the temple's two main hallways are only off by three millimeters. The temple's contractors, NCC Rakennus OY, were so pleased with their work that they received permission to hold a special reception in the temple exclusively for their top twenty customers.

In a land where religion is too personal to talk about and discussions about God are uncomfortable, the events surrounding the temple's three-week open house will always be remembered as a miracle. For a brief period, people on the streets, busses, in stores, and throughout the media were suddenly

SITE
7.4 acres

GROUNDBREAKING
March 29, 2003, by D. Lee Tobler

DEDICATION
October 22, 2006, by
Gordon B. Hinckley

EXTERIOR
Light gray Italian granite and
Finnish brown granite (stone
walls surrounding temple)

TOTAL FLOOR AREA
16,350 square feet

DIMENSIONS
212 feet by 103 feet by 139 feet

HIDDEN IMAGE
The Savior is depicted
among the trees.

talking about the Church and its new temple. Church officials who set a goal of 25,000 visitors were amazed when 56,000 attended, comprising roughly one percent of the total population of Finland. Visitors lined up for up to two hours in the rain to see the temple.

Finland public affairs director Ville-Matti Karumo shared the following personal thoughts on the open house miracle: "Members have a very difficult time sharing their testimony because their neighbors and friends do not want to hear it. Now . . . their neighbors are *coming here* and *asking* questions! So many thousands and thousands coming to the temple, asking questions and then leaving with a tear in their eye while holding hands. Members see this and they can't believe it! It has been a remarkable change."

Brother Karumo shared one of his tender memories of the open house: "I arrived early one day to the temple site and found in the parking lot a couple asleep in their car. I did not want to wake them. I later learned they had traveled in the night from four hours away. They were not members but wanted to be among the first to tour the temple in the morning."

On October 22, 2006, President Gordon B. Hinckley dedicated the house of the Lord. To attend the dedication, members traveled from as far away as the Arctic Circle in northern Finland, while others traveled for up to four days from areas across Russia. During the four dedicatory sessions, members who were once political enemies gathered together in love.

Some 1,000 members viewed the dedication's proceedings in the temple and another 15,000 members scattered throughout the district participated via satellite broadcasts. In total, sixty-two sites around the world received the historic satellite transmission of dedicatory sessions, including forty-four in Russia and still others in the Baltic states and in Armenia. Other sites included five in Salt Lake City.

The ninety-sixth member of the Church in Finland, Patriarch Tauno Savolainan, who was baptized in 1949, declared, "There's a new spirit in Finland. Spiritually the temple has made a difference—a big difference."

Rexburg Idaho Temple

Rexburg, in southeastern Idaho, was established in 1883 by a small band of Mormon pioneers who rolled into this cold, unfriendly land within view of the Grand Tetons. In 1888, the Bannock Stake Academy was founded, which later became Ricks College. In August 2001, Rexburg put itself on the national map when Ricks College, the city's two-year learning institution, formally became Brigham Young University–Idaho and began to offer four-year degrees. The BYU–Idaho expansion spurred Rexburg in becoming the fastest-growing city in Idaho and paved the way for the need of a temple.

In a December 12, 2003, letter to priesthood leaders in Idaho, the First Presidency stated: "We are pleased to announce that a temple will be constructed in Rexburg, Idaho. This temple is being made possible by a generous donation from faithful members of the Church."

The property upon which the temple is positioned was purchased by Ricks College on October 6, 1948, for $5,500. For many years, the land was used as part of the agricultural classes at Ricks College. J. Wendell Stucki operated a dairy farm and pastured his cows on the land. This beautiful ridge was an ideal location for the region's soon-to-be greatest landmark.

Construction commenced approximately seventeen months following the announcement. On July 30, 2005, more than 8,000 people poured onto the temple site for the groundbreaking ceremony.

125

Among the immediate challenges facing the temple builders was excavating the solid volcanic bedrock foundation. A rock-boring machine was bought on site to bore holes in which explosives were inserted. Nearly an entire month was required to blast, loosen, and remove the submerged volcanic earth. The rock and debris were bucketed into trucks, which required an incredible 1,000 loads to remove.

Landscaping the ten-acre temple hillside property required a great deal of planning and a large quantity of vegetation. Over the spring and summer of 2007, more than 800 truckloads of topsoil were brought to the site. Nearly 400 trees and 2,000 shrubs were planted. Many white and red roses were strategically placed on the grounds. To further beautify the grounds, nearly four acres of sod were rolled into place.

The construction schedule worked perfectly to allow the angel Moroni to be hoisted on top of the temple steeple on September 21, 2006—the 183rd anniversary of Moroni's appearance to Joseph Smith. When the angel was placed on the steeple, a cold rain and wind made it difficult to position the statue. Three hours later, the sky cleared and the sun shone.

The exterior is covered with 637 precast panels created from forty different molds. The material, a mix of concrete and white quartz, is called China White. The temple features five sealing rooms on the third floor. One of the sealing rooms accommodates more than eighty people and is one of the largest sealing rooms in the entire Church. The bride's room is truly spectacular. A large oval-shaped dome in the ceiling houses a beautiful chandelier. Various interior finishes were imported, including wood trim from Africa and stone and tile from Israel.

Original murals depicting the natural beauty of eastern Idaho grace the walls of the temple's ordinance rooms. Leon Parson, Rexburg native and a member of the art faculty at BYU–Idaho, was selected to create the murals. Parson, a renowned wildlife painter and illustrator, tackled the monumental task of painting eight panels, ten feet high and twenty-seven feet long, as murals for two rooms in the temple. The murals include

SITE
10 acres

GROUNDBREAKING
July 30, 2005, by John H. Groberg

DEDICATION
February 10, 2008, by
Thomas S. Monson

EXTERIOR
Precast concrete panels with
white quartz rock finish

TOTAL FLOOR AREA
57,504 square feet

DIMENSIONS
85 feet wide by 190 feet
long by 169 feet high

HIDDEN IMAGE
The Savior is kneeling with
clasped hands among the trees
looking up at the temple.

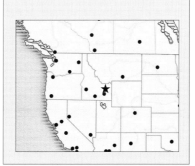

local landscapes from the River Bottoms to the glorious Teton Mountains. Nearly life-size aspens, cottonwoods, willows, pines, and sage further enhance the reality of the painting. Wildlife includes white-tailed and mule deer, elk, great blue heron, mountain bluebirds, and ruffed grouse. Sharing his personal thoughts about the project, Parson said, "Let me just quietly say that without the help of the Lord, the murals would not look the way that they do. I have been literally assisted by the Spirit. It has been a chance for me to give something of myself to all the people here in this community that I love."

Enhancing the beauty of the temple's interior and exterior are the nearly 700 hand-crafted art glass windows that include a subtle wheat stalk motif. Each window required as many as 350 pieces of cut glass to create the intricate designs. The windows are rich in color, beauty, and symbolism. According to the glass artist, Tom Holdman, the windows in the bride's room are made of colorless crystal, which represent purity and virtue. All the windows get noticeably more intricate as you move higher, representing drawing closer to God. Additional meanings include the wheat representing harvesting the souls of men. The shades of wheat are represented by white for the other side of the veil and a darker color for mortality.

The oxen in the baptistry are significant because they are organized in groups of three, with each group facing a major point of the compass. This specific arrangement is patterned after the oxen found in Solomon's temple (see 1 Kings 7:25).

Following an open house, the temple was ready to be dedicated. The scheduled dedication was delayed one week due to the passing of the beloved prophet Gordon B. Hinckley. The temple was then dedicated on February 10, 2008. The day of dedication was shrouded with heavy fog, which blended seamlessly with the high banks of snow. The new latter-day prophet, Thomas S. Monson, said at the event, "I can't think of anything I'd rather do as my first official act than dedicate this holy house of the Lord." More than 7,300 members attended four dedicatory sessions while thousands more felt the spirit of the event remotely at area stake centers.

Curitiba Brazil Temple

The city of Curitiba is recognized as a leading cultural, political, and economic center for all of Latin America. It is located in the southern region of Brazil only sixty-five miles from the coast. Referring to its architecture and environmentalism, the city is known as both "Model City" and "Ecological Capital of Brazil." The construction of the Curitiba Brazil Temple lived up to these established standards.

Approximately 37,000 Latter-day Saints live in the state of Paraná. Of these members, 25,000 live in metropolitan Curitiba. For decades, these members demonstrated their dedication to family history work and temple attendance. Brother Lenilton Cardoso, a former bishop and a stake president in Ponta Grossa, said temple trips happened frequently. "We would leave the Ponta Grossa stake center in three buses. When the temple used to be open overnight, from Fridays to Saturdays, we would work all night long for our ancestors." These demonstrations of faith contributed to the building of a sacred temple in their own area.

The history and legacy of Church members in the Curitiba area is full of inspiring stories that demonstrate the faith and hard work of a humble people who are dedicated to the Lord. The Church's history in Curitiba goes back to April 22, 1938, when a meeting was held in the house of an American family gracious enough to open their home for services, although not members of the Church themselves. Attending the meeting were only four individuals, including investigators

126

254

and missionaries. It likely never entered the minds of those early pioneer members that they were building a tradition of faithfulness that would someday culminate in receiving a house of the Lord.

In 1953, President Spencer W. Kimball visited Santa Catarina to dedicate the Ipomeia meetinghouse, located 150 miles from Curitiba. In the dedication services, President Spencer W. Kimball declared: "One day, in this region, there will be a temple of the Lord." Over fifty years later, the fulfillment of that prophecy began with the announcement of the Curitiba Brazil Temple on August 23, 2002. Two years after the announcement, the site was personally chosen by President Gordon B. Hinckley while in Brazil for the rededication of the São Paulo Temple.

On the beautiful morning of March 10, 2005, Church members, government officials, and other guests gathered under ancient Araucaria trees to break ground for the fifth Brazilian temple. Araucaria trees are uniquely beautiful and only grow in limited regions of the world. Many of these massive and rare specimens add an exotic presence to the temple's eight-acre property.

One of the distinguished guests at the groundbreaking was the city's vice-mayor, Luciano Ducci, who expressed that the construction of the temple was the greatest gift the city could ever receive, because it "will unite families at a time when so many of them are falling apart."

The temple was built on spacious property surrounded by a canopy of lush vegetation and is conveniently located near bus stops and shopping centers. Decorating the exquisite grounds are a substantial water feature, expansive gardens, and numerous tree varieties. Modified versions of the temple's floor plan were used for several temples, including the Vancouver British Columbia Temple and Manaus Brazil Temple. The gold-leafed angel Moroni statue was installed atop the spire of the Curitiba Brazil Temple on January 11, 2008.

The temple's stately facade is clad in sienna white granite native to the nearby state of Espírito Santo. Thirty colorful art glass window panes adorn the facade's exterior. Interior highlights include trim crafted from the exquisite Brazilian hardwood Ipê. Compared to steel in strength, this dense wood

SITE
8.15 acres

GROUNDBREAKING
March 10, 2005, by Russell M. Nelson

DEDICATION
June 1, 2008, by Thomas S. Monson

EXTERIOR
Sienna white granite over reinforced concrete; granite native to the state of Espírito Santo, Brazil

TOTAL FLOOR AREA
27,850 square feet

DIMENSIONS
125 feet high to the top of the angel Moroni statue (the statue is 14 feet, 2 inches tall)

HIDDEN IMAGE
The world-famous Christ the Redeemer statue, located in Rio de Janeiro, is positioned among the trees left of the temple.

was used by master craftsmen in many of the temple rooms. The temple's original murals were painted by renowned local artist Alexandre Reider. Other highlights include stone and tile imported from Spain and native Brazilian ceramics and vases.

During unseasonably warm weather the temple held a successful two-week open house from May 10 to 24, 2008. Over 42,000 visitors took the opportunity to visit the newly completed temple. Among them was a man who became noticeably anxious during his tour. At the conclusion of the tour, the man almost ran out of the final room. The next day, the visitor returned with his wife, children, and grandchildren and explained the cause of his anxious behavior. "I felt something in my heart that I had never felt before [that] filled me with happiness," he said. "I wanted my family to feel what I was feeling. That's why I ran; I was in a hurry to tell my wife about this and ask her to come back with me." Of the thousands that toured the temple, 2,000 guests requested missionaries.

Robert T. Owens served a portion of his 1957 Brazil mission in Curitiba and attended the open house. While standing on the temple grounds, he said, "We didn't have a chapel here; we met in a member's home. We baptized some good people. It's amazing to see how the Church has grown. I can't tell you what it feels like to think that I was a missionary here, and now to see a temple here, to know that the Church has grown from having only one chapel to having thousands in the country, to see the city I opened with just five members now a thriving stake, to see membership in the country grow from 2,000 to a million members."

On his first trip outside North America after becoming the leader of Church, President Thomas S. Monson dedicated the Curitiba Brazil Temple on Sunday, June 1, 2008. Recognizing the Church's legacy in the region, the prophet noted this was "a long-awaited day" for Church members in Brazil and missionaries who have served here. The temple was filled to capacity during four dedicatory sessions. Throughout the temple district, thousands of members participated in the sacred proceedings by attending satellite broadcasts in their stake centers.

Panama City Panama Temple

Panama is an isthmus country that links not only two continents but also two oceans. Bridging the narrow neck of land is the world's most famous international waterway, the Panama Canal. The canal is fifty miles long, is crossed by more than thirty ships every day, and is a key conduit for international maritime trade. Perched on a hill less than a mile from the constant procession of seafaring vessels is the serene Panama City Temple.

This Central American country is home to more than 51,000 Latter-day Saints. The first known members of the Church to visit Panama arrived in 1941, when military personnel stationed in the Canal Zone held meetings and organized the nation's first branch. However, official missionary efforts did not begin until 1965, when the Church was officially recognized. After years of rapid growth, one in every seventy-four Panamanians are Church members.

Dreams came true and consistent prayers answered on August 23, 2002, when the First Presidency announced a temple would be built in Panama's capital city. Three years later, on October 30, 2005, Elder Spencer V. Jones of the Seventy broke ground upon land partially occupied by the existing Cárdenas Ward meetinghouse.

During the days preceding the much-anticipated groundbreaking, members had been following the path of category-three Hurricane Beta as it ravaged the coastline of Nicaragua and Costa Rica. Hurricane Beta was the seventh and final major hurricane of

127

the record-breaking 2005 Atlantic hurricane season. Panama's citizens were placed on alert as they prepared for potential disaster. Faithful Panamanian members placed their faith in God that the weather would improve. Although heavy rains caused flooding and landslides, the hurricane moved north the day of the groundbreaking, leaving blue skies for the ceremonial beginning of construction.

In addition to the construction, the adjacent meetinghouse was extensively remodeled and updated. A large facility at the rear of the property was constructed to provide housing for the temple presidency, temple missionaries, and temple patrons. The exotic landscape was further beautified with additional palm trees, colorful foliage, and a serene water feature.

The temple's environment and property vistas are uniquely Panamanian. Although located in the boundary of Panama City, the temple property provides a lush jungle setting with an abundance of tropical plants, animals, and birds. From its elevated perch, temple visitors have difficulty seeing the canal through the dense vegetation. However, travelers along the Panama Canal can see the temple's white spire and golden Moroni contrasted against the canopy of green.

The 19,000-square-foot temple features several original murals, wood doors and decorations crafted from Panama mahogany, and floors and countertops made of Spanish stone.

Unlike other temples, patrons of the Panama City Temple are able to feel and *see* the Holy Ghost within the walls of the temple. Panama's national flower is the *Holy Ghost Orchid (Peristeria elata)*. The plant received its unique name because of its white cup-shaped flowers that clearly resemble a white dove in the center. The Holy Ghost Orchid motif is on display throughout the temple on door handles, glass ornamentation, and a decorative wall painting.

The Church's public affairs team worked diligently to build goodwill and promote the temple's open house. The result of this highly proactive campaign was nearly 100% positive press coverage. For example, the nation's newspaper gave the temple a front-page story. A radio commentator reportedly told his audience that if they didn't visit the "Mormon temple," they were missing a once-in-a-lifetime experience.

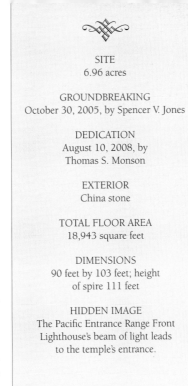

SITE
6.96 acres

GROUNDBREAKING
October 30, 2005, by Spencer V. Jones

DEDICATION
August 10, 2008, by
Thomas S. Monson

EXTERIOR
China stone

TOTAL FLOOR AREA
18,943 square feet

DIMENSIONS
90 feet by 103 feet; height
of spire 111 feet

HIDDEN IMAGE
The Pacific Entrance Range Front
Lighthouse's beam of light leads
to the temple's entrance.

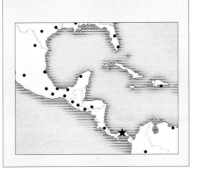

Almost 33,000 people participated in the two-week open house activities. The open house ended with a last-minute flurry of activity when some 10,000 visitors toured the temple in the final two days. The open house ran July 11 through July 26, 2008. Among the highest-profile visitors were the country's vice president and first lady.

The many comments collected during the open house provide insight into how impressed and uplifted visitors were: "I enjoyed the temple and would one day like to be sealed to my family for eternity." "I'm not a member of your Church, but this building is the best thing I've seen in my life." "I think this is the most special place I have ever visited. I felt the Creator's presence." "The peace felt inside the temple is incredible. In every room, you feel close to the Lord." "Being inside the temple is like being in heaven. It's special."

Although President Thomas S. Monson's tenure as a General Authority spanned more than four decades, the prophet had never before visited this Central America nation. After months of dedicated practice and preparation, nearly 1,000 youth from the nation's seven stakes performed a variety of local folkloric and cultural dances that included cumbias, salsas, and the conga. At the conclusion of the event, President Monson briefly addressed the crowd and said, "I've long wanted to come to Panama. Since I make the assignments, I assigned myself to be here."

On August 10, 2008, several years after the temple was announced, the Church's 127th temple was dedicated in four sessions by President Monson. Soon after the temple's dedication, the country's president requested to meet with Church officials inside the temple. Although Church leaders accommodated his meeting request, they did inform him that the meeting would have to take place at another location.

The sacred words of the dedicatory prayer include the following message of peace and truth: "May this House provide a spirit of peace to all who observe its majesty, and especially to those who enter for their own sacred ordinances and to perform the work for their loved ones beyond the veil. Let them feel of Thy divine love and mercy." In this country that links continents, a house of the Lord now links generations for eternity.

Twin Falls Idaho Temple

The Twin Falls Idaho Temple is located in southern Idaho's "Magic Valley," only half a mile from the Snake River. The name "Magic Valley" is a reference to the use of water that transformed the uninhabitable area into some of the most productive farmland in the northwestern United States. Likewise, the Twin Falls Idaho Temple provides the living water of the gospel to all those who are worthy and prepared.

The Twin Falls Idaho Temple was announced by President Gordon B. Hinckley during the October 2004 general conference. Almost immediately after the temple announcement, local residential building lots doubled in value. The forty-eight-unit subdivision near the temple site was promptly named after the LDS magazine, the *Ensign*.

On June 16, 2004, Twin Falls West Stake President Brent Nielson received a phone call from President Gordon B. Hinckley. The prophet asked President Nielson to meet him at the airport and then be an escort to potential temple locations. The entourage toured eight sites, and in the end, all in the group felt good about the Candleridge Golf Course location. The course was already planned to close and was for sale because the owner had deemed it unprofitable. Of the experience, President Nielson recorded in his journal, "I was impressed as I met with the prophet that he is truly in charge of this Church. . . . It was amazing to me to watch him as he went through the process of making this decision. . . . I marveled that a man of 94 was so incredibly sharp and so insightful. I was

128

Temples of the New Millennium

most impressed that it was clear that his main purpose in being in Twin Falls was to move the work of the Lord forward and bless the Saints of the Magic Valley."

Some 1,000 local members of the Church gathered on April 15, 2006, for the ground-breaking of the Twin Falls Idaho Temple. Presiding and offering the dedicatory prayer was Elder Neil L. Andersen. Beneath the surface of the temple site are thick layers of solid basalt volcanic rock. The very hard stone provided an ideal foundation for the temple but made digging the foundation impossible. Dynamite had to be used to blast away the rock and make way for the lower portions of the temple. Neighbors were given notice and nearby traffic was stopped before every blast.

A highlight of the temple grounds is massive rustic stone. In all, over 8,000 tons of stone were brought in from a location in Montana near the Canadian border. Using the same kind of stone, the temple features two waterfalls, each with about a four-foot drop, based upon the town's name, "Twin Falls."

Just before Christmas of 2007, stonemasons were working on the temple's exterior when weather conditions became treacherous. For safety's sake, the day's work was canceled and the workmen began to climb down the high scaffolding. The last man on the scaffolding slipped while trying to get down. He fell twenty-four feet and landed on the concrete below, where he appeared "white as a sheet" and was unconscious. Paramedics quickly arrived and determined that his trauma justified a Life Flight emergency trip to Salt Lake City. "All we could do is pray," said Elder Barnes. "At the hospital he received a priesthood blessing, they did not have to operate and two days later he was released. Not even a broken bone . . . it was a miracle."

Members living in Twin Falls can thank temple construction missionary Vern E. Barnes for overseeing construction of the temple and for building the 350-foot-high Hansen bridge that spans the Snake River Gorge. "After 53 years of engineering, I have built many impressive structures in my life, but none of them are like the temple. You feel the Spirit here and

SITE
5.10 acres

GROUNDBREAKING
April 15, 2006, by Neil L. Andersen

DEDICATION
August 24, 2008, by Thomas S. Monson

EXTERIOR
Precast concrete panels with quartz rock finish

TOTAL FLOOR AREA
31,245 square feet

DIMENSIONS
152 feet, 10 inches high by 178 feet, 10 inches long by 87 feet, 10 inches wide

HIDDEN IMAGE
A full-length image of the Savior is within this drawing. Additionally, the famous Shoshone Falls are illustrated among the trees to the right of the temple.

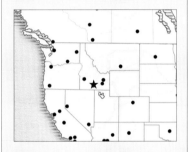

that is what makes it so special. This will be my last building and the capstone of my career and Church service."

While the temple was under construction, a seasoned contractor visited the site and commented to Elder Barnes that in his opinion, the temple was "over engineered." Elder Barnes described the conversation: "He told me that he could have built the temple using half the material and that all the extra is a waste. I asked him how long he planned his buildings to last. He responded by saying, 'Forty to fifty years at least.' 'Well that is the difference,' I told him. 'We are building for eternity.'"

As the temple neared completion, Primary children from a few nearby wards turned memorizing the Articles of Faith into a wonderful way to contribute to the temple fund. As the children memorized Articles of Faith, they were allowed to contribute that article's number in pennies to the temple savings. When the landscaping trees arrived to the temple site, the entire Primary and their leaders arrived to select a tree to pay for and call their own. A specific maple tree was selected, and the saved funds were sent to the Temple Department to pay for "their" tree.

The temple features a motif of the syringa flower, Idaho's state flower, and a mural of Shoshone Falls created by Idaho artist Leon Parson. Parson created the mural that covers three walls of the ordinance room, featuring scenes of south-central Idaho's most beautiful natural features, from Shoshone Falls and Thousand Springs to the South Hills.

In a town with a population of about 45,000 people, the temple's six-week open house attracted 159,867 visitors. The temple was dedicated by Thomas S. Monson on August 24, 2008, and was simulcast live to fourteen stake centers. As President Monson drove from the temple to the airport, he saw small groups of families holding signs: "We love the temple." "We love the prophet." "We love the scriptures." For more than a mile, other sentiments followed on similar signs. President Monson called it "The mile of farewell."

Draper Utah Temple

Salt Lake Valley's third temple is nestled in the valley's southeast foothills. From its panoramic perch, views stretch northward to Salt Lake City and beyond the Oquirrh Mountain Temple to the west. The temple's white granite spire towers over 1,000 acres of pristine open space in the canyon below, which is a habitat for deer, elk, and other wildlife. This permanent open space was formally approved by the Draper City Council a year before the temple's groundbreaking. Referring to the temple and its close proximity to the preserve, Draper Mayor Darrell Smith said, "I don't think it's any coincidence that we happened to preserve 1,025 acres here."

The temple was announced by President Gordon B. Hinckley in his opening remarks at the October 2004 general conference. The exact location of the temple was not known until it was formally disclosed in a letter dated November 17, 2004, in which the First Presidency announced the temple's location would be Corner Canyon. It stated, "We are confident that this temple will be a blessing to the many faithful Saints in this rapidly-growing area. It will accommodate the overcrowded evening and weekend sessions now experienced in the Jordan River Utah Temple."

With the temple resting at an elevation of 5,145 feet, "High on the Mountain Top" was an apt choice for the opening hymn at the groundbreaking. In a season of rapid, worldwide temple expansion, it was rare to have the President of the Church preside and break ground for a temple. It was even

129

rarer for the event to be attended by the entire First Presidency. Such was the occasion on August 5, 2006, when ninety-six-year-old President Gordon B. Hinckley and counselors Thomas S. Monson and James E. Faust participated in the historic proceedings.

During his address, President Hinckley explained that he frequently gets asked why the Church has so many temples in Utah. "Because we need them," he said. "It's a tribute to our people, so faithful in temple attendance." While costly to construct and costly to maintain, "We must have them," he said, noting that as the Utah population grows, there may be a need to build one or two more temples in the valley. "But it will be a while," he said. "Don't count on it tomorrow."

According to Steve Goodwin, an architect for the temple, the original plans were for a larger temple, but constraints made it necessary to change the design. At 58,300 square feet, the temple is considered to be a medium-size temple. Goodwin said that this temple is on the convergence of two fault lines, and the plans specified that it would be engineered and designed to last well beyond a hundred years, and probably several hundred.

Within the temple, a recurring motif is Utah's state flower, the sego lily. The sego lily motif is also carved into the carpet in the celestial room and the paneling and ceilings of other parts of the temple. The limestone for the floors originates from France, and much of the wood is exotic Makore hardwood from Central Africa. The artwork of Linda Curley Christensen is featured throughout the temple.

Accomplished Colorado artist Keith Bond created the stunning murals in the temple. The story of these murals begins with the Twin Falls Idaho Temple. Keith was asked to submit a mural proposal for that temple. He visited the area to explore and connect with the region's rugged wilderness. While among the rolling hills, he discovered a thriving aspen grove blazing with autumn color. His submission featured these colorful aspen groves. The designers were impressed with the layout, skill, and vision of the proposal, but they thought the artwork would be better suited for the Draper Utah Temple. "To prepare my mural for the Draper Temple I slightly changed the composition, but eighty percent remained the same. I opened up the

SITE
12 acres (including adjoining meetinghouse)

GROUNDBREAKING
August 5, 2006, by
Gordon B. Hinckley

DEDICATION
March 20–22, 2009, by
Thomas S. Monson

EXTERIOR
Temple white granite from China

TOTAL FLOOR AREA
58,300 square feet

HIDDEN IMAGE
The Good Shepherd is depicted in the landscaping cradling one of His sheep.

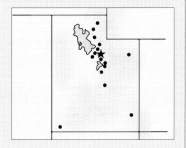

grove and added a lake in the distance. There are no animals in the painting."

The temple's splendid windows are a colorful 30,000-piece glass puzzle. Soldered iron holds the individual pieces to make up the 700 windows. Tom Holdman and his team spent two and a half years planning, styling, cutting, joining, and mounting the windows. The windows incorporate the Log Cabin quilt pattern used by the early pioneers.

A major catastrophe threatened the temple's stained-glass windows as they were being manufactured. Holdman had been working on the temple windows for eighteen months when a fire devastated the warehouse where the windows were stored. Tom arrived at the scene along with the fire department and watched in horror as his precious work was about to be destroyed. Holdman asked if he could rescue his artwork before the roof collapsed. The firefighters agreed, and together they ran into the blaze to drag the windows to safety. Although the warehouse contained bottles of highly flammable chemicals, none were ignited. Among the ashes, only one window was damaged.

The Draper open house was one of the most widely attended open houses in Church history. During its two-month open house from January 15 to March 14, 2009, the temple attracted 684,721 visitors, and the temple committee served 1,030,000 cookies. To make the event possible, an average of 600 Church members a day volunteered their time directing traffic, working in security, hosting, and cleaning the building.

Over a three-day period, March 20–22, 2009, President Thomas S. Monson presided over twelve sessions to dedicate the Draper Utah Temple. In addition to offering the dedicatory prayer in each of the sessions, he addressed several of the sessions. Some 16,000 members attended dedicatory sessions in the temple, while thousands of others attended a live broadcast to stake centers. The words of the dedicatory prayer reflect the temple's sacred purpose: "May this House provide a spirit of peace to all who observe its majesty, and especially to those who enter for their own sacred ordinances and to perform the work for those beyond the veil. Let them feel of Thy divine love and mercy."

Oquirrh Mountain Temple

Resting on a gradual bluff that rises over the highly traveled Bangerter Highway, the Oquirrh Mountain Utah Temple sits six miles east of the Oquirrh Mountains. The stately temple faces eastward toward a panoramic view of the Wasatch Mountains and the valley's three other temples.

The origins of the Oquirrh Mountain Temple are directly related to the tremendous activity and consistent use of the Jordan River Utah Temple. At the peak of its attendance, the temple served 110 stakes and required the assistance of over 4,500 temple workers. Jordan River Temple President Robert L. Backman (2005–2008) observed that the south valley members were indeed ready for additional temples. "They've demonstrated this by their activity in the temple," he said.

During his opening remarks at the first session of the 175th Semiannual General Conference, President Gordon B. Hinckley announced that a new temple would be built in the western part of the Salt Lake Valley. "You may ask why we favor Utah so generously," he said. "It is because the degree of activity requires it."

Christmas came a few days early when Church leaders and members gathered beneath the shelter of a massive white tent to celebrate the temple's ceremonial groundbreaking. On December 16, 2006, the entire First Presidency broke ground for the temple. During the historic event, President Hinckley announced the temple's official new name. "Hereafter this temple will be known as the Oquirrh Mountain

130

Utah Temple. They won't know how to spell it, but they don't come to the temple to spell, they come to serve in the work of the Lord."

Originally referred to as the "South Jordan Utah Temple," the future temple's name was changed to differentiate it from the nearby Jordan River Utah Temple. The name "Oquirrh" connects with a Goshute Indian word meaning "wooded mountain."

The temple site covers a little more than eleven acres on a small bluff that was at the bottom of the prehistoric Lake Bonneville. The site's silt, sand, and gravel materials are all deposits from this ancient lake.

The spire of the Oquirrh Mountain Utah Temple was installed atop the temple on July 11, 2008. Rather than assembling the spire on the roof of the temple, contractors applied the layers of stone to the spire's steel frame on the ground and then lifted it as a completed piece. Before assembling the tower, structural engineers estimated the weight of the tower would be 19,000 pounds. However, once assembled, the actual weight of the tower was 32,000 pounds. To accommodate this massive increase in weight, a more powerful crane was needed. With nearly 1,000 spectators watching, the new crane lifted the tower successfully, clearing the roof by only six inches. According to project superintendent Ron Wilkins, "We watched, hoped, and prayed that the tower would clear the roofline. It was so close that I think it was a miracle." Immediately following the installation of the spire, the angel Moroni was hoisted into its permanent position.

Every window in the building was created and installed by master craftsman John D. Quist. John invented a technique and equipment that are truly unique to his craft. His method allows him to sculpt relief and glass designs in a revolutionary way. Describing the design and patterns created for the Oquirrh Mountain Temple's glass, John said, "The design has stars and a veil-like pattern so to me the windows are like looking into heaven."

Throughout John's career, his brother Mike has been his trusted assistant. Together they have worked on multiple temples. While working on the Oquirrh Mountain Temple,

SITE
11 acres

GROUNDBREAKING
December 16, 2006, by
Gordon B. Hinckley

DEDICATION
August 21–23, 2009, by
Thomas S. Monson

EXTERIOR
Light beige granite from China

TOTAL FLOOR AREA
60,000 square feet

DIMENSIONS
108 feet by 209 feet; height is 183 feet to top of angel Moroni statue

HIDDEN IMAGE
The Savior is kneeling with clasped hands among the trees looking up at the temple.

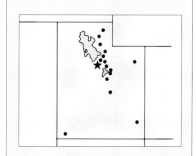

Mike was diagnosed with a terminal disease. As a tribute, John gave Mike the privilege of installing the last piece of glass in the temple. This final sixteen-inch-square piece of glass is located on the third floor's main hallway on the ceiling's northeast corner. After completing their project together, the brothers went into a sealing room, where John gave Mike a priesthood blessing. Remembering the experience, John said, "It was probably the most tender moment of any temple I have worked on."

Shortly after the beginning of the temple's open house, the angel Moroni statue was struck by lightning. The strike left the gold-leafed, thirteen-foot, eight-inch statue blackened across the face, trumpet, and right arm. A new Moroni statue in perfect condition replaced the damaged statue ten days prior to the temple's dedication.

In preparation for the open house, members of the South Jordan Daybreak Stake worked hard to make sure the approach to the temple was as beautiful as possible. Some 300 youth and leaders gathered 6,000 pounds of trash strewn along Bangerter Highway just east of the temple. The successful service project demonstrates the length members will go to show their respect for the Lord's house.

On August 21, 2009, President Thomas S. Monson dedicated the Oquirrh Mountain Utah Temple on his eighty-second birthday. Some 14,500 members participated inside the temple during the dedicatory sessions. Tens of thousands of others from across the entire state joined in the sacred celebration. Traditional Sabbath meeting schedules on August 23 were canceled so members could view one of the sessions. The Sunday dedicatory sessions were observed in 657 church buildings.

The Oquirrh Mountain Temple is the only temple with the word "Mountain" in its name. With the temple now dedicated, patrons can literally go up to the *mountain,* as Isaiah wrote anciently: "And many people shall go and say, Come ye, and let us go up to the mountain of the Lord, to the house of the God of Jacob; and he will teach us of his ways, and we will walk in his paths" (Isaiah 2:2–3).

Vancouver British Columbia Temple

In February 2010, the world focused on the XXI Olympic Winter Games hosted by Vancouver, British Columbia. The worldwide sporting spectacle was a once-in-a-lifetime event for citizens of British Columbia. Three months later, Latter-day Saints again focused on Vancouver as it celebrated the dedication of the Church's 131st temple. Lyn Sloan of Surrey, British Columbia, recalled that Latter-day Saints in the area were excited for the Olympics, but the temple dedication "was always foremost in our minds. We have talked about this day for years and dreamed about it. Really, it is a dream come true."

For many years, Church members in British Columbia received their temple blessings by traveling to the Seattle Washington Temple. However, there was a significant number of Saints who could not cross the border for various reasons. Thus, many members could not attend the temple. These factors, in addition to the increased strength of Church members in British Columbia, prompted the need for a temple in Vancouver.

In the fall of 2005, Paul D. M. Christensen, who was serving at the time as stake president of the Abbotsford B.C. Stake, received a phone call from the Temple Department requesting his assistance to immediately begin the search for potential temple sites. Sites were identified and logistical arrangements made to prepare for site inspection by the prophet. In December 2008, President Gordon B. Hinckley, President Thomas S. Monson, and vital staff arrived to tour the locations.

131

After briefly inspecting the prospective site where the temple would eventually be built, President Hinckley declared, "That would be a good site for a temple." Two additional locations were visited, but within thirty seconds at each, it was clear to President Hinckley that they were not suitable for a temple.

The selected temple site is a beautiful location on the peak of the largest hill in the township. The twelve-acre location was assembled from three separate parcels that were originally not for sale. The site would also accommodate a new meetinghouse. Over a period of several months, properties were acquired and necessary city permits and exemptions were granted.

The Vancouver British Columbia Temple was announced on May 25, 2006 in a letter to mission presidents, stake presidents, and all General Authorities and affected Church leaders. In the words of President Christensen, "Within a matter of hours the announcement was known throughout the world, showing the efficacy of the Church communication network."

One of the site's previous property owners had planted thousands of trees and shrubs as part of their business. This stock vegetation was not going to be used in the temple landscaping, so members of a local stake were invited to dig up the plants and relocate them in their yards as a reminder of the temple. Many members participated and enjoyed sharing in the bounty.

On August 4, 2007, the groundbreaking took place for a meetinghouse, a temple president's residence, and Canada's seventh temple. Nearly 400 members attended the occasion on a sunny summer morning in an area surrounded by evergreen trees.

The temple's interior features include expansive use of beautifully grained Makore hardwood from the west coast of Africa. British Columbia's provincial flower, the Pacific dogwood, is a highlighted motif in the decorative painting and intricate carpet sculpting. Uniform interior colors include green, light blue, and soft gold, all reminiscent of the natural colors in the sea, sky, and evergreens of the Pacific Northwest. Artwork by Leon Parson graces the walls of one of the instruction rooms. The spire rises 140 feet and is crowned with a gilded statue of the angel Moroni.

SITE
11.6 acres

GROUNDBREAKING
August 4, 2007, by Ronald A. Rasband

DEDICATION
May 2, 2010, by Thomas S. Monson

EXTERIOR
Bianco Sienna granite from Brazil

TOTAL FLOOR AREA
28,165 square feet

DIMENSIONS
87 feet by 165 feet

HIDDEN IMAGE
The Christus statue is seen among the clouds. An inuksuk, a stone landmark built by the indigenous people of the Arctic region, is placed among the distant trees.

Thanks to the dedicated support of 4,000 local members, the temple's open house was an organized success. From April 7 to 24, 2010, more than 40,000 people toured the newly completed temple.

On a drizzly and cold morning, crowds from across British Columbia gathered on the temple grounds for the dedication and cornerstone ceremony of the new temple. Upon arriving, President Thomas S. Monson said, "I helped pick the site, and now see a lovely temple here. It couldn't have been created for a more noble purpose. We came with a prayer in our hearts," President Monson said. "You look, first of all, at what the Lord has given: the terrain, the grasses, the trees, the setting. Then you figure if the Lord can do all that, the best you can do is build a temple to grace the land He has pointed out. The best we can do is build a temple."

Elder William R. Walker, Executive Director of the Temple Department of the Church, witnessed a tender moment that illustrates the genuine, warm, and friendly nature of the prophet. He explained how President Monson had completed a dedicatory session and then exited the celestial room. While walking down the hallway, he waved and greeted members in each room. As the prophet passed by one room, "He looked across the room and noticed an older woman, probably in her 80s, sitting in a wheelchair near the front of the room. She was leaning over in her wheelchair looking back trying to see the prophet, who was standing at the door. When he saw her, instead of continuing down the hall, he went right through the room to this older sister who was in the wheelchair. He reached over and shook her hand, then he bent down and kissed her on the forehead . . . I had the feeling, 'That is the way Jesus would be.' He would find the person in the crowd who was aged or had heartache and would express His love and kindness to them."

The following sacred words of the dedicatory prayer describe a divine purpose of the temple: "The Plan of Salvation, taught in Thy temples with simplicity yet with power, will be as a never-failing beacon of divine light to guide our footsteps and keep us constantly on the pathway to eternal life."

The Gila Valley Arizona Temple

The Gila Valley is a small agricultural region surrounded by rivers that provide life to the desert earth. The small communities of Thatcher, Pima, and Safford are nestled together near the base of the majestic Gila Mountains. Among these larger cities, the smaller town of Central is the home of The Gila Valley Arizona Temple.

Mormon settlers first came to the area in 1879. These hardworking Saints brought with them their faith and desire for a temple. Early records dating back to 1882 note that Church leaders promised the Saints a temple in The Gila Valley. During a conference held on January 30, 1898, visiting Apostle John W. Taylor made the Saints an unforgettable promise: "One of the most beautiful temples that was ever built among the Saints in the Rocky Mountains will be built in this valley."

The eagerness of Latter-day Saints for a temple is demonstrated by financial contributions made without a temple being announced. According to a 1921 publication, "The first donation toward this end was recorded January 24, 1887, in the name of Mrs. Helena Roseberry, a poor widow of Pima, who gave $5 toward the building of a temple in Arizona, handing the money to Apostle Moses Thacher. This widow's mite ever since has been held by the Church in Salt Lake."

Although decades passed, the memory of these temple promises did not fade. In a letter dated May 1, 1973, President Spencer W. Kimball referenced the

132

266

temple again: "About 80 years ago approximately, one of the conference visitors from Salt Lake predicted that there would be a temple in The Gila Valley. In the many years that the stake has carried on but has not grown greatly and with the realization that one could hardly see any future that would bring a great population to The Gila Valley, yet if that prophecy was made by inspiration, then the Lord will find a way to do it."

The day after Christmas in 2007, Pima Arizona Stake President Mark S. Bryce received a phone call inviting him to assist in the search for a temple site. President Bryce and a group of officials from Church Headquarters visited several locations. The group's tour ended at a large tract of land where a local stake had built a baseball park. As the brethren walked the grounds, President Bryce said, "A feeling fell on us, like a ton of bricks." The Spirit was so strong that it caused him to weep and exclaim, "This is the place, this is the right place!"

Though anticipated more than 125 years earlier, the faith and patience of generations of Latter-day Saints was rewarded on April 26, 2008, when President Thomas S. Monson announced a temple for The Gila Valley.

Excitement was felt throughout the valley on the day of the temple's historic groundbreaking. Thousands gathered at the site to witness the event, and many more participated via a live broadcast. Special care was made to ensure the ceremonial groundbreaking would take place in a specific location. Shovels turned over the soil precisely where the celestial room would be located.

The official name of the temple is "The Gila Valley Arizona Temple." The capital "T" on the word "The" is used to reference the formal name of the valley in which it is built, "The Gila Valley." President Spencer W. Kimball's son Andrew Kimball said that his father "loved this area. He loved the people." He said his father always wanted the temple in his hometown community to bear one name: "The Gila Valley Temple."

Once the temple was announced, an anonymous Church member contributed "a very large donation" for the purpose

SITE
17 acres (including adjacent meetinghouse)

GROUNDBREAKING
February 14, 2009, by
Neil L. Andersen

DEDICATION
May 23, 2010, by Thomas S. Monson

EXTERIOR
Architectural precast stone

TOTAL FLOOR AREA
18,561 square feet

DIMENSIONS
27 feet by 104 feet

HIDDEN IMAGE
The Savior is depicted in the motion of inviting all to receive the blessings of the temple.

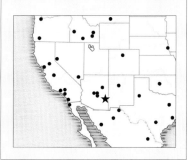

of "enhancing the beauty of the temple." The interior beauty of the temple includes original oil murals depicting the beauty of the Arizona desert. Other commissioned oil paintings bring to life a cotton field, flower garden, and a waterfall on Mt. Graham.

Building the temple's solid concrete foundation was the responsibility of contractor Dennis Wilkins. One aspect of pouring the concrete around the steel re-bar according to unique specifications was extremely challenging and technical. "I was not sure how to accomplish the specific task and had worried about it for weeks," he said. "One night I woke up and as clear as bell I knew what to do. It was one of the times in my life when I *knew* the Holy Ghost had taught me. I knew exactly what to do and exactly how to do it."

The doors of the temple were opened to the public from April 23 to May 15, 2010. The open house attracted 90,865 visitors, which is a significant total considering the region's small population and remote location.

On the day prior to the temple's dedication, President Monson and accompanying Church leaders arrived at the Safford airport. As the entourage traveled along an isolated stretch of highway, they were greeted by a small group of members holding signs to welcome the prophet. The prophet surprised everyone when he instructed the drivers to pull over so he could greet the members.

The temple was dedicated on May 23, 2010, in three sessions. The dedication followed a youth cultural celebration Saturday evening, during which more than 1,600 young people retold through song, dance, and spoken word the rich cultural history of eastern Arizona.

Members living in the temple district demonstrated their faith and dedication to temple service following the temple's dedication. In slightly more than two years, over 2,000,000 sacred ordinances were performed. For as long as it stands, the temple will serve as a tribute to the faithful generations of the past and a source of fulfillment for the future generations of The Gila Valley.

Cebu City Philippines Temple

On April 24, 2005, President Gordon B. Hinckley addressed over 100,000 members in twenty-seven stakes on the islands of the southern Philippines. In a live broadcast originating from Salt Lake City, he spoke of the Church's progress and the requirements to have a temple built in the Cebu City area. After acknowledging their desire for another temple, President Hinckley challenged all the adult members to qualify for a temple recommend. Then he said, "If enough of you can do this, we shall be obliged to build another temple in the Philippines more convenient to where you live."

Less than a year later, The First Presidency announced construction of a new temple in Cebu City by a letter to priesthood leaders dated April 18,

2006. The announcement stated, "We are confident this will be a blessing to the many faithful Saints in this and surrounding areas who have had to travel long distances to enjoy the blessings of the temple."

"The news of the announcement of the new temple to be built in the Cebu Island spread like wildfire throughout the Visayan Islands and in Mindanao," said President Ray W. Nelson, the Manila Philippines Temple president. "This has become an answer to the prayers of the Saints, who are eager to have a temple constructed nearer their area. These Saints have exercised determination in their temple trips to Manila and normally experience a great deal of sacrifice to the point of selling material possessions just to allocate funds for their

133

trip." For example, in 2005, a group of Saints from the southern part of the Philippines traveled twelve hours aboard a flatbed truck under inhospitable weather and road conditions to perform ordinances for themselves and their ancestors.

Twenty-three years after the dedication of the temple in Manila, ground was broken for the nation's second temple. Elder Dallin H. Oaks broke ground for the temple complex on November 14, 2007. The 11.6-acre complex includes a temple, patron housing, a meetinghouse, homes for the temple and mission presidents, and a mission office. Some 400 members and local community leaders gathered for this historical event. During the event, Cebu City Mayor Tomas Osmeña remarked: "It is with great honor that I am here to witness the groundbreaking of what is to be the place for a beautiful temple." The mayor shared the history of the property and explained that the site was used to defend freedom and that treasures were rumored to be buried there.

Although no "treasures" were found, Mayor Osmeña's comments proved to be very true. The temple is located on higher ground in Cebu City. When the Japanese invaded the Philippines during World War II, they occupied the area and fortified it as a stronghold. During the occupation, the Japanese built a labyrinth of underground tunnels to facilitate movement and the storage of ammunition and explosives. These twenty-foot-deep tunnels were discovered while excavating the temple's foundation in front of the main entrance. Ultrasound equipment was used and care was given to determine the extent of the tunnels and remove equipment and unexploded bombs. Soil was stabilized by filling the tunnels with at least twenty-eight truckloads of concrete.

Some 1,200 workers labored on the temple. None of them had ever worked on a project requiring such high level of detail and care. Subsequently, nearly all the local workers and tradespeople had to be retrained on aspects of their craft so they could provide "temple quality" workmanship. Temple project manager Knut Klavenes said, "I had to get them to understand that they were not just building another building; they were building something special." One area in the temple had to be

SITE
11.6 acres

GROUNDBREAKING
November 14, 2007

DEDICATION
June 13, 2010, by Thomas S. Monson

EXTERIOR
Mountain gray granite from China

TOTAL FLOOR AREA
29,556 square feet

HIDDEN IMAGE
The Savior is depicted among
the trees left of the temple.

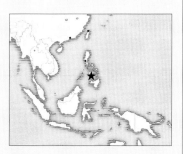

repainted eighteen times until it was finally done to the level of superiority required in a temple. All the workers left the project grateful for having learned new skills. Additionally, as a gesture of appreciation, the Church provided all workers with a new set of tools.

Several of those involved with the construction were converted and baptized during the building of the Lord's house in Cebu City. Among them was project manager Knut Klavenes. Philippines Cebu City Mission President D. Parke Hansen related the experience of presenting Knut with a Book of Mormon: "One day we were driving together in the city and I had the impression that I should give him a Book of Mormon. I told him that I thought he was ready for exposure to the Book of Mormon. His comment to me was, 'I think you are right. I think I am ready.' Knut was soon baptized and President Hansen confirmed him a member.

Describing his conversion experience, Knut said, "My biggest moment was in the sealing room. I came back from Manila, where I had been inspecting furniture, on a Friday evening. It was quite late, but I thought 'I'll just go by the temple to make sure everything is OK.' I went inside the sealing room, and as soon as I went in, I could tell the Spirit was there. It was very, very strong. As soon as I walked in, I just wanted to cry. It was the nicest feeling. I was there for about 10 or 15 minutes, crying like a little baby."

President Thomas S. Monson dedicated the second temple in the Philippines in three sessions on June 13, 2010. At the time of dedication, the temple served some 200,000 members living in the Visayas and Mindanao island groups in the southern part of the Philippines.

On October 15, 2013, a 7.2-magnitude earthquake shook the Cebu City Philippines Temple, causing the angel Moroni to rotate ninety degrees. Only weeks later, category-5 typhoon *Haiyan* ravaged the Philippine islands, causing further damage to the statue. As a temporary solution, workers climbed 140 feet of scaffolds to fix the problem by repositioning the statue to again point east. An entirely new statue was placed on the temple the following year.

Kyiv Ukraine Temple

Kyiv is one of the oldest cities in Eastern Europe and has always been the heart and soul of Ukraine. This city of nearly three million residents is one of the most handsome and progressive cities in all of the former Soviet Union. The marvelously rich agricultural heartland of Ukraine is found to the west of the city and is known as the "The Breadbasket of Europe."

On September 12, 1991, President Boyd K. Packer pronounced an Apostolic blessing upon Ukraine and dedicated it for the preaching of the gospel. President Packer offered the words at the base of a monument honoring the Grand Prince Vladimir, who brought Christianity to the Slavic world in AD 988. Eastern Orthodox scholars report that Vladimir believed in the importance of performing baptisms for the dead.

Reflecting on the historic day, President Packer reminisced, "It is interesting that on the same day we stood near Prince Vladimir's statue to offer a blessing on the land of Ukraine, the statues of Lenin, who was the image or symbol of communism, were being pulled down." In offering the blessing upon the land he also prophesied of a future temple. President Packer said, "We are gathered here as missionaries and as members, a small group. This gathering is prescient of the tens and the hundreds and the thousands and the hundreds of thousands that will yet join Thy Church. . . . And in due time, the spires of temples will be seen across this great land."

It did not take long for this prophecy to be fulfilled. The Church in Kyiv quickly developed as a

134

center of strength shortly after the introduction of missionaries, as indicated by prolific congregational growth and the announcement of the temple only eight years after missionaries entered the country. Amazingly, the temple was announced six years before the nation's first stake was formed. At the time, the Church had but a single chapel in the country. Except for the early years of the Restoration, it is the fastest temple to be built after missionaries were first introduced to a country. Having the knowledge that a temple was going to be built helped the evolution of the Church while it was yet in its infancy.

The scene at the groundbreaking was unimaginable considering that seventeen years earlier, Ukraine was in the communist Soviet Union and had no freedom of religion. Nine years transpired from the time of the temple's announcement until the groundbreaking ceremonies on June 23, 2007. The delay was partly due to difficulty finding the correct location along with legal, governmental and financial challenges. The temple's architecture was changed from the originally planned smaller temple design to a robust structure that reflects Ukrainian history and style. The central spire reaches skyward from a structure that is massive, heavy, and solid. The edifice rightfully commands formal respect and still appears welcoming. Some have observed that the temple resembles a striking resemblance to the famous *Golden Gates of Kyiv* (ca. AD 1024) located six miles away. When the angel Moroni was hoisted to the pinnacle of the temple on September 21, 2010, the trumpet seemed to announce the presence of the restored gospel to all of Eastern Europe.

The temple reflects two main Ukrainian design motifs: sheaves of wheat and decorated Easter eggs. The Easter egg symbolizes the Resurrection and Atonement of Christ. The yellow in the Ukrainian flag represents the wheat, and the blue represents the sky.

As the temple neared completion, full-time missionaries were given unique opportunities to assist. On one occasion, temple project manager Hanno Luschin walked over to the

SITE
12.35 acres

GROUNDBREAKING
June 23, 2007, by Paul B. Pieper

DEDICATION
August 29, 2010, by
Thomas S. Monson

EXTERIOR
Amarelo Macieira granite
with quartzite crystals

TOTAL FLOOR AREA
22,184 square feet

DIMENSIONS
About 138 feet high, crowned with
a gilded angel Moroni statue

HIDDEN IMAGE
The national and spiritual
symbol of wheat is depicted in
the shadows of the trees.

mission home and requested the service of dozens of elders and sisters. The missionaries were put to work uncrating furniture and carrying the delicate furnishings into the temple. Among the items they moved into position were the fiberglass baptistry oxen. A few days later, a sister missionary from Armenia had an experience that she will never forget. At the conclusion of her mission, she was in the mission offices waiting to be taken to the airport later. Help was needed to assemble the celestial room chandelier, and she was asked if she would help. The last act of service this sister performed on her mission was to carefully attach hundreds of delicate crystals onto the chandelier in the house of the Lord.

In addition to the temple, the property is home to a meetinghouse, mission offices, temple housing, a distribution center, and a genealogical library. The temple open house was heavily marketed in media outlets and on billboards and metro signs. The full-time missionaries serving in and around the city used this time to assist in a variety of ways relating to the temple.

The evening before the temple's dedication, President Thomas S. Monson addressed 4,000 members who had gathered at the youth celebration. At the conclusion of his remarks, he expressed his genuine love for the members when he said, "I'm so glad that I've come. At my age I ought to stay home. But I've come to see you, to thank you for all the good that you do. . . . You look so wonderful to me, so bright and happy. I wish I could come down and put my arms around every one of you and say thank you. I'm sorry I can't do that. We would be here all night. Please know, that's how I feel," he said, reminding them that they have now personally heard the prophet bear testimony of God and His Church.

It was a thousand years ago that Christian baptisms for the dead were performed in Kyiv, Ukraine. On August 29, 2010, the Kyiv Ukraine Temple was dedicated, allowing for true baptisms for the dead and other eternal ordinances to be performed by Latter-day Saints who hold the divinely restored priesthood authority to do so.

San Salvador El Salvador Temple

El Salvador is the smallest and most densely populated country in Central America. The small nation is well known for its stunning volcanic landscape, deep green vegetation, and friendliness. Contrasting these favorable attributes, El Salvador has endured chronic political and economic instability, earthquakes, and civil unrest. Through these difficult realities, Salvadoran Saints have desperately clung to the source of true peace—the gospel of Jesus Christ. With the beautiful temple in San Salvador, a new beacon of peace is now available.

The first convert baptisms in El Salvador took place in 1951. Eight years later, pioneer member Rosa Solis was also converted to the restored gospel. Since that time, Sister Solis and other early converts have witnessed and participated in the rapid growth of the Church throughout their country. As people partook of the sweet taste of the gospel, branches, wards, and stakes started to fill the land. Missions were established and the culture of the gospel began to be passed on to forthcoming generations.

Rosa Solis admits that a temple in El Salvador never crossed her mind when she was baptized in 1959. At the age of seventeen, she and a few other members gathered each Sunday in a rented house. Sister Solis first obtained her temple blessings in the Mesa Arizona Temple (2,420 miles away) and then later was able to visit the temple in Mexico City (967 miles away). "I don't have a fancy car and I don't own a big house on the beach, but the Lord has helped me prosper," said

135

272

Sister Solis. "I have children, grandchildren, and even a great-grandchild that love God. And now there is a temple in El Salvador."

In a letter from the First Presidency read in sacrament meetings on November 18, 2007, members first learned of the plans to construct a temple in El Salvador. Longtime Salvadoran member Fidel Bonilla remembers hearing the happy news that a temple would be built in his homeland. "We all started to cry," he said. No longer would members need to make lengthy trips to the Guatemala City Guatemala Temple and deal with the threat of highway robberies.

Just six weeks after President Thomas S. Monson dedicated the Panama City Panama Temple, construction began on another temple in Central America. Situated in the affluent Antiguo Cuscatlán district, the temple location is highly visible and easily accessible. Major roads and highways seem to flow around the temple on three sides. The temple also stands only 1,000 feet away from one of the most premier and exclusive shopping centers in Central America. Residing on the temple complex is a meetinghouse, a patron housing facility with a residence for the temple president, a cafeteria, and Distribution Services. Protecting the complex and all who visit there are security fences and guards.

Located comfortably on a spacious six and a half acres, the temple's Spanish colonial architecture is encased with Bianco Sienna Brazilian granite. The distinctly Salvadoran edifice features arches and decorative features picturing El Salvador's national flower. The Flor de Izote is highlighted in art glass windows and other interior ornamentation. Other interior details include mahogany wood from Honduras and limestone flooring from Israel.

The temple's open house dates were June 28 through July 23, 2011. Members throughout the country made the most of

SITE
6.5 acres

GROUNDBREAKING
September 20, 2008,
by Don R. Clarke

DEDICATION
August 21, 2011, by Henry B. Eyring

EXTERIOR
Bianco Sienna Granite from Brazil

TOTAL FLOOR AREA
27,986 square feet

DIMENSIONS
113 feet by 94 feet

HIDDEN IMAGE
The Savior is depicted in the motion of inviting all to receive the blessings of the temple.

the historic event by inviting their neighbors and friends and explaining why the temple is important. The open house enjoyed visits from many of the nation's top business and government leaders. Several national newspaper and television stories covered the event. In all, 165,790 people toured the temple interior and explored the lush exterior grounds.

A day before dedicating the San Salvador El Salvador Temple, President Henry B. Eyring and several other General Authorities visited the President and First Lady of El Salvador. Their visit marked the first time a member of the First Presidency had met with a president of El Salvador.

Several thousand young Salvadoran members performed in a cultural celebration preceding the temple's dedication. For months, Church youth from the nation's sixteen stakes gathered to practice a variety of Salvadoran folk dances celebrating their rich culture and their unified testimonies of the Lord and His newest temple. Once gathered at the National Gymnasium in San Salvador, the youth gave their best as they performed for a large audience, which included President Eyring and several other General Authorities.

The following day, President Eyring dedicated the temple in three dedicatory sessions. Thousands participated in the services inside the temple, while many more viewed the proceedings remotely via closed-circuit broadcast to meetinghouses across El Salvador and several other Central American nations.

In the words of the sacred dedicatory prayer is the following message of hope and purpose: "We pray that Thy Saints may gather here to carry forward the work of receiving their own ordinances, and offering these ordinances to those beyond the veil of death that Thine eternal purposes may be accomplished."

Quetzaltenango Guatemala Temple

Quetzaltenango, Guatemala, is the second largest city in the Central American nation and is considered by many to be "the capital of the Mayas." The mountainous and lush landscape surrounding Quetzaltenango offers a peek into the indigenous past of the Americas, where ancient Mayan ruins are found and Mayan languages of Kiche and Mam are still spoken.

The faithful Saints of the area have a long history of living the gospel and finding a way to obtain temple blessings. Some of the area's early converts were Ricardo and Ignacia Perez. Both are descendants of the Mayans of the Quetzaltenango highlands. Ricardo, Ignacia, and their three oldest children were baptized January 26, 1954. Their commitment to

their new faith led them to seek the blessings of the temple. After being sealed as a couple in the Mesa Arizona Temple in 1965, they longed to be sealed as an eternal family with their children who were unable to originally accompany them to the temple. To financially accommodate their goal, Sister Perez worked diligently selling tortillas. After years of hard work and saving, the success of her tortilla business allowed the Perez family to again travel to the Mesa Arizona Temple and be sealed as a family. In 1975, Brother Perez was called as the patriarch of the newly created Quetzaltenango Stake.

In 1984, the first temple in Central America was dedicated in Guatemala City. However, traveling to the nation's capital still presented significant

136

challenges for the quickly growing LDS population in western Guatemala. Julio Alvarado, a former Area Authority Seventy who once presided over the Guatemala Quetzaltenango Mission, said, "I'm well aware of the limitations that many have had trying to regularly attend the temple in the capital. For example, the members who live in Canquixaja Momostenango have to travel via pick-up truck two hours to the town of Momostenango, and then travel another four to six hours by bus to Guatemala City."

While presiding at the December 16, 2007, groundbreaking ceremony for the Oquirrh Mountain Utah Temple, President Gordon B. Hinckley announced plans to build a temple in Quetzaltenango in western Guatemala. Referencing the busy schedule of the Guatemala City Temple, President Hinckley said, "The temple in Guatemala City (dedicated in 1984) can't accommodate all those who wish to come."

News of the coming temple to western Guatemala spread quickly throughout the country. Members rejoiced and considered the news to be the best Christmas gift of the season. The announced temple would provide unprecedented access and growth to the thousands of devout members living in western Guatemala. After years of lengthy and costly temple visits, members in Quetzaltenango would be able to attend the temple and return to their homes on the same day.

The groundbreaking ceremony for the temple and patron housing facility occurred on a lovely spring-like morning on March 14, 2009. More than 700 members attended the historic event, which was enriched by an eighty-voice choir featuring many women dressed in the indigenous style typical of the region. Central America Area President Don R. Clarke, who presided at the historic ceremony, referenced the faithful temple attendance of members in the area by saying, "It is because of your obedience and diligence that the Lord has permitted the construction of this sacred house."

The Mayan-inspired temple architecture stands atop a knoll at the city's western edge near the popular zoo. The temple's exterior is clad with precast concrete originating from Mexico. The Mayan-influenced motif can also be found in the temple's ornate interior stone, glass, and woodwork. The artistic design provides an aesthetic homage to the region's rich indigenous history and proud culture.

SITE
6.47 acres

GROUNDBREAKING
March 14, 2009, by Don R. Clarke

DEDICATION
December 11, 2011, by
Dieter F. Uchtdorf

EXTERIOR
Precast concrete panels from Mexico

TOTAL FLOOR AREA
21,085 square feet

HIDDEN IMAGE
The Mayan Tikal Temple has been placed among the distant landscaping.

Keith Bond created the masterful murals that adorn the temple's interior. Prior to beginning his work, he traveled to Guatemala to collect reference material for his mural proposal. Upon arriving, he hired a Church member to drive him to remote locations and guide him through the country. It did not take long for him to be impressed with the people and culture. He said, "The people are so friendly and loving. I quickly learned to absolutely love that country." One day while traveling in the countryside, his car was in an accident with another vehicle. While waiting several hours for assistance, he set up his easel at the edge of the road and started painting the landscape. "As I painted, children from a nearby village slowly approached and watched me paint. They crowded me so much that I almost couldn't paint." This unexpected experience actually assisted Keith with his painting in two ways. The time he spent being stranded allowed him to focus on the vegetation and interact with the people in a way that he had not before been able to do. He explained, "The accident enabled me to immerse myself and connect with the landscape and see details I had not before noticed because of my rushed schedule. I also connected with the people more at that time than any other part of my trip. That moment allowed me to interact with the people and connect with the country."

Keith thought it would be important to include the well-known Lake Atitlán. This lake is one of the country's most popular tourist destinations and is beloved by Guatemalans. Surrounded by ancient volcanoes, the lake is a distant feature in the mural, depicted from a pristine perspective. Other visual elements include waterfalls, a black jaguar, a deer, and the national bird, the quetzal.

The temple's successful fifteen-day public open house accommodated more than 126,000 visitors, including about 16,500 on the event's final day. The temple was dedicated under temperate skies on December 11, 2011, by President Dieter F. Uchtdorf. Of the sacred occasion, President Uchtdorf said, "After today's dedication, the [Quetzaltenango] temple will be as sacred as the temple of Solomon, the temple in Nauvoo, the temple in Salt Lake City, or any of the temples in the world."

Kansas City Missouri Temple

T he story of the Church returning to Missouri and Kansas is a story of bricks and mortar, faith, hard work, and patience. The peace of today starkly contrasts with the turbulent past scenes of adversity and sacrifice. Church members have returned to a land of their ancestors to preserve sacred places and establish future generations of Saints. The progression of these events serves as a reminder that the Lord proceeds according to His due time. The pinnacle of this story is the dedication of the Kansas City Missouri Temple.

The temple location is in Clay County on property purchased by the Church in 1980. After the First Presidency approved a temple for the greater Kansas City area, President Dieter F. Uchtdorf was assigned to select the temple location. After reviewing several potential sites, he approved the temple's beautiful current location.

The temple was formally announced by President Thomas S. Monson in the morning session of general conference on Saturday, October 4, 2008. Eighteen months later, ground was broken for the temple on an unseasonably cold spring day. Some 1,700 members and invited guests attended the event.

The architectural design of the Kansas City Temple was crafted to be reminiscent of temples with pioneer heritage. For example, the two towers and elongated windows are patterned after the temples in Logan, Manti, and Salt Lake City.

The temple's architects and designers learned

137

early on that Kansas City is known as the "City of Fountains." With over 250 fountains around town, the city is thought to have more fountains than Rome. Thus, the decision to add a fountain to the temple site was "too obvious to miss."

The temple was built with extraordinary craftsmanship and a passion for perfection. This commitment to excellence is displayed in many of the features that make this temple so unique. As the design team began working on the temple, someone had the impression that the olive branch should be used. David B. Hall. Jr., the Director of Temple Design and Services, explained how the olive branch theme "seemed to develop a life of its own," and in fact "became larger than life" throughout the temple. The olive branch can be found in such places as the exterior stone carvings, the cut and stained-glass windows, the lights, wallpaper, wrought-iron trim on the banisters, and the sculpted carpeting.

Carefully placed details and furnishings throughout the temple enhance the beauty and purpose of the temple. Among these details in the temple's celestial room and sealing rooms is the Celtic knot, also known as the eternal knot. The naturally beautiful wood in the temple is the African hardwood anigre from Africa and white oak harvested sixty miles away from the sacred site of Adam-ondi-Ahman. The wood from Adam-ondi-Ahman was masterfully crafted into the recommend desk and is among the first things visitors see as they enter the temple. Chandeliers were designed specifically for the temple and include custom details. For example, the chandelier in the bride's room manifests the blossom of the state tree, the flowering dogwood.

Local artist Michael Albrechtsen received the commission of a lifetime when he was informed that he had been selected to paint the murals for the first instruction room. He created the murals in a rented warehouse space that was about the same size as the instruction room. Working twelve to thirteen hours a day for four months, he created a masterpiece that depicts landscapes from Kansas and Missouri, including a valley reminiscent of Adam-ondi-Ahman. His desire was to create a "feeling that would enhance the temple experience" and "allow those who entered to feel the presence of Heavenly Father in

SITE
8.05 acres

GROUNDBREAKING
May 8, 2010, by Ronald A. Rasband

DEDICATION
May 6, 2012, by Thomas S. Monson

EXTERIOR
Precast concrete

TOTAL FLOOR AREA
32,000 square feet

HIDDEN IMAGE
A full-length image of the Savior is in the motion of inviting all to the temple. An olive branch is also included in the drawing.

that room and to remember all that God has done for us."

One evening in mid-March 2011, a semi-truck and trailer arrived on the temple grounds. Although it looked like an ordinary delivery, the cargo it carried was anything but common. Inside lay the temple spires and the twelve-foot-tall, 1,200-pound statue of angel Moroni. By March 24th, both spires had been hoisted into position and the statue was permanently placed on the temple's 151-foot spire.

With the temple a year away from completion, a new tradition began to support a wonderful cause. The Kansas City Temple Run is a 5k race that does not charge an entry fee but does encourage food donations. All food items benefit the local charity "In as Much Ministries," which provides food and other necessities to the less fortunate. The race begins and ends at the temple. Nearly 2,000 runners, walkers, and stroller-pushers participate in this annual event.

The temple's highly successful open house attracted 91,960 people from forty-eight states and eleven countries. Nationwide media covered the open house, including CNN, who shared with its print and television viewers a story called "a rare tour of a Mormon temple." One of the many groups attending the temple was a special extended family of approximately 120 guests that had one thing in common—all were descendants of the Prophet Joseph Smith Jr.

At the conclusion of the tour, visitors were invited to a hospitality location, where they could spend some time discussing their experience and enjoying refreshments. The tour guests consumed a total of 118,008 snickerdoodle cookies.

During the dedicatory services that took place on May 6, 2012, President Thomas S. Monson noted that 170 years had passed since those difficult days in LDS history and feelings have softened since then. He mentioned how the Missouri Governor Jay Nixon had recently attended the open house for the temple and referred to the event and upcoming dedication as "a time of healing." President Monson concluded his message by noting how the Prophet Joseph walked here and that the temple will be a beacon of righteousness.

Manaus Brazil Temple

Manaus, Brazil, is an isolated city of 2.2 million people and is accessible only by boat or plane. Located in the heart of the Amazon River Basin, the city is engulfed by large rivers and dense rain forests. Manaus is situated near the confluence of the dark-colored Rio Negro and the lighter Rio Solimões. Where the rivers meet, their contrasting colors famously flow for several miles without blending and eventually become the Amazon River. Manaus is now home to a temple. When visiting the city to dedicate the temple, President Dieter F. Uchtdorf likened the faith and commitment of Latter-day Saints living there to the Amazon River. He said, "Both flow deep and strong."

From its early beginnings, the temple-loving pioneer legacy of the Manaus Saints is to be respected and admired. The first congregation was established in 1978, and continued growth led to the first stake in 1988. Members attended the temple in Sao Paulo by traveling a total of seven days by boat and eight days by bus. Epic stories of sacrifice, faith, and hardship abound during this time of dedicated temple attendance. Some became sick, while others suffered from muscle cramps. Still "they arrive absolutely happy, with hope in their hearts, with faith that they did what was acceptable to God," said Elder Claudio R. M. Costa of the Seventy. "They gave all that they had to receive the blessings to be an eternal family."

Dorivaldo Graciano served as a temple worker in Sao Paulo. He often welcomed the Saints who caravanned from Manaus. In 2001, after masked robbers

138

attacked a group of members traveling to the temple, Brother Graciano said the Manaus members arrived in Sao Paulo without money, travel documents, or other possessions. "They proved their faith," he said. "They returned home happy and the caravans continued."

Manaus became a part of the Caracas Venezuela Temple District in 2005. Members were excited to have a temple so close. When preparing to make their first journey to Caracas, they declared, "Now it takes us only 40 hours to get to the temple!" Even though traveling time was reduced by almost nine days, the journey still required overcoming many challenges, such as travel costs, lack of vacation days from work, bus malfunction, robbers, and difficulty getting passports. The Saints endured the long journey by singing hymns and having firesides on the bus.

Based upon the members' faith and many years of dedicated sacrifices to attend distant temples, the First Presidency determined that Manaus was deserving of a temple. The Manaus Brazil Temple was announced on May 23, 2007. "It is not possible to express the joy that I feel as a result of the announcement," said Geraldo Diogo Lima, a local Church leader in Manaus. "I often find myself in tears as I ponder the blessing of having a temple in our city."

Ground was broken for the temple and patron housing complex on the banks of the mighty Rio Negro on Friday, June 20, 2008. Interior designers and artisans worked diligently to create an experience that is unique to the Amazon. The interior designs include the colors reflective of the area. Rich greens and blues mimic those found in the adjacent river and surrounding jungle. Careful attention was given to the decor, specialized woodwork, detailed staircases, and stained-glass windows. The exterior of the Manaus temple is coated with white Paris granite.

The Manaus Brazil Temple is the only temple with its own

SITE
7.7 acres

GROUNDBREAKING
June 20, 2008, by Charles A. Didier

DEDICATION
June 10, 2012, by Dieter F. Uchtdorf

EXTERIOR
Branco Paris granite from Brazil

TOTAL FLOOR AREA
32,032 square feet

HIDDEN IMAGE
The world-famous Christ the Redeemer Statue, located in Rio de Janeiro, is positioned among the trees right of the temple.

dock. The dock provides easy access for those arriving to its grounds by boat.

Some 42,000 people visited the Manaus Brazil Temple during its open house May 15 to June 2. Each day, loaded busses arrived full of members and their friends. Many visitors traveled long distances to attend the open house. For example, members from Maues, Itacoatiara, and Teffe journeyed by boat for two to three days. These trips were made at great personal and family sacrifice. It was common to see people emotional, with tears in their eyes, at the end of the visit.

Following the open house and preceding the dedication, members enjoyed their highly anticipated cultural celebration, which featured 1,200 participants in nine dances. The event featured regional music and a choir of a thousand voices. In an area known for its life-giving water and lush rain forests, youth members danced to the song of the birds and the music of the rain. A climactic scene occurred during the final moments of the production when more than 1,000 choir members spread a huge work of art depicting their temple across one section of the arena.

The never-forgotten journeys taken by early members began on the banks of the Rio Negro and culminated on June 10, 2012, when President Dieter F. Uchtdorf dedicated the Manaus Brazil Temple. The temple's three dedicatory sessions were broadcast to congregations of the Church within the temple district.

Manuel Viracu Macedo, patriarch of the Ponta Negra Stake, joined the Church in 1982 in Manaus. Reflecting on the temple's dedication, he said, "I always knew in my heart we would have a temple in Manaus. We had the privilege to see the growth of the Church in Manaus and now the temple." Members, he said, never looked at the long temple caravans as a sacrifice. "We looked at it as a blessing."

Brigham City Utah Temple

A mong the earliest industries in Box Elder County was the fruit-growing business. The earliest settlers discovered that the Brigham City area was particularly adapted for peaches, berries, and small fruits. For generations, local farmers worked the same orchards and served customers from the same fruit stands. Annual peach crops became so successful that an annual harvest celebration, known as "Peach Days," was started in 1904.

Within the temple, homage is given to the importance of peaches to the community. Delicate peach blossoms are expertly portrayed in the temple's colorful art glass windows. Additional impressions of peach blossoms are repeated throughout the temple and are found in the exterior walls, sealing room

carpet, bride's room woven rug, door handles, crown moldings, decorative painting, and furniture details. The upper floors of the temple feature elaborate, painted designs using a technique known as "Damask Stenciling." Imagery in these patterns depicts peach blossoms and poppies that flourish in the neighboring town of Mantua.

The site for the Box Elder Stake Tabernacle was selected by President Brigham Young. This location, known as "Sagebrush Hill," was chosen because it was the highest point on Main Street and would be visible for many miles throughout the valley. Completed in 1897, the building has served the community well by housing civic events and religious services. The tabernacle is an icon of the city's industrious past,

139

and the forthcoming temple would be a great symbol of its promising future.

The temple's orientation and building materials strategically complement the neighboring tabernacle. The temple doors are lined up exactly across from the tabernacle doors across the street. The rock used on the planter and parking garage walls comes from the same quarry used for the tabernacle's construction. Within the temple, woodwork details include "egg-and-dart" handcrafted ornamentation patterned after motifs found in the tabernacle. These details were carved by hand using patterns, basic tools, and a great deal of patience. Although subtle, these expert details create a visual harmony that bonds these two iconic structures.

The temple site formerly housed Central Elementary School, a three-story school that was completed in 1901 and rebuilt after a fire in 1947. The school served the community and thousands of children for nearly 100 years. "I am home." So began President Boyd K. Packer as he addressed the sea of onlookers at the groundbreaking of the temple. President Packer, who grew up in Brigham City, called the three acres "sacred ground." As he detailed the area's history, he mused, "Can you imagine what it would take to preserve this spot for 150 years, to wait until a temple could be built here?"

In the year 2000, the school was razed after its closure. As an empty lot, the city's most prime real estate was on the market for nearly ten years. Although it was nearly sold multiple times, each of the transactions was never finalized.

The architectural design of the Brigham City Temple was crafted to be reminiscent of Utah's pioneer heritage. For example, the placement of the elongated and circular windows is patterned after the temples in Logan, Manti, and Salt Lake City.

The purpose of the temple is not to show art; however, art does set the tone for the rooms and the service performed there. A painting in the baptistry represents the history of the area by depicting Native Americans being baptized. One of the instruction rooms features the artwork of Gary Ernest Smith. A goal of his painting was to make the visitors feel at home. To accomplish this, he depicted familiar landscapes indigenous to the area, including the wildlife preserve and a mountain called the "Three Presidents."

The temple's exquisite interior marble originates from Turkey. Church building managers traveled to Turkey to

SITE
3.14 acres

GROUNDBREAKING
July 31, 2010

DEDICATION
September 23, 2012, by
Boyd K. Packer

EXTERIOR
Precast concrete

TOTAL FLOOR AREA
36,000 square feet

HIDDEN IMAGE
Among the leaves above the temple,
an image of the Savior is rendered
in the motion of inviting all to
receive the blessings of the temple.

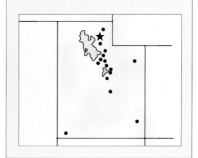

personally inspect and select marble grades and color. Once approved, semi-trailer-sized blocks of marble were shipped to China to be milled, cut, and polished according to exact specifications. Once the marble arrived at the temple site, every piece was identified and installed.

Among the 160 trees on the temple grounds are many fruit trees. Although very few temples include fruit-bearing trees, the Brigham City Temple features peach, apricot, cherry, pear, and apple. Temple construction missionaries Gregory and Michele Peck were able to harvest the first fruit crop prior to the temple's open house. Elder Peck explained, "That first year we were able to collect some very nice apricots. We gave them to President Packer. He was among the first to have fruit from the temple."

According to Elder Peck, "The support the builders received from the city and members was incredible. Members took initiative and started bringing meals for the workers. Once word got out, meals were brought for the entire crew (ranging from 100 to 200 servings) several times a week. Sometimes they would even bring treats in the afternoon for the workers to take as they left for the day. The workers were amazed and appreciative. . . . They couldn't believe that anyone cared about them."

Nearly 404,500 visitors toured the building during the one-month public open house from August 18 to September 15, 2012. The largest number of visitors to tour the temple was 25,000 on Labor Day, averaging more than 600 people per hour. To accommodate refreshments to the visitors, a local Smith's grocery store delivered 26,000 cookies every day of the open house.

On September 23, 2012, President Boyd K. Packer returned to dedicate the temple in three sessions. Before the first session began, President Packer went outside to apply mortar to the cornerstone as it was set in place. Among the unique items placed within the temple's cornerstone were an actual railroad spike and a brick from the foundation of the school that had previously occupied the property. The event was broadcast to stake centers in Utah and parts of Idaho. The Brigham City Utah Temple will serve some 40,000 Latter-day Saints from thirteen stakes in northern Utah and southeastern Idaho.

Calgary Alberta Temple

Picturesque Calgary is situated at the confluence of the Bow River and the Elbow River and is only fifty miles east of the Canadian Rockies. It celebrates the world-renowned Calgary Stampede annually and in 1988 was the host city of the XV Olympic Winter Games. For Latter-day Saints, it is also the home of Alberta's third temple. Since the dedication of the Cardston Alberta Temple in 1923, southern Alberta has been the bedrock of the Latter-day Saints in Canada.

The ten-acre site where the temple now stands is located on property acquired by the Church in 1980. After the building of the Royal Oak Chapel, officials in Salt Lake City encouraged local stake leadership to sell the excess land not being used by the chapel. However, Calgary West Stake President Richard

Melchin recommended that his stake retain the property, although the Church did not have plans to build a temple in Calgary at the time. The First Presidency ultimately decided not to sell the property per the recommendation of President Melchin.

In August 2008, President Henry B. Eyring visited Calgary to attend a Priesthood Leadership Conference. President Eyring had been given the special assignment from President Monson to privately visit the Royal Oak site to determine if the location would be suitable for a temple. Following the conference, Elder Richard Melchin drove President Eyring to the site where the Royal Oak Chapel is situated. At the site, the two leaders walked the five or six feet up a slope

140

to a plateau to enjoy the panoramic view of the mountains to the west, the river valley to the south, and downtown Calgary to the east. President Eyring commented that "the Lord always prepares the way" and then asked, "What direction is the east?" He took a few steps and turned and said, "I think you'll get your temple." Two months later, in an opening address of general conference in October 2008, President Monson announced five new temples, including one in Calgary, Alberta, Canada.

In the years prior to the announcement of the temple, the Royal Oak Ward members organized and worked with community leaders on causes such as barbecues, breakfasts, community spring cleanups, and food bank drives. As a result, Church members became trusted friends with community leaders and neighbors. These trusted relationships greatly helped the temple to be welcomed and approved by the community.

The groundbreaking and site dedication was held on May 15, 2010, presided over by Elder Donald L. Hallstrom of the Presidency of the Seventy. Over 1,500 people witnessed the ceremony in person. The historic event was also broadcast to surrounding stake centers in Calgary, allowing more than 3,000 others to view the event.

During the last three weeks of construction, members volunteered to aid the workers by providing appreciation meals. The hearty food included pizza, tacos, burgers, professionally decorated cupcakes, cinnamon twists, and even a lemonade stand. Of course the meals and kindness were a raging success with the hungry crews of 150 workers.

As the temple's construction neared completion and the open house approached, an increasing amount of focus was placed on the incomplete landscaping. Problems of late delivery of materials and an insufficient workforce put the landscaping far behind schedule. Through priesthood channels, an emergency call of help was sent out to local congregations. The response was immediate, and the number of volunteers was staggering. While the army of landscape volunteers labored outside, dedicated members worked inside doing final cleanup. An astounding 16,000 man-hours of volunteer labor were contributed. Thanks to the dedicated and speedy work of these volunteers, the required work on the grounds and inside the

SITE
10.17 acres

GROUNDBREAKING
May 15, 2010

DEDICATION
October 28, 2012, by
Thomas S. Monson

EXTERIOR
Gray granite from China

TOTAL FLOOR AREA
33,000 square feet

HIDDEN IMAGE
Based upon the temple's wheat theme, on both sides of the temple and among the landscaping and sky are shafts of wheat.

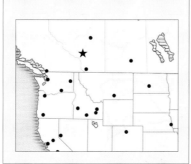

temple was completed one hour prior to the temple's first open house tour.

The stained glass of the temple is remarkably beautiful and offers an appropriate tribute to Alberta's golden prairies. The blue represents the sky over the tan and golden colors of stylized wheat. A wheat motif is also found in the marble detailing, stained-glass windows, railings, doorknobs, and furniture throughout the building. The wild rose is another motif that honors the natural beauty of the region and is exquisitely painted on the ceiling of the bride's room.

Renowned artist Leon Parson had a "distinct feeling" that he should submit a proposal for the Calgary Temple. Once selected as the artist, he traveled to Calgary to learn about the area and take reference photography. "I asked the Lord where I should go and He said, 'Carburn Park.'" Leon collected thousands of helpful reference photos from areas in Alberta, British Columbia, and Wyoming. However, elements from Carburn Park are included on both sides of the murals. At the request of the interior designer, he included three elk, five mule deer, thirteen Canada geese, a great horned owl (Alberta's official bird), a pair of western tanagers, fourteen antelope, two white-tailed deer, a harrier hawk, some bees, and some butterflies.

The celebrated open house brought Church members from across the region together in a sweet spirit of love and unity. The temple was open for public viewing from September 28 to October 20, 2012. Just over 100,000 people attended the open house, where the Spirit of the Lord welcomed all guests.

The frosty bite of a Canadian winter arrived early in Calgary on the morning of the temple dedication. A blanketed white landscape was the setting for the thousands who arrived to participate in the day's sacred event. The Calgary Alberta Temple was dedicated by President Thomas S. Monson on October 29, 2012. The dedicatory sessions were broadcast to stake centers in Alberta and Southern British Columbia. Over 33,000 people participated in the three dedicatory sessions. The magnificence of the Calgary Alberta Temple is surpassed only by the majesty and power of the ordinances presented there. For decades, the Saints of Calgary have faithfully traveled distances through all kinds of Canadian weather to serve in the temple. Now, it's their privilege to have one of their own.

Tegucigalpa Honduras Temple

The Church was first introduced in Honduras 1952, when Elders Spencer W. Kimball and Marion G. Romney of the Quorum of the Twelve Apostles left a Book of Mormon with a hotel waiter. The waiter was later baptized, and missionaries soon arrived in the country. Following the first few convert baptisms, the nation's first congregation was formed in Tegucigalpa in March 1953. From its infant beginning, the Church has experienced dramatic and steady growth. As of 2015, Honduras has four missions and 165,000 members and is one of the fastest-growing countries in Church membership.

For members living in Honduras, attending the temple often included danger, hardship, and sacrifice. Bishop Gustavo Adolfo Andara of the Comayagua Ward described a memorable trip to the Guatemala City Guatemala Temple: "Members of the Church here are very poor, and we have to make great sacrifices to attend the temple. Bus rides are very hard and twelve hours long on damaged roads. I remember when the constant rains caused a hillside by the road to collapse. Members were clean but the mudslide made our hands and clothes dirty. It took an entire day to get out of the mud. We arrived at the temple very muddy and without water to get clean but we were happy. That day we realized that the Lord had given us that obstacle so we could learn to move forward regardless of the challenges in our way. It was a wonderful temple trip that we will never forget."

The First Presidency announced in a June 9,

141

2006, letter that a temple would be built in the Honduran capital of Tegucigalpa. News of the temple spread fast across the country, causing a wave of rejoicing. One sister shared her thoughts when she first learned of the temple: "One of my greatest blessings of my life is to know the gospel of Jesus Christ and have the opportunity to enter the holy temple." She continued, "I am profoundly grateful that we will soon have our temple in Honduras where we can perform sacred ordinances and where our children enter into the covenant of marriage."

Unfortunately, the members of Honduras had to wait three years before the groundbreaking. Land disputes, military coups, government overthrows, and pervading national security issues were only a few of the challenges encountered while building Honduras's first temple. The original project began in 2007 but was halted due to concerns regarding its location. The media reported on concerns that the temple would put the view of "the main Catholic church of Honduras in jeopardy." After a year of negotiations, a new site was selected and construction could proceed—only to be delayed again by a military coup.

Construction procedures in Honduras do not include strict safety guidelines. Despite the best efforts and training of project leaders, accidents did occur. Project superintendent Dennis Pack shared a few unfortunate incidents that could have had a much worse ending. "I feel that the workers were protected by our Heavenly Father," Brother Pack recorded. "Despite working in a third-world country with total safety ineptness, we only had three accidents during the thirty-seven-month project. On one occasion two men fell off a scaffold, . . . and one of them continued working the same day and the other came back two days later. On another occasion, a man was using a grinder without a guard on it at face level. The grinder kicked and buried itself in his face, going down toward his neck. In a fraction of a second another worker was able to unplug the grinder before the man very possibly could have died. The man returned to work one week later. These were both very unusual incidents."

More than 210,000 people attended a three-week open house prior to the temple dedication, including special guests Honduran President Porfirio Lobo Sosa, First Lady Rosa Elena

SITE
13.6 acres

GROUNDBREAKING
September 12, 2009,
by Don R. Clarke

DEDICATION
March 17, 2013, by Dieter F. Uchtdorf

EXTERIOR
Mountain gray granite from China

TOTAL FLOOR AREA
28,254 square feet

HIDDEN IMAGE
Among the trees and landscaping
to the right of the temple is an
image of the Savior kneeling and
looking up at the temple.

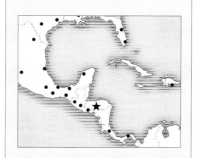

de Lobo, and a large government delegation that included ten cabinet ministers. These visitors toured the 28,254-square-foot temple with designs inspired by Mayan culture. Other interior features include original murals depicting Honduran landscapes. Motifs of the orchid, national flower of Honduras, are found on the furniture, doors, and other places in the temple.

Just forty-eight hours before the temple's dedication, Honduran President Porfirio Lobo accepted an invitation to have breakfast with President Dieter F. Uchtdorf and other visiting Church leaders at the temple annex building. The Honduran leader returned the kindness by inviting President Uchtdorf to join him the next morning for breakfast at his presidential palace. The two respective leaders exchanged gifts and discussed the new temple and the Church's rapidly growing presence in Honduras.

The Tegucigalpa Honduras Temple was dedicated on March 17, 2013, by President Dieter F. Uchtdorf in three sessions that were broadcast to all Church units in Honduras and Nicaragua.

In addition to economic trials, the Saints in Honduras face challenges of crime, violence, and physical safety. Honduras has the highest homicide rate in the world, and unfortunately these dangers have directly affected the temple. Multiple security guards are on the temple property at all times. A member of the temple presidency, Don Cazier, described these serious challenges: "One of our aged temple workers was shot. The wife of another dear temple worker was shot and killed. One time someone entered the property and robbed the distribution center. This kind of violence has affected almost every family. It is not without sacrifice that members serve in the Church. We would often let our workers leave the temple early so they could travel home before dark. That is the kind of thing they are dealing with there. In spite of this, we have wonderful members who are serving faithfully."

Elder Kevin R. Duncan, Second Counselor in the Area Presidency, praised the faithful resilience of members who worship in Honduras's first temple. Many, he said, come from notoriously violent, unstable communities—but they are gentle, happy people thanks to their faith and temple devotion.

Gilbert Arizona Temple

For several decades, precious water turned the area's thirsty desert soil into thriving dairy farms and alfalfa fields. In the early 1900s, the agricultural success of Gilbert, Arizona, earned it the name of "Hay Capital of the World." Today, living water provides a spiritual oasis where the doctrines of Christ are learned and eternal covenants are made.

On April 26, 2008, plans to build two new temples in Arizona were announced, one in The Gila Valley and another in Gilbert. President Thomas S. Monson remarked, "It is my personal priority to make sure members of the Church have access to the blessings of the temple." The temple's location in Gilbert was the last temple site chosen by President Gordon B. Hinckley.

Thousands gathered to witness the groundbreaking ceremony on November 13, 2010. Before construction could begin, temple builders were faced with major challenges. The site's lower grade would predictably result in the collection of excessive storm runoff water. To prevent inevitable flooding, a massive underground storage system for storm water was constructed beneath the parking lot. A second challenge was the high-voltage overhead power lines. This obstacle was overcome by miraculously being allowed to bury the large power lines deep in the earth. Finally, the busy intersection with all its noisy traffic provided an unwanted contrast to the peaceful seclusion that should dwell in the temple. Many soundproofing techniques

142

were employed, including seven-inch-thick temple walls with insulation.

To keep the highly complex temple working in unobstructed unison, the latest technology was utilized. Using 3-D printing and computer models, every aspect of the temple was designed digitally before it was installed or built physically.

The tranquil fountains surrounding the exterior prepare visitors for their temple experience. Dennis A. Call designed the water features and patterned them after childhood memories of growing up close to the site where the temple is now located. He explained, "My memories of the Gilbert hay fields being irrigated influenced my design of the Gilbert Temple water features. The flat, green, marble water tables of the fountains at the temple with their raised, light-colored dividers are reminiscent of the Gilbert alfalfa fields being irrigated. The fountain springs at the head of each fountain are reminiscent of the water coming from the wells that fed the canals and ditches. It seems appropriate to remember the farming heritage of Gilbert and the people who have farmed there for many years."

Local members followed the progress of their temple during all phases of construction. No one knows this more than temple construction missionaries Wayne and Patricia Miller. Elder Miller said, "We managed to entertain about 70,000 visitors to the temple site during its construction. One ward made a three-day trek to the temple site. Wards and stakes would journey to the temple with hundreds of kids. We built a viewing platform to allow people to see the progress."

Among the many unique features within the temple are the brushed bronze oxen in the baptistry. Long hours and tender care were given to each piece to ensure luster and perfection. Another highlight of the temple is the curving and graceful grand staircase. The staircase is extremely complex and is a marvel of craftsmanship and resourceful ingenuity. A theme repeated throughout the temple is the agave plant. According to the temple's head architect, Greg Lambright, the agave plant

SITE
15.38 acres

GROUNDBREAKING
November 13, 2010, by
Claudio R. M. Costa

DEDICATION
March 2, 2014, by Thomas S.
Monson (read by Henry B. Eyring)

TOTAL FLOOR AREA
85,326 square feet

HIDDEN IMAGE
Standing along the right side
of the temple is a full-length
image of the Savior.

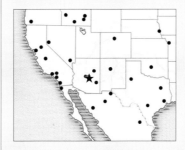

was selected because of beauty and symbolism. "Besides the beauty, color, and rich texture of these plants, at the end of the life cycle, many of the agave plant species willingly and beautifully give up their life for those who will follow, in a like manner as what the Savior did for us."

The completed temple was open to the public from January 13 to February 15, 2014. The open house attracted approximately 400,000 visitors, utilized the service of 9,312 volunteers, and was directed by 764 trained tour guides. Among the special guests to attend the temple were Senator John McCain, Sandra Day O'Connor, and Arizona's governor Jan Brewer. Governor Brewer was thoroughly impressed and described the temple as "a beacon of hope, faith and love to all those who come to this sacred building and its beautiful grounds. It is a special place . . . a place of spiritual refuge in this troubled world. This temple is also a testament to those who came before you. With faith, fortitude and devotion to God, Mormon pioneers settled much of this state, including what would become the town of Gilbert."

The heavens opened up on the youth cultural celebration on March 1, 2014. With the temple in the background, an army of 12,000 youth performed beautifully during a torrential downpour. The evening's theme was "Live True to the Faith" and paid tribute to heroes, both ancient and modern, who remained true in spite of persecution and trials.

Arizona's fourth temple was dedicated in three sessions on March 2, 2014. President Thomas S. Monson presided over the three sessions. Among the unique items honoring the area's history that were included in the time capsule were alfalfa seeds and a hay hook. The dedicatory prayer included the following inspiring message: "May this, Thy house, be a sanctuary of serenity, a refuge from the storms of life and the noise of the world. May it be a house of quiet contemplation concerning the eternal nature of life and of Thy divine plan for us."

Fort Lauderdale Florida Temple

Southern Florida is a worldwide magnet for beach vacations, Caribbean cruises, ocean boating, exotic animals, and unique natural beauty. The Fort Lauderdale Florida Temple is in the vicinity of many of these attractions and natural wonders: Everglades National Park, Hollywood Florida, coastal beaches, the Bahamas, and Key West. Contrasting from the things of the world, the holy temple in Fort Lauderdale provides peace and blessings for those who are focused on their eternal destination.

President Thomas S. Monson opened the Church's 179th Semiannual General Conference, held on Saturday and Sunday, October 3 and 4, 2009, by announcing the locations of five new temples, including the Fort Lauderdale Florida Temple.

Before construction could commence, local zoning permits and city approvals needed to be received. To earn these approvals and in an effort to be a good neighbor in the community, the Church agreed to several requests. including lowering the spire from 115 to 100 feet, maintaining empty portions of the property, and following nighttime lighting guidelines. As an added gesture of good will, the Church agreed to promptly purchase and install a streetlamp at the roundabout entrance to the neighborhood. At a Davie Town Council meeting on February 16, 2011, all ordinances were approved without dissent, and the mayor said with a smile, "Welcome to Davie!"

On June 18, 2011, more than 200 invited guests attended the one-hour groundbreaking event.

143

Included in the audience was Mayor Judy Paul of Davie. Mayor Paul expressed her excitement for the new addition to the community. "We embrace diversity, and we embrace all new-comers to the town," she said. "We will make it as easy and comfortable as possible [for you] to be here."

As construction progressed on the temple, so did spiritual work progress in the lives of members in the temple district. In the words of Miami Lakes Florida Stake President James Robinson, "The time leading up to the opening of the Fort Lauderdale Temple were days never to be forgotten. Missionary work in South Florida boomed, with the stakes in the Fort Lauderdale Mission having more baptisms than any other time in mission history. The Spirit of Elijah also moved on the hearts of the Saints. In our Miami Lakes Stake, for example, we had more—MANY more—active temple recommend holders than at any time in our stake's history. And there was a spirit of cooperation and unity among the Saints that I have never before witnessed. I did not think anything could top that."

Renowned landscape artist Brad Aldridge received the commission to paint the murals for the temple's interior. To collect reference material, Brad visited the Everglades, the Keys, and the beaches near Fort Lauderdale. At the end of his trip, he had captured over 1,700 photographs. His goal was to "paint a native landscape as it would appear before it was touched by man," he said. "I always hope I will find the perfect spot to paint, but that never happens. I always have to combine elements from a variety of locations, a tree from one location, a rock from another and plants from another." The massive undertaking required six months, with Brad frequently working twelve- to fourteen-hour days.

The ten-foot-tall mural was painted in an old turkey hatchery warehouse. Brad needed a large space to build an exact replica of the temple room. He then stretched the canvas in the walls of the room and painted his masterpiece. In addition to including white-tailed deer and several indigenous species of birds, he included smaller critters. "People like to discover things each time they look at a mural, so I gave them a lot to look at and included smaller things like butterflies and geckos. I painted three butterflies for my three daughters and two gecko lizards representing my two sons. I tried to create a religious experience on a beach. The details of the painting

SITE
16.82 acres

GROUNDBREAKING
June 18, 2011, by Walter F. González

DEDICATION
May 4, 2014, by Dieter F. Uchtdorf

EXTERIOR
Architectural precast concrete

TOTAL FLOOR AREA
30,500 square feet

HIDDEN IMAGE
Standing along the right side
of the temple is a full-length
image of the Savior.

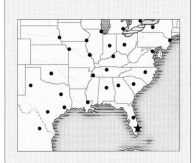

are mostly behind you, and then the complexity gives way as you look forward toward the ocean."

During the process of creating the murals, Brad learned a few life lessons. "I always start my day with scripture study and prayer. As I was praying for inspiration for the painting I had the thought 'Get to work so that I can inspire you. Put some paint on the canvas and then I can inspire you . . . but just get to work.' That is what I needed to learn, 'Get to work first, then I can inspire you.'"

As the temple neared completion, it earned the adoration of a panel of judges in the construction trade industry. In the year of its dedication, it was named the best cultural/worship construction project by ENR Southeast's annual project excellence program. Among the reasons cited for winning is the use of "less commonly used" materials, "which provided the strength required to exceed the Florida Building Code impact requirements while maintaining the design aesthetics."

During the open house, the temple quickly solidified itself as a new landmark in south Florida. Tens of thousands of visitors toured the building. The distinctly Floridian structure features an interior color scheme of cool blues and greens, reflecting the state's tropical environment. Sawgrass leaves, palm fronds, and other local natural elements are represented in ornate glass and metalwork in the baptistry and several other areas of the temple.

The dedication of the Fort Lauderdale Florida Temple made The Sunshine State even brighter. The state's second temple was dedicated on May 4, 2014, by President Dieter F. Uchtdorf. More than 2,000 members participated in the three dedicatory sessions inside the temple. Thousands more viewed the proceedings via closed-circuit broadcasts to meetinghouses throughout Florida and portions of Georgia.

Several months after the dedication, local member Eliza Gomez observed the temple's positive impact among the area's teenagers and young adults, who have flocked to the Lord's house to do baptisms for the dead. "Now that the temple is in our midst, it seems they have caught fire even more," she said. "They're going so much more often. It's so powerful and special. The lens, the focus is off the Fort Lauderdale Temple now, but seeing them be so valiant and diligent is a special honor and brings a sweet spirit that is strengthening our wards and stakes."

Phoenix Arizona Temple

President Thomas S. Monson publicly announced a new temple for "The Valley of the Sun" on May 24, 2008. On ground that used to be dirt roads and spacious farmland, Arizona's capital city temple now provides members convenient access to the house of the Lord.

The announcement of the temple brought with it a maelstrom of protests and obstacles. For nearly two years, many neighbors organized to express their disagreement with the temple's location, size, height, lighting, and even color. Although the temple complied with all zoning requirements, many complained it would block their views and bring unwanted traffic. After many meetings, media interviews, and debates, the Church offered a modified plan at a special neighborhood meeting on August 17, 2010. "We want the neighbors to understand that their concerns were considered as the new design was drawn up," said Church spokesman Jennifer Wheeler. The temple was completely redesigned, turning the two-story building into a single-story building with a full basement. The Church agreed to not build a visitors' center, hold pageants, or display Christmas lights. Many members consider the final temple design to be a blessing because the added basement dramatically increased the overall interior space.

Before construction began, the Church held a "Why do Mormons Build Temples?" event at the adjacent meetinghouse. Among the visitors at the event were curious neighbors Cynthia and her fifteen-year-old son Jeffrey. "What I learned and felt brought me

144

peace," Cynthia said, "so we started attending church services." Growing up a faithful Christian, she had experienced spiritual promptings in her life and thus recognized the Spirit when she met with the Mormons. In her words, "Everything I learned about the Church I somehow already knew to be true. The teachings provide me direction and give me the peace I have always looked for. I look forward to going to the temple *so* much. This temple will always be *my* temple because when it came to my neighborhood, my son and I found the Church and were baptized."

During most of the two-year construction process, wards were given the opportunity to provide treats and snacks for each worker (about 200 each time). Each treat included a spiritual thought, inspirational quote, or "thank-you." This wonderful tradition was greatly appreciated by the workers and provided an opportunity for wards to be involved with "their" temple. Temple special project missionary Elder Don Lamb always enjoyed delivering the treats to the workers. He recalled, "As we approached the workers with the treats, the workers would often shout out 'Cookie Day.' It was not just about the cookie, it was just as much about the note that came with each treat. The workers would often take the notes home and share them with their families."

A beautiful design feature within the temple is the masterful use of clay-based terra cotta. In an effort to visually connect the Mesa Arizona Temple with the temple in Phoenix, interior designers used terra cotta designs and turquoise colors originating in the Mesa Temple. Among the places where terra cotta is extensively used is in the baptistry. According to Elder Lamb, the baptismal font's exterior adornment is "literally a massive jigsaw puzzle of terra cotta." The same company that created the terra cotta material for the Mesa temple in 1927 also provided the material for the Phoenix Arizona Temple.

Enhancing the beauty of the instruction room are three large oil mural panels. "In preparation for the painting," commented artist Keith Bond, "I camped for a week northwest of Phoenix and immersed myself in the desert landscape. I did several plein-air paintings and took thousands of reference photos." The mural does not depict a single location or scene.

SITE
5.19 acres

GROUNDBREAKING
June 4, 2011 by Ronald A. Rasband

DEDICATION
November 16, 2014, by
Thomas S. Monson

EXTERIOR
Precast integral colored
concrete panels

TOTAL FLOOR AREA
66,000 square feet

HIDDEN IMAGE
The Good Shepherd is cradling
one of His sheep among the
temple's landscaping and trees.

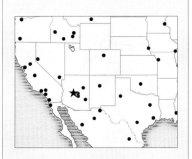

Keith explained, "I paint bits and pieces from my reference material so it does feel like the area." Included in the stunning Sonoran Desert landscape are rugged mountains, specimens of cacti, mesquite, fauna, and blooming Palo Verde tree. Wildlife includes the Cactus Wren, cardinals, deer, rabbits, lizards, and a family of quail. "When I include animals, I do not want it to look like a zoo," Keith said. "I paint the animals where they would be found naturally. I try to paint them subtly, because when you are outside among nature, you typically only get brief glimpses of wildlife."

Sisters living within the temple district were given the unique opportunity to create altar cloths for the building. Within six months, forty-five cloths were completed and presented to the temple. Additionally, members included a note describing what the opportunity meant to them. All of these notes were included in the temple's official history. Among these heart-felt submissions was the following: "As I walk into a temple, I immediately feel reverence of the Spirit and the quality that is in the Lord's house. I wanted to put this into my work. I started by making sure my hands were clean and I kept the cloth in clean containers. I made sure every stitch was counted and correct. I also prayed for strength and guidance, as this work was not mine but the Lord's."

The evening before the temple's dedication, 4,300 youth participated in the Phoenix Arizona Temple youth cultural celebration, titled "Be a Light." Each group had its own script, song, dance, and name. According to Allyson Morris, director of the cultural celebration, "hundreds and hundreds of hours" were put into writing, editing, and practice. Of the evening, she said, "The kids were amazing and the performance went on without a hitch. It all went so well. I felt inspired and did what was in my heart, and those kids followed me with exactness. It was the Lord's production, and they are His youth. This was His message. The experience was absolutely one of the most wonderful things to ever happen to me. It was great."

President Thomas S. Monson dedicated Arizona's fifth temple in three sessions on November 16, 2014. The building sits on 5.19 acres and serves 60,000 Latter-day Saints from sixteen stakes.

Córdoba Argentina Temple

The city of Cordoba, Argentina, is known throughout Latin America for its culture, commerce, and having the first campus established for higher learning. It is located in the geographical center of the country at the foothills of the Sierras Chicas along the beautiful Suquia River. Amid the city's many great attractions of sporting venues, museums, and historical monuments is a sacred structure that focuses on things of eternal worth. It is the Córdoba Argentina Temple.

The Church has deep roots in this region of Argentina's heartland. Church membership has grown dramatically since the 1920s, when the first members who were European immigrants requested missionaries. In 1986, the members were blessed to receive a temple in Buenos Aires. As the nation's

Church membership grew, so did the need for a second temple. The Church's sixty stakes and member population of over 430,000 put a strain on the lone temple in the capital city of Buenos Aires. For decades, members faithfully made costly flights or ten-hour bus excursions to Buenos Aires. For these reasons, members cheered on October 4, 2008, when President Thomas S. Monson announced plans to build Argentina's second temple in Cordoba.

After months of negotiations, the Church finalized the acquisition of property adjacent to the Villa Belgrano meetinghouse for construction of the temple. After the properties were legally joined into a single parcel, temple plans were presented to the city. Ground was broken on October 30, 2010, and

145

the temple site was dedicated by Elder Neil L. Anderson. The groundbreaking marked a time of celebration for members living in northern Argentina. Many viewed the building of the nation's second temple as the realization of Elder Melvin J. Ballard's 1925 prophecy that the area "will become a power in the Church."

After the groundbreaking, Miriam Hadid de Chehda, a local member, said, "The Córdoba temple is a reward for the endurance of many members of the Church in the area. I didn't even imagine that I could see it during my life. Now I know that my children and grandchildren will be married here, that the eternal vows that my husband and I began more than 30 years ago will continue for generations."

The temple property has served the purpose of the Restoration for nearly fifty years. The first chapel in Cordoba was built on the corner of the property, along with a mission office. Elder Richard G. Scott lived on the site in the early 1960s while he served four years as the president of the Argentina North Mission. Elder D. Todd Christofferson walked the property as a young missionary serving under President Scott. Considering the property's meaningful past, members thought it appropriate that it would become the site of the house of the Lord.

Progress on the temple proceeded slowly because the former stake center and sports complex needed to be razed and the land cleared. Finally, in February 2012, building permits were secured and the site was prepared to allow full-scale operations to commence. The temple's drawings were produced in Spanish with an emphasis on local building materials and construction methods due to difficulties with import fees into Argentina.

Elder Mark Fenn and Sister Carrie Fenn cherished their four years of service as the temple's special project missionaries. Sister Fenn performed clerical duties in the on-site office while Elder Fenn assisted the Church-employed project manager. He helped greatly by translating between the architect from the United States and the local subcontractors. Another vital task performed by Elder Fenn was helping project managers find or create materials and components locally that were required for the temple. During construction, political troubles in Argentina essentially prevented the importation of desperately needed supplies. Through the power of faith and prayer, a few

SITE
3.2 acres

GROUNDBREAKING
October 30, 2010

DEDICATION
May 17, 2015, by Dieter F. Uchtdorf

EXTERIOR
Light gray granite quarried in Cordoba

TOTAL FLOOR AREA
34,369 square feet

DIMENSIONS
90 feet to the top of the angel Moroni

HIDDEN IMAGE
The angel Moroni statue is illustrated among the foreground shadows.

exceptions were made, allowing the Church to import items unavailable in Argentina.

After waiting nearly seven years since the temple's announcement, members were understandably eager for the opening of the temple. "We've waited so long for this temple, it didn't seem like it would ever really open," said Grisilda Morena de Martinez, a local member. "We watched the temple being built through every stage of construction."

Prior to the temple dedication, more than 49,000 people attended the two-week open house to view the building's beauty and learn about the purpose of temples. The open house guests were welcomed to a quiet place of worship ornate in carved exterior stone, inlaid marble flooring, intricate woodwork, and art glass windows. The interior's natural colors complement the red marble counters and accent stone from Spain. Hand-sculpted carpet designs mirror the extensive decorative painting and gold stenciling. The 34,369-square-foot, gray stone building is beautiful without being extravagant.

The temple dedication was preceded by a cultural celebration Saturday night. The event included a variety of colorful folk dances that told the story of Argentina's indigenous history, its fight for independence, the legacy of countless immigrants and, lastly, the ongoing emergence of the Church. It was a once-in-a-lifetime opportunity for the youth to showcase their talent with the theme "The Light of the Gospel Shines." The performance concluded with the entire cast unrolling a massive mural emblazoned with the image of the Córdoba Argentina Temple. Those who participated in the event were impressed by how amazing the experience was. A young man said, "It was very nice because it gave me the chance to know members from other provinces and cities—in reality, it was a beautiful experience."

On a pleasant and sunny autumn day, more than 2,000 members joined in the temple's three dedicatory sessions. President Dieter F. Uchtdorf presided at the services and gave the dedicatory prayer.

Attending the dedication services was Elder D. Todd Christofferson. At the conclusion of the day, he said, "It's almost surreal. Something beyond my fondest imaginations that we [the Church] would be here dedicating a temple, some 50 years, more or less, from my mission service time. It's a great blessing, a miracle, really."

Payson Utah Temple

The Payson Utah Temple, nestled among the foothills of the Wasatch Mountain Range, is distinguished by four distinct mountain peaks: Mount Timpanogos, Santaquin Peak, Loafer Mountain, and Mount Nebo. This majestic setting naturally causes local members to refer to the temple as a "mountain of the Lord." Positioned on a gently sloping hill, the temple prominently greets travelers from the south and can even be seen from northern parts of Utah County.

Pioneer history and faith resonate among the members living in Payson, Utah. In 1850, Brigham Young sent members to settle near what was then known as Peteeneet Creek. For over 150 years, the area's faithful members lived among pastoral farms, alfalfa fields, and fruit orchards. On January 25, 2010,

President Thomas S. Monson announced plans to construct a temple in Payson. A special groundbreaking ceremony conducted by Elder Dallin H. Oaks took place on October 8, 2011. Some 6,000 members gathered on a rainy day to witness the historic occasion.

Throughout all phases of construction, enthusiasm for the temple was evidenced by a constant flow of people driving by the temple site to inspect the work in progress. Additionally, members provided regular service to inspire those building the temple. Relief Society sisters provided treats and warm meals, groups were organized to sing, and thank-you cards were delivered.

Elder DeVeri Stoddard and Sister Patty Stoddard served for three years as the temple's special project

146

missionaries. As they faithfully oversaw all aspects of the temple's construction, they developed close relationships with many tradespeople, subcontractors, and construction managers. Elder Stoddard related how a tile and stone foreman had difficulty with his responsibilities because he could not find qualified individuals to properly perform the technical installation. Discouraged and prepared to quit, the foreman decided to walk through the temple for the last time. All the workers had gone home and he was alone in the temple. Suddenly, entering the foreman's mind were the words, "You do the work and I will provide the workers." Shortly thereafter, qualified individuals became available and were hired.

From the art glass windows to the color palette of cream, light green, and light burgundy, the temple reflects in quiet tones the history and landscape of the area. The temple's precast concrete panels capture a pioneer flavor by depicting classical quilting motifs. Payson is also known for its heritage of apple orchards and wheat, both of which are visible throughout the temple. With 600 exterior windows and 600 interior windows, the Payson Utah Temple has more art glass than any other temple. The glasswork displays apple blossoms in different stages. Starting on the bottom floor in the baptistry, the apple blossoms are barely buds. Advancing to higher floors of the temple, the apple blossoms grow until they are in full bloom on the top floor of the temple.

The Payson Utah Temple features nineteen original pieces of art, many of which were created by local artists. The baptistry mural is a reproduction of a Leon Parson original painting created for the Calgary Alberta Temple. This mural includes forty-one animals, along with some bees and butterflies.

Further beautifying the temple's interior are delicate lace altar cloths. The altar cloths serve a practical purpose while being artistic expressions of faith. Local lace maker Jordan Anderson learned meaningful lessons as she crocheted her cloth for the temple. She explained, "Although I was provided a pattern, there were times I thought I knew better than the pattern . . . but I didn't. It wasn't until I humbled myself enough to really study the instructions that I gained an understanding of how to be successful with each motif. I had a moment of inspiration and felt the Spirit remind me that the scriptures and the words of the prophets are the pattern for our lives. Disregarding this pattern only brings frustration. Even more touching, was how

SITE
10.63 acres

GROUNDBREAKING
October 8, 2011

DEDICATION
June 7, 2015, by Henry B. Eyring

EXTERIOR
Concrete precast panels

TOTAL FLOOR AREA
96,630 square feet

DIMENSIONS
212-foot-tall central spire

HIDDEN IMAGE
Among the trees and landscaping to the right of the temple is an image of the Savior kneeling and looking up at the temple.

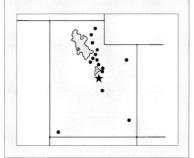

the experience helped my testimony of the Atonement grow. I made many, many mistakes in the process of completing the altar cloth. With every mistake I ripped out the mistake and changed my stitches to fix the problem. Once the cloth was completed, there was no evidence that mistakes were made and the result was a complete and flawless whole. The Savior does the same for us when we turn our mistakes over to Him for healing and grace."

The temple began blessing and changing lives soon after it was announced. Less-active member Arnold Beddoes said, "The Payson Temple has had a deep impact upon my life and my entire family." After forty-seven years of smoking three packs a day, a chain of events during the temple's construction turned a near tragedy into an eternal blessing. Brother Beddoes attended the temple's groundbreaking ceremony and listened to the prayer given by Elder Dallin H. Oaks. "I listened to the prayer intently," said Brother Beddoes. "He called the angels down to guard and protect the site. Those words really touched my heart, and the Holy Ghost testified to me that he is truly a man of God." Although Brother Beddoes began attending church and serving in his ward, he still had difficulty breaking the chain of daily smoking and drinking coffee. A few months later, he suffered a heart attack. He recalled, "As I recovered in the ICU, I couldn't smoke, so I thought, *this is my chance*. From that time on, I never had another cigarette or cup of coffee . . . not one! In my estimation, the Lord blessed me with a heart problem." Shortly after recovering, Brother Beddoes attended the Provo Utah Temple, accepted the call to be high priests group leader, and was eventually sealed with his eternal companion. Considering how his life had changed, he surmised, "People say I quit my habits because of my heart attack, but that's not what happened. . . . My heart was changed because of the grace of Jesus Christ. I believe it was the Spirit that comes with the temple that has the power to influence and change lives."

The month-long open house attracted over 500,000 visitors. Youth participated in a cultural celebration at BYU's LaVell Edwards Stadium on June 6, 2015. The following day, President Henry B. Eyring dedicated the temple in three sessions. The temple in Payson ranks as the tenth largest temple and was designed to support a significant volume of temple work. This beautiful temple is a direct reflection on members' faithful past and a tribute to the anticipated needs of a promising future.

Trujillo Peru Temple

Trujillo is northern Peru's largest city and is home to many of the nation's greatest treasures of antiquity. The warm Sechura desert and ocean breezes in this coastal city have contributed to the city being known as *La Ciudad de la Eterna Primavera*—"The City of Everlasting Spring." This city has also become a home to everlasting blessings.

For over half a century, Peru has been a stronghold for the Church and a fertile land of growth. The Trujillo Peru Stake was organized in 1978, and in 2013, Peru became just the fourth country to reach the 100-stake milestone. During this season of growth, the Peruvian Latter-day Saints have made the temple the anchor of their membership. Since the temple in Lima was dedicated in 1981, members began lengthy bus, train, and river excursions to the temple. Some days, the Lima Temple was so busy that patrons were required to patiently wait for hours before entering.

Members in northern Peru were understandably overjoyed when the First Presidency announced in December 2008 the building of a temple in Trujillo. On September 14, 2011, construction of the Trujillo Peru Temple formally commenced. The temple is in the archeological buffer zone of the UNESCO World Heritage Site of Chan Chan. Due to this close proximity, the Church was required to receive a special building permit before excavation could begin. During the excavation, a licensed state archeologist was on site to inspect the grounds for possible antiquity discoveries. Thankfully, nothing of

147

296

historical value was unearthed, and construction proceeded without delay.

Johnny and Kay Anderson faithfully served as the temple's special project missionaries. Elder Anderson's vast construction experience and love for others quickly earned him the respect of all those laboring on the temple. Early in his assignment, he approached a few workers and asked them if they were feeling okay. They responded that they were feeling fine. He asked if they were sure they were feeling fine. The workers again said they were just fine. Elder Anderson then said, "I don't think you are. I think you need this 'pill' to make you feel better." He then presented delicious candies and gave them to the workers to make them "feel better." Workers quickly realized that Elder Anderson always carried these tasty treats with him. As he walked around the construction site, workers occasionally played along by pretending to cough, which resulted in promptly receiving a candy from Elder Anderson.

"When we build a temple in a developing nation it creates a new standard for construction in the entire country," said a Church construction official. "The Church is a demanding client, and the workers need to rise to our standard. . . . The contractors always rise to the occasion, learn new skills, and accomplish something they never had before. They leave the project as better workers who then apply these skills on their future jobs. . . . It's a big step forward."

Renowned landscape artist Brad Aldridge received the commission to paint the murals for the temple's interior. To collect reference material, he traveled to Trujillo and explored the region's vast deserts, mountains, rivers, and unique vegetation. He explained his experience and painting as follows, "When I arrived in Trujillo to take reference photos for my mural, I was provided a cab driven by a member of the Church. I shared with him what I was looking for, and he always seemed to know where to go. I found a beautiful mango tree that I photographed and included in my painting. . . . To me this mango tree represents the Peruvian 'Tree of Life.' The mural's general design is based upon the valleys associated with the Rio Moche and Rio Chicama. The rainbow depicted on the back wall was painted from a photo taken near Machu Picchu. . . . At the end of the day, we picked up the cab driver's wife and went out to dinner. She had a nice yucca plant by her front door. I included

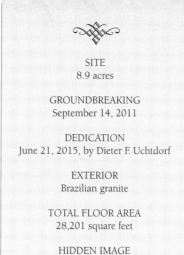

SITE
8.9 acres

GROUNDBREAKING
September 14, 2011

DEDICATION
June 21, 2015, by Dieter F. Uchtdorf

EXTERIOR
Brazilian granite

TOTAL FLOOR AREA
28,201 square feet

HIDDEN IMAGE
An image of the Christus statue is located among the clouds above the temple.

this exact yucca plant on the sisters' side of the painting in honor of their kindness."

The three tall windows between the small chapel and baptistry are clear with colored art glass around the edges. They were specifically designed to allow those in the adjoining small chapel to view the proceedings of the baptistry. As installation began, it was noticed that the colored edge along the bottom was blocking the view into the baptistry. Changing the glass windows at this late phase of construction presented challenges and additional cost. As Church authorities considered how to proceed, an accident occurred that shattered one of the three windows. Without explanation, one of the windows fell out of its position. Promptly after the event, newly designed clear windows were ordered and installed. A worker involved with the situation said, "The Lord wanted clear windows, and He got it."

Once complete, the temple doors were opened and Trujillo residents and their neighbors were invited for a look inside. Almost 100,000 people participated in the three-week open house. Sister missionaries served as hostesses during the entire open house. They welcomed guests by showing an introductory video, and after the tours they mingled with guests, answering questions and assisting visitors who wanted further information.

The day of the temple's dedication dawned with an overcast morning that gave way to sunshine. The peaceful Sabbath of June 21, 2015, will always be remembered by the 90,000 members the temple will serve. This sacred day was also celebrated as Father's Day in much of the world. This important holiday was not overlooked by President Uchtdorf, who noted that Father's Day was the perfect day to dedicate a new temple. "We are told to celebrate, honor and worship our Father in Heaven—and this is Father's Day," he said at the cornerstone ceremony of the dedication. "What an honor and a wonderful privilege it is to give to our Heavenly Father this house of the Lord."

In a land of remarkable history and people, including the Incas and other indigenous peoples, the house of the Lord has become a great spiritual symbol. In Trujillo, some of the world's greatest archeological treasures are located within walking distance of the eternal treasures found in the holy temple. The spiritual treasures of the restored gospel of Jesus Christ will help build the people and families who call Trujillo their home.

Indianapolis Indiana Temple

The Indianapolis Indiana Temple marks a milestone in the growth of Hoosier Mormonism. Compared to neighboring states, Indiana has been peripheral to Church history. As the Church moved west from New York in the 1800s, ultimately settling in Utah, missionaries often commuted through Indiana to the eastern states. Church roots began to be established as little congregations appeared in the early 1900s. These gatherings, often consisting of one or two families, would occur in members' homes. In recent years, the state's membership has grown to more than 43,000 members and 100 congregations. Church members are excited to finally see their dream of a temple come to fruition.

In early 2010, members of the Indianapolis Indiana North Stake were issued a formal challenge by their stake president to index one million names by the end of the year. While diligently working to achieve their ambitious goal, stake members were unknowingly preparing themselves for an upcoming incredible announcement. Within days of accomplishing their one-million-name goal, President Thomas S. Monson announced plans to build a temple in Indianapolis. Describing the reaction to the historic announcement, local member Emily Freeze said, "It was amazing for our stake to achieve our goal and then learn of our new temple. I think every member in our stake could tell you where they were when they found out that the temple was announced. . . . Members have been working hard and for a long time to prepare for a temple."

148

The Church acquired fifty acres of undeveloped farmland for the temple site in the Indianapolis suburb of Carmel. The temple grounds also include the newly completed Indianapolis Indiana North Stake Center and temple president's residence.

As Church representatives presented development plans to the Carmel board of zoning, local residents expressed concerns, which included open space retention, traffic patterns, retention pond preservation, and tree buffer maintenance. Church authorities promptly visited these residents to respectfully discuss their concerns and provide possible solutions. On May 23, 2011, favorable resolutions were made and the board of zoning voted 5–0 in favor of the temple project.

On a fall morning, September 29, 2012, some 500 Latter-day Saints, local dignitaries, and members of the media gathered for the temple's groundbreaking ceremonies. After nearly two years of steady construction progress, the temple reached a construction milestone when it received its angel Moroni statue on October 17, 2014. The statue weighs 900 pounds and required only a few minutes to be hoisted into position. For the Church members in attendance, the placement of the statue was a day to celebrate because it symbolized the near completion of the temple.

Much of the temple's exterior reflects prominent Indiana landmarks. In preparation for designing the temple, Church architects from Salt Lake City visited Indianapolis. They were shown the downtown area and visited war memorials and monuments celebrating Indiana history. The temple spire closely resembles the obelisk-shaped "Soldiers' and Sailors' Monument" located in the middle of a large traffic circle in the heart of the city.

Just north of the circle is the massive Indiana World War Memorial. This mausoleum-style limestone and marble structure has a unique pillared entrance and large brass doors. These features are reflected in the temple's front entrance with its large bronze doors.

The temple's principle design motifs are the Celtic knot pattern and the blossom of the tulip poplar—the Indiana state tree. These themes are tastefully integrated into the fencing, door handles, art glass, light fixtures, carpet, furniture, decorative painting, and cherry woodcarvings. Other repeated designs reference two nicknames of Indiana's capital city. The

SITE
18.11 acres

GROUNDBREAKING
September 29, 2012

DEDICATION
August 23, 2015, by Henry B. Eyring

EXTERIOR
Limestone cladding quarried
in Myra, Turkey

TOTAL FLOOR AREA
34,025 square feet

DIMENSIONS
106 feet, 4 inches tall, crowned with
a seven-foot angel Moroni statue

HIDDEN IMAGE
An image of the Christus statue is
located behind the water fountain.

shape of an "X" in the stained glass subtly reminds temple visitors that the city is known as the Crossroads of America. The round circles located in the stained glass and the outside fountain make reference to "the Circle City." These touches of "Indiana" in the temple anchor the temple to the community and state.

As the temple's highly anticipated open house approached, some out-of-state Christian opponents stirred controversy by distributing an antagonistic twelve-page advertising supplement in community newspapers. Their aggressive campaign backfired and only piqued curiosity about the temple and increased empathy for the Church. Leaders of interfaith groups responded by publically voicing their support for the Church and temple. Chris Duckworth, pastor of New Joy Lutheran Church in Westfield, said, "We don't treat people, who have been seriously picked on, in that way. We know better than that. We are better than that."

A newspaper editorial submitted by the Center of Interfaith Cooperation stated, "In our experience of working directly with members of the Mormon community, we have witnessed overwhelming generosity and a dedication to service that emulates the very best of American values. We encourage you to join us in extending our tradition of Hoosier hospitality as The Church of Jesus Christ of Latter-day Saints (Mormons) dedicate their new temple this summer."

The level of excitement for the open house far exceeded expectation. The final total of visitors participating in the three-week event was 90,109. Summarizing the event's positive outcome are the words written by a seven-year-old boy who submitted the first comment card. He wrote, "I was so happy I thought my heart would pop."

Prior to the temple dedication, on August 22, 2015, a cultural celebration entitled "Gather to the Light" was held commemorating the heritage of the Indianapolis region through narration, song, and dance. The celebration was held at the Michael Carroll Track & Field Stadium on the campus of Indiana University–Purdue University Indianapolis. Local composer Garrett Breeze created an inspired song exclusively for the celebration. The following finely crafted lyrics seem to capture joyous emotions of the newly completed House of the Lord: "We've waited long to see His word fulfilled; Our lives will shine with his truth revealed."

Tijuana Mexico Temple

Tijuana Mexico is located just twenty miles south of San Diego, California and is a border town on the Baja California Peninsula. Since 1993, faithful members of the Church have been making great sacrifices to cross the border to worship and receive their temple blessings at the San Diego California Temple. On October 2, 2010, at the commencement of the 180th general conference, President Thomas S. Monson provided fresh optimism for the Baja Saints by announcing the building of the Tijuana Mexico Temple. The Saints received the news with jubilation and were humbled at the privilege of having a house of the Lord in their midst. For the approximately forty-five percent of faithful recommend holders who cannot enter the United States and attend the temple

in San Diego, the presence of a temple in Tijuana means the twelve-hour bus ride to the nearest temple in Hermosillo will no longer be necessary.

The groundbreaking for Mexico's thirteenth temple was held on August 18, 2012. The 2,000 Latter-day Saints in attendance gathered under the dusty desert sun while the event was broadcast to stake centers throughout the temple district. By the time construction workers began the task to build the temple, members had already started a work of preparing 300,000 new names for temple service.

Church leaders wanted the temple to be more than just a religious edifice; they wanted the building to make a powerful statement to the people of Tijuana. According to the temple's principal architect,

149

Wally Cooper, "There was a conscientious effort to create a temple that said: 'you are incredibly important to our Church and your temple is equal to any other.'" The temple designers pushed the limit to create a more visually striking structure that would stand out against the crowded Tijuana backdrop. "It had to be something that was truly outstanding," he says. Even before completion, the temple had earned the 2015 Design Award Winner: Best International Building Structure, awarded by a leading trade organization.

While the Temple maintains a respectful appearance as a house of the Lord, it also reflects the historical flavor of Mexican and Spanish Colonial styles. "For nearly three years," explained Cooper, "we did a great deal of careful precedent study in areas throughout Tijuana, Arizona, and even Spain. When we submitted our final design to the Church, we were worried that it would not be accepted because it was so different from anything else previously built. We were delighted when we received word that 'the Brethren loved it.'"

Elder Benjamin De Hoyos of the Seventy compared the temple to the old Spanish Missions and colonial churches in the area. "Those early Spanish friars were very valiant in their preaching and building," he said. "And today, we in Mexico are very comfortable with the style of those churches. The temple will be an emblem for the entire Tijuana community."

Enhancing the beauty of the instruction room is a large mural created by master landscape artist Keith Bond. "I traveled the Baja Peninsula for a week to collect reference material for my painting," the artist explained. "I wanted my painting to depict an entire scene that would be recognizable for members living along the coast and those who live inland. I had a clear vision of how the mural would look, however, the mural was going to wrap around walls within the temple and I did not know how I should create a transition from one wall to the next. My trip was nearly over, and I did not have a solution for the transition. On the last day of my trip, my father [who was with me on the trip] asked if we could go back to speak with someone who he had spoken to earlier and give him a Book of Mormon. So we went back, and as my dad gave him a Book of Mormon, I saw the missing piece I had been searching for. I saw the transition area my painting needed. In my mind, it is not a coincidence that the man who received the Book of Mormon was in the exact spot that needed to be in my painting."

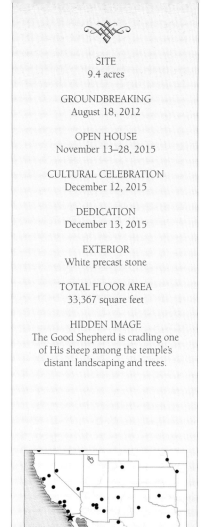

SITE
9.4 acres

GROUNDBREAKING
August 18, 2012

OPEN HOUSE
November 13–28, 2015

CULTURAL CELEBRATION
December 12, 2015

DEDICATION
December 13, 2015

EXTERIOR
White precast stone

TOTAL FLOOR AREA
33,367 square feet

HIDDEN IMAGE
The Good Shepherd is cradling one of His sheep among the temple's distant landscaping and trees.

With 108 mature palms, 292 trees, over 14,000 shrubs and perennials, and two stunning water features, the temple oasis has become a standout landmark in the region. "There is nothing remotely close to this in Tijuana," explained landscape project manager Perry Brätt. "All of the plant stock originated within Mexico, so the largest challenge was simply finding the required vegetation. We had to travel as far away as Mexico City (nearly 2,000 miles away). We often traveled two to three days with fully loaded and refrigerated semi-trailers. . . . People did not mind selling us their trees, but it was quite a challenge to locate healthy trees that were all the same height and size. Our goal was to find trees that would look unified once they were planted."

As the building neared completion, the temple's first president was selected and called. "Our call came as a great surprise," explained Clark B. Hinckley. "Sister Hinckley and I had actually submitted papers to serve a temple mission in the United States. A few days after submitting our papers, we received an invitation to meet with President Henry B. Eyring. President Eyring indicated that he had a new calling for us and asked if we were willing to accept it—without telling us what it was! It was a great lesson in being willing to do whatever we are asked."

Prior to completion, the Mormon temple was solidifying its position as a highly respected and prized part of the community. The city demonstrated its appreciation by enhancing the surrounding area by rebuilding a roundabout and adding street medians and landscaping. Additionally, eight months before the temple's dedication, the building was featured in highway billboards and posters around the city to advertise the Tijuana Grand Prix. This annual mega-event is a road race that adjusted its 2015 course to pass in front of the temple.

The temple's three dedicatory sessions occurred on December 13, 2015. The dedicated temple is the nation's thirteenth temple. The Tijuana Mexico Temple is a tribute of faith representing how far the Church has progressed and how the gospel has taken firm root in the soil of Mexico. The faithful Mexican Latter-day Saints have a reputation for finding a sparkle of joy in trials. This temple in their midst means they won't have to look quite as hard for that joy.

Provo City Center Temple

In the cold, early-morning hours of Friday, December 17, 2010, a fire raged undetected for hours in the attic of the Provo Tabernacle. Provo Firefighter B Platoon was dispatched at 2:43 a.m., and within minutes, numerous fire trucks and emergency vehicles raced through the early morning darkness to the centerpiece of downtown Provo. The expanding inferno engulfed the roof's large wooden timbers and exceeded the capacity of firefighters to extinguish the blaze and salvage the building. By 6:00 a.m., most of the tabernacle's roof had collapsed, pulling down the brick gables on the sides of the building. By Friday afternoon, what had once been a Utah landmark and treasured icon was little more than a charred shell heaving ash onto mourning onlookers.

As news of the disaster spread and the shock of the event was becoming a reality, the Church issued the following statement: "The fire at the Provo Tabernacle is tragic. The building not only serves our members and the community, but is a reminder of the pioneering spirit that built Utah. The damage appears severe and until we make a structural assessment we won't know whether this historic treasure will be able to be saved."

After more than 130 years of bringing the community together to celebrate and worship, the building's scorched brick shell sat cold and dormant for nearly a year. Throughout this time, members speculated on how the Church would determine the building's fate. Finally, during the October 2011 general

150

conference, President Thomas S. Monson made the following historic announcement, "After careful study, we have decided to re-build it with full preservation and restoration of the exterior, to become the second temple of the Church in the city of Provo." This news was received by gasps throughout the Conference Center. It has been called a phoenix rising out of the ashes.

Before construction could begin, archeological teams were given a five-month assignment to look for artifacts and learn more about the property. The team uncovered the remains of the first LDS baptistry in Utah County and a basement of the site's original meetinghouse built in the late 1850s. Archaeologists sifted through dirt, rock, and other debris in the basement and discovered artifacts including beads, horseshoes, scissors, slate pencils, pieces of ceramics, a small doll pin, marbles, and even two bullets. Richard Talbot, director of BYU's Office of Public Archaeology, explained, "This has been sacred ground since the Old Tabernacle was dedicated in 1867. I hope people see the parallels and the connections between the soon-to-be constructed temple and the Old Tabernacle. I believe there is a bond between the past and the present that is manifest in this site. I like to imagine how excited the first pioneers who built this meetinghouse would be to know that their sacrifice and toil has ultimately resulted in a temple of God."

President Thomas S. Monson set the tone and direction of the Provo City Center project when he announced the temple by using the words "preservation" and "restoration." These two words declared the temple's design and materials would preserve and restore the legacy of the old tabernacle. The action of preserving the tabernacle actually began the day of the fire. Church historians and curators immediately began a six-month effort to painstakingly go through the rubble to document the building's details and retrieve any salvageable items.

In order to build a new temple within and under the tabernacle while preserving the original structure, cutting-edge construction and engineering technologies were used. Workers first stabilized the building's shell by giving the walls more strength. Once the exterior was stabilized, crews rested the 6.8-million-pound tabernacle on 40-foot steel stilts. For months, the tabernacle remained suspended in air while workers excavated the ground underneath. Although the pile-supported elevation technique had been previously used, it had never before been

GROUNDBREAKING
May 12, 2012

DEDICATION
March 20, 2016

EXTERIOR
Fully restored brickwork

ORIGINAL TABERNACLE
30,000 square feet

TOTAL FLOOR AREA
Approximately 85,084 square feet

DIMENSIONS
127 feet to top of spire

HIDDEN IMAGE
Among the trees is an image of the Savior. Additionally, the Provo Utah Temple is rendered in the distant vegetation behind the temple.

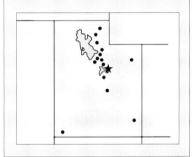

attempted on a structure nearly 130 years old. Andy Kirby, the temple's project manager, said, "As a construction project, it is unique in all the world." Laser monitors and load sensors were used to alert engineers of any changes in elevation or material stress, no matter how slight.

The successful transformation from tabernacle to temple is a testament of the commitment the Church has to historical preservation. David Hall, director of temple design services in the Church's special projects department, said, "With the building being repurposed as a temple, it is not possible to restore the building interior in its entirety. Rather significant efforts have been made to cast the new temple's interior design consistent with the architectural styles used in the original tabernacle. Upon entering the new temple, its familiarity to the historic tabernacle will be evident."

The Victorian theme is carried throughout the interior design and furnishings. The building features oak and walnut woods, rich colors in the wallpaper, and decorative stencil painting. The upper floors of the temple are in a pioneer gothic style featuring a number of arches. The exterior finish includes fully restored brickwork, and the entire temple is detailed with installations of art glass, finials, and original hardware salvaged from the Provo Tabernacle remains. Three of the spires, which have original timbers on the inside, were repaired and placed back on the temple. The fourth spire sustained extensive fire damage and was completely replaced. Scalloped slate shingles matching the original 1800s design were used on the roof. On the south side, a seventeen-foot, four-tiered bronze Victorian fountain with ornamental nozzles graces the grounds near the gazebo.

Throughout the construction process, the tabernacle's dramatic rebirth garnered interest throughout the western United States. Church leaders therefore anticipated receiving over 750,000 visitors during its celebrated seven-week open house. More than five years after flames emblazed the Provo night, the tabernacle became a house of the Lord on March 20, 2016. The three dedicatory sessions were broadcast to all stakes and districts in Utah.

The Provo City Center Temple is a tangible bond between the past and the present. The heavenly structure stands as a memorial to pioneer craftsmanship and faith. Their sacrifice and toil ultimately resulted in the Provo City Center Temple—THE 150TH TEMPLE OF THE CHURCH.

150 Interesting Temple Facts

1. In December 2001, the Christmas lights surrounding the Washington D.C. Temple glowed in red, white, and blue to honor those who died in the tragic events of September 11th, 2001.

2. The St. George Utah Temple's baptismal font weighs nine tons.

3. The two most distant temples from Church headquarters in Salt Lake City are the Johannesburg South Africa Temple (9,930 miles) and the Perth Australia Temple (9,723 miles).

4. The Kona Hawaii Temple has special nighttime flood lighting that shines down on the temple. The temple is lit after dark with special lights that have hoods permitting only downward light. This is due the city's building codes preventing upward light from reaching the Big Island's Mauna Kea Observatory.

5. On April 7, 1893, at the close of the Salt Lake Temple's dedicatory services, Emma Bennett of Provo, Utah, gave birth to a son in the temple. Eight days later Emma returned with her husband and new son for a blessing, in which Joseph F. Smith named the baby boy "Joseph Temple Bennett."

6. Joseph F. Smith was the only man to serve as prophet and as a temple president (of the Salt Lake Temple) at the same time.

7. On Friday, September 21, 2001, the angel Moroni statue was placed on top of the Nauvoo Illinois, The Hague Netherlands, and the Boston Massachusetts Temples. The day marked the 178th anniversary of Moroni first appearing to Joseph Smith.

8. Five temples have names that do not reflect their city of origin: the Jordan River Utah Temple, Mount Timpanogos Utah Temple, Winter Quarters Nebraska Temple, Columbia River Washington Temple, and Oquirrh Mountain Utah Temple.

9. The rebuilt Nauvoo Illinois Temple was dedicated June 27–30, 2002. The first dedicatory session began during the hour and on the day of the 158th anniversary of the martyrdom of Joseph Smith and his brother Hyrum at Carthage Jail.

10. In 2002, the Christmas lights at Temple Square remained lit until the conclusion of the historic Salt Lake City 2002 Olympics. The colors were modified to appeal to both Christmas and Olympic visitors. Many more clear bulbs were used rather than the traditional red, green, and gold.

11. Following the announcement of rebuilding of the Nauvoo Illinois Temple, thousands of tradespeople and contractors requested the opportunity to bid on the temple's construction.

12. Both the original Nauvoo Temple (1846) and the rebuilt Nauvoo Illinois Temple (2002) have the same base and width dimensions (128 feet by 88 feet).

13. In May 2001, Briggs & Stratton, a manufacturer of lawn mowers and other outdoor power equipment, called the gardens at Temple Square and Church Office Building Plaza one of the top ten most impressive lawns and landscapes in the country.

14. The Salt Lake Temple and Anchorage Alaska Temple are the only temples to feature the constellation Ursa Major (Big Dipper) on the exterior.

15. The American Society of Landscape Architects honored the Church in July 1999 with a "once-in-a-century medallion award for its world-renowned landscaping and gardens at Church headquarters in Salt Lake City."

16. Six Subway sandwich shops in the Tri-Cities Washington area provided a variety of gourmet cookies for the 65,000 visitors attending the Columbia River Washington Temple open house.

17. At the dedication of the Stockholm Sweden Temple on March 17, 1984, the temperature was so cold that torches were used to thaw the icy ground in preparation for the ceremonial first turning of the soil.

18. During construction of the Snowflake Arizona Temple, the number eight green of the neighboring Snowflake Municipal Golf Course was purchased by the Church. The golf course facilitated the purchase by creating another green and adjusting other greens and fairways.

19. During construction of the Raleigh North Carolina Temple, category-4 Hurricane Floyd was headed toward the city. Four proselyting missionaries quickly tied loose items down and rid the site of anything that could cause damage. On September 16, 1999, the storm's path changed, causing no damage to the temple and leaving only puddles on the construction site.

20. The state of Illinois manufactured 600 official auto license plates that bear the image of the Nauvoo Illinois Temple with the temple's originally scheduled 2002 open house dates.

21. Prior to receiving an angel Moroni statue, the spire of the Provo Utah Temple was once struck by lightning, causing temple's fire alarm to automatically be set off.

22. The Visitors' Center on Temple Square celebrated its 100-year anniversary on August 4, 2002.

23. On June 29, 2002, the Mormon Tabernacle Choir recorded *Music and the Spoken Word* from the grassy hill west of the newly dedicated Nauvoo Illinois Temple.

24. Most temples feature baptistries underground. The Manhattan New York Temple was built out of an existing structure and features a baptistry on the first floor in a location originally occupied by two restaurants.

25. A recumbent horizontal angel flew briefly on the Assembly Hall on Temple Square in Salt Lake City.

26. The Nauvoo Illinois Temple is the only temple to feature a bell and exterior clock. The four clocks display specially designed hands patterned after those on the original Nauvoo Temple.

27. Visitors' centers are located near the Idaho Falls Idaho, Laie Hawaii, London England, Los Angeles California, Mesa Arizona, Mexico City, Nauvoo Illinois, Hamilton New Zealand, Oakland California, Rome Italy, St. George Utah, Salt Lake, and Washington D.C. Temples.

28. Over 720,000 visitors attended the San Diego California Temple open house. The temple's carpet is wear dated for fifteen years. One week's worth of open house visitor traffic is equal to three years of normal wear.

29. The Nauvoo Temple is such a tall building that the Nauvoo Fire Department received a new aerial ladder fire truck in order to be prepared for it. The Church and a number of other state and local entities provided the funding.

30. Moonstones on the perimeter of the Palmyra New York Temple depict twenty-one phases of the moon at moonrise in two-week intervals. The moonstone found on the center of the temple's west side represents June 27, 1844, the date of the Prophet Joseph's martyrdom. The stone is placed on the temple's west side to face the Sacred Grove.

31. The unique acoustics of the celestial room in the Lubbock Texas Temple allow for whispers to travel across the room.

32. An enclosed garden at the site commonly called Temple Beach is located 2,500 feet away from the Laie Hawaii Temple. This peaceful garden is a place for quiet meditation and can facilitate baptisms in the Pacific Ocean.

33. The architecture of three temples includes bell towers: the Nauvoo Illinois, Redlands California, and Tijuana Mexico Temples. Of these, only the Nauvoo Temple has a bell.

34. In December 2010, the Provo Tabernacle fire occurred when a lighting technician mistakenly set a 300-watt light fixture on a wooden speaker box in the attic.

TEMPLE FIRSTS

First Temple Built outside the United States
Cardston Alberta Temple

First Temple in Southern Hemisphere
Hamilton New Zealand Temple

First European Temple
Bern Switzerland Temple

First Temple Built in the State of Utah
Ogden Utah Temple (earlier temples were dedicated in Utah Territory)

First Temple to Present Ordinances in a Language Other Than English
Mesa Arizona Temple (Spanish)

First Temple to Perform Endowments for the Dead
St. George Utah Temple

First Temple to Be Converted from Existing Building
Vernal Utah Temple

First Temple to Use a Movie Instead of Live Actors
Bern Switzerland Temple

First Temple to Be Built in a Communist Nation
Freiberg Germany Temple

First Temple Capable of Holding More Than One Endowment Session at a Time
Oakland California Temple

35. Near disaster was averted in July 2003, when an arson fire engulfed the hillside where the Reno Nevada Temple sits. High winds whipped the fast-moving blaze within feet of the temple. Thanks to fast-acting firefighters, no injuries or structural damage was reported.

36. Occasionally, neighbors raise concerns over newly announced temples. These concerns frequently include the height of the spire, nighttime lighting, and an increase of traffic.

37. The original bell that was once in the Nauvoo Temple is now housed in a monument on Temple Square. In observance of a National Day of Prayer and Remembrance in the wake of the September 11th, 2001, attacks, the Nauvoo Bell tolled for three minutes at noon.

38. The Vernal Utah Temple, Copenhagen Denmark Temple, Manhattan New York Temple, and Provo City Center Temple were built from existing structures.

39. Idaho Falls Idaho Temple architect John Fetzer Sr. based his temple design on "an ancient Nephite temple" that was revealed to him in a dream.

40. While building The Hague Netherlands Temple, workers climbed the scaffolding in their traditional wooden shoes as part of a Dutch tradition known as "het hoogste punt."

41. On November 14, 1962, a plastic explosive device was attached to the doorknobs of the east doors of the Salt Lake Temple. Once detonated, windows were shattered and the original pioneer doors and hardware were damaged or destroyed.

42. At least one session of the April 1893 general conference was held in the upper room of the Salt Lake Temple when President Wilford Woodruff dedicated the temple.

43. The Temple Riders Association breaks the mold of the typical biker club. These motorcycle-riding brothers and sisters make cross-country trips to serve in temples and visit scenic locations.

44. The greatest number of viewers to witness the placing of an angel Moroni statue was on the Nauvoo Illinois Temple. On September 21, 2001, at least 500 people witnessed the event in person and an untold number participated remotely via a live Internet stream.

45. Located at twenty-three feet below sea level, The Hague Netherlands Temple is built at the lowest elevation of any temple.

46. At 2° 9' 22.49" S latitude, the Guayaquil Ecuador Temple is the closest temple to the equator.

47. The Manhattan New York Temple cornerstone contains a time capsule that includes a commemorative white satin

handkerchief with gold detailing patterned after one Joseph Smith commissioned for the dedication of the first latter-day temple in Kirtland, Ohio.

48. The underground parking garage of The Hague Netherlands Temple allows for the parking of as many bicycles as cars.

49. Four prophets have also served as temple presidents: Wilford Woodruff (St. George Utah Temple, Lorenzo Snow (Salt Lake Temple, Joseph F. Smith (Salt Lake Temple), Joseph Fielding Smith (Salt Lake Temple).

50. The Manhattan New York Temple's cornerstone is the only one located on a temple's interior wall, between the entrance and the elevator to the chapel.

51. During the years of above-ground nuclear testing in Nevada, the light of the massive nuclear explosions could be seen 370 miles away in Salt Lake City. In 1955, photos demonstrating this were taken of the Salt Lake Temple, showing the temple silhouetted against the glowing nuclear sky.

52. The most interesting phone number associated with a temple was for the Washington D.C. Temple Visitors' Center. During the United States Bicentennial celebration in 1976, visitors could dial 667–6667 to schedule visits to the temple. On a phone number keypad, the phone number spells M-O-R-M-O-N-S.

53. The most temples dedicated in the shortest amount of time occurred on May 20–21, 2000, when the Tampico Mexico Temple, Nashville Tennessee Temple, and Villahermosa Mexico Temple were dedicated.

54. Ten temples had their angel Moroni statues added after their dedication: the Idaho Falls, Bern Switzerland, London England, Ogden Utah, Provo Utah, São Paulo Brazil, Tokyo Japan, Freiberg Germany, Boston Massachusetts, and Manhattan New York Temples.

55. The dedication of the Johannesburg South Africa Temple on August 24, 1985, marked the first time when a temple was located on every inhabited continent.

56. The Andean language of Quechua, dating back to before AD 500, is thought to be the oldest language in which the temple ceremony has been given. Offered only in temples in Peru, it is the most widely spoken language family of the indigenous peoples of the Americas.

57. The Manhattan New York Temple is built in a remodeled building that once occupied a heath club's racquetball courts.

TEMPLE DIMENSIONS AND LOCATIONS

Tallest Temple
Washington D.C. Temple (288 feet)

Largest Temple Site
Washington D.C. Temple (52 acres)

Smallest Temple Site
Hong Kong China Temple (.3 acres)
Manhattan New York Temple (.3 acres)

Largest Temple
Salt Lake Temple (382,207 square feet including annex)

Smallest Temple
Colonia Juárez Mexico Temple (6,000 square feet)

Lowest Elevation
The Hague Netherlands Temple (23 feet below sea level)

Highest Elevation
Cochabamba Bolivia Temple (8,738 feet above sea level)

Northernmost Temple
Anchorage Alaska Temple (61.1 degrees latitude)

Southernmost Temple
Melbourne Australia Temple (-37.8 degrees latitude)

Largest Temple Outside the U.S.
Mexico City Mexico Temple (116,642 square feet)

58. Those who know and revere the musical accomplishments of American composers will appreciate the Manhattan New York Temple being located adjacent to a street named Leonard Bernstein Place.

59. Due to the unique schooling, career, and performing arts opportunities of New York City, an unusually large number of the Manhattan New York Temple workers are young single adults.

60. Volunteers skilled in calligraphy helped address 650 envelopes containing invitations to the Raleigh North Carolina VIP open house tour.

61. On January 2, 1901, Emma Ray Riggs and David O. McKay became the first couple in the twentieth century to be married in the Salt Lake Temple.

62. Among the temples located closest to a coastline are the Laie Hawaii Temple (2,093 feet), Suva Fiji Temple (2,613 feet), and Apia Somoa Temple (3,235 feet).

63. During the dedication ceremony of the San Diego California Temple, a chirping bird was trapped in the celestial room. President Gordon B. Hinckley made remarks about the bird during the dedicatory proceedings.

64. Many Native Americans of the Washakie Tribe labored to build the Logan Utah Temple and considered it an honor to do so.

65. The first 150 temples are located in forty-two different countries.

66. The images of only two temples are reflected in neighboring waterways: the Idaho Falls Idaho Temple in the Snake River and The Hague Netherlands Temple in a traditional Dutch canal that flows behind the temple.

67. In June 2000, four temples were completed and ready for dedication almost simultaneously. On a single extended trip, President Gordon B. Hinckley dedicated the Fukuoka Japan Temple on June 11, Adelaide Australia Temple on June 15, Melbourne Australia Temple on June 16, and Suva Fiji Temple on June 18.

68. Due to strategic placement of clear windows, the angel Moroni statue is visible from within the San Diego California Temple and Billings Montana Temple.

69. The Freiberg Temple was constructed from 1983 to 1985 under the Communistic rule of the German Democratic Republic.

70. The Nauvoo Illinois Temple and Apia Samoa Temple are the only two temples to be destroyed by fire and later rebuilt.

71. The Redlands California Temple sits on the original Mormon landholdings of the San Bernardino colony, established in 1851 under the direction of Brigham Young.

72. The historic Washington D.C. chapel was the inspiration for the exterior design of the Houston Texas Temple. The Washington D.C. chapel was the first LDS church built east of the Rocky Mountains after the Saints left Nauvoo.

73. Of the first 150 temples, thirty-two operate with a primary language of Spanish.

74. What do the Houston Texas Temple and Westminster Abbey have in common? Both places of worship are beautified by art glass designed by London artist Graham Jones. He designed the art glass for the entire Houston Temple and replaced some Westminster Abbey glass that was destroyed during World War II.

75. In 1945, at the conclusion of World War II, a German prisoner-of-war camp was established directly across from the Idaho Falls Idaho Temple. The temple gardener, Robert Frederick August Woller, a native of Germany, visited the camp on many occasions. He recorded that it was "a great privilege to preach the gospel to the German prisoners of war in the German language."

76. The Kyiv Ukraine Temple is positioned directly on the approach of runway 26 of Kyiv's large Zhuliany International Airport and has an airplane-warning beacon on its spire.

77. The Harrision New York Temple was announced on September 30, 1995. Due to overwhelming opposition, legal battles, and the need for a temple in the heart of New York City, the Harrison temple was abandoned and focus was placed on the Manhattan New York Temple.

78. The Helsinki Finland Temple experienced overwhelming attendance during its three-week open house. Church officials who set a goal of 25,000 visitors were amazed when 56,000 attended.

79. During the construction of many worldwide temples, "temple cams" have been strategically positioned to allow curious online viewers to follow construction process.

80. In the early morning of October 15, 2006, a magnitude-6.7 earthquake struck the Hawaiian Islands. No damage was reported to the Laie Hawaii Temple and the Kona Temple received only chandelier damage.

81. In Accra, Ghana, city officials were slow to provide building permits because in their estimation, the temple was not elaborate enough. Knowing the temple would beautify and add prestige to the republic's capital, city officials strongly encouraged the Church to aggrandize the temple as much as possible.

82. Encompassing twelve time zones and two continents, the Helsinki Finland Temple has the largest district of any temple.

ANGEL MORONI STATUES

First Temple with an Angel
Nauvoo Temple

First Temple Statue Designated as Moroni
Salt Lake Temple

Versions of the Angel Moroni Statue
6

Only Temple to Feature Moroni in Unique Clothing
Los Angeles Temple (Mayan designs)

Tallest Moroni
Jordan River Utah Temple (20 feet)

Only Temple to Have a White Moroni
Monticello Utah Temple (later replaced with a gold version)

Only Chapel with an Angel Moroni Statue
The Washington D.C. Chapel

Only Statue Not Placed on Top of a Building
The Hill Cumorah Monument

Heaviest Moroni
Washington D.C. Temple (4,000 pounds)

83. The Oquirrh Mountain Temple and the Jordan River Temple are the only temples located in same city and sharing the same zip code (84095). The Provo Utah Temple and the Provo City Center Temple are located in the same city.

84. The Freiberg Germany Temple was dedicated on June 29, 1985. Less than a year later, the city of Freiberg celebrated its 800th anniversary.

85. On February 1, 1883, the first telephone exchange was opened in Logan, Utah. The city's original telephone poles were purchased from the Logan Temple. These poles had been used for the scaffolding in building the temple.

86. For nearly ninety years, the Mesa Arizona Temple was the last temple built without a spire. Future temples without spires include the Meridian Idaho Temple and Paris France Temple.

87. Prior to the Church owning the property where the Freiberg Germany Temple now stands, two elderly couples owned the land. These owners had been ejected from the land during the Communistic reign of the German Democratic Republic. Laws at that time required the Church to pay the landowners only a fraction of its real retail value, but the Church volunteered to pay nearly three times the required price.

88. Nearly nine years after its announcement, ground was broken for the Kyiv Ukraine Temple on June 23, 2007. The historic event served as a tribute to President Gordon B. Hinckley on his ninety-seventh birthday.

89. The Communistic rule of the German Democratic Republic had a Ministry of State Security know as the "Stasi." Thousands of citizens were recruited to act as covert informants. It is on record that at least twenty-one undercover informers were assigned to monitor the Freiberg Temple's 1985 open house.

90. Likely Utah's most sacred mountain, Ensign Peak has an elevation of 5,414 and is located behind the Utah State Capitol, only about 1,100 feet above the city streets. Not long after the pioneers arrived in the Salt Lake Valley, Ensign Peak was also used for a brief period as an outdoor temple until the Endowment House was constructed.

91. In a sense, the open house of the Mesa Arizona Temple lasted for two years and the Cardston Alberta Temple open house lasted for three years. Public tours were frequently given during the final years of construction of those temples.

92. Moroni statues are obvious targets for lightning strikes. They are metallic-covered objects perched on high temple spires.

Lightning damage and pollution are the two main causes for the statues to be replaced or repaired.

93. When pressure from mobs forced the Saints to evacuate Nauvoo, members of the Lamoreaux family recovered the temple's bell before they headed west. On a stormy night, the bell was put in a wagon, pulled by hand to the edge of the Mississippi River, and carefully concealed in the water. Andrew Lamoreaux and his brother David brought the bell to Utah with their families.

94. In 1967, President David O. McKay and Mark Garff, chairman of the Church's building committee, considered the building of a "Temple Ship." The ship would sail into ports, "making a continuous tour of where there are people needing the blessing of the temple and the holy endowment." The project was never finalized.

95. If the Independence Missouri Temple had been built in the earlier years of the Church, it would have looked very similar to the Kirtland Temple. As recorded by Frederick G. Williams, both temples were to have similar window layouts, floor plan, and interior details.

96. In the unfinished Nauvoo Temple, on Sunday, October 5, 1845, the Church held its first general conference in three years. With newly installed windows and a temporary floor, it became the only general conference ever held within a temple after its enclosure.

97. On May 27, 1850, a tornado demolished much of what was left of the Nauvoo Temple. Sizeable fragments of carved stone, including parts of the stone oxen and the sun, moon, and star stones, were removed for souvenirs.

98. With the threat of losing temples to the U.S. government because of polygamy, Wilford Woodruff issued the Manifesto repealing polygamy, which saved the temples.

99. Many people are familiar with the story that the Founding Fathers of the United States appeared to Wilford Woodruff in the St. George Utah Temple and requested that their temple work be completed. Interestingly, not only was temple work completed for them but also for other historical figures, including Henry Clay, Christopher Columbus, Frederick the Great, Washington Irving, Thomas "Stonewall" Jackson, Sir Walter Scott, Amerigo Vespucci, Daniel Webster, John Wesley, Jane Austen, Charlotte Brontë, Marie Antoinette, and Martha Washington.

100. Many years prior to the completion of the Freiburg Germany Temple, a little-known proposal was made in the late 1970s to provide temple blessings to faithful members living

BUILDING MATERIALS

Gilbert Arizona Temple
180,000 pieces of hand-cut art glass

Logan Utah Temple
24,000 pounds of nails; 2,144 yards of homemade carpet

Fort Lauderdale Florida Temple
70 tubes of paint (300 mL each) required for murals

Oquirrh Mountain Utah Temple
17,096 exterior stones; 47 miles of wood; 80 miles of electrical wiring

Sacramento California Temple
10 million pounds of concrete

St. George Utah Temple
1,000,000 feet of lumber

Rexburg Idaho Temple
8,000 crystals in celestial room chandelier

Newport Beach Temple
200 tons of rebar; over 3,000 cubic yards of concrete (earthquake engineering)

Redlands California Temple
2,702,000 pounds of granite

Nauvoo Illinois Temple
30 sunstones, moonstones, and star stones

Payson Utah Temple
900 tons of high-quality structural steel

behind the Iron Curtain. Although never built, an endowment house was considered to feature a meetinghouse on one side and an endowment facility on the other.

101. The Logan Utah Temple's rugged exterior is formed out of dark-colored limestone. Originally, the temple's dark color was covered by a stunning white paint. Within a few years, the paint was wearing off and a decision was made to leave the stone's natural beauty exposed.

102. The Laie Hawaii Temple was the first temple to be built beyond the continental limits of the United States; it was the first to be dedicated of three temples of a similar design; it was also the first wherein Saints residing in Asian and Polynesian countries received living endowments.

103. An estimated 200,000 people toured the Mesa Arizona Temple during its final two years of construction. Mesa's total population was less than 4,000, and 200,000 was about half the population of Arizona.

104. In 1953, a young staff member in the Missionary Department named Gordon B. Hinckley was given the assignment by President David O. McKay to create a method of presenting the temple ordinances in eight languages. Weeks later, the future President Hinckley proposed portraying the ordinances in movie form. Once the idea was approved, the fifth floor of the Salt Lake Temple was organized into a sacred movie set.

105. On the temple property adjacent to the Oakland California Temple is a large meetinghouse that originally served the three stakes in the area. The building features a large 1,800-seat auditorium and a massive cultural hall. When the NBA's Philadelphia Warriors moved to San Francisco in 1962, they used the building as their practice facility for a brief time.

106. Adjacent to the Salt Lake Temple, Ogden Utah Temple, and Brigham City Utah Temple are previously built tabernacles.

107. Incredibly, about twenty people who attended the dedication of the Salt Lake Temple in 1893 also made it to the Jordan River Temple dedication, which took place 88 years later in 1981.

108. In July 2009, the Atlanta Georgia Temple was closed for extensive renovations. New uses were found for many of the original building materials, including a piece of stonework that was fashioned into a podium for the chapel.

109. The first three temples to have six spires are the Salt Lake, Washington D.C., and Boise Idaho Temples.

110. The new Nauvoo Illinois Temple features a 1,000-pound bronze-alloy replica of the original bell. The new bell features

the engravings of two years, 2001 (the year of its casting) and 2002 (the year of the temple's completion). On September 21, 2001, spectators cheered as a statue of the angel Moroni was set into place and the bell chimed seven times.

111. Many of the world's temples are located on streets named after the temple. A few of these include the Salt Lake (North Temple Street), Manti Utah (Temple Hill), Bern Switzerland (Tempelstrasse), Hamilton New Zealand (Temple View), Provo Utah (Temple Hill Drive), Manila Philippines (Temple Drive), Las Vegas (Temple View Drive), Stockholm Sweden (Tempelvägen), Madrid Spain (Calle del Templo), Palmyra New York (Temple Road), Preston England (Temple Way), Aba Nigeria (Temple Road [nickname given by locals]), and Indianapolis Indiana (Temple Drive).

112. It is a common misconception that the Freiberg Germany Temple did not originally feature an angel Moroni statue because of reasons relating to the Communist regime. However, the fact is that Church officials never requested permission to position a statue on the temple's spire. On December 20, 2002, twelve years after the German reunification, the golden statue was added to the temple's spire.

113. For more than a century, Portland Oregon has been knows as the "City of Roses." In 1994, the Portland Oregon Temple was awarded first place in the category of commercial rose plantings by the Royal Rosarians of Portland Oregon.

114. A bomb exploded on July 29, 1988, outside a side door of the Stockholm Sweden Temple. No one was injured, and the temple only suffered minor damage.

115. In the Panama City Panama Temple, patrons are able to see the Holy Ghost while in the temple. Panama's national flower is the Holy Ghost Orchid (Peristeria elata), or the *flor del Espiritu Santo*. The Holy Ghost Orchid motif is on display on door handles, glass ornamentation, and decorative wall painting.

116. As a result of the increasing number of temples worldwide, the First Presidency announced a uniform naming guideline for temples in October 1999. The guideline provides for the temple names to primarily include the city and state or province, or the city and country in which they are located. Only the Salt Lake Temple retained its original name.

117. At the time of its dedication, the Helsinki Finland Temple served some 26,000 members in six countries: Finland, Estonia, Latvia, Lithuania, Belarus, and Russia.

118. The countries with the most dedicated temples are the United States (73), Mexico (13), Canada (8), and Brazil (6).

STAINED-GLASS WINDOWS

Salt Lake Temple
Adam and Eve being expelled
from the Garden of Eden

Joseph Smith receiving
the golden plates

The First Vision

Vernal Utah Temple
The Good Shepherd among
a flock of sheep

Palmyra New York Temple
The First Vision

Snowflake Arizona Temple
Christ instructing a circle
of children and adults

Winter Quarters Nebraska Temple
Many pioneer themes

Nauvoo Illinois Temple (2002)
Baptism of Christ

Redlands California Temple
The First Vision

Manhattan New York Temple
Christ with two Apostles on
the road to Emmaus

**Sao Paulo Brazil Temple
(Remodeled)**
Christ appearing to the
Nephites in Bountiful

119. The oxen under the baptismal font in the Vernal Utah Temple have a unique history—they were on public display for more than twenty years in the South Visitors' Center on Temple Square in Salt Lake City.

120. On March 23, 2007, a six-inch water pipe burst in the basement of the Anchorage Alaska Temple. Water flooded up to the first floor. Firefighters pumped thousands of gallons of water out of the building. The temple was closed for about a week.

121. The St. Paul Minnesota Temple has the distinction of being the last temple to have an open house in 1999 and the first to be dedicated in the year 2000. Thus, the panel on the cornerstone of the temple is engraved "Erected 1999—Dedicated January 2000."

122. Three temples have been built directly upon sites that were once used as burial locations. At all three locations, graves needed to be relocated (Hamiliton New Zealand Temple, Stockholm Sweden Temple, and the Winter Quarters Temple).

123. An estimated 1.5 million members participated in the Palmyra New York Temple dedication ceremonies by attending either the live broadcast or the rebroadcast. The ceremony aired in twelve languages and in six time zones.

124. Occasionally, temples with similar floor plans work together to provide each other with refreshed interiors. For example, in 2014, the furniture from the Montreal Canada Temple was sent to replace the furnishings in the Edmonton Canada Temple. The furniture in the Edmonton Temple was sent to replace the furniture of the Bismarck North Dakota Temple.

125. When angel Moroni statues are damaged, they are often replaced rather than repaired in position because of the expense and difficulty of working suspended in the air.

126. The shortest distance between two operating temples is between the Provo Utah Temple and the Provo City Center Temple (2.34 miles).

127. According to an article published on Mormon Newsroom, temple sites are constructed in areas "with enough members (there's no required number) to warrant construction, or where great distances exist between temples."

128. On the evening before the dedication of the Manhattan New York Temple, a special celebration was hosted at the famed Radio City Music Hall. More than 2,400 teens, the largest cast to ever play at the renowned music hall, performed a variety of dances to the delight of nearly 6,000 people attending.

129. Many people do not realize that there is a dedicated temple in Bethlehem. The San Jose Costa Rica Temple is located in the suburb town of San Antonio de Belén. *Belén* is the Spanish word for "Bethlehem."

130. President Gordon B. Hinckley and his wife, Marjorie, traveled together to the Guadalajara Mexico Temple dedication. On the day of dedication, April 29, 2001, President and Sister Hinckley celebrated their sixty-fourth wedding anniversary.

131. Very unique features of the Brigham City Utah Temple are the fruit trees adorning the grounds: peach, apricot, cherry, pear, and apple.

132. The recommend desk of the Kansas City Missouri Temple was made of white oak wood harvested from the sacred location of Adam-ondi-Ahman.

133. The Kyiv Ukraine Temple was announced only eight years after missionaries entered Ukraine. It is the fastest temple to be built after missionaries were introduced to a country.

134. The Copenhagen Denmark Temple was built out of an existing chapel that was used as a public bomb shelter during World War II.

135. Three temples were built on property previously used as a golf course: the Denver Colorado Temple, Snowflake Arizona Temple, and Twin Falls Idaho Temple.

136. Due to a political/military coup a few weeks prior to the Suva Fiji Temple's dedication, the June 19, 2000, event was reduced from four sessions open to all members to only a single private session.

137. The Baton Rouge Temple is the only temple built in a swamp. A portion of the temple property extends into the Bluebonnet Swamp. The 103-acre swamp is the home of hundreds of bird species, alligators, snakes, turtles, opossums, armadillos, squirrels, and foxes.

138. Only two temples contain the word "The" in the formal name of the temple: The Hague Netherlands Temple and The Gila Valley Temple.

139. There are forty-nine "smaller temples" designed to bring temples to the members. The first smaller temple was the Monticello Utah Temple, dedicated in 1998, and the last was the Aba Nigeria Temple, dedicated in 2005.

140. Although multiple temples are located in rain forests, the only temple to be situated in a jungle is the Panama City Panama Temple.

HOLINESS TO THE LORD
THE HOUSE OF THE LORD

German
DAS HAUS DES HERRN
HEILIG DEM HERRN

Finnish
HERRALLE PYHITETTY
HERRAN HUONE

Spanish
SANTIDAD AL SEÑOR
LA CASA DEL SEÑOR

Portuguese
SANTIDADE AO SENHOR
A CASA DO SENHOR

Swedish
HERRENS HUS
HELIGHET ÅT HERREN

Danish
HELLIGET HERREN
HERRENS HUS

Dutch
DE HERE GEWIJD
HET HUIS DES HEREN

Samoan
E PAIA I LE ALII
O LE MAOTA O LE ALII

Tongan
MĀʻONIʻONI KI HE ʻEIKÍ
KO E FALE ʻO E ʻEIKÍ

141. During excavation of the San Antonio Texas Temple, a cavern containing well-formed stalactites and stalagmites was discovered. These natural formations were carefully removed and cut with precision to be used in the temple's stained-glass windows.

142. The San Salvador El Salvador Temple includes the word *Savior* twice in its name. *Salvador* is Spanish for "Savior."

143. Located on the Aba Nigeria Temple complex are a security house, water pump, filtration structure, and a power building used to supply the temple with backup electricity.

144. Reflecting mirrors on the opposite walls in temple sealing rooms is a beautiful and symbolic feature in most temples. To achieve as many reflections as possible, special glass with very low lead content is used. Installers of the mirrors use a highly specialized tool that allows for perfect alignment and an exact reflection pattern.

145. Three temples feature a central spire encompassed by four additional corner towers: the Oakland California Temple, Cochabamba Bolivia Temple, and Provo City Center Temple.

146. The shortest distance between two temples outside the United States is 51 miles, between the São Paulo Brazil Temple and Campinas Brazil Temple.

147. The street on the north side of the Campinas Brazil Temple is named after President James E. Faust. Former mayor of Campinas Dr. Helio de Oliveira Santos unveiled the street "Rua James Esdras Faust" in 2008.

148. Temples are paid for promptly by Church funds earmarked for that purpose. Executive Director of the Temple Department Elder William R. Walker explained, "We would not build a temple unless we could pay for the temple as the temple was built."

149. The Manaus Brazil Temple is the only temple with its own dock. The dock provides easy access for those arriving to its grounds by boat. The temple is located 250 feet away from the massive Rio Negro river.

150. While excavating the foundation for the Cebu City Philippines Temple, tunnels were found that were created by Japanese soldiers in World War II. These interconnected tunnels were located fifteen to twenty feet down and contained leftover bombs and gases. All of the tunnels were filled with at least twenty-eight truckloads of concrete.

Sources

A significant portion of this book's content originates from hundreds of personal interviews with the author. The majority of the quotations in this book are taken from those interviews and are shared with permission. The remaining sources quoted are listed below.

1. Tim Beery, "Alder tells history of St. George Temple," *The Spectrum*, 11 Apr. 2015.

   N. B. Lundwall, *Temples of the Most High* (1954), 79, 81.

   James E. Talmage, *The House of the Lord: A Study of Holy Sanctuaries, Ancient and Modern* (1976), 181.

2. Nolan P. Olsen, "Logan Temple: The First 100 Years" (1978), 6, 73, 152–53, 199.

   Joel E. Ricks, *The History of a Valley: Cache Valley, Utah-Idaho* (1956), 282.

   Lundwall, *Temples of the Most High*, 98.

3. Barbara Lee Hargis, "A Folk History of the Manti Temple: A Study of the Folklore and Traditions Connected with the Settlement of Manti, Utah, and the Building of the Temple" (1968), 36.

   Dennis Lyman, *History at Temple Hill: Manti* (2003).

   "Spiritual Manifestations in the Manti Temple," *Millennial Star*, 13 Aug. 1888, 521.

   Orson F. Whitney, *Life of Heber C. Kimball, an Apostle; The Father and Founder of the British Mission* (1888), 436.

   Victor J. Rasmussen, *The Manti Temple* (1988), 5, 25, 104, 118.

   Lundwall, *Temples of the Most High*, 116.

4. Richard O. Cowan, in *Salt Lake City: The Place Which God Prepared*, ed. Scott C. Esplin and Kenneth L. Alford (2011), 47–68.

   Jennifer Barrett, "Mission offered gift of art," *The Salt Lake Tribune*, 3 Feb. 2006.

   Richard Neitzel Holzapfel, *Every Stone a Sermon: The Magnificent Story of the Construction and Dedication of the Salt Lake Temple* (1992), 9.

   Lisa Ann Jackson, "Saints in the Shadow of Mount Timpanogos," *Ensign*, Dec. 1996.

5. "Temple in Hawaii," *Liahona: The Elders' Journal*, vol. 13, Oct. 26, 1915, 279.

   Valerie Thorne, "Temple designer inspires through beauty," *Deseret News*, 4 Oct. 2010.

   Joseph H. Spurrier, "The Hawaii Temple: A Special Place in a Special Land," *Mormon Pacific Historical Society*, vol. 7, no. 1 (1986), 29, 31, 33.

   Hyrum C. Pope, "About the Temple in Hawaii," *Improvement Era*, vol. 23, Dec. 1919.

6. Susa Young Gates Files, "Letter to Stake Relief Society Presidents," 25 Apr. 1916.

   Joseph F. Smith, in Conference Report, Apr. 1901, 69.

   V. A. Wood, *The Alberta Temple: Centre and Symbol of Faith* (1989), 25–27, 35, 66, 50–59, 64, 74, 93, 102–3, 173.

   Melvin S. Tagg, *A History of the Mormon Church in Canada* (1968), 74.

   Richard O. Cowan, *Temples to Dot the Earth* (1994), 126.

7. Jay Mark, "LDS Mesa Temple opening in 1920s also attracted thousands," *The Republic*, 5 Feb. 2014.

   Lundwall, *Temples of the Most High*, 170, 181.

8. Delbert V. Groberg, *The Idaho Falls Temple: The First LDS Temple in Idaho* (1985), 47, 63.

   Cowan, *Temples to Dot the Earth*, 142–44.

   Russell M. Nelson, "Honoring the Priesthood," *Ensign*, May 1993.

   Judith M. Felt, "On the Bright Side," *Church News*, 16 Sept. 1995.

9. Sheri L. Dew, *Go Forward with Faith: The Biography of Gordon B. Hinckley* (1996), 176–79.

   Dale Kirby, *The History of the Swiss Temple* (1969), 8, 16–18.

   "Blessings of house of the Lord reach faithful in many lands," *Church News*, 24 Sept. 1994.

   Marba C. Josephson, "A Temple Is Risen to Our Lord," *Improvement Era*, Sept. 1955.

   David O. McKay, in Conference Report, Oct. 1955, 7.

   Gerry Avant, "LDS officials rededicate Swiss Temple," *Deseret News*, 24 Oct. 1992.

   Avant, "Thousands tour London and Swiss Temples," *Church News*, 24 Oct. 1992.

10. Edward O. Anderson, "The Los Angeles Temple," *Improvement Era*, Apr. 1953.

    Cowan, *Temples to Dot the Earth*, 153, 155–56.

    "Grounds at Los Angeles Temple ablaze with light," *Deseret News*, 12 Dec. 1998.

11. Lundwall, *Temples of the Most High*, 215–16.

    New Zealand Temple—A Brief History, Visitors' center brochure.

    Brian W. Hunt, *Zion in New Zealand: A History of the Church of Jesus Christ of Latter-day Saints in New Zealand, 1854—1977* (1977), 9, 81, 85, 87–89.

    Allie Howe, "A Temple in the South Pacific," *Improvement Era*, Nov. 1955.

    Glen L. Rudd, *Treasured Experiences of Glen L. Rudd* (1995), 222–25.

12. "Seedlings sprout from ancient oak named in honor of Pres. McKay," *Deseret News*, 2 Nov. 1963.

    Terry Warner, "A Temple for Great Britain," *Millennial Star*, 9 Sept. 1958.

    Avant, "Thousands tour London and Swiss Temples," *Church News*, 24 Oct. 1992.

13. Greg Hill, "Oakland's Temple Hill—A beacon for members," *Church News*, 15 Sept. 2007.

    Evelyn Candland, *An Ensign to the Nations: History of the Oakland Stake* (1992), 60, 63, 65, 67–69, 71.

    Heber J. Grant, in Conference Report, Apr. 1943.

    John L. Hart, "Heroes emerge amid devastation," *Church News*, 28 Oct. 1989.

    "Temple unscathed in Oakland fire," *Church News*, 26 Oct. 1991, 5.

14. "Ogden Temple to Get Architectural Facelift," Mormon Newsroom, 17 Feb. 2010.

    Tom Christensen, "Ogden LDS Temple to reopen this year," *Standard-Examiner*, 30 Jan. 2014.

    Sarah Jane Weaver, "President Monson rededicates Ogden Utah Temple," *Church News*, 21 Sept. 2014.

    Ida Mae D. Hipwell, *Ogden Utah Weber North Stake History* (1980), 151.

15. Richard O. Cowan and Justin R. Bray, "Provo Utah Temple: Four decades of service," *Church News*, 28 Jan. 2012.

    Doyle L. Green, "Two Temples to Be Dedicated," *Ensign*, Jan. 1972, 9.

    "Temple experiences in 'Deseret,' reflect reverence, warmth," *Church News*, 23 Apr. 1994, 10.

16. "Model of Washington D. C. Temple on Public Display," Mormon Newsroom, 10 Jan. 2015.

    Belnap and Belnap, "Washington Temple Visitors' Center."

    Keith W. Wilcox, *The Washington, DC Temple: A Light to the World: A History of Its Architectural Development* (1995).

    "Angel Moroni statue chosen for temple," *Deseret News*, 10 July 1971.

    Donita Painter and Pete Pichaske, "Landmark to most, temple is sanctuary for area's Mormons," *The Montgomery County Journal*, 8 Nov. 1999.

17. J. M. Heslop, "Area conference in Brazil," *Church News*, 8 Mar. 1975.

    "In many countries, great efforts made to attend the temple," *Church News*, 25 June 1994.

18. Carol Moses, "To Build a House of the Lord," *Liahona*, Oct. 1980.

    Spencer J. Palmer, *The Church Encounters Asia* (1970), 83.

    "Temple plan thrills members," *Church News*, 23 Aug. 1975.

19. Anna Kay Price, *The History of the Seattle Temple— The Early Years, 1960–1984*, 6–7, 9, 14–15.

20. Trent Toone, "Looking back on the rich history of the Jordan River Temple," *Deseret News*, 2 July 2012.

    "Jordan River Temple Architectural Design Announced," *Ensign*, July 1978.

    Dell Van Orden, "Ground is broken for temple," *Deseret News*, 16 June 1979.

    "Temple Service Extends the Spirit of Christmas," *Church News*, 14 Dec. 1991.

21. Mathew R. Lee, "Former Georgia Governor Busbee: 'First Mormon Temple in the entire southern United States,'" *Church News*, 12 Apr. 2011.

    Rob Jenkins, "Remodeled Georgia Atlanta Temple features exotic materials, natural light," *Church News*, 12 Apr. 2011.

    "Church President Thomas S. Monson rededicates Atlanta Georgia Temple after renovation," Mormon Newsroom, 1 May 2011.

22. Richard O. Cowan, in *Regional Studies in Latter-day Saint Church History: The Pacific Isles* (2008), 145–60.

    Taralyn Trost, "Fire Destroys Samoa Temple," *Ensign*, Sept. 2003.

    Jerry L. King, "Samoan Temple to be rebuilt on site," *Deseret News*, 25 Oct. 2003.

    Jason Swensen, "Precious gift returns to Samoa," *Church News*, 10 Sept. 2005.

23. Weaver, "LDS Tonga Temple rededicated," *Deseret News*, 6 Nov. 2007.

    Eric B. Shumway, *Tongan Saints: Legacy of Faith* (1991), 143–44, 166, 195.

24. Carole Mikita, "President Hinckley to Travel Temple Open House in Chile," *KSL News*, 8 Mar. 2006.

    Swensen, "Chile greets Pres. Hinckley," *Deseret News*, 12 Mar. 2006.

Gregory Encina Billikopf, "On Sacred Ground," *Liahona*, Feb. 1993.

"In many countries, great efforts made to attend the temple," *Church News*, 25 June 1994.

Hart, "Temple Dedicated in an Oasis of Calm," *Church News*, 25 Sept. 1983, 10.

25. Thorne, "Temple designer inspires through beauty," *Deseret News*, 4 Oct. 2010.

Weaver, "Faithfulness blesses lives of temple-bound Tahitians," *Church News*, 30 Dec. 2006.

R. Lanier Britsch, *Unto the Islands of the Sea: A History of the Latter-day Saints in the Pacific* (1986), 78.

26. Swensen, "Prophet rededicates historic temple," *Church News*, 22 Nov. 2008.

John Forres O'Donnal, *Pioneer in Guatemala: The Personal History of John Forres O'Donnel Including the History of the Mormons in Guatemala* (1997), 283.

"Saints Throng to Temple in Mexico City," *Ensign*, Feb. 1984.

27. David Self Newlin and Linda Williams, "LDS Church Pres. Monson Re-Dedicates Boise Temple," *KSL News*, 18 Nov. 2012.

Bob Cazier, "Boise Temple Dedicated," *Ensign*, Aug. 1984.

28. Britsch, *Unto the Islands of the Sea*, 248–49.

"Temple moments: Prayer, determination," *Church News*, 5 Sept. 1998.

Lynda Bakker, "News of the Church: Among Australian Landmarks," *Ensign*, Nov. 1984.

29. "Manila Philippines Temple," *Liahona*, Apr. 2010.

"Pohnpei members make first temple trip," *Church News*, 16 Sept. 2006.

"Houses of the Lord in far-away places cause great rejoicing," *Church News*, 13 Aug. 1994.

30. Susan Cobb, "Dallas Temple Dedication Opens New Era for Southwestern Saints," *Ensign*, Dec. 1984.

"Temple in Dallas Means Blessings for Southwestern Saints," *Ensign*, Oct. 1984.

Ivan L. Hobson, *Dallas Texas Temple: An Early History* (1991), 70.

"Dallas Temple Is Underway," *Ensign*, Apr. 1983.

31. Adam C. Olson, "Turning Hearts in a Land of Temples," *Ensign*, Oct. 2007.

Jensen and Liu, "Taiwan Saints Eager for Temple Blessings," *Ensign*, Nov. 1984.

32. "Guatemala City Temple Dedicated," *Ensign*, Feb. 1985.

Craig A. Hill, "New facility evidence of growth," *Church News*, 19 July 1992.

"In many countries, great efforts made to attend the temple," *Church News*, 25 June 1994.

33. Raymond M. Kuehne, "The Freiberg Temple: An Unexpected Legacy of a Communist State and a Faithful People," *Dialogue*, June 2004.

Eugene and Claire Freedman, "Angel statue added to Freiberg Temple," *Church News*, 12 Jan. 2002.

Shaun D. Stahle, "Skies Clear for Freiberg Temple Open House," *Church News*, 31 Aug. 2002, 6.

1999–2000 Church Almanac, 324.

Thomas S. Monson, *Faith Rewarded: A Personal Account of Prophetic Promises to the East German Saints* (1996), 85, 88, 103, 105.

34. Ingvar Olsson, "The Stockholm Sweden Temple–Built on Historic Ground," Oct. 2004.

Reid H. Johnson, *Open Doors* (1998), 133.

Avant, "Temple in Sweden is as spiritual magnet to grateful members," *Church News*, 11 Nov. 1995.

35. Karen Winfield, "Rites begin construction of new temple near Chicago," *Church News*, 21 Aug. 1983.

Chicago Herald, 13 July 1985, 1.

"Chicago Saints: Reaching Out for Spiritual Blessings," *Ensign*, Aug. 1985.

"Chicago Temple Dedicated," *Ensign*, Oct. 1985.

36. R. Val Johnson, "South Africa: Land of Good Hope," *Ensign*, Feb. 1993.

"Madagascar's first temple trip," *Church News*, 19 Jan. 2002.

"Johannesburg Temple Dedicated," *Ensign*, Nov. 1985.

Mary Mostert, "Trip to temple 'special' for Kenya family," *Church News*, 25 Apr. 1992.

37. Newby, Younger, and Le Cheminant, *For Those Who Dare to Dream* (1986), 11, 35, 44, 54, 59–60.

Jerry P. Cahill, "Times of Great Blessings: Witnessing the Miracles," *Ensign*, Jan. 1981.

"Houses of the Lord in far-away places cause great rejoicing," *Church News*, 13 Aug. 1994.

38. Swensen, "Faithful Peruvians claim temple blessings," *Church News*, 19 May 2001.

"The Church in Bolivia, Colombia, Ecuador, Peru, and Venezuela," *Ensign*, Jan. 1997.

"In many countries, great efforts made to attend the temple," *Church News*, 25 June 1994.

"Lima Temple Dedication Brings Blessings to Saints in Peru, Bolivia," *Ensign*, Mar. 1986.

39. Swensen, "Thousands celebrate in rededication of Mormon Temple in Buenos Aires, Argentina," *Deseret News*, 10 Sept. 2012.

"Buenos Aires Temple Will Be a Focal Point for Saints," *Ensign*, Jan. 1986.

"Buenos Aires Temple Fulfills Desire of Saints," *Ensign*, Mar. 1986.

Nestor Curbelo, "New training center, temple housing facility dedicated in Argentina," *Church News*, Mar. 19, 1994.

DeAnne Walker, "Facing the Challenge in Argentina," *Liahona*, Sept. 1998.

40. Twila Bird, *Build Unto My Holy Name* (1987), 22–23, 28–29, 53–54, 71.

R. Scott Lloyd, "LDS fill Denver arena to celebrate 100 years of Church's presence," *Church News*, 20 Sept. 1997.

41. F. Enzio Busche, *Yearning for the Living God* (2004) 209, 212.

Erika F. Mueller, "Friedrichsdorf, a Hallowed Refuge," *Ensign*, Sept. 1990.

"Blessings of house of the Lord reach faithful in many lands," *Church News*, 24 Sept. 1994.

42. Toone, "LDS Church's Portland Oregon Temple turns 25," *Deseret News*, 7 Aug. 2014.

"Portland Oregon Temple Visitors' Center Opens," Mormon Newsroom, 28 Feb. 2012.

Lois G. Kullberg, *Saints to the Columbia: A History of the Church of Jesus Christ of Latter-day Saints in Oregon and Southwestern Washington, 1850—1998* (2002), 103, 108, 113.

"300,000 visitors tour Portland Temple," *Church News*, 15 July 1989.

"Many receive sweet blessings as they attend holy temples," *Church News*, 5 Mar. 1994.

"Portland Oregon Temple: Temple is 'gift of a thankful people,'" *Church News*, 26 Aug. 1989.

43. Aaron Shill, "For many in Vegas, temple has been fulfillment of dream," *Deseret News*, 22 Jan. 2009.

"Fifteen Thousand Attend Las Vegas Regional Conference," *Ensign*, Apr. 1987.

Hart, "New temple inspires visitors," *Church News*, 18 Nov. 1989.

44. Dell Van Orden, "Valiant acts of early LDS are 'forever etched into history,'" *Church News*, 1 Sept. 1990.

Richard Robertson, "Toronto: A Growing Light in the East," *Ensign*, Sept. 1988.

"Toronto Temple Dedicated," *Ensign*, Nov. 1990.

"Apostles testify of temples' importance," *Church News*, 1 Sept. 1990.

45. Tony Perry, "Mormon Temple Rises above Ordinary," *Los Angeles Times*, 4 Jan. 1993.

"Portland, San Diego Temples given special recognition," *Church News*, 12 Mar. 1994.

Van Orden, "San Diego Temple: 45th house of the Lord dedicated in 'season of temple building,'" *Church News*, 8 May 1993.

46. "Carter wants new vote to deny Mormon Temple," *Orlando Sentinel*, 13 Feb. 1991.

Mark Skousen, *Sunshine in the Soul: One Hundred Years of the Mormon Church in Florida* (1996), 61, 80–81.

"Temple to bring 'brighter day' to Florida," *Church News*, 27 June 1992.

Lloyd, "90,000 tour temple; give glowing reports," *Church News*, 1 Oct. 1994.

47. John Paul Barlow, *Bountiful Utah Temple Site History* (1969), 52–53.

"'Elegance to complement the Spirit'—Bountiful Temple's interior welcomes, teaches visitors," *Church News*, 12 Nov. 1994.

48. Monte J. Brough and John K. Carmack, "How the Hong Kong Temple Came to Be," *Ensign*, Dec. 2006.

Avant, "Hong Kong Temple Dedicated," *Church News*, 1 June 1996.

"Guests feel peace at open house in Hong Kong Temple," *Church News*, 18 May 1996.

49. Hart, "Mt. Timpanogos Utah Temple," *Church News*, 16 Oct. 1993.

Cannon, "Dressing temple grounds in green—family donates sod, then helps lay it for Mount Timpanogos Temple," *Church News*, 4 Nov. 1995.

Van Orden, "Mount Timpanogos Temple dedicated," *Church News*, 19 Oct. 1996.

50. *St. Louis Temple Book of Remembrance*, 23.

Hart, "Ground is broken on cold day for temple in St. Louis, Mo.," *Church News*, 6 Nov. 1993.

51. Lloyd, "Vernal Temple doors open to public," *Church News*, 18 Oct. 1997.

"Temple experiences in 'Deseret' reflect reverence, Warmth," *Church News*, 23 Apr. 1994.

52. Peter J. Trebilcock, "The House of the Lord is completed."

Avant, "Hearts brim full of gratitude," *Church News*, 13 June 1998.

Avant, "Temple is 'great symbol of our message to the world,'" *Church News*, 26 Dec. 1998.

53. Hill, "Monticello Temple expands to match faith of members," *Church News*, 23 Nov. 2002.

"Monticello Temple Rededicated," *Ensign*, Feb. 2003.

Lloyd, "Ground broken for the first of Church's new 'small' temples," *Church News*, 22 Nov. 1997.

Lloyd, "20,000 tour new temple prior to its dedication," *Church News*, 25 July 1998.

Van Orden, "Inspiration came for smaller temples on trip to Mexico," *Church News*, 1 Aug. 1998.

54. Patricia B. Jasper and Diane Lommel, *A Gathering of Saints—An Informal Chronicle of the Church of Jesus Christ of Latter-day Saints in the Stake of Alaska* (1999), 320.

Carl G. Liungman, *Dictionary of Symbols* (1995), 318.

55. Debra R. Spilsbury, "Temple moments: a powerful influence," *Church News*, 16 Mar. 2002.

"Colonia Juárez Temple dedication," *Church News*, 13 Mar. 1999.

"Temple started for Mexico colonies," *Church News*, 14 Mar. 1998.

56. Avant, "Pres. Hinckley in Spain for dedication of temple: LDS leader visits royal couple at Madrid palace," *Church News*, 18 Mar. 1999.

Carol Mikita, "Saints in Spain: A Faith Defined," KSL Television Special, 1999.

Hart, "Ground broken for temple in Madrid," *Church News*, 22 June 1996.

Avant, "Temple dedicated in Madrid, Spain," *Church News*, 27 Mar. 1999.

"Pres. Hinckley dedicates Madrid Spain Temple," *Deseret News*, 19 Mar. 1999.

"Construction well under way on Madrid Temple," *Church News*, 16 Nov. 1996.

57. Marvin K. Gardner, "The Saints of Colombia: An Example of Strength," *Ensign*, Mar. 2005.

"Work begins on Colombia Temple," *Deseret News,* 3 June 1995.

58. Hart, "Guayaquil Ecuador Temple dedication: 'A wondrous day' for members," *Church News,* 7 Aug. 1999.

"In many countries, great efforts made to attend the temple," *Church News,* 25 June 1994.

59. "Weather clears as 1,000 watch groundbreaking in Spokane," *Church News,* 24 Oct. 1998.

Julie Dockstader, "Amid rays of sunshine, 59th temple dedicated," *Church News,* 28 Aug. 1999.

60. "Columbus Ohio Temple: Spiritual celebration surrounds dedication," *Church News,* 27 Oct. 1999.

David W. Martin and Ernie J. Shannon, *Columbus Ohio Temple* (1999), 21, 99.

Stahle, "Spiritual celebration—Columbus Ohio Temple dedicated," *Church News,* 11 Sept. 1999.

61. Lowell L. Cheney, *Miracles of the Bismarck North Dakota Temple Site.*

Janet Kruckenberg, "Ground broken for two more temples," *Church News,* 24 Oct. 1998.

Van Orden, "Shortening the vast distances," *Church News,* 25 Sept. 1999.

62. "Columbia South Carolina Temple Ground-breaking," *Ensign,* Mar. 1999.

Linda Franklin-Moore, "South Carolina Temple opens for tours," *Church News,* 2 Oct. 1999.

Lloyd, "New temple in a 'place of history,'" *Church News,* 23 Oct. 1999.

"Temple sustains couple in trial," *Deseret News,* 23 Oct. 1999.

63. Matthew Baker and Laury Livsey, "A Temple of Our Own," *New Era,* July 2001.

Hill, "A temple in their midst," *Church News,* 30 Oct. 1999.

Kruckenberg, "Ground broken for two more temples," *Church News,* 24 Oct. 1998.

Jeanne Cady, "Angel Moroni statue tops Detroit Temple," *Church News,* 17 July 1999.

Patricia Michalek, "Detroit open house visitors feel 'serenity of the temple,'" *Church News,* 23 Oct. 1999.

64. Gordon B. Hinckley, "Some Thoughts on Temples, Retention of Converts, and Missionary Service," *Ensign,* Nov. 1997.

Stahle, "Thousands attend open houses in Canada," *Church News,* 13 Nov. 1999.

"'What a happy day' as 700 attend Halifax Temple ceremony," *Church News,* 17 Oct. 1998.

Stahle, "Historic Sabbath in Canada," *Church News,* 20 Nov. 1999.

65. Lloyd, "Ground broken for temple on Canada's plains," *Church News,* 21 Nov. 1998.

"Plane problem leads to LDS first: Halifax, Regina Temples rites both planned for today," *Deseret News,* 14 Nov. 1999.

67. Kruckenberg, "Announcements of new holy edifices brings joy and tears," *Church News,* 20 Feb. 1999.

Lloyd, "Ground is broken for temple in Canada, 'a monument of faith,'" *Deseret News,* 6 Mar. 1999.

68. Lloyd, "While building temple, he embraced the gospel," *Church News,* 25 Dec. 1999.

69. Kruckenberg, "Ground broken for temple," *Church News,* 3 Oct. 1998.

Kruckenberg, "Announcements of new holy edifices brings joy and tears," *Church News,* 20 Feb. 1999.

71. Hart, "Resolute LDS in Ciudad Juarez," *Church News,* 10 Feb. 2001.

Hart, "Juarez Temple is an island of calm in bustling city," *Church News,* 4 Mar. 2000.

72. John Clark, "Temple moments: felt a different spirit," *Church News,* 25 Mar. 2000.

Hart, "Impact on lives begins even before completion of Hermosillo Temple," *Church News,* 4 Mar. 2000.

73. Weaver, "Temple melding members of three cultures," *Church News,* 11 Mar. 2000.

74. Kristine Miner, "The Church in Oaxaca, Mexico," *Ensign,* Apr. 2001.

"Seven Temples Dedicated," *Ensign,* May 2000.

Hart, "Oaxaca Mexico Temple: New horizons open for a faithful people," *Church News,* 18 Mar. 2000.

75. Hart, "Temple blesses distant corner of rural Mexico," *Church News,* 13 Jan. 2001.

"Springtime ceremony begins temple in southern Mexico," *Church News,* 27 Mar. 1999.

76. Charles Pearl, "Don Poulsen Put Heart and Soul into the Temple," *The Oldham Era,* 9 Mar. 2000.

77. Roger J. Adams, "Palmyra Temple History," 5.

Carrie A. Moore, "'Jewel' adorns Palmyra: LDS Church gets ready for the dedication of its 79th temple," *Deseret News,* 5 Apr. 2000.

78. Mark Gudmundsen, "An artist's vision for Fresno Temple," *Deseret News,* 17 Sept. 2009.

79. Lynn Howlett, "Rise of sacred edifice reflects rebuilt lives," *Church News,* 22 Apr. 2000.

81. Jeff DeLong, "Brush fire threatens temple, homes," *Reno Gazette-Journal,* 2 July 2003.

82. Jerry Johnston, "Worthy of the heart of a people," *Church News,* 13 May 2000.

Hart, "Prophet breaks ground for new temples," *Church News,* 23 Nov. 1996.

83. Swensen, "Sacred hill now site of Tampico Temple," *Church News,* 27 May 2000.

84. "Letter to the editor," *Tennessean,* 26 Nov. 1994.

85. Swensen, "Villahermosa Temple stands like a ceiba tree," *Church News,* 27 May 2000.

Sergio A. Sosa Soberano, "Groundbreaking ceremony held in southern Mexico: 'Land of temples,'" *Church News,* 23 Jan. 1999.

86. Barbara Jean Jones, "Five New Temples Dedicated in Four Countries," *Ensign,* Aug. 2000.

Don L. Brugger, "Teaming Up for Temple Work," *Ensign,* June 1995.

Dockstader, "Montreal Temple highlight of 40 years of progress," *Church News,* 10 June 2000.

John A. Farrington, "Temple moments: Wonderful news!" *Church News,* 24 Apr. 1999.

87. LaRene Porter Gaunt, "Costa Rica: Rising in Majesty and Strength," *Ensign,* Dec. 1996.

Swensen, "A new landmark by shining seas," *Church News,* 10 June 2000.

88. Hill, "Church members rejoice over temple in southern Japan," *Deseret News,* 17 June 2000.

Takuji Okata, "Japan's second temple, in Fukuoka, celebrates groundbreaking," *Church News,* 27 Mar. 1999.

89. Phillip Howes, "Rain, clouds in Adelaide do not dampen spirits during groundbreaking," *Church News,* 5 June 1999.

"'Spiritual sanctuaries' for faithful Adelaide, Melbourne members," *Church News,* 24 June 2000.

90. "'Spiritual sanctuaries' for faithful Adelaide, Melbourne members," *Church News,* 24 June 2000.

Lindsay J. Sanders, "Ground is broken for Melbourne Temple," *Church News,* 3 Apr. 1999.

Kruckenberg, "Announcements of new holy edifices brings joy and tears," *Church News,* 20 Feb. 1999.

91. "Gospel shines in faces of members in Fiji," *Church News,* 26 May 2001.

"'Fortress of faith' prompts brotherhood and tears," *Church News,* 24 June 2000.

92. "Temple moments: Temple for Mayans," *Church News,* 17 Apr. 2004.

Lee Warnick, "Yucatán: Promising future amid ancient ruins," *Church News,* 5 Sept. 1992.

Blanca Pinelo de Ferraez, "Temple 'will add to peace in the Yucatan Peninsula,'" *Church News,* 30 Jan. 1999.

Swensen, "Modern temple rises among Mayan ruins," *Church News,* 15 July 2000.

93. "President Hinckley Stresses Family, Book of Mormon," *Ensign,* Apr. 1996.

"Ground broken for eighth temple in Mexico," *Church News,* 12 Jan. 1999.

95. Dockstader, "Oklahoma City Temple: A sacred building on sacred ground," *Church News,* 5 Aug. 2000.

96. Swensen, "Church leaders work to buoy members' spirits," *Church News,* 25 Jan. 2003.

Gordon B. Hinckley, "May We be Faithful and True," *Ensign,* May 1997.

Swensen, "Venezuela Saints rejoicing at new Caracas Temple," *Church News,* 26 Aug. 2000.

97. Wendy Nielsen and Miken Johnson, *Gift of Love— The Houston Texas Temple* (2002), 19, 21.

Steven Cook, *Beginning of the Houston Temple: Site Selection History.*

98. "Ground broken for temple in Alabama," *Church News,* 16 Oct. 1999.

Greg Garrison, "Mormon President Conducts Ceremony," *Birmingham Alabama News,* 4 Sept. 2000.

99. Swensen, "Caribbean's first temple prompts rejoicing," *Church News,* 23 Sept. 2000.

Jason Swensen and Chris Morales, "Widespread flooding," *Church News,* 10 Nov. 2007.

Crystal Powell, "Jamaicans' journey of faith to the LDS temple," *Deseret News,* 9 June 2014.

"Excitement growing as members prepare for Caribbean temple," *Church News,* 11 Jan. 1997.

100. "Mitt Romney's speech about Boston Temple," *Deseret News,* 9 Dec. 2011.

Stahle, "Picture-perfect temple dedication in Boston," *Deseret News,* 2 Oct. 2000.

Moore, "Boston LDS Temple tumult called beneficial to Church," *Deseret News,* 28 May 2005.

Dew, *Go Forward with Faith,* 530.

Stahle, "This has been a banner year," *Deseret News,* 7 Oct. 2000.

102. "Five new temples are announced," *Church News,* 11 Oct. 1997.

Nestor Curbelo, "'Glorious event' completes historic year of temples," *Church News,* 23 Dec. 2000.

103. Curbelo, "Groundbreaking begins 'a new era for Uruguay,'" *Church News,* 15 May 1999.

Curbelo, "Uruguay's president tours new Montevideo Temple," *Church News,* 17 Mar. 2001.

Curbelo, "Dream of many decades now a reality," *Church News,* 24 Mar. 2001.

104. Michael Kelly, "Two miracles named Lance," *Omaha World-Herald,* 5 Sept. 2000.

Julia McCord, "Strong finances, central control propel Church," *Omaha World-Herald,* 29 July 2000.

105. "Mexico's 9th temple begins," *Church News,* 26 June 1999.

Swensen, "New temples in Mexico are making eternal impact in thousands of lives," *Church News,* 12 Aug. 2000.

Swensen, "New temple a sacred blessing, responsibility," *Church News,* 5 May 2001.

106. Alan Wakeley and Richard Hunter, "Temple in far corner received with gratitude," *Church News,* 26 May 2001.

107. Mike Lee, "Mormons to build temple in Tri-Cities," *Tri-City Herald,* 3 Apr. 2000.

"The offering of our hearts and our hands," *Church News,* 24 Nov. 2001.

Harriet Sutherland, "Temple inspires public," *Church News,* 3 Nov. 2001.

108. *Snowflake Arizona Temple, An Inheritance of Faith* (2002).

109. Beth Pratt, "Mormons readying temple for dedication," *The Lubbock Avalanche-Journal,* 23 Mar. 2002.

Don L. Searle, "The Temple Effect," *Ensign,* Feb. 2005.

110. "Mexicans Block Mormon Temple," *The Quarterly Journal,* vol. 16, no. 3, 1996.

Hart, "Million member milestone expected in 2004," *Church News*, 18 May 2002.

Brenton G. Yorgason, *Two Fond Hearts—The Eran A. and Katherine G. Call Story* (2006).

111. "Third temple announced for Brazil, in Campinas," *Church News*, 12 Apr. 1997.

"'Like a Dream,'" *Church News*, 18 Oct. 1997.

"President Faust Honored, Breaks Ground for Two Brazil Temples," *Ensign*, Aug. 1998.

"Ground broken for two temples in Brazil," *Church News*, 9 May 1998.

Fernando Assis, "Beacon of light in Campinas," *Church News*, 25 May 2002.

"President Hinckley Dedicates Two Temples, Meets with Members," *Ensign*, Aug. 2002.

112. Swensen, "Gospel is welcome," *Church News*, 20 July 2002.

"President Hinckley Dedicates Two Temples, Meets with Members," *Ensign*, Aug. 2002.

"Paraguay temple nears completion," *Church News*, 1 Dec. 2001.

Curbelo, "It's 'our temple,' say Paraguayans," *Church News*, 18 May 2002.

113. Don L. Searle, "Nauvoo: A Temple Reborn," *Ensign*, July 2002.

"An Interview with the Nauvoo Temple Architect," *Meridian Magazine*.

Jay Hughes, "Nauvoo Temple reconstruction a blend of the historic and modern," Associated Press, 11 Mar. 2002.

Moore, "Furnishings reflect an era," *Deseret News*, 2 May 2002.

Swensen, "Nauvoo history comes full circle," *Church News*, 29 June 2002.

Avant, "Crowning objective of Joseph's life," *Church News*, 29 June 2002.

114. "A temple in the land of tulips and windmills," *Church News*, 24 Aug. 2002.

115. Kristy Sexton, "Temple Draws 15,000," *The Sunday Mail*, 4 May 2003.

"Ground broken, site dedicated for Brisbane Australia Temple," *The Brisbane Temple Times*, Issue 3, Sept. 2001.

"The Religion Report," Australian Broadcasting Corporation, 14 May 2003.

116. Priscilla Nordyke Roden, "Latter-day Saints' new temple goes on display," *San Bernardino County Sun*, 6 Aug. 2003.

Redlands California Temple Times, May 2003.

Andrea Feathers, "Mormon Church president lays cornerstone to complete temple," *Redlands Daily Facts*, 16 Sept. 2003.

117. Glenn L. Pace, *Safe Journey* (2003), 185.

Eddie O'Gorman, "African temple award for NI firm," BBC Northern Ireland.

"U.S. ambassador tours temple site," *Church News*, 16 Aug. 2003.

118. "Danish chapel will become new temple," *Deseret News*, 29 May 1999.

Avant, "Faithful heritage in Denmark," *Church News*, 29 May 2004.

"News of the Church," *Ensign*, Aug. 2004.

119. Julie Dockstader Heaps, "Members in New York flourishing a year later," *Church News*, 7 Sept. 2002, p. Z04.

Robert Langfod Hall, "New York Saints praise temple announcement," BYU NewsNet, 12 Aug. 2002.

Moore, "LDS temple set in N.Y.C.," *Deseret News*, 8 Aug. 2002.

Cathy Lynn Grossman, "Mormons open temple doors to share beliefs," *USA TODAY*, 26 Apr. 2004.

Stahle, "Miracle in Manhattan," *Church News*, 19 June 2004.

120. Swensen, "A temple on a hill," *Church News*, 28 May 2005.

121. Henry Umahi, "Peep into Aba's Sacred place," *The Sun News*, 6 July 2005.

Donna and Vern Whisenant, "His Name Is Temple," *Meridian Magazine,* Aug. 2005.

123. Maurine Proctor, "Sacramento Temple Dedication—More than Meets the Eye," *Meridian Magazine*, Sept. 2006.

Laurel Rosen, "Church breaks temple ground," *Sacramento Bee*, 23 Aug. 2004.

124. Nina Weckström, "Mormon Temple Opens its doors," *Hufvudstadsbladet*, 19 Sept. 2006.

Scot and Maurine Proctor, "A Promised Day Arrived," Meridian Magazine, Nov. 2006.

125. Leon Parson, "The artist's touch," *LDS Life*, 6 Jan. 2008.

Peggy Fletcher Stack, "Monson dedicates Rexburg Temple," *Salt Lake Tribune*, 11 Feb. 2008.

126. Ana Claudia Soli, "Curitiba temple nearing completion," *Church News*, 28 Apr. 2007.

Fernando Assis, "Ground broken for temple in Curitiba," *Deseret News*, 19 Mar. 2005.

Avant, "Temple is answer to many prayers," *Church News* 31 May 2008

Avant, "New Brazil temple thrills Utahn," *Church News*, 25 May 2008.

Avant, "President Monson presides, notes 'long-awaited day,'" *Church News*, 2 June 2008.

127. Swensen, "Panama temple is ready for dedication," *Church News*, 9 Aug. 2008.

Swensen, "LDS Church's 127th temple is dedicated in Panama," *Church News*, 11 Aug. 2008.

128. Avant, "New temple is dedicated in Idaho," *Church News*, 30 Aug. 2008.

129. Amelia Nielson-Stowell, "Site of Draper Temple dedicated," *Deseret News*, 6 Aug. 2006.

Lloyd, "Temple location to be a canyon in Draper," *Church News*, 27 Nov. 2004.

Jennifer Dobmer, "Church leaders break ground for LDS temple in Draper," Associated Press, 5 Aug. 2006.

130. Swensen, "South valley members prepare for temples," *Church News*, 4 Oct. 2008.

Gordon B. Hinckley, "Opening Remarks," *Ensign*, Nov. 2005.

Swensen, "Utah's 13th temple: 'A great and wonderful day,'" *Church News*, 23 Dec. 2006.

131. Weaver, "Vancouver British Columbia Temple: Church's 131st temple dedicated," *Church News*, 2 May 2010.

Avant, "'Beautiful day'—Vancouver British Columbia Temple," *Church News*, 8 May 2010.

William R. Walker, *Conversations*, Episode 47, Mormon Channel.

132. Weaver, "Temple is beautiful, just as foretold 110 years ago," *Church News*, 29 May 2010.

W. Bradford Perkinson, *The Ninth Temple—A Light in the Desert,* Granite Publishing, 2002.

"'The Gila Valley,' plain and simple," *Church News*, 29 May 2010.

133. "Notable progress in the Philippines," *Church News*, 30 Apr. 2005.

"Temple announced," *Deseret News*, 29 Apr. 2006.

"New Temple Announcement Answers Members' Prayers," *Liahona*, Sept. 2006.

"Groundbreaking Held for Cebu Philippines Temple Complex," *Deseret News*, Nov. 27, 2007.

Maurine Proctor, "Knute Klavenes: Building the Temple Converted Him," *Meridian Magazine*, July 2010.

134. Avant, "Kyiv Ukraine Temple fulfills 1991 prophecy," *Church News*, 25 Aug. 2010.

Stahle, "4,000 gather in Ukraine for Pres. Hinckley," *Church News*, 21 Sept. 2002.

135. Swensen, "'A local treasure' San Salvador El Salvador Temple," *Church News*, 27 Aug. 2011.

136. Jason Swensen and Chris Morales, "Joyous day awaits western Guatemala," *Church News*, 13 Jan. 2007.

Moore, "Ground broken for LDS temple," *Deseret News*, 17 Dec. 2006.

Julio Alvarado, "Guatemala Temple construction begins," *Church News*, 21 Mar. 2009.

Swensen, "President Uchtdorf dedicates second LDS temple in Guatemala," 11 Dec. 2011.

137. Jeremiah J. Morgan, Cynthia McDavitt, and Lori Tubbs Garcia, *Kansas City Missouri Temple: For Such a Time as This*, Donning Company Publishers, 2012.

Avant, "LDS Church dedicates temple in Kansas City," *Deseret News*, 7 May 2012.

138. Weaver, "LDS Church dedicates temple in Brazil, its 138th," *Church News*, 10 June 2012.

Weaver, "Manaus Brazil temple: Legacy of sacrifice, 'The hands of God have touched the people of Manaus,'" *Church News*, 16 July 2012.

Claudio R.M. Costa, "Gather to the Temple," *Ensign*, Dec. 2008.

"New Temple to Be Built in Manaus, Brazil," Mormon Newsroom, 7 June 2007.

139. "The Perfect Spot for a Temple," *The Leader*, 31 July 2010.

141. "Mormons to build gigantic temple in front of Marian shrine in Honduras," Catholic News Agency, 30 Jan. 2009.

142. "Two new temples: Gilbert, Gila Valley," *Church News*, 26 Apr. 2008.

"Arizona governor visits Mormon Gilbert temple open house," *Church News*, 22 Jan. 2014.

"Gilbert Arizona Temple: 'A refuge from the storms of life,'" *Church News*, 8 Mar. 2014.

143. Jennifer Samuels and Calli Benzion, "Groundbreaking for Ft. Lauderdale temple," *Church News*, 25 June 2011.

"South Florida Mormon Temple Showcases Design Aesthetics," ENR Southeast, 3 Nov. 2014.

Tad Walch, "LDS temples grow ever closer to members," *Deseret News*, 4 Oct. 2014.

144. Betty Reid, "LDS Church unveils Phoenix temple redesign," *The Arizona Republic*, 18 Aug. 2010.

145. Swensen, "Ground is broken for Córdoba Argentina Temple," *Church News*, 2 Nov. 2010.

Swensen, "Córdoba Argentina Temple: Already uplifting spirits, changing lives," *Church News*, 17 May 2015.

"Church Holds Cultural Celebration and Dedicates Córdoba Argentina Temple," Mormon Newsroom, 17 May 2015.

"Church Dedicates Córdoba Argentina Temple," Mormon Newsroom, 17 May 2015.

147. Swensen, "President Uchtdorf dedicates Trujillo Perú Temple," *Church News*, 21 June 2015.

148. Cathy Knapp, "Christian opponents object to Mormon temple in Indiana," *USA TODAY*, 14 July 2015.

Don Knebel, Lindsey Mintz, and Charlie Wiles, "Letter: We welcome the Mormon Temple," *Current in Carmel*, 16 July 2015.

Garrett Breeze, "Gather to the Light," Breeze Tunes Productions, 2015.

149. Jerry Earl Johnston, "Emblem to the community: Temple ground breaking in Tijuana, Mexico," *Church News*, 25 Aug. 2012.

150. "Fire Damages Historic Provo Tabernacle," Mormon Newsroom, 17 Dec. 2010.

Thomas S. Monson, "As We Meet Again," *Ensign*, Nov. 2011.

Steve Fidel, "Tabernacle excavation reconnects Provo with pioneer history," KSL, 30 Mar. 2012.

Joseph Walker, "Provo City Center Temple a feat of engineering, hard work and faith," *Deseret News*, 28 Apr. 2013.

Genelle Pugmire, "LDS Church: New Provo temple to stay true to historic roots," *Daily Herald*, 27 Jan. 2013.